Problematic Relationships
IN THE Workplace | VOLUME 2

This book is part of the Peter Lang Media and Communication list.
Every volume is peer reviewed and meets
the highest quality standards for content and production.

PETER LANG
New York • Washington, D.C./Baltimore • Bern
Frankfurt • Berlin • Brussels • Vienna • Oxford

Problematic Relationships
IN THE Workplace | VOLUME 2

EDITED BY *Becky L. Omdahl &*
Janie M. Harden Fritz

PETER LANG
New York • Washington, D.C./Baltimore • Bern
Frankfurt • Berlin • Brussels • Vienna • Oxford

Library of Congress Cataloging-in-Publication Data
Problematic relationships in the workplace / edited by
Becky L. Omdahl, Janie M. Harden Fritz.
p. cm.
Includes bibliographical references and indexes.
1. Conflict management. 2. Organizational behavior. 3. Interpersonal conflict.
4. Problem employees—Psychology. 5. Courtesy in the workplace.
I. Omdahl, Becky Lynn. II. Fritz, Janie M. Harden.
HD42.P755   658.3'145—dc22   2005027351
ISBN 978-0-8204-7400-7(volume 1, paperback)
ISBN 978-1-4331-1799-2 (volume 2, hardcover)
ISBN 978-1-4331-1798-5 (volume 2, paperback)
ISBN 978-1-4539-0926-3 (volume 2, e-book)

Bibliographic information published by **Die Deutsche Nationalbibliothek**.
Die Deutsche Nationalbibliothek lists this publication in the "Deutsche
Nationalbibliografie"; detailed bibliographic data is available
on the Internet at http://dnb.d-nb.de/.

The paper in this book meets the guidelines for permanence and durability
of the Committee on Production Guidelines for Book Longevity
of the Council of Library Resources.

© 2012 Peter Lang Publishing, Inc., New York
29 Broadway, 18th floor, New York, NY 10006
www.peterlang.com

All rights reserved.
Reprint or reproduction, even partially, in all forms such as microfilm,
xerography, microfiche, microcard, and offset strictly prohibited.

Printed in the United States of America

CONTENTS

Preface   ix
Becky L. Omdahl & Janie M. Harden Fritz

Introduction to Problematic Relationships

CHAPTER 1.   A Review of Concepts Relevant to Problematic   3
Relationships in the Workplace
Janie M. Harden Fritz

CHAPTER 2.   The Role of Emotion in Problematic Relationships   18
in the Workplace
Becky L. Omdahl

Part I: Problematic Behaviors Impacting Relationships

CHAPTER 3.   Hostile Work Relationships   43
Loraleigh Keashly

CHAPTER 4.   Workplace Bullying as Interpersonal Violence?   68
A Reconceptualization in Progress
Terry A. Kinney

CHAPTER 5. The Relative Predictability of Incivility on Interpersonal   85
and Organizational Trust
Beverly Davenport Sypher & Matthew J. Gill

CHAPTER 6. Exclusive or Exclusory: Workplace Relationships,   105
Ostracism, and Isolation
Patricia M. Sias

Part II: Frameworks for Understanding Problematic Relationships in the Workplace

CHAPTER 7. Out of Sight, Out of…the Loop? Relationship Challenges   125
for Teleworkers and Their Co-Located Peers, Managers,
and Organizations
Martha J. Fay

CHAPTER 8. The Bureaucrat as Problematic Other: Arendt's Warning   145
Ronald C. Arnett

CHAPTER 9. Contemplating an Upward Spiral: When Cultural   163
Diversity Emerges in Problematic Workplace Relationships
Lisa M. Millhous

CHAPTER 10. Explaining Tensions in Workplace Relationships: 190
Toward a Communicative and Situated Understanding
of Tokenism
Brittany L. Collins, Rebecca Gill, & Jennifer J. Mease

Part III: Maintaining and Restoring Effective Relationships

CHAPTER 11. "The Most Vulnerable…[and] Most Resilient People":   215
Communicatively Constituting Palestinian
Refugees' Resilience
Abrar Hammoud & Patrice M. Buzzanell

CHAPTER 12. Communication Strategies to Restore Working Relations: 235
Comparing Relationships That Improved with Ones That
Remained Problematic
Jon A. Hess & Katelyn A. Sneed

CHAPTER 13. Protecting and Promoting Workplace Relationships: 257
Professional Civility
Janie M. Harden Fritz

CHAPTER 14. Communicating Forgiveness in Work Relationships 267
Vincent R. Waldron & Dayna N. Kloeber

CHAPTER 15. Resilience, Civility, Positive Communication, 289
and Forgiveness in the Academy
Becky L. Omdahl

Contributors 309

Author Index 315

Subect Index 329

PREFACE

BECKY L. OMDAHL & JANIE M. HARDEN FRITZ

We have all experienced challenging behavior in the organizations in which we work. It might be a flaming e-mail from a coworker on a tirade about a request (e.g., "How dare Susan tell us that textbook orders are due on April 20th. Faculty cannot possibly have time to review new books for fall courses by that date"), or a supervisor claiming sole credit for an important report he or she didn't write, or a subordinate wasting everyone's time with hours of stories about personal family matters. We might work in organizations in which those concerned primarily with their own career ambitions make high-level decisions injurious to both the long-term interests of the organization and authentic needs of most employees.

Not surprisingly, repeated behaviors like these often create the realization that certain relationships are problematic. Nearly all of us have struggled with workplace relationships that we find difficult, and we often recognize their costs. Micromanaging bosses, harassing peers, unprofessional coworkers, and a host of others claim mental energy, increase communication challenges, and impose personal and organizational costs.

Given the prevalence and apparent downsides to bad behavior and problematic workplace relationships, over a decade ago a group of us began to study them intensely. Our first volume of *Problematic Relationships in the Workplace* (Fritz &

Omdahl, 2006) addressed how relationships with disliked others can be conceptualized. We identified the behaviors that cluster and give rise to "types" of problematic others like "the bully" and "the abrasive harasser" (Fritz, 2006). We learned that no matter how clear the type, it is better to avoid labeling the other as "difficult" and use the time to analyze and resolve causes contributing to difficulties outside the person (Duck, Foley, & Kirkpatrick, 2006). We reviewed cases revealing that people face greater challenges when stereotypes and biases are operating (e.g., workplace pregnancy; Liu & Buzzanell, 2006), and we looked at what happens when workplace friendships are challenged (Sias, 2006). We also learned that while most relationships headed south continue to deteriorate, there are cases in which problematic relationships turn around (Hess, Omdahl, & Fritz, 2006).

This group of scholars also studied harms caused by problematic relationships, and the findings evoked great concern. Problematic workplace relationships contribute significantly to stress, burnout, depression, and anxiety (Omdahl & Fritz, 2006), as well as reduced job satisfaction, diminished commitment, and increased workplace cynicism (Fritz & Omdahl, 2006). Not surprisingly, interactions with disliked others elicit negative emotions, and the management of those relationships becomes an important element of the communication process (Kramer & Tan, 2006). The very perception that a message is negative elicits self-protection and negative affect, and once negative affect is triggered, psychological states and symptoms of decreased well-being follow (Kinney, 2006). The symptoms of decreased well-being are more likely to be reversed by actions that avoid contact or direct challenge than by actions that appease the other person (Kinney, 2006).

Finally, the first volume offered ways to maintain and rebuild relationships. Distancing from problematic relationships facilitates the regulation of distress/arousal (Hess, 2006). By learning to focus on the organization's mission, developing expectations appropriate to the public sphere, and adopting a commitment to community, workplaces become productive and conducive to constructive relationships (Arnett, 2006). When transgressions do occur, forgiveness, as an emotionally transformative experience, can enable people to move forward (Metts, Cupach, & Lippert, 2006). These and other steps, like marrying a call for civility with genuine listening, and efforts in minimizing shame in how we communicate, can foster healthier workplaces, making greater progress toward the mission (Omdahl, 2006).

Building on the research and reviews presented in Volume 1, this new volume presents an entirely new slate of research and reviews. Introducing the book are chapters on the concepts used to address problematic relationships in the workplace (Fritz) and the five roles emotions play in these relationships (Omdahl). In looking at problematic behaviors, the volume focuses on hostile work relationships (Keashly), bullying (Kinney), incivility (Davenport Sypher and Gill), and ostracism and isolation (Sias). Several frameworks engender greater understanding, including working remotely (Fay), the rise of bureaucracy (Arnett), diversity in the workplace (Millhous), and tokenism (Collins, Gill, and Mease). Finally, the last section explores how we can maintain and restore relationships through resilience (Hammoud and Buzzanell), communication strategies (Hess and Sneed), professional civility (Fritz), forgiveness (Waldron and Kloeber), and, for those of us working in organizations (especially the academy), fostering individual and organizational actions that lead to healthy and productive workplaces (Omdahl).

This new volume promises to hold heuristic value for researchers and scholars as well as practical applications for those trying to lead and contribute in organizations. We remain sobered by the significant costs of problematic relationships in the workplace and confident that the findings, understandings, and strategies offered throughout this book offer a path to greater personal and organizational achievement and well-being.

References

Arnett, R. C. (2006). Professional civility: Reclaiming organizational limits. In J. M. H. Fritz & B. L. Omdahl (Eds.), *Problematic relationships in the workplace* (pp. 233–248). New York, NY: Peter Lang.

Duck, S., Foley, M. K., & Kirkpatrick, D. C. (2006). Uncovering the complex roles behind the "difficult" coworker. In J. M. H. Fritz & B. L. Omdahl (Eds.), *Problematic relationships in the workplace* (pp. 3–20). New York, NY: Peter Lang.

Fritz, J. M. H. (2006). Typology of troublesome others at work: A follow-up investigation. In J. M. H. Fritz & B. L. Omdahl (Eds.), *Problematic relationships in the workplace* (pp. 21–46). New York, NY: Peter Lang.

Fritz, J. M. H., & Omdahl, B. L. (2006). Reduced job satisfaction, diminished commitment, and workplace cynicism as outcomes of negative work relationships. In J. M. H. Fritz & B. L. Omdahl (Eds.), *Problematic relationships in the workplace* (pp. 131–152). New York, NY: Peter Lang.

Hess, J. A. (2006). Distancing from problematic coworkers. In J. M. H. Fritz & B. L. Omdahl (Eds.), *Problematic relationships in the workplace* (pp. 205–232). New York, NY: Peter Lang.

Hess, J. A., Omdahl, B. L., & Fritz, J. M. H. (2006). Turning points in relationships with disliked coworkers. In J. M. H. Fritz & B. L. Omdahl (Eds.), *Problematic relationships in the workplace* (pp. 89–106). New York, NY: Peter Lang.

Kinney, T. A. (2006). Should I stay or should I go now? The role of negative communication and relational maintenance in distress and well-being. In J. M. H. Fritz & B. L. Omdahl

(Eds.), *Problematic relationships in the workplace* (pp. 179–204). New York, NY: Peter Lang.
Kramer, M. W., & Tan, C. L. (2006). Emotion management in dealing with difficult people. In J. M. H. Fritz & B. L. Omdahl (Eds.), *Problematic relationships in the workplace* (pp. 153–178). New York, NY: Peter Lang.
Liu, M., & Buzzanell, P. M. (2006). When workplace pregnancy highlights difference: Openings for detrimental gender and supervisory relations. In J. M. H. Fritz & B. L. Omdahl (Eds.), *Problematic relationships in the workplace* (pp. 47–68). New York, NY: Peter Lang.
Metts, S., Cupach, W. R., & Lippert, L. (2006). Forgiveness in the workplace. In J. M. H. Fritz & B. L. Omdahl (Eds.), *Problematic relationships in the workplace* (pp. 249–278). New York, NY: Peter Lang.
Omdahl, B. L. (2006). Towards effective work relationships. In J. M. H. Fritz & B. L. Omdahl (Eds.), *Problematic relationships in the workplace* (pp. 279–294). New York, NY: Peter Lang.
Omdahl, B. L., & Fritz, J. M. H. (2006). Stress, burnout, and impaired mental health: Consequences of problematic work relationships. In J. M. H. Fritz & B. L. Omdahl (Eds.), *Problematic relationships in the workplace* (pp. 109–130). New York, NY: Peter Lang.
Sias, P. M. (2006). Workplace friendship deterioration. In J. M. H. Fritz & B. L. Omdahl (Eds.), *Problematic relationships in the workplace* (pp. 69–88). New York, NY: Peter Lang.

Introduction to Problematic Relationships

· 1 ·
A REVIEW OF CONCEPTS RELEVANT TO PROBLEMATIC RELATIONSHIPS IN THE WORKPLACE

JANIE M. HARDEN FRITZ

In the mid-1990s, Vardi and Wiener (1996) published an article proposing the general organizing term "misbehavior in organizations" for employee misconduct, identifying behaviors such as theft, unconventional practices at work, counterproductive behavior in organizations, issues of problematic management ethics, white-collar crime, whistle-blowing, deviant behavior of professionals, concealing pertinent information, substance abuse, sexual harassment at work, and vandalism within the concept's broad scope (p. 152). By the time their book-length treatment of the topic (Vardi & Weitz, 2004) was published, several of these terms (and a number of new ones) had taken on prominent conceptual status within the arena of what Griffin and O'Leary-Kelly (2004) referred to as the "dark side" of organizational behavior, paralleling the growing interest in "dark side" behaviors in the interpersonal communication and relationship domain (Cupach & Spitzberg, 1994; Spitzberg & Cupach, 1998; see also Cupach & Spitzberg, 2011). These terms included aggressive, antisocial, counterproductive, deviant, and dysfunctional behavior in organizations, incivility, and bullying. These concepts were adapted from several domains of social scientific inquiry in addition to organizational behavior and related areas (e.g., sociology, e.g., Hollinger, 1986; see also Griffin & Lopez, 2005; anthropology, see Brodsky, 1976) as issues relevant to the workplace, and they were investigated primarily within the broad fields of organizational behavior, management, and organizational psychology.

At the time of the current volume's preparation, the field of communication has witnessed a number of edited volumes addressing problematic workplace behavior, with an eye to their specifically communicative nature (e.g., Fritz & Omdahl, 2006; Lutgen-Sandvik & Davenport Sypher, 2009). These volumes typically include sections or chapters addressing recommendations for ameliorating the effects of these problematic issues or for preventing them altogether. At the same time, a turn to positive organizational behavior (Luthans, 2002) and positive organizational scholarship (Cameron, Dutton, & Quinn, 2003) has emerged as a research focus in response to the preponderance of work on problematic behaviors in the workplace. Communication scholars have turned attention in this direction, examining communicative practices related to positive phenomena in organizations (e.g., Lutgen-Sandvik, Riforgiate, & Fletcher, 2011) as well as exploring the positive side of interpersonal communication more generally (Socha & Pitts, 2012). Clearly, the study of problematic workplace behaviors is part of a larger background concern for the well-being of persons and institutions, which requires a focus on both positive and negative elements of communicative interaction in the workplace.

This chapter presents a selective review of the terminological scope of problematic workplace behaviors, including a brief review of negative supervisory behavior, within which I situate the contents of the current volume. As has become evident through continued research in this vast and important area, these problematic behaviors are, both conceptually and operationally, communicative behaviors and must be addressed within a communication framework.

Problematic Workplace Behaviors: Terminological Multiplicity

Research focusing on what I term here as problematic behavior in the workplace has resulted in an extensive body of literature designed to define, explore, and refine an ever larger pool of related, yet arguably distinct, concepts (e.g., Griffin & Lopez, 2005; O'Leary-Kelly, Duffy, & Griffin, 2000; Robinson & Greenberg, 1998; Vardi & Weitz, 2004). Studies of workplace aggression (Neuman & Baron, 1997, 1998; O'Leary-Kelly, Griffin, & Glew, 1996), antisocial work behavior (Aquino & Douglas, 2003; Giacalone & Greenberg, 1997; O'Leary-Kelly et al., 2000; Robinson & O'Leary-Kelly, 1998), counterproductive work behavior (Fox & Spector, 2005a), organizational deviance (Robinson & Bennett, 1995; Warren, 2003), dysfunctional workplace behavior (Griffin, O'Leary-Kelly, & Collins, 1998), organizational misbehavior (Vardi & Weitz, 2004; Vardi & Wiener, 1996), organizational retaliatory behavior (Skarlicki & Folger, 1997), problematic relationships in the workplace (Fritz & Omdahl, 2006), destructive organizational communication (Lutgen-Sandvik & Davenport Sypher, 2009), and, the latest to appear on the scene, insidious workplace behavior (Greenberg, 2010), make regular appearances in the academic literature of various disciplinary domains, including communication, education, management studies, organizational behavior, organizational/industrial psychology, applied psychology, and social psychology (see Fritz, in press, for a review, and Keashly, this volume, for additional concepts in this area).

Competing Constructs

This proliferation of concepts has resulted in what some researchers refer to as a "battle of competing constructs" (Bies & Tripp, 2005, p. 69) or, in a more benign frame, as a dilemma of labeling and definitions (Keashly & Jagatic, 2003, p. 32). Contributing to the confusion is researchers' lack of agreement on the status of these constructs; although some investigators claim that these terms refer to essentially identical phenomena (e.g., Sagie, Stashevsky, & Koslowski, 2003, p. 3), others argue that terms that appear to be similar are, in fact, distinct because of a given conceptualization's definitional explicitness as a specific instance of a particular problematic behavior (e.g., Robinson & Bennett, 1995). However, despite variations in this research, including conceptual starting points, labels, orientations, and emphases, consistency holds in this regard: almost all of the behaviors are perpetrated by members of the organization, directed at the organization and its members, and intentional and (potentially) harmful (Bennett & Robinson, 2003, pp. 250–251).

One factor that adds to the complexity of sorting out various conceptual articulations of problematic workplace behaviors is the fact that researchers in this area vary in the extent to which they focus on a limited number of concepts or pursue work in several areas. For example, Baron and Neuman (1996; Neuman & Baron, 1998) worked with a limited number of closely associated terms (e.g., workplace violence, workplace aggression). Some researchers maintain a focus on one term (see Bennett and Robinson's research on workplace deviance, Robinson & Bennett, 1995; Robinson & Greenberg, 1998) and pursue it as a contributing research agenda to various overarching conceptual umbrellas, either by collaborative work with others involving a term considered broader in scope (e.g., workplace deviance as one of many subcategories of antisocial behavior; see Thau, Crossley, Bennett, & Sczesny, 2007) or by their own agreement to affiliate their work with a collection under a particular term (e.g., Bennett, Aquino, Reed, & Thau, 2005, published in Fox & Specter's [2005a] volume on counterproductive work behavior). However, Greenberg addresses antisocial behavior (Giacalone & Greenberg, 1997), organizational deviance (Robinson & Greenberg, 1998), and insidious workplace behavior (Greenberg, 2010), along with the more specific behavior of employee theft (e.g., Greenberg, 1990), and R. W. Griffin is associated with organization-motivated aggression (O'Leary-Kelly et al., 1996), dysfunctional work behaviors (Griffin & Lopez, 2005), and dysfunctional organizational culture (Van Fleet & Griffin, 2006).

A final complicating factor in the research on problematic workplace behaviors is that the pursuit of similar concepts in different continents and countries has resulted in terminology specific to a particular region. Bullying and mobbing, for instance, first emerged as a recognized and salient research focus in Europe, particularly in the Scandinavian countries, and these terms take on different conceptual contours depending on the country (Einarsen, Hoel, Zapf, & Cooper, 2011b). As Einarsen, Hoel, Zapf, and Cooper (2011b) and Keashly and Jagatic (2011) pointed out, the European tradition and the North American tradition show different patterns of development and focus on different specific constructs, with the North American tradition showing more fragmentation than the European tradition. These perspectives are now intersecting in volumes that bring the two traditions together (e.g., Einarsen, Hoel, Zapf, & Cooper, 2011a).

Attempts to Systematize

In response to what could be considered a confusing and chaotic panoply of terms populating an ever-more-crowded conceptual space of negative interactive workplace phenomena, researchers call for integration and unification and subsequent systematic conceptual development (Fox & Spector, 2005b; Keashly & Jagatic, 2011; Neuman & Baron, 2005; O'Leary-Kelly et al., 2000; Robinson & Bennett, 1995; Robinson & Greenberg, 1998; Vardi & Weitz, 2004) to lend order and definitional rigor to this multidisciplinary and interdisciplinary (but apparently undisciplined) conceptual family. Attempts to systematize the area emerge as researchers in a given area offer a framework to differentiate terms or to subsume competing terms under one overarching, preferred term or organizing/integrating construct, such as dysfunctional behavior (e.g., Griffin & Lopez, 2005), workplace aggression (Neuman & Baron, 1997, 2005), or counterproductive work behavior (Fox & Spector, 2005a).

Efforts to systematize according to an organizing framework may include identifying dimensions along which these terms can be characterized and thereby differentiated. Robinson and Greenberg (1998), for instance, employed five dimensions of perpetrator, intentionality, target, modality of action (e.g., direct/indirect, active/passive, verbal/physical), and consequences to organize and differentiate antisocial behavior, workplace deviance, employee vice, organizational misbehavior, workplace aggression, organizational retaliation behavior, noncompliant behavior, and organization-motivated aggression. Griffin and Lopez (2005) distinguished workplace deviance, workplace aggression, antisocial behavior, and workplace violence in their construction of a typology of "bad behavior" in the workplace, organized under the conceptual umbrella of dysfunctional behavior, tracing the etiology of these concepts and identifying different perspectives within these areas. The workplace aggression research appears to have two distinct strands, identified as the Neuman and Baron conceptualization of workplace aggression and the O'Leary-Kelly, Griffin, and Glew perspective of organization-motivated aggression, with different sets of researchers working from these models. Robinson and Bennett's (1995) work on workplace deviance is widely recognized, and Griffin and Lopez suggested that recent work on workplace deviance framing the concept differently—in particular, recognizing that deviance could, in some instances, be constructive—is an extension rather than a variant (p. 990). This analytic work provides clarity in its highlighting of similarities and differences among conceptualizations of terms, as well as other factors, such as theoretical clarity of terms and definitional precision (Griffin & Lopez, 2005). Other examples include efforts to differentiate or characterize incivility and/or rudeness (Fritz, 2009; Pearson, Andersson, & Porath, 2005), bullying (e.g., Keashley & Jagatic, 2011; Lutgen-Sandvik, Tracy, & Alberts, 2007), and counterproductive work behavior (Fox & Spector, 2005b).

One result of attempts to systematize and integrate this research is the appearance of edited collections gathering research together under one of the terms: "dark side" behavior in organizations (Griffin & O'Leary-Kelly, 2004), dysfunctional workplaces (Langan-Fox, Cooper, & Klimoski, 2007), counterproductive work behavior (Fox & Spector, 2005a), organizational deviance (Kidwell & Martin, 2005), antisocial work behavior (Giacalone & Greenberg, 1997), misbehavior in organizations (Vardi & Weitz, 2004), problematic work relationships (Fritz & Omdahl, 2006; this volume), and insidious behavior in organizations (Greenberg, 2010). These collections are distinct from other volumes dedicated to conceptual advances in organizational behavior or other particular domains, which often include topical contributions on one or more of these problematic behaviors in addition to selections on a broad range of general topics. To name just two examples of these general collections, *Organizational Behavior: The State of the Science* (Greenberg, 2003) contains Bennett and Robinson's (2003) review of organizational deviance, and Griffin et al. (1998) contributed a chapter on dysfunctional work behaviors in organizations to Cooper and Rousseau's (1998) *Trends in Organizational Behavior* collection. The appearance of an edited collection gathering research under one umbrella term suggests that the construct has sufficient public recognition to gather publishing interest and contributors and provides access to studies and reviews that can be considered conceptually related to the general term.

The fact that most of these volumes include scholars from almost all terminological camps (for example, Neuman and Baron have a chapter on workplace aggression in Giacalone & Greenberg's [1997] volume on antisocial behavior in the workplace and in Fox and Spector's [2005a] volume on counterproductive work behavior) suggests that the outcome of the struggle is not yet determined and perhaps matters less than that research continue in these areas, as Bennett and Robinson (2003) noted. Two terms that have emerged from the fray with some enduring appeal, perhaps because of public recognition of their status as both popular and academic terms, are "bullying" and "incivility." These terms manifest a high degree of identity distinction, finding a conceptual place among their various cousin terms and also enjoying popular recognition as viable labels with just enough specificity and public acknowledgment to lend them conceptual credibility and shore up their resistance to complete subsumption within other terms, although they are, by rare common agreement, considered subcategories of other terms.

Bullying, typically classified as workplace aggression, has given rise to many volumes itself, both academic and for the popular press (see Keashly, this volume, and Kinney, this volume, for several references, as well as Lutgen-Sandvik, Namie, & Namie, 2009; an extensive interdisciplinary and multidisciplinary literature on bullying has burgeoned over the last decade). Incivility is mentioned in Vardi and Weitz's (2004) book on misbehavior in organizations (authored rather than edited, with their own conceptual development of misbehavior in organizations encompassing multiple other terms). A chapter on incivility appears in Griffin and O'Leary-Kelly's "dark side" edited volume (Pearson & Porath, 2004), in Fox and Spector's edited volume (2005a) on counterproductive work behavior (Pearson et al., 2005), and in Greenberg's (2010) volume on insidious workplace behavior (Pearson, 2010).

Incivility, according to the conceptualization of the researchers who brought it to popularity in the organizational behavior literature, overlaps several other constructs (see Pearson et al., 2005), but it does not gather a number of stand-alone terms under its conceptual canopy. Pearson et al. (2005) identified counterproductive work behavior as the broadest term, one that encompasses all the other terms. Deviance is the next most general term, followed by aggression, which deviance subsumes. Aggression, in turn, encompasses violence, mobbing, and bullying. Counterproductive behavior and deviant behavior encompass incivility completely, and incivility and aggression overlap partially. Bullying also includes incivility, shows some overlap with mobbing, and falls completely within aggression. Bullying and incivility are included in our volume as distinct conceptualizations; see Davenport Sypher and Gill (this volume) and Kinney (this volume).

Negative Supervisory Behavior: More Multiplicity

Partially overlapping these frameworks of problematic interpersonal processes in the workplace is the category of abusive, destructive, dysfunctional, or toxic supervisory behavior or leadership. Because of the nature of power relations in organizations, positions of management and leadership are particularly salient as locations of workplace bullying, which involves supervisors as the perpetrator in as many as 89% of reported incidents (Einarsen, Aasland, & Skogstad, 2007). Studies of hostile supervisory behavior include destructive leadership behavior (Einarsen et al., 2007), petty tyranny (Ashforth, 1994), abusive supervision (Tepper, 2007), bosses as a type of troublesome other in the workplace (Fritz, 2002, 2006), and dysfunctional leadership (Kets de Vries, 2004), to name a few. The concepts of dysfunctional leadership and dysfunctional organizations have been approached from the perspective of psychopathology (e.g., Kets de Vries, 2004), whereas the term's connotative, nonclinical meaning emerges with broader treatments of dysfunctional behavior in organizations (e.g., Griffin et al., 1998) and will not be addressed here as unique to the supervisory level.

The literature on problematic supervisory behavior is beset by conceptual and operational challenges similar to those faced by problematic work behavior in general—multiplicity (Einarsen et al., 2007), fragmentation (Tepper, 2007), and lack of integration (Tepper, 2007). Tepper (2007) identified abusive supervision as the term under which most of the work on the destructive side of supervision has taken place, with Ashforth's (1994) petty tyranny, Schat, Desmarais, and Kelloway's (2006) supervisor aggression (as cited in Tepper, 2007), and Duffy, Ganster, and Pagon's (2002) supervisor undermining also emerging as terms identifying similar behaviors. As noted by Keashley, Trott, and MacLean (1994), abusive supervision is characterized by nonphysical actions such as angry outbursts and ridiculing employees (p. 262).

Varied Approaches

Einarsen et al. (2007) defined destructive leadership as "the systematic and repeated behavior by a leader, supervisor or manager that violates the legitimate interest of the organization by undermining and/or sabotaging the organization's goals, tasks, resources, and effectiveness and/or the motivation, well-being or job satisfaction of subordinates" (p. 208) and identified abusive supervisors (Tepper, 2000), health-endangering leaders (Kile, 1990, cited in Einarsen et al., 2007), petty tyrants (Ashforth, 1994), toxic leaders (Lipman-Blumen, 2005), bullies (Namie & Namie, 2000), derailed leaders (Shackleton, 1995), intolerable bosses (Lombardo & McCall, 1984), psychopaths (Furnham & Taylor, 2004), and harassing leaders (Brodsky, 1976) as conceptual categories that fall within the domain of destructive leadership with subordinates as targets.

Tepper (2007) focused on research exploring the process of abusive leadership, while Einarsen, Aasland, and Skogstad highlighted research identifying types of problematic leaders. Two other studies of problematic supervisors merit mention here. Fritz (2002) identified six clusters of troublesome bosses defined by their positions on 10 factors, described as lording power, busybody behavior, backstabbing, being different from the respondent, sexual harassment, poor work ethic, unprofessional focus of attention, distracting, excessive demands, and defensiveness (p. 418). These troublesome boss types ranged from highly problematic to bosses who were seen simply as different from the respondent: the defensive tyrant, the taskmaster, the different other, sand in the gears, the extreme unprofessional, and the okay boss. A follow-up study (Fritz, 2006) identified nine factors (self-promoting, unethical incompetence, interfering, lording power, distractingly different, unprofessional focus of attention, sexual harassment, obnoxiousness, and social undermining), resulting again in six clusters: the different boss, the good old boy/girl, the okay boss, the toxic boss, the self-centered taskmaster, and the intrusive harasser.

Einarsen et al.'s (2007) definition of destructive leadership was designed to be inclusive of the extant set of conceptualizations, capturing behaviors directed toward subordinates and the organization. Such behaviors included physical and verbal behaviors, unlike Tepper's (2000) conceptualization, which focused only on nonphysical behavior. Einarsen, Aasland, and Skogstad's destructive leadership was conceptualized to fit within Buss's (1961) aggression framework, which included dimensions of physical and verbal, passive and active, and direct and indirect aggression. Tepper's (2007) abusive supervision was based on subordinates' perceptions of supervisors' sustained display of nonphysical, hostile verbal and nonverbal behavior and is defined as willful, ongoing, patterned behavior that may or may not be intended to harm. Because the intent of abusive supervision may be to increase productivity or benefit the organization in some other way, Tepper (2007) considered it distinct from general workplace aggression. Because Ashforth's (1994) petty tyranny was characterized as lording power over others but was not necessarily characterized by hostility, Tepper (2007) did not include this broader concept as equivalent to abusive supervision. Fritz's (2002, 2006) work was designed to capture subordinates' perceptions of troublesome bosses on the basis of behavioral factors; she did not distinguish troublesome boss behaviors from other conceptualizations.

The Problematic Nature of Negative Supervisory Behavior

Because of the power supervisors wield over subordinates, bullying behavior by bosses is particularly destructive. Research related to these types of behaviors adds to our knowledge of the deleterious effects of leadership behavior that, instead of supporting and nurturing productivity, organizations, and people, strikes against them in destructive ways. Given the responsibility of bosses to prevent problematic behaviors such as incivility, bullying, and related problematic behaviors in the workplace (Pearson et al., 2005; Pearson & Porath, 2004, 2009; Sutton, 2007), supervisors who contribute to an unhealthy, destructive organizational culture through systematic and repeated exhibition of these behaviors encourage incivility, bullying, and other destructive behaviors on the part of other organizational members, compromising the potential of the institution and the persons within it.

Contributions of this Volume to the Study of Problematic Workplace Behaviors

The behaviors reviewed here have been addressed by scholars in the communication field as instances of communication phenomena relevant to the workplace (e.g., Davenport Sypher, 2004; Fritz, 2009, 2012). Other behaviors have communicative dimensions, but these communicative dimensions have not been studied exclusively as organizational phenomena. Aggression, for instance, has been studied as verbal aggression (e.g., Infante & Rancer, 1996); although this concept has been explored in workplace contexts (e.g., Infante, Anderson, Martin, Herington, & Kim, 1993), it is a term of broad scope; the focus has been the behavior in general rather than a particular manifestation peculiar to the workplace. Antisocial communication (Kinney & Pörhölä, 2009) manifests a wide range of applications, as well, although Kinney and Pörhölä's (2009) collection contains a chapter on workplace bullying relationships (Rainivaara, 2009).

The work presented in this volume adds to the conversation on the nature of problematic relationships in the workplace and, in particular, on the relevance of communication processes to these problematic behaviors and relationships. The work on ostracism and cliques by Sias (2009; this volume) focuses on communicative behavior as the defining feature of the phenomenon of exclusion. Fay's chapter (this volume) on telecommuting as a context for problematic workplace behaviors identifies, through the lived communicative experience of teleworkers, defining communicative coordinates of potential exclusion. Davenport Sypher and Gill (this volume) offer new and important evidence of the influence of perceptions of organizational and interpersonal incivility on trust, an element integral to the good of relationships. Kinney's conceptualization of bullying as violence (this volume) demonstrates the powerful effect of interpersonal communication in its contribution to the bullying relationship and of institutional communication on how seriously bullying is taken. Kinney offers an important reflection of the importance of naming: when bullying is labeled as an unacceptable act of violence and organizational policy follows suit, the social construction of this problematic behavior takes a new turn, legitimizing organizational action to penalize, and thereby prevent, this destructive behavior. Keashly's chapter on hostile work relationships (this volume) adds to the conceptualization of these phenomena as communicative in nature, offering a review of the latest research on the dynamic nature of the communication process in multiple types of hostile relationships and the interactive nature of processes such as bullying.

What these chapters offer to the literature is a careful working out of implications of communication processes in relation to problematic behaviors in the workplace as they constitute both work relationships and organizational phenomena such as culture and climate. As our knowledge of factors contributing to problematic behaviors and to problematic behaviors' trajectory into problematic work relationships continues to grow, we will be able to address the problem at its roots. Of particular importance is the juxtaposition of these chapters on behaviors affecting problematic workplace relationships with chapters exploring contexts and potential remedies. As was the case with the first volume treating problematic relationships in the workplace (Fritz & Omdahl, 2006), we find it important to include a holistic picture of both problems and potential solutions, as have others pursuing related research (e.g., Lutgen-Sandvik & Davenport Sypher, 2009).

References

Aquino, K., & Douglas, S. (2003). Identity threat and antisocial behavior in organizations: The moderating effects of individual differences, aggressive modeling, and hierarchical status. *Organizational Behavior and Human Decision Processes, 90*, 195–208.

Ashforth, B. (1994). Petty tyranny in organizations. *Human Relations, 47*, 755–778.

Baron, R. A., & Neuman, J. H. (1996). Workplace aggression—the iceberg beneath the tip of workplace violence: Evidence on its forms, frequency and targets. *Public Administration Quarterly, 21*, 446–464.

Bennett, R. J., Aquino, K., Reed, A., II, & Thau, S. (2005). The normative nature of employee deviance and the impact of moral identity. In S. Fox & P. Spector (Eds.), *Counterproductive work behavior: Investigations of actors and targets* (pp. 107–125). Washington, DC: American Psychological Association.

Bennett, R. J., & Robinson, S. L. (2003). The past, present, and future of workplace deviance research. In J. Greenberg (Ed.), *Organizational behavior: The state of the science* (2nd ed., pp. 247–281). Mahwah, NJ: Lawrence Erlbaum.

Bies, R. J., & Tripp, T. M. (2005). The study of revenge in the workplace: Conceptual, ideological, and empirical issues. In S. Fox & P. E. Spector (Eds.), *Counterproductive work behavior: Investigations of actors and targets* (pp. 65–81). Washington, DC: American Psychological Association.

Brodsky, C. M. (1976). *The harassed worker.* Lexington, MA: Lexington Books.

Buss, A. H. (1961). *The psychology of aggression.* New York, NY: Wiley.

Cameron, K. S., Dutton, J. E., & Quinn, R. E. (Eds.). (2003). *Positive organizational scholarship: Foundations of a new discipline.* San Francisco, CA: Berrett-Koehler.

Cooper, C. L., & Rousseau, D. M. (Eds.). (1998). *Trends in organizational behavior.* New York, NY: Wiley.

Cupach, W. R., & Spitzberg, B. H. (Eds.). (1994). *The dark side of interpersonal communication.* Hillsdale, NJ: Lawrence Erlbaum.

Cupach, W. R., & Spitzberg, B. H. (Eds.). (2011). *The dark side of close relationships—II.* New York, NY: Routledge.

Davenport Sypher, B. (2004). Reclaiming civil discourse in the workplace. *Southern Communication Journal, 69,* 257–269.

Duffy, M. K., Ganster, D., & Pagon, M. (2002). Social undermining in the workplace. *Academy of Management Journal, 45,* 331–351.

Einarsen, S., Aasland, M. S., & Skogstad, A. (2007). Destructive leadership behavior: A definition and conceptual model. *The Leadership Quarterly, 18,* 207–216.

Einarsen, S., Hoel, H., Zapf, D., & Cooper, C. L. (Eds.). (2011a). *Bullying and harassment in the workplace: Developments in theory, research, and practice* (2nd ed.). Boca Raton, FL: CRC Press/Taylor & Francis.

Einarsen, S., Hoel, H., Zapf, D., & Cooper, C. L. (2011b). The concept of bullying and harassment at work: The European tradition. In S. Einarsen, H. Hoel, D. Zapf, & C. L. Cooper (Eds.), *Bullying and harassment in the workplace: Developments in theory, research, and practice* (2nd ed., pp. 3–39). Boca Raton, FL: CRC Press/Taylor & Francis.

Fox, S., & Spector, P. E. (Eds.). (2005a). *Counterproductive work behavior: Investigations of actors and targets.* Washington, DC: American Psychological Association.

Fox, S., & Spector, P. E. (2005b). Introduction. In S. Fox & P. E. Spector (Eds.), *Counterproductive work behavior: Investigations of actors and targets* (pp. 3–10). Washington, DC: American Psychological Association.

Fritz, J. M. H. (2002). How do I dislike thee? Let me count the ways: Constructing impressions of troublesome others at work. *Management Communication Quarterly, 15,* 410–438.

Fritz, J. M. H. (2006). Typology of troublesome others at work: A follow-up investigation. In J. M. H. Fritz & B. L. Omdahl (Eds.), *Problematic relationships in the workplace* (pp. 21–46). New York, NY: Peter Lang.

Fritz, J. M. H. (2009). Rudeness and incivility in the workplace. In S. Wright & R. Morrison (Eds.), *Friends and enemies in organizations: A work psychology perspective* (pp. 168–194). Hampshire, England: Palgrave Macmillan.

Fritz, J. M. H. (2012). Interpersonal crisis communication in the workplace: Professional civility as ethical response to problematic interactions. In S. A. Groom & J. M. H. Fritz (Eds.), *Communication ethics and crisis: Negotiating differences in public and private spheres* pp. (67–86). Madison, NJ: Fairleigh Dickinson University Press.

Fritz, J. M. H. (in press). Organizational misbehavior. In L. Crothers & J. Lipinski (Eds.), *Bullying in the workplace: Symptoms, causes and remedies.* New York, NY: Routledge.

Fritz, J. M. H., & Omdahl, B. L. (Eds.). (2006). *Problematic relationships in the workplace.* New York, NY: Peter Lang.

Furnham, A., & Taylor, J. (2004). *The dark side of behavior at work. Understanding and avoiding employees leaving, thieving and deceiving.* New York, NY: Palgrave Macmillan.

Giacalone, R. A., & Greenberg, J. (1997). *Antisocial behavior in organizations.* Thousand Oaks, CA: Sage.

Greenberg, J. (1990). Employee theft as a response to underemployment inequity: The hidden cost of pay cuts. *Journal of Applied Psychology, 75,* 399–432.

Greenberg, J. (Ed.). (2003). *Organizational behavior: The state of the science* (2nd ed.). Mahwah, NJ: Lawrence Erlbaum.

Greenberg, J. (Ed.). (2010). *Insidious workplace behavior.* New York, NY: Routledge.

Griffin, R. W., & Lopez, Y. P. (2005). "Bad behavior" in organizations: A review and typology for future research. *Journal of Management, 31,* 988–1005.

Griffin, R. W., O'Leary-Kelly, A., & Collins, J. (1998). Dysfunctional work behaviors in organizations. In C. L. Cooper & D. M. Rousseau (Eds.), *Trends in organizational behavior* (pp. 65–82). New York, NY: Wiley.

Griffin, R. W., & O'Leary-Kelly, A. M. (2004). An introduction to the dark side. In R. W. Griffin & A. M. O'Leary-Kelly (Eds.), *The dark side of organizational behavior* (pp. 1–19). San Francisco, CA: Jossey-Bass.

Hollinger, R. C. (1986). Acts against the workplace: Social bonding and employee deviance. *Deviant Behavior, 7,* 53–75.

Infante, D. A., Anderson, C. M., Martin, M. M., Herington, A. D., & Kim, J. (1993). Subordinates' satisfaction and perceptions of superiors' compliance-gaining tactics, argumentativeness, verbal aggressiveness, and style. *Management Communication Quarterly, 6,* 307–326.

Infante, D. A., & Rancer, A. S. (1996). Argumentativeness and verbal aggressiveness: A review of recent theory and research. In B. R. Burleson (Ed.), *Communication yearbook 19* (pp. 319–351). Thousand Oaks, CA: Sage.

Keashly, L., & Jagatic, K. (2003). By any other name: American perspectives on workplace bullying. In S. Einarsen, H. Hoel, D. Zapf, & C. L. Cooper (Eds.), *Bullying and emotional abuse in the workplace: International perspectives in research and practice* (pp. 31–61). New York, NY: Taylor & Francis.

Keashly, L., & Jagatic, K. (2011). North American perspectives on hostile behaviors and bullying at work. In S. Einarsen, H. Hoel, D. Zapf, & C. L. Cooper (Eds.), *Bullying and harassment in the workplace: Developments in theory, research, and practice* (2nd ed., pp. 41–71). Boca Raton, FL: CRC Press/Taylor & Francis.

Keashly, L., Trott, V., & MacLean, L. M. (1994). Abusive behavior in the workplace: A preliminary investigation. *Violence and Victims, 9,* 125–141.

Kets de Vries, M. F. R. (2004). Dysfunctional leadership. In N. Nicholson, P. Audia & M. Pillulta (Eds.), *Encyclopedic dictionary of organizational behavior* (pp. 368–373). Oxford, England: Blackwell.

Kidwell, R. E., Jr., & Martin, C. L. (Eds.). (2005). *Managing organizational deviance.* Thousand Oaks, CA: Sage.

Kinney, T., & Pörhölä, M. (Eds.). (2009). *Anti and pro-social communication: Theories, methods, and applications.* New York, NY: Peter Lang.

Langan-Fox, J., Cooper, C. L., & Klimoski, R. J. (2007). Introduction. In J. Langan-Fox, C. L. Cooper, & R. J. Klimoski (Eds.), *Research companion to the dysfunctional workplace: Management challenges and symptoms* (pp. xiii–xvi). Cheltenham, England: Edward Elgar.

Lipman-Blumen, J. (2005). *The allure of toxic leaders. Why we follow destructive bosses and corrupt politicians—and how we can survive them.* Oxford, England: Oxford University Press.

Lombardo, M. M., & McCall, M. W. J. (1984). *Coping with an intolerable boss.* Greensboro, NC: Center for Creative Leadership.

Lutgen-Sandvik, P., & Davenport Sypher, B. (Eds.). (2009). *Destructive organizational communication: Processes, consequences, and constructive ways of organizing.* New York, NY: Routledge.

Lutgen-Sandvik, P., Namie, G., & Namie, R. (2009). Workplace bullying: Causes, consequences, and corrections. In P. Lutgen-Sandvik & B. Davenport Sypher (Eds.), *Destructive organizational communication: Processes, consequences, & constructive ways of organizing* (pp. 27–52). New York, NY: Routledge.

Lutgen-Sandvik, P., Riforgiate, S., & Fletcher, C. (2011). Work as a source of positive emotional experiences and the discourses informing positive assessment. *Western Journal of Communication, 75*, 2–27.

Lutgen-Sandvik, P., Tracy, S. J., & Alberts, J. K. (2007). Burned by bullying in the American workplace: Prevalence, perception, degree, and impact. *Journal of Management Studies, 44*, 837–862.

Luthans, F. (2002). The need for and meaning of positive organizational behavior. *Journal of Organizational Behavior, 23*, 695–706.

Namie, G., & Namie, R. (2000). *The bully at work. What you can do to stop the hurt and reclaim your dignity on the job.* Naperville, IL: Sourcebooks.

Neuman, J. H., & Baron, R. A. (1997). Aggression in the workplace. In R. A. Giacalone & J. Greenberg (Eds.), *Antisocial behavior in the workplace* (pp. 35–67). Thousand Oaks, CA: Sage.

Neuman, J. H., & Baron, R. A. (1998). Workplace violence and workplace aggression: Evidence concerning specific forms, potential causes, and preferred targets. *Journal of Management, 24*, 391–419.

Neuman, J. H., & Baron, R. A. (2005). Aggression in the workplace: A social-psychological perspective. In S. Fox & P. E. Spector (Eds.), *Counterproductive work behavior: Investigations of actors and targets* (pp. 13–40). Washington, DC: American Psychological Association.

O'Leary-Kelly, A. M., Duffy, M. K., & Griffin, R. W. (2000). Construct confusion in the study of antisocial work behavior. *Research in Personnel and Human Resources Management, 18*, 275–303.

O'Leary-Kelly, A. M., Griffin, R. W., & Glew, D. J. (1996). Organization-motivated aggression: A research framework. *Academy of Management Review, 21*, 225–253.

Pearson, C. M. (2010). Research on workplace incivility and its connection to practice. In J. Greenberg (Ed.), *Insidious workplace behavior* (pp. 149–173). New York, NY: Routledge.

Pearson, C. M., & Porath, C. L. (2004). On incivility, its impact, and directions for future research. In R. W. Griffin & A. M. O'Leary-Kelly (Eds.), *The dark side of organizational behavior* (pp. 403–425). San Francisco, CA: Jossey-Bass.

Pearson, C., & Porath, C. (2009). *The cost of bad behavior: How incivility is damaging your business and what to do about it.* New York, NY: Portfolio.

Pearson, D., Andersson, L., & Porath, C. (2005). Workplace incivility. In S. Fox & P. E. Spector (Eds.), *Counterproductive workplace behavior: Investigations of actors and targets* (pp. 177–200). Washington, DC: American Psychological Association.

Rainivaara, S. (2009). Workplace bullying relationships. In T. Kinney & M. Pörhölä (Eds.), *Anti and pro social communication: Theories, methods, and applications* (Language as Social Action, Vol. 6, pp. 59–70). New York: Peter Lang.

Robinson, S. L., & Bennett, R. J. (1995). A typology of deviant workplace behaviors: A multidimensional scaling study. *Academy of Management Journal, 38*, 555–572.

Robinson, S. L., & Greenberg, J. (1998). Employees behaving badly: Dimensions, determinants, and dilemmas in the study of workplace deviance. In C. L. Cooper & D. M. Rousseau (Eds.), *Trends in organizational behavior* (Vol. 5, pp. 1–30). Chichester, England: John Wiley & Sons.

Robinson, S. L., & O'Leary-Kelly, A. M. (1998). Monkey see, monkey do: The influence of work groups on the antisocial behavior of employees. *Academy of Management Journal, 41*, 658–672.

Sagie, A., Stashevsky, S., & Koslowsky, M. (2003). Introduction: Misbehaviour in organizations. In A. Stagie, S. Stashevsky, & M. Koslowsky (Eds.), *Misbehaviour and dysfunctional attitudes in organizations* (pp. 3–10). Hampshire, England: Palgrave MacMillan.

Schat, A. C. H., Desmarais, S., & Kelloway, E. K. 2006. *Exposure to workplace aggression from multiple sources: Validation of a measure and test of a model.* Unpublished manuscript, McMaster University, Hamilton, Canada.

Shackleton, V. (1995). Leaders who derail. In V. Shackleton (Ed.), *Business leadership* (pp. 89–100). London, England: Thomson.

Sias, P. (2009). *Organizing relationships: Traditional and emerging perspectives on workplace relationships.* Thousand Oaks, CA: Sage.

Skarlicki, D. P., & Folger, R. (1997). Retaliation in the workplace: The roles of distributive, procedural, and interactional justice. *Journal of Applied Psychology, 82,* 424–443.

Socha, T. J., & Pitts, M. J. (2012). *The positive side of interpersonal communication.* New York, NY: Peter Lang.

Spitzberg, B. H., & Cupach, W. R. (Eds.). (1998). *The dark side of close relationships.* Mahwah, NJ: Lawrence Erlbaum.

Sutton, R. (2007). *The no asshole rule.* New York, NY: Warner Business Books.

Tepper, B. J. (2000). Consequences of abusive supervision. *Academy of Management Journal, 43,* 178–190.

Tepper, B. J. (2007). Abusive supervision in work organizations: Review, synthesis, and research agenda. *Journal of Management, 33,* 261–289.

Thau, S., Crossley, C., Bennett, R. J., & Sczesny, S. (2007). The relationship between trust, attachment, and antisocial work behaviors. *Human Relations, 60,* 1155–1179.

Van Fleet, D. D., & Griffin, R. W. (2006). Dysfunctional organizational culture: The role of leadership in motivating dysfunctional work behavior. *Journal of Managerial Psychology, 21,* 698–708.

Vardi, Y., & Weitz, E. (2004). *Misbehavior in organizations.* Mahwah, NJ: Lawrence Erlbaum.

Vardi, Y., & Wiener, Y. (1996). Misbehavior in organizations: A motivational framework. *Organization Science, 7,* 151–165.

Warren, D. E. (2003). Constructive and destructive deviance in organizations. *Academy of Management Review, 28,* 622–632.

· 2 ·

THE ROLE OF EMOTION IN PROBLEMATIC RELATIONSHIPS IN THE WORKPLACE

BECKY L. OMDAHL

Across the well-over one thousand surveys compiled by the team of Fritz, Hess, and Omdahl, over 99 percent identified emotions as part of their experiences with problematic relationships in the workplace (see Fritz & Omdahl, 2006). The emotions reported vary from mild to intense states, and they range from pure (e.g., anger or fear) to same-valence blends (e.g., anger and fear) to developmentally complex, opposite-valence blends (e.g., anger and happiness). In only one case did a person report no emotion elicited by a problematic relationship in the workplace.

Positive emotional experiences are also plentiful in the workplace. In a study of 835 employees, Lutgen-Sandvik, Riforgiate, and Fletcher (2011) identified seventeen different kinds of positive emotional experiences (e.g., recognition, social support, triumph) that represented five social discourses (i.e., power-empowerment, individualism-uniqueness, success-accomplishment, belonging-affiliation, and safety-security). Throughout the reported kinds of emotional experiences, most are rooted in workplace relationships.

Regardless of whether the focus is on destructive or constructive relationships, experiences with others at work potentially bring a wealth of emotions, and those emotions play distinct roles. In some cases, emotional expressions are the behaviors that people find problematic (e.g., the boss who "blows up," the coworker who cries at the most carefully delivered constructive feedback). Emotions can also be the drivers of patterns characterizing problematic interaction (e.g., shame as the driver of aggressive behaviors). These first two roles often lead to the third: Emotions are experiences that must be managed in order to meet personal, relational, or organizational goals. Emotions also play a fourth role, as mediators between the situation and the initiation of coping responses which, to greater or lesser extent, stave off deleterious outcomes. Finally, emotions play a transformative role in some of the constructive responses to problematic relationships in the workplace.

This chapter explores these five roles in detail. For each role, emotion theory and research are offered as an explanatory backdrop and then examples are offered from research as well as from chapters in this volume.

Emotional Displays as Problematic Behavior in the Workplace

In 1872, Darwin (1872/1965) confronted his readers with detailed drawings of the postures and facial expressions for different emotions. In *Expression of the Emotions in Man and Animals*, Darwin (1872/1965) argued that the gestures associated with different emotions have survival-enhancing action orientations. The primate with squared lips, displaying bared teeth, readily reflected an action orientation of "attack" to readers in the year 1872. Not surprisingly, the same expression of unbridled anger displayed by a colleague is capable of sending the same message to modern-day coworkers.

Lutgen-Sandvik (2006) offered the following examples of participant descriptions from her bullying research: "She would scream at us, her face getting all red and her eyes watering. It was almost like she wanted to reach out and choke you" (p. 411); "I could see his eyes bulging, his veins and everything, spitting, and pointing his finger" (p. 412); and, "So his face would get beet-red, and he'd *slam* his hands down, stand up, and start shaking his finger at you, and *screaming* 'Get out of here. Get out of my sight.' Everyone waiting outside heard all of it, and you'd go out, and the next person went in for the kill" (p. 413).

Whether it is a boss destroying trust by turning red and screaming or a highly sensitive colleague derailing productive work with tears, emotional expressions are often identified as problematic behaviors in the workplace. Fritz's (2002) typology pointed out behaviors grouped under the term "unprofessional" that are prime emotional displays (e.g., yelling). These unprofessional behaviors characterized specific types of problematic others in the subsequent cluster analysis as in "The Extreme Unprofessional" boss and the "Abrasive, Incompetent Harasser" coworker (Fritz, 2006, p. 23).

Behaviors described as bullying, hostile, and uncivil permeate this volume. Many of the behavioral displays described involve emotional expressions. For example, Kinney (this volume) overviews compliance gaining and influence strategies, including those involving aggression in the forms of hitting, kicking, or offering insults. Keashly (this volume) offers a framework for hostile work relationships that "captures all manner of behavior ranging from the more overt physical violence (e.g., assault) as physical, active and direct to yelling and cursing as verbal, active, and direct to the silent treatment as verbal, passive, and direct." The examples provided here highlight emotional displays that can lead to evaluations of problematic workplace relationships.

So why are the displays of human emotion so powerful? Numerous studies have demonstrated that human facial expressions of emotions (e.g., Ekman, 1972, 1982, 1984; Ekman & Friesen, 1975, 1978), human vocal expressions (Scherer, 1986; Scherer, London,& Wolf, 1973), and even body movement and gestures communicate emotional states at far better than chance levels. Emotional states are associated with action orientations that signal what a person is likely to do next (e.g., anger: attack; fear: run; happiness: approach/ engage; Frijda, 1986). Thus, the emotional displays of others have strong predictive value of what's coming next, and if what's coming next is costly in terms of human energy or, worse yet, dangerous, it warrants a protective response.

Even without the information of particular emotional states, behavior enabling people to deduce some basic underlying tendencies may be sufficient to result in labels of "problematic." A recent study using 144 features representing appraisals, psycho-physiological states, motor expressions, action tendencies, subjective experiences, and emotion regulation identified four underlying dimensions of emotion: evaluation-pleasantness, potency-control, activation-arousal, and unpredictability (Fontaine, Scherer, Roesch, & Ellsworth, 2007). Messages reflecting core dimensions underlying emotions (e.g., a hand unexpectedly smacking a table reflecting potency, arousal, and unpredictability) may enable observers to anticipate what is coming and respond accordingly.

Real-life experience leads me to conclude that a common cost for colleagues frequently offering emotion displays is that they are sometimes excluded from work groups. Hot-tempered, aggrandizing, or overly sensitive people are easily exempted from meetings with the simple and polite dropping of a name (e.g., "Tom, Mary, and John should be able to work this one out." Where's Rhonda in this list?). While exclusion (Sias, this volume) can arguably be an uncivil act toward a member of a workforce, exclusions may result when costly behaviors are recurrent.

Emotions as Drivers of Patterns of Interaction

Kinney's chapter (this volume) on bullying and Keashley's work (this volume) on hostile work relationships move the focus on repeated acts of aggression directed toward or between workers. Both Kinney (this volume) and Keashly (this volume) include documentation that behaviors often move from indirect, covert messages to more direct, overt aggressive messages as the relationship goes on. As Keashly (this volume) states, "Both the conflict (Keashly & Nowell, 2003, 2011) and aggression (e.g., Barling, 1996; Glomb, 2002; Glomb & Miner, 2002) literatures provide evidence that subtle, covert, and more psychological forms of aggressive behavior precede more overt and direct forms of hostility, including physical violence."

Retzinger (1991, 1995) offered tremendous insight into why hostile behaviors recur and often escalate. According to Retzinger (1991, 1995), shame is the driver of aggressive nonverbal and verbal behaviors. Shame is triggered when the words or actions of the other signal abandonment (e.g., an employee who repeatedly contacts his or her boss and receives no response) or engulfment (e.g., a colleague who asks questions that are perceived as overly personal). While not everyone would experience abandonment or engulfment as a response to the examples embedded here, Retzinger (1991) provided an explanation of why some people do. Interdependence is a psychological space in which a person's unique self must co-exist with dyadic interactions. She argues that a "flexible bonding system" in which a person can maintain a basic level of differentiation even while being emotionally close is crucial to tolerance for times of separation and intimacy. In contrast, when self-identity feels lost, as in the case of engulfment (i.e., the perception that the other is defining, controlling, subsuming self) or when the security of the relationship is challenged, as in the case of abandonment, shame is triggered. While anyone is vulnerable to an occasional "shame attack," as childhood or repetitive situations damage self-identities and boundaries and increase the insecurity about the stability of a relationship, it becomes much more difficult to manage "flexible bonding" or the psychological space of independence. Under these conditions, it becomes much more likely that messages will be perceived as threatening self (engulfment) or relationship (abandonment).

Retzinger (1991, 1995) further argued that shame is a very painful emotion. While shame motivates people to follow the morals essential for social interaction, the experience of shame feels debilitating. Shame involves the whole self and "the sudden exposure of deficiency in one's own eyes as well in the eyes of the other" (Retzinger, 1991, p. 41). While experiencing shame, people feel helpless and exposed and want to hide to escape the purview of others (Retzinger, 1991).

The extremely painful nature of shame motivates people to "bypass" it, and the way it is typically bypassed is to substitute anger or rage (Retzinger, 1991). The reason for this particular substitution is simple. Anger is the perfect antidote: While shame feels debilitating, anger feels empowering. Thus, rather than directly displaying or addressing feelings of inferiority, attacking, demeaning, angry messages are displayed or expressed (Retzinger, 1991).

Messages *interpreted* as attacking or demeaning lead to *perceptions* of engulfment or abandonment on the part of the receiver. This process initiates a spiral in which the aggressive message from one party trips shame in the receiver who covers the shame and responds with an increasingly aggressive message, and so on. If a person is highly skilled at articulating an experience of shame (e.g., "Just now when you said, 'The reports weren't finished,' I felt terrible."), and the other is a person capable of responding with support and affirmation ("I'm sorry I said it that way. I know you unexpectedly had to go to that conference all last week and had no chance to finish them."), they have a good chance of escaping escalation. However, without these skills, it is likely that shame-rage spiral will continue and escalate.

While I have chosen to present Retzinger's (1991, 1995) explanation in detail, there are numerous other scholars positing shame as the driver of hostile behaviors between people. Paralleling the work of Retzinger, Scheff (1994) proposed that there is a need to balance the focus on the individual and the group. Solidarity occurs when there is balance: The individual has a healthy self-identity that has meaning and connection to the group. When individuals feel alienated from important groups, they experience isolation (too much focus on the self) or engulfment (too much focus on the group). In Scheff's (1994) approach, both isolation and engulfment give rise to shame, and shame drives aggressive behaviors such as bullying.

The shame/rage spiral proposed by Retzinger (1991) and the model of social integration offered by Scheff (1994) offer rich explanations for shame as the emotional driver of hostile work relationships (Keashly, this volume) and bullying behavior (Kinney, this volume). As noted earlier, Keashly points out that the conflict and aggression literatures point to subtle, covert, psychological forms of aggressive behavior occurring in advance of direct, overt forms of hostility (e.g., Barling, 1996; Glomb, 2002; Glomb & Miner, 2002; Keashly & Nowell, 2003). Similarly, the research by Einarsen (1999) documented escalation in bullying behaviors. Paralleling these observations, Retzinger (1991) observed spirals in which the conversations began with seemingly innocuous statements that would be responded to with the subtlest of shame cues (e.g., rolling in a lip, offering a slight smile). Micro-seconds later the person rolling the lip or offering the slight smile would respond with a message ever so slightly increasing the level of aggression. Retzinger's exhaustive coding scheme and data provide convincing evidence that shame was the driver behind the increasingly direct, overt, and aggressive spiral of behaviors. This pattern is totally consistent with claims that reciprocation of rude or uncivil comments can give rise to a spiral of increasing hostility (Anderson & Pearson, 1999).

Rainivaara (2009, cited by Keashly, this volume) talked about a "tipping point" for people in bullying or hostile relationships. Similarly, Hess and Sneed (this volume) talk about the difficulty people have holding back from behavior that inflames the situation. What explains this difficulty in escaping inflammatory behavior and moving toward de-escalation? The basic answer is that they experienced an inability to regulate emotion. This is the focus of the next role of emotion.

Emotion as an Experience to Be Managed

There are two very different discussions in the literature about the management of emotion in the workplace. The first focuses on the demands of the organization while the second focuses on the desires of the individual to navigate his or her difficult psychological space. Ultimately, both are addressing the same processes of regulating emotion.

Hochschild (1983) introduced the concept of "emotional labour" in her study of flight attendants. She argued that many jobs require people to manage their emotion consistently with the norms (or display rules) of the organization. In the case of flight attendants, they must wear the prescribed mask of the airline, smiling while enduring turmoil on the flight deck (Hochschild, 1983). For many, Hochschild (1983) argued, this was real work, "emotional labour." In order to carry out the labor, two levels of emotion management, surface acting and deep acting, are performed (Hochschild, 1983). Surface acting occurs when an employee recognizes that his or her emotional state does not match the display rules expected by the organization, and the person strives to control the display of his or her emotion (e.g., to avoid expressing anger). This action is consistent with Ekman and Friesen's (1971) discussion of intentionally managing emotional expression to fit display rules honoring cultural norms. Deep acting is when the employee attempts to alter or change his or her actual emotional state to that expected by the organization (e.g., to actually not be angry; Hochschild, 1983). These concepts continue to receive attention, with particular focus on the dissonance that drives them (e.g., Glomb & Tews, 2004) and moderators (e.g., genuinely focusing on meeting the needs of customers) that may reduce the stress (e.g., Allen, Pugh, Grandey, & Groth, 2010).

Fineman (1993) argued that there is

> an intricate order of permissible emotion display attached to different categories of jobs and situations. For instance, while a waitress in an informal restaurant might playfully "flirt" with a male customer, a dentist would not do so with a patient....A local shopkeeper might tell a regular customer about some work worries; a counter clerk in a bank would be less likely to reveal such news. (p. 19)

Much of the original research on emotion in the workplace focused on specific industries in which employees needed to manage emotions because of the branding of the organization (e.g., Disney), the nature of the service provided (e.g., flight attendants), or the challenging emotional work directly attributable to the clientele served (e.g., nurses; Fineman, 1993). As Mann (2004) pointed out, workers engaged in "people-work" must engage in high levels of emotion management as they convey appropriate emotions. While failed efforts to manage emotion in some lines of work might result in the loss of a customer, "within the 'caring' business, such as the counseling and guidance professions, a failure to display the appropriate emotion (e.g., sympathy) or a leakage of an inappropriate one (e.g., boredom) can have much more serious implications for the well-being of the client and their continued relationship with the professional" (Mann, 2004, p. 205). Jobs vary considerably in the degree to which they require pervasive and highly skilled emotional labor, and some argue that a disservice is done when all positions are viewed as requiring the same level of emotion management skill (Payne, 2009).

While there are countless studies arguing that high levels of emotional labor are incurred to a greater extent within certain professions, scholars also increasingly address the fact that nearly all people are required to bring emotional management skills to the workplace. Payne (2009, p. 354) summarized the trend clearly: If one argues that emotional labor occurs "between workers and managers, and between workers and their peers, then one might argue that it is essential to all jobs." So how do all these people in all these different lines of work manage emotion?

According to the newer approaches to emotion management, the cognitive regulation of emotion occurs at multiple levels. This assertion is based on an approach to emotion that is ultimately an integration of two lines of theorizing about emotion (Philippot, Baeyens, Douilliez, & Francart, 2004). In an effort to foster an understanding of this approach, this section begins with an overview of the physiological and cognitive approaches to emotion that are wed together in the multiple level approach. The evolving argument is that people are managing both the physiological activation described beginning with Darwin (1872/1965) and James (1884/1984) to the present day (Philippot et al., 2004), and emotion arising from cognitive appraisal and reappraisal (e.g., Higgins, 2011; Scherer, 1984a)

Analysis of the physiological nature of emotion began with Darwin (1872/1965) and was followed by James (1884/1984). James offered a theory reversing the common belief that humans experienced a subjective emotional state and then expressed that state through facial and bodily configurations. He (James, 1884/1984) argued that "the bodily changes follow directly the perception of the exciting fact, and that our feeling of the same changes as they occur is the emotion" (p. 128). This theory is a logical extension of Darwin's (1872/1965) evolutionary claims: Immediate physical changes and actions made survival possible while subjective states were secondary in importance. While this was the central theme, James recognized the existence of mental emotions outside the expressions of the peripheral nervous system.

The rebuttal to James came years later from Cannon (1914, 1927). Cannon honored the order (physiological changes, then subjective state) but challenged the mechanisms proposed by James. According to Cannon (1914), changes in the slow, insensitive, undifferentiated viscera could not produce emotional states as hypothesized by James. The alternative theory posited by Cannon claimed that changes in the thalamic region determined subjective emotional experience. Thus, both James and Cannon maintained that distinct physiological changes were associated with discrete emotions.

Physiological theories of emotion continue in the literature today. Tomkins (1962, 1963) and Izard (1977) argued that the subjective emotional states are determined by unique neural firing patterns for several primary emotions. Building on evidence from facial displays of discrete emotions (Eibl-Eibesfelt, 1970; Ekman & Friesen, 1975; Ekman & Oster, 1979; Izard, 1977), Tomkins and Izard argued that neural firings from the facial region are received by the cortex and determine or strongly affect the subjective state. As a refinement, Izard (1977) also argued that when facial expressions are triggered but not expressed (e.g., when a person is neutralizing expression to follow display rules), neural firings are still transmitted to the cortex and impact the person's subjective state.

The failure to find distinct physiological changes for specific emotions in research conducted in the 1950s, 1960s, and 1970s dampened enthusiasm for physiological theories. The cross-cultural research by Ekman and Izard and colleagues (e.g., Ekman, 1972, 1982; Izard, 1977) was one of the few strains of research keeping discrete emotion theory alive. The 1980s produced isolated studies documenting distinct physiological patterns for a few discrete emotions for which there are universal facial displays (e.g., Ekman, Levenson, & Friesen, 1983).

As interest in searching for physiological bases of discrete emotions waned in the 1950s, 1960s, and 1970s, the exploration of the cognitive underpinnings of emotion took off. Schacter (1959) discovered that anxious research participants preferred to wait for an upcoming experimental session with someone rather than alone. He argued that the behavior of others offered information about how to interpret one's own arousal. The role of attributions in determining subjective emotional experience became the main focus of emotion research.

The most famous study from this time period was Schacter and Singer's (1962) exploration of how participants would "attribute" the experience of being injected with epinephrine. Subjects given a clear explanation for their physical changes were not as affected by the performances of highly emotive confederates. In contrast, subjects not given a clear explanation but provided with overt emotional displays of happy and angry confederates did explain their physiological arousal consistently with actions of the confederate (i.e., happy or angry). The problem in the results came from the control condition: Subjects who were not given any epinephrine (i.e., had no induced "arousal" to label as an emotional state) reported higher levels of the confederates' emotion than subjects given epinephrine and experimenter-provided rationales for their experience of arousal.

At approximately the same time as social science was wrestling with the Schacter and Singer (1962) results, information processing models were introducing a paradigm shift. Originating in computer science, artificial intelligence models were increasingly used to explain emotion (e.g., see Oatley, 1988; Ortony, 1988; Pfeifer, 1988). Social scientists began to propose emotion theories emphasizing information processing rather than physiological changes as causal mechanisms leading to different subjective states. For example, Mandler (1975, 1984) proposed that schema discrepancies are the basis for emotions. Specifically, Mandler (1975, 1984) argued that when a stimulus is encountered, there are two basic cognitive processes that may be elicited. If the stimulus is easily identified, it is assimilated based on existing cognitive structures. Assimilation elicits low levels of arousal; these low levels are typically positively labeled. If the stimulus cannot be easily identified or integrated into existing cognitive structures, the person must accommodate the stimulus. Accommodation trips of relatively high levels of arousal are elicited, and the person engages in heightened cognitive processing to determine whether this arousal is positive or negative. Mandler's schema discrepancy explanation of emotion was adopted by other social scientists (e.g., Berscheid, 1983).

The 1980s and 1990s were characterized by the interweaving of philosophical treatises, physiological theories, and cognitive approaches to emotion. Cognitive appraisal theories of emotion (e.g., Arnold, 1960; de Rivera, 1977; Ellis, 1985; Ellsworth & Scherer, 2003; Frijda, 1986; Ortony, Clore, & Collins, 1988; Roseman, 1984; Scherer, 1982, 1984a, 1984b, 1988a, 1988b; Smith & Ellsworth, 1985; Weiner, 1985) explain the cognitive processing that leads to specific emotional states. They argue that people arrive in emotional states by evaluating incoming information in terms of appraisals (e.g., Is it novel or known? Is it pleasant or unpleasant?). Configurations of appraisals lead to complete packages of emotional responses (i.e., physiological changes, behavioral expressions, action orientations, and subjective states).

The multi-level approach asserts that both the physiological and cognitive approaches to emotion are operating (Philippot et al., 2004). In this approach, an immediate reaction to a situation may originate in schematic memory. A former graduate student described wandering into a townhouse under construction while in the Caribbean. As she reached for a doorknob, a massive orange spider landed on her hand. The argument posed by the multi-level approach to emotion management is that the spider landing would elicit a "wholly-prepared, immediate response" because it is a very challenging situation in which the body is prepared to act (Philippot et al., 2004). This schema could be elicited by peripheral feedback (e.g., the fear taking over the musculature of her face), the redirection of attention (e.g., to the spider), and/or the elaboration of emotional information (e.g., a pounding heart). The argument is that the schematic response induces a set of automatic behaviors that are not deliberately processed. When the schema leads to an intense emotion, it is likely that this response will overwhelm the person and delay the person's ability to *self-direct* his or her expressions and behaviors.

Beyond the immediately produced schema is another level of response involving slower, deliberate, cognitive elaboration (Philippot et al., 2004). In terms of emotion regulation, the slower, elaborative level allows for emotion regulation. Elements of the situation, one's response, similar situations, meanings, possible actions, and standards for action can be processed with much greater ability to regulate the emotional experience.

One set of models offering interesting examples and applications of both schema-driven emotion and emotion arising within cognitive elaboration is offered by Fruzzetti and the late Neil Jacobson (1990). Fruzzetti and Jacobson (1990) offered two contrasting models for people encountering conflict that offer an explanation for the "tipping point" (i.e., the point at which people seem to be unable to regulate actions to move toward desired ends). People with histories marked by problematic conflict resolution experience the immediate elicitation of high levels of emotion (or what Gottman, 1995, would call "flooding"), making it difficult to devote sufficient cognitive processing capacity to problem solving when so much effort must be devoted to managing the high levels of emotion. Fruzzetti and Jacobson (1990) argued that they basically adopt one of two paths: Either they shut down or attack. In this state of overwhelming negative emotion, he argued, it is nearly impossible for people to devote sufficient cognitive processing capacity to engage in problem solving. The second model represents people with prior histories of good conflict resolution. When people in this group sense a conflict emerging, minimal to low levels of emotion are elicited. Given that vast proportions of cognitive processing are not consumed with the emotional experience, the abilities to assess their own and others' feelings, identify the concerns of both parties, and engage in communication moving toward resolution are retained. Thinking of the multi-level emotion regulation model, those with good conflict resolution histories are in the cognitive elaboration/appraisal mode with the ability to regulate emotion.

Additional research on the regulation of emotion suggests that negative emotions impair "best self" regulation more than positive states. The self-regulation of emotion is impaired by emotional distress (Tice, Baumeister, & Zhang, 2004; Baumeister, Bratslavsky, Finkenauer, &Vohs, 2001). When people feel good, they are much more capable of regulating emotion to achieve goals or other ideals, but when they feel bad, the ability to regulate both internal states and behaviors breaks down (Tice et al., 2004). This is because navigating the subjective realm of negative emotions claims a higher priority than regulating outward displays. Consistent with this reprioritization, in negative states, people abandon their tendency to choose maximally rewarding actions in favor of immediate gratification (i.e., feeling better; Tice, et al., 2004). Negative emotions are compelling; they place getting rid of the negative state at the top of the priority list.

This research also offers considerable support to Hochschild's (1983) term "emotional *labour*." The very act of regulating emotion has been demonstrated to take energy (Baumeister, Bratslavsky, Muraven, & Tice, 1998; Muraven, Tice & Baumeister, 1998). Tice et al. (2004) used the term "ego depletion" to refer to the resulting state. Research conducted in work environments reveals that job demands for self-control (e.g., avoiding distraction, controlling impulses, overcoming resistance to work projects) resulted in greater job strain, especially for people facing high levels of concentration requirements or high work pressure (work load; Diestel & Schmidt, 2009).

The good news is that positive emotion replenishes the depletion of energy occurring after efforts to engage in self-control (Tice et al., 2004). This restoration of energy enables people to again make better emotion regulation decisions and effectively respond to demands (Tice et al., 2004).

A related, but distinct, approach to the regulation of emotion in problematic relationships is offered in the work of Hess and colleagues (2002, 2003, 2006; Hess, Omdahl, & Fritz, 2006) in their study of distancing in problematic relationships. In relationships that must be maintained, physical or psychological distancing (e.g., being overly polite, limiting the topics to be discussed) often serves to regulate emotion.

The emotion regulation findings and models provide an excellent background for understanding behaviors discussed by authors in this volume. First, every chapter directly or indirectly calls for people to expend the emotional labor required to manage harmful emotional displays and engage others in mutually respectful communities. Admonitions to prevent and address bullying (Kinney, this volume), hostile work relationships (Keashly, this volume), incivility (Davenport Sypher & Gill, this volume), and ostracism and isolation (Sias, this volume) are all calls to expend emotional labor. Similarly, understanding frameworks and counteracting the challenges they impose require emotional labor. Specifically, noticing, involving, and communicating with teleworkers (Fay, this volume), engaging true leadership rather than being a bureaucrat (Arnett, this volume), and embracing diversity rather avoiding or harming the "different-than-me" other (Millhous, this volume) or selecting "token" others (Collins, Gill, & Mease, this volume) all demand investment. Finally, choosing to build and restore effective work relationships takes emotional labor. Developing resilience and good coping strategies (Hammoud & Buzzanell, this volume), selecting effective communication strategies (Hess & Sneed, this volume), enacting civil behaviors (Fritz, this volume), and forgiving (Waldron & Kloeber, this volume) also expend, but also build up, reserves for emotional labor.

Second, many chapters in this volume address debilitating situations in which people seem incapable of managing emotion to choose more constructive actions due to the intense emotional package that has been elicited. Kinney (this volume) and Keashly (this volume) address bullying and hostile work relationships, which are characterized by a very complicated mix of schema-driven, poorly controlled emotional responses and very deliberative, cognitive processes fostering attack through behaviors that remain beneath the radar or fail to elicit severe sanction. In their exploration of forgiveness, Waldron and Kloeber (this volume) address many facets of forgiveness involving the regulation of emotion. They note that forgiveness calls for a heightened need to communicate feelings while "listening for emotions, venting, labeling feelings, legitimizing emotions, proposing a 'cooling off' period, and resisting the temptation to rush the process (with comments like 'get over it')." While there may be moments in which an emotion schema is elicited, for most, the process of forgiveness is presented as a slow, deliberative process, with twists and turns in the underlying attributions. As Waldron and Kloeber (this volume) state, "the process can take not just days, but weeks, months, and even years as hurt subsides, grudges gradually erode, and the partners come to new understandings of the moral codes that will guide their interactions in the future."

Emotion as a Mediator

The fourth role of emotion is as a mediator, and this role permeates the literature on problematic relationships in the workplace. Some of the research on emotions as mediators stems from the discussion in the last section: Emotions must be managed. This approach posits that emotions signal the need for coping strategies, which in effect address or ameliorate the aversive state. The second approach treats emotions as direct mediators between environmental problems (e.g., problematic workplace relationships) and outcomes.

Hans Selye (1974) initiated the concept of stress. In studies, organisms facing a variety of threats (e.g., extreme temperatures, viral and bacterial agents, and demands for over-exertion) experienced a sequence of changes. Selye (1974) labeled the sequence the "general adaptation syndrome," and he described the stages as (1) a mobilization of defenses as a reaction to an alarm, (2) resistance reflected in defenses and adaptation, and (3) collapse of the adaptive mechanisms as exhaustion set in.

Shortly after introduction of the stress concept, theorists began trying to explain the interface between external stimuli and the general adaptation syndrome (e.g., Cox, 1978; Lazarus, 1991; Lazarus, Kanner, & Folkman, 1980; Perlin, Menaghan, Lieberman, & Mullan, 1981). Cognitive, behavioral, and physiological coping methods were explored (e.g., Cox, 1978; Lazarus & Folkman, 1984) to determine their relative effectiveness in staving off the harmful effects of stress.

Selye's (1974) and other research suggested that perpetuation of high levels of greater demand than resources (imbalance) culminates in burnout (Maslach, 1979; 2003; Maslach & Leiter, 1997). Maslach and Jackson (1981) defined burnout as a negative psychological experience characterized by three components: (1) depersonalization, which is exemplified by perceiving care recipients as objects or difficult, disliked people; (2) reduced personal accomplishment, which occurs when the caretaker perceives that self is a failure in some or all phases of work largely due to ineffective patterns of interaction; and (3) emotional exhaustion, which is evidenced by fatigue, feeling worn out, and generally being unable to generate energy to perform responsibilities adequately.

Resilience was introduced as the opposite of burnout. Rather than experiencing a deterioration of energy and ability to cope with the demands, a person who is resilient has the ability to engage in ways that maintain greater resources than demands. As such, resilience signifies that a person is successfully mediating between the demands of the situation and outcomes.

Hammoud and Buzzanell (this volume, originally presented in Buzzanell, 2010) identify five processes that characterize and sustain resilience: (1) the person crafts normalcy; (2) the person affirms identify anchors; (3) the person develops, maintains, and uses communication networks; (4) the person puts alternative logics to work; and (5) the person legitimizes negative feelings but remains focused on productive action.

In the stress and coping literature, the processes that characterize and sustain resilience identified by Buzzanell (2010, cited in Hammoud & Buzzanell, this volume) would be called coping strategies. Lazarus and Folkman (1984) explained the role of coping strategies as follows: External demands that pose threats to internal resources (stressors) engender emotion. In order to address the situation, people engage in one of two types of coping. Emotion-focused strategies attempt to deny or sooth one's emotional state while problem-focused coping attempts to either solve the problem or reframe it to be a more positive/redeeming experience. These coping strategies mediate between the emotion and the ultimate outcome. Research has generally found that problem-focused coping (e.g., attempting to solve the problems, identifying what is/can be learned or gained through the challenge) is more effective than Emotion-focused coping (e.g., attempting to block it out of one's mind by sleeping, drinking, seeking social support) in averting negative outcomes (Lazarus & Folkman, 1984).

Gender differences have been observed in the effectiveness of problem-focused coping strategies. In a longitudinal study, Yamasaki, Sakai, and Uchida (2006) found that for men, problem solving at time one significantly impacted positive affect at time two. However, for women, cognitive reappraisal at time one significantly impacted positive affect at time two (Yamasaki, Sakai, & Uchida, 2006), and the alternative (cognitive appraisal for men and problem solving for women) did not yield significant results.

Keashly (this volume) points out the range of coping strategies implemented by people who are bullied. According to Lutgen-Sandvik (2006, as cited by Keashly, this volume), these strategies include the following: exodus (e.g., intending to quit, quitting, requesting a transfer), collective voice (e.g., sharing experiences with coworkers, exploring ways to stop the abuse, discussing plans to find other jobs), reverse discourse (e.g., turning repressive language and actions to liberating advantages), subversive disobedience (e.g., withdrawing output, working to rule), and confrontation (e.g., face-to-face conversations or humorous retorts).

Einarson and Mikkelson (2003) and Mikkelson and Einarson (2002) also addressed the relationships among workplace bullying, the mediation effects of affect and coping, and the resulting health complaints. They defined bullying as when a person is repeatedly and over a period of time exposed to negative acts by supervisors, coworkers, or subordinates such as offensive remarks or teasing, ridicule, or social exclusion. Coping strategies and emotion are believed to mediate between exposure to bullying behavior and deleterious consequences, such that people with better appraisal and coping strategies will be resilient in the face of bullying. The two mediating variables corresponding to appraisal and coping used in the study by Mikkelson and Einarson (2002) were affect and self-efficacy. Two hundred and twenty-four workers at a Danish manufacturing company participated in the study. Participants rated bullying behavior, psychological health complaints (anxiety, depression, and other physical symptoms), psychosomatic health concerns, as well as positive affect, negative affect, and self-efficacy. The results revealed that bullying did lead to significantly more negative affect, psychological health consequences, psychosomatic concerns, and negative affect, but it was not significantly correlated with self-efficacy. Negative affect was significantly associated with both psychological health complaints and psychosomatic health concerns, and it was a partial mediator of both (i.e., it increased the variance explained). Self-efficacy ended up being a weak mediator between bullying and negative health consequences and psychosomatic health concerns.

In addition to studies arguing that emotions and coping strategies mediate between events and outcomes, some studies look at emotion as a direct mediator. For example, positive emotions have been found to be a significant moderator between events at work and job satisfaction (Meeussen, Van Dam, Van Zundert, & Knape, 2010). Experiencing pride at the end of the day was the most important positive emotion in mediating between negative events and job satisfaction.

Further evidence of emotions as mediators between challenging feedback at work and undesirable outcomes (i.e., counterproductive work behavior, turnover, citizenship, and affective commitment) is provided by Den Hartog and Belschak (2007). They found that emotional reactions were controlling mediators for all four of the dependent behaviors named earlier. In receiving challenging feedback from supervisors, whether or not the employee negatively shifted behavior and commitment was totally dependent on the emotional response to the feedback.

Emotion, either alone or as a causal variable leading to coping strategies, plays a significant role as mediator for many of the behaviors characterizing problematic relationships in the workplace. How a person feels about behaviors of others is a key determinant of outcomes such as job satisfaction, organizational commitment, and personal well-being.

Emotion as Transformation

The final role for emotion is as an experience that can be transformed. After the end of apartheid in South Africa, amnesty was granted to those who came forward to account for their crimes against humanity, and Desmond Tutu was a key participant in the amnesty tribunals (Tippett, 2012). Neither apologies nor remorse was required for people to receive amnesty. For those who had experienced pain or lost loved ones, Desmond Tutu acknowledged, "this felt wrong—like a harsh blow." However, as a witness to the work of those listening to accounts and granting amnesty, Tutu said it was the rare testimony that did not contain the expression of genuine apology. In the end, he came to believe that the rules for amnesty were brilliant in that had apologies been required, those who had suffered could easily have attributed them to a requirement. Instead, those who had suffered were able to perceive them as voluntary and hence motivated by genuine emotion in remorse for the harm done. This opened the door to forgiveness, and the ability of those who harmed and the harmed to reflect and correct, said Desmond Tutu, is why he believes that there is true hope for humanity.

In this volume, Waldron and Kloeber define forgiveness as "a relational process whereby harmful conduct is acknowledged by one or both partners, the harmed partner extends undeserved mercy to the perceived transgressor, one or both partners experience a transformation from negative to positive psychological states, and the meaning of the relationship is renegotiated, with the possibility of reconciliation" (wording from Waldron and Kelley, 2008, p. 5). In this process, Waldron and Kloeber (this volume) note the importance of the explicit acknowledgment of wrongdoing and/or harm by the offending party, the organization's support for this process, the right of the victimized party to forgive or not, the distinction between forgiveness and reconciliation, and the moral nature of this work.

This volume addresses numerous behaviors injurious to relationships in the workplace for which the process of forgiveness outlined by Waldron and Kloeber may be a healing path. Keashly (this volume) points to forgiveness and reconciliation as approaches increasingly studied as responses to norm violation. Not surprisingly, whether forgiveness is likely to occur depends in large part on whether the aggressor has sympathy for or anger toward the person targeted. Sympathy for the person harmed is more likely to lead to forgiveness and reconciliation than is anger (Crossley, 2009, cited by Keashly, this volume).

Both Keashly (this volume) and Waldron and Kloeber (this volume) carefully differentiate forgiveness, which is an emotional transformation, from reconciliation, which is a behavioral action. Across the literature, scholars addressing forgiveness point out that it may be possible for a person to let go of the anger/rage/blame resulting from the other's egregious actions without finding it safe to restore the relationship (Aquino, Tripp, & Bies, 2006; Metts, Cupach, & Lippert, 2006; Waldron & Kloeber, this volume). Thus, people can experience the emotional transformation of forgiveness without taking behavioral actions to interact with the person or persons as before the transgression occurred. The emotional transformation described is likely to evoke an appraisal-reappraisal process that elicits a chain of changing emotions over a period of time (Higgins, 2011). In this sense, forgiveness is not a single emotional transformation but a sequence of them.

In conclusion, people experience a full array of negative and positive emotions in response to the rich and varied situations encountered in the workplace. The five roles played by emotions are explicated by theory and research, and they are readily exemplified in the scholarship and anecdotes offered in chapters in this volume. For those witnessing bulging eyes, red faces, and screaming, emotional expressions are problematic workplace behaviors signaling the action orientation of the other. In the case of targeted aggression, the emotion of shame functions as a hidden driver. Emotion eliciting situations call for management—requiring emotional labor to guide experiences and implement wise decisions. Those situations eliciting a package of strong emotion are particularly difficult, if not impossible, to manage. Emotion also plays the role of mediating between stressful experiences and coping strategies or outcomes. People who can develop highly effective coping strategies become resilient to the same stresses debilitating to others. Finally, emotions can be transformed as forgiveness and other constructive behaviors to restore personal well-being and possibly reconcile relationships.

References

Allen, J. A., Pugh, S. D., Grandey, A. A., & Groth, M. (2010). Following display rules in good or bad faith?: Customer orientation as a moderator of the display rule-emotional labour relationship. *Human Performance, 23*, 101–115.

Anderson, L. M., & Pearson, C. M. (1999). Tit for tat? The spiraling effect of incivility in the workplace. *Academy of Management Review, 24*, 452–471.

Aquino, K., Tripp, R. M. , & Bies, R. J. (2006). Getting even or moving on? Power, procedural justice, and offense as predictors of revenge, forgiveness, reconciliation and avoidance in organizations. *Journal of Applied Psychology, 91*, 653–668.

Arnold, M. B. (1960). *Emotion and personality*. New York, NY: Columbia University Press.

Barling, J. (1996). The prediction, psychological experience, and consequences of workplace violence. In G. Vanden Bos & E. Q. Bulatao (Eds.), *Violence on the job: Identifying risks and developing solutions* (pp. 29–50). Washington, DC: American Psychological Association.

Baumeister, R. F., Bratslavsky, E., Finkenauer, C., &Vohs, K. D. (2001). Bad is stronger than good. *Review of General Psychology, 5*, 323–370.

Baumeister, R. F., Bratslavsky, E., Muraven, M., & Tice, D. M. (1998). Ego depletion: Is the active self a limited resource? *Journal of Personality and Social Psychology, 74*, 1252–1265.

Berscheid, E. (1983). Emotion. In H. H. Kelley, E. Berscheid, A. Christensen, J. H. Harvey, T. Huston, G. Levinger, E. McClintock, L. Peplau, and D. R. Peterson (Eds.), *Close relationships* (pp. 110–168). New York, NY: Freeman.

Cannon, W. B. (1914). Recent studies of bodily effects of fear, rage and pain. *Journal of Philosophy, Psychology, and Scientific Methods, 11*, 162–165.

Cannon, W. B. (1927). The James-Lange theory of emotion: A critical examination and an alternative theory. *The American Journal of Psychology, 39*, 106–124.

Cox, T. (1978). *Stress*. Hong Kong: The MacMillan Press Ltd.

Crossley, C. D. (2009). Emotional and behavioral reactions to social undermining: A closer look at perceived offender motivations. *Organizational Behavior and Human Decision Processes, 108*, 14–24.

Darwin, C. (1965). *The expression of the emotions in man and animals*. London, England: Murray. (Original work published 1872)

Den Hartog, D. N., & Belschak, F. D. (2007). Personal initiation, commitment, and affect at work. *Journal of Occupational and Organizational Psychology, 80*, 601–622.

de Rivera, J. (1977). A structural theory of the emotions [Monograph]. *Psychological Issues, 4*, Monograph 40.

Diestel, S., & Schmidt, K. H. (2009). Mediator and moderator effects of demands on self-control in the relationship between work load and indicators of job strain. *Work and Stress, 23*(1), 60–79.

Eibl-Eibesfeldt, I. (1970). *Ethology: The biology of behavior*. New York, NY: Holt, Rinehart & Winston.

Einarsen, S. (1999). The nature and causes of bullying at work. *International Journal of Manpower, 20*, 16–27.

Einarsen, S., & Mikkelson, E. G. (2003). Individual effects of exposure to bullying at work. In S. Einarson, H. Hoel, D. Zapf, & C. L. Cooper (Eds.), *Bullying and emotional abuse in the workplace: International perspectives in research and practice* (pp. 127–144). London, England: Taylor & Francis.

Ekman, P. (1972). Universals and cultural differences in facial expressions of emotion. In J. R. Cole (Ed.), *Nebraska Symposium of Motivation, Vol. 19* (pp. 207–283). Lincoln: University of Nebraska Press.

Ekman, P. (1982). Methods of measuring facial action. In K. R. Scherer & P. Ekman (Eds.), *Handbook of methods in nonverbal behavior research* (pp. 45–90). Cambridge, England: Cambridge University Press.

Ekman, P. (1984). Expression and the nature of emotion. In K. R. Scherer & P. Ekman (Eds.), *Approaches to emotion* (pp. 319–344). Hillsdale, NJ: Lawrence Erlbaum.

Ekman, P., & Friesen, W. V. (1971). Constants across culture in the face and emotion. *Journal of Personality and Social Psychology, 17*, 124–129.

Ekman, P., & Friesen, W. V. (1975). *Unmasking the face*. Englewood Cliffs, NJ: Prentice Hall.

Ekman, P., & Friesen, W. V. (1978). *Manual for the facial action coding system*. Palo Alto, CA: Consulting Psychologists Press.

Ekman, P., Levenson, R. W., & Friesen, W. V. (1983). Autonomic nervous system activity distinguishes among emotions. *Science, 221*, 1208–1210.

Ekman, P., & Oster, H. (1979). Facial expressions of emotion. *Annual Review of Psychology, 30*, 527–554.

Ellis, A. (1985). Cognition and affect in emotional disturbance. *American Psychologist, 40*, 471–472.

Ellsworth, P., & Scherer, K . R. (2003). Appraisal processes in emotion. In R. J. Davidson, K. R. Scherer, & H. Goldsmith (Eds.), *Handbook of affective sciences* (pp. 572–595). New York, NY: Oxford University Press.

Fineman, S. (1993). Organizations as emotional arenas. In S. Fineman (Ed.), *Emotion in organizations* (pp. 9–35). Newbury Park, CA: Sage.

Fontaine, J. R., Scherer, K. R., Roesch, E. B., & Ellsworth, P. (2007). The world of emotions is not two dimensional. *Psychological Science, 18*(12), 1050–1057.

Frijda, N. H. (1986). *The emotions*. New York, NY: Cambridge University Press.

Fritz, J. M. H. (2002). How do I dislike thee? Let me count the ways: Constructing impressions of troublesome others at work. *Management Communication Quarterly, 15*, 410–438.

Fritz, J. M. H. (2006). Typology of troublesome others at work: A follow-up investigation. In J. M. H. Fritz & B. L. Omdahl (Eds.), *Problematic relationships in the workplace* (pp. 21–46). New York, NY: Peter Lang.

Fritz, J. M. H., & Omdahl, B. L. (Eds.). (2006). *Problematic relationships in the workplace.* New York, NY: Peter Lang.

Fruzzetti, A. E., & Jacobson, N. S. (1990). Toward a behavioral conceptualization of adult intimacy: Implications for marital therapy. In E. A. Blechman (Eds.), *Emotions and the family for better or worse* (pp. 117–135). Hillsdale, NJ: Lawrence Erlbaum.

Glomb, T. M. (2002). Workplace aggression: Informing conceptual models with data from specific encounters. *Journal of Occupational Health Psychology, 7*, 1, 20–36.

Glomb, T. M., & Miner, A. G. (2002). Exploring patterns of aggressive behaviors in organizations: Assessing model-data fit. In J. M. Brett &F. Drasgow (Eds.), *The psychology of work: Theoretically based empirical research* (pp. 235–252). Mahwah, NJ: Lawrence Erlbaum.

Glomb, T. M., & Tews, M. J. (2004). Emotional labor: A conceptualization and scale development. *Journal of Vocational Behavior, 64*, 1–23.

Gottman, J. (1995). *Why marriages succeed or fail: And how you can make yours last.* New York, NY: Simon & Schuster.

Hess, J. A. (2002). Distance regulation in personal relationships: The development of a conceptual model and a test of representational validity. *Journal of Personal and Social Relationships, 19*, 663–683.

Hess, J. A. (2003). Measuring distance in personal relationships: The Relational Distance Index. *Personal Relationships, 10*, 197–215.

Hess, J. A. (2006). Distancing from problematic coworkers. In J. M. H. Fritz & B. L. Omdahl (Eds.), *Problematic relationships in the workplace* (pp. 205–232). New York, NY: Peter Lang.

Hess, J. A., Omdahl, B. L., & Fritz, J. M. H. (2006). Turning points in relationships with disliked coworkers. In J. M. H. Fritz & B. L. Omdahl (Eds.), *Problematic relationships in the workplace* (pp. 89–108). New York, NY: Peter Lang.

Higgins, E. T. (2011). Accessibility theory. In P. A. M. Van Lange, A. Kruglanski, & E. T. Higgins (Eds.), *Handbook of theories of social psychology* (pp. 75–96). Thousand Oaks, CA: Sage.

Hochschild, A. R. (1983). *The managed heart: Commercialization of human feeling.* Berkley: University of California Press.

Izard, C. E. (1977). *Human emotions.* New York, NY: Plenum.

James, W. (1984). What is an emotion? In C. Calhoun &R. Solomon (Eds.), *What is an emotion?* (pp. 127–141). New York, NY: Oxford University Press. (Original work published 1884)

Keashly, L., & Nowell, B. L. (2003). Conflict, conflict resolution and bullying. In S. Einarson, H. Hoel, D. Sapf, & C. Cooper (Eds.), *Bullying and emotional abuse in the workpace: International research and practice perspectives* (pp. 339–358). London, England: Taylor & Francis.

Keashly, L., & Nowell, B. L. (2011). Conflict, conflict resolution, and bullying. In S. Einarsen, H. Hoel, & D. Zapf, & C. L. Cooper (Eds.), *Workplace bullying: Developments in theory, research, and practice* (2nd ed., pp. 423–455). Boca Raton, FL: CRC Press/Taylor & Francis.

Lazarus, R. S. (1991). Psychological stress in the workplace. *Journal of Social Behavior and Personality, 6*, 1–14.

Lazarus, R. S., & Folkman, S. (1984). *Stress, appraisal and coping*. New York, NY: Springer.
Lazarus, R. S., Kanner, A. D., & Folkman, S. (1980). Emotions: A cognitive-phenomenological analysis. In R. Plutchik & H. Kellerman (Eds.), *Emotion: Theory, research, and experience: Vol. 1, theories of emotion* (pp. 189–217). New York, NY: Academic Press.
Lutgen-Sandvik, P. (2006). Take this job and…: Quitting and other forms of resistance to workplace bullying. *Communication Monographs, 73*, 406–433.
Lutgen-Sandvik, P., Riforgiate, S., & Fletcher, C. (2011). Work as a source of positive emotional experiences and the discourses informing positive assessment. *Western Journal of Communication, 75*, 2–27.
Mandler, G. (1975). *Mind and emotion*. New York, NY: Wiley.
Mandler, G. (1984). *Mind and body*. New York, NY: Norton.
Mann, S. (2004). "People work": Emotion management, stress, and coping. *British Journal of Guidance and Counseling, 32*, 205–221.
Maslach, C. (1979). The burn-out syndrome and patient care. In C. Garfield (Eds.), *Stress and survival* (pp. 111–120). St Louis, MO: Mosby.
Maslach, C. (2003). *Burnout: The cost of caring*. Cambridge, MA: Malor.
Maslach, C., & Jackson, S. E. (1981). The measurement of experienced burnout. *Journal of Organizational Behavior, 2*, 99–113.
Maslach, C., & Leiter, M. P. (1997). *The truth about burnout: How organizations cause personal stress and what to do about it*. San Francisco, CA: Jossey-Bass.
Meeussen, V., Van Dam, K., Van Zundert, A., &Knape, J. (2010). Job satisfaction among Dutch nurse anaesthetists: The influence of emotions on events. *International Nursing Review, 57*, 85–91.
Metts, S., Cupach, W. R., & Lippert, L. (2006). Forgiveness in the workplace. In J. M. H. Fritz &B. L. Omdahl (Eds.), *Problematic relationships in the workplace* (pp. 249–278). New York, NY: Peter Lang.
Mikkelson, E. G., & Einarson, S. (2002). Basic assumptions and symptoms of post-traumatic stress among victims of bullying at work. *European Jounal of Work and Organizational Psychology, 11*, 87–101.
Muraven, M., Tice, D. M., & Baumeister, R. F. (1998). Self control as a limited resource: Regulatory depletion patterns. *Journal of Personality and Social Psychology, 74*, 774–789.
Oatley, K. (1988). Plans and the communicative function of emotions: A cognitive theory. In V. Hamilton, G. H. Bower, & N. H. Frijda (Eds.), *Cognitive perspectives on emotion and motivation* (pp. 345–364). Boston, MA: Kluwer Academic Publishers.
Ortony, A. (1988). Subjective importance and computational models of emotions. In V. Hamilton, G. H. Bower, & N. H. Frijda (Eds.), *Cognitive perspectives on emotion and motivation* (pp. 321–344). Boston, MA: Kluwer Academic Publishers.
Ortony, A., Clore, G. L., & Collins, A. (1988). *The cognitive structure of emotions*. New York, NY: Cambridge University Press.
Payne, J. (2009). Emotional labour and skill: A reappraisal. *Gender, Work, and Organization, 16*, 348–367.
Perlin, L. I., Menaghan, E. G., Lieberman, M. A., & Mullan, J. T. (1981). The stress process. *Journal of Health and Social Behavior, 22*, 337–356.
Pfeifer, R. (1988). Artificial intelligence models of emotion. In V. Hamilton, G. H. Bower, &

N. H. Frijda (Eds.), *Cognitive perspectives on emotion and motivation* (pp. 345–364). Boston, MA: Kluwer Academic Publishers.

Philippot, P., Baeyens, C., Douilliez, C., & Francart, B. (2004). Cognitive regulation of emotion: Application to clinical disorders. In P. Philippot & R. Feldman (Eds.), *The regulation of emotion* (pp. 71–100). Mahwah, NJ: Lawrence Erlbaum.

Rainivaara, S. (2009). Workplace bullying relationships. In T. A. Kinney & M. Porhola (Eds.), *Anti and pro-social communication: Theories, methods, and applications* (pp. 59–70). New York, NY: Peter Lang.

Retzinger, S. (1991). *Violent emotions: Shame and rage in marital quarrels*. Newbury Park, CA: Sage.

Retzinger, S. (1995). Identifying shame and anger in discourse. *American Behavioral Scientist, 38*, 1104–1113.

Roseman, I. J. (1984). Cognitive determinants of emotion: A structural theory. In P. Shaver (Ed.), *Review of personality and social psychology, Vol. 5: Emotions, relationships, and health* (pp. 11–36). Beverly Hills, CA: Sage.

Schacter, S. (1959). *The psychology of affiliation*. Stanford, CA: Stanford University Press.

Schacter, S., & Singer, J. E. (1962). Cognitive, social, and physiological determinants of emotional state. *Psychological Review, 69*, 379–399.

Scheff, T. J. (1994). *Bloody revenge: Emotions, nationalism, and war*. Boulder, CO: Westview Press.

Scherer, K. (1986). Vocal affect expression: A review and a model for future research. *Psychological Bulletin, 99*, 143–165.

Scherer, K. R. (1982). Emotion as a process: Function, origin, and regulation. *Social Science Information, 21*, 555–570.

Scherer, K. R. (1984a). On the nature and function of emotion: A component process approach. In K. R. Scherer & P. Ekman (Eds.), *Approaches to emotion* (pp. 293–317). Hillsdale, NJ: Lawrence Erlbaum.

Scherer, K. R. (1984b). Emotion as a multicomponent process: A model and some cross-cultural data. In P. Shaver (Ed.),*Review of personality and social psychology, vol. 5: Emotions, relationships, and health* (pp. 37–63). Beverly Hills, CA: Sage.

Scherer, K. R. (1988a). Criteria for emotion-antecedent appraisal: A review. In V. Hamilton, G. Bower, & N. H. Frijda (Eds.), *Cognitive perspectives on emotion and motivation* (pp. 89–126). Dordrecht, The Netherlands: Kluwer Academic Publishers.

Scherer, K. R. (Ed.). (1988b). *Facets of emotion*. Hillsdale, NJ: Lawrence Erlbaum.

Scherer, K. R., London, H., & Wolf, J. (1973). The voice of confidence: Paralinguistic cues and audience evaluation. *Journal of Research in Personality, 7*, 31–44.

Selye, H. (1974). *Stress without distress*. New York, NY: The New American Library.

Smith, C. A., & Ellsworth, P. C. (1985). Patterns of cognitive appraisal in emotion. *Journal of Personality and Social Psychology, 48*, 813–838.

Tice, D. M., Baumeister, R. F., & Zhang, L. (2004). The role of emotion in self-regulation: Differing roles of positive and negative emotion. In P. Philippot & R. S. Feldman (Eds.), *The regulation of emotion* (pp. 213–226). Mahwah, NJ: Lawrence Erlbaum.

Tippett, K. (2012, February 25). On Being: Interview with Desmond Tutu [Radio broadcast]. Retrieved from American Public Media at http://americanpublicmedia.publicradio.org/programs/; http://www.onbeing.org/; http://www.onbeing.org/program/desmond-tutus-god-surprises/85

Tomkins, S. S. (1962). *Affect, imagery, consciousness: Vol. I, the positive affects*. New York, NY: Springer.
Tomkins, S. S. (1963). *Affect, imagery, consciousness: Vol. II, the negative affects*. New York, NY: Springer.
Waldron, V., & Kelley, D. L. (2008). *Communicating forgiveness*. Thousand Oaks, CA: Sage.
Weiner, B. (1985). An attributional theory of achievement motivation and emotion. *Psychological Review, 92*, 548–573.
Yamasaki, K., Sakai, A., & Uchida, K. (2006). A longitudinal study of the relationship between positive affect and both problem-and emotion-focused coping strategies. *Social Behavior and Personality: An International Journal, 34*(5), 499–509.

PART I

Problematic Behaviors Impacting Relationships

· 3 ·

HOSTILE WORK RELATIONSHIPS

Loraleigh Keashly

Work is inherently relational (Blustein, 2010). What we accomplish is done in and through our connection to others, particularly our bosses, peers, subordinates, clients, and customers. Further, work and its associated experiences are intimately connected to our sense of self, providing meaning, matter, and dignity (Blustein, 2010). To the extent that this is true, the more constructive our relationships are with others at work, the more likely we, our colleagues, and, by extension, the organization, will be productive and work itself will be satisfying and energizing. More personally, our sense of competence as workers and our identity as persons of worth will be strengthened.

In her 2003 book, *Energizing Your Workplace*, Jane Dutton highlighted the importance of relationships for productive and constructive work by describing *high quality connections*, relationships characterized by respectful engagement, trust, task enabling, and support. She described interactions that not only lacked these qualities but also were demeaning, dismissive, undermining, and diminishing to all involved. She aptly labeled these relationships *corrosive connections*. While most work connections and interactions are likely to be neutral to positive, many workers have relationships that are negative and, in some cases, corrosive to them and to their work. While such relationships may be in the minority of a particular worker's experience, they have a proportionally greater impact on workers' sense of self, satisfaction, and productivity than more positive experiences (e.g., Baumeister, Bratslavsky, Finkenauer, & Vohs, 2001).

This disproportionate effect has been demonstrated in a variety of relational contexts, including schools, families, marriages, and friendships. Research has focused on identifying the number of positive interactions needed to offset negative interactions within a relationship. For example, John Gottman (1995) identified the "magic relationship ratio" of 5:1 for successful marriages (i.e., for every "put-down," there needed to be five "put-ups"). Barbara Frederickson (2009) identified a 3:1 "positive ratio" in her work with children, and she argued that this ratio generalizes to other relationships. Regardless of the specific ratio, what is clear from other relational contexts is that the quality and character of the interaction within the relationship have significant implications for the parties involved and for those that surround them (e.g., Andersson & Pearson, 1999; Totterdell, Hershcovis, Niven, Reich, & Stride, in press). These findings draw our attention to the nature and impact of negative relationships at work.

In this chapter, I focus on a specific set of negative relationships that are characterized by hostility and aggression. Specifically, I focus on hostile relationships with organizational insiders, since employees work with them the most often. Organizational insiders create many opportunities for relational development, both positive and negative. Drawing on literatures addressing aggression, abusive treatment, conflict, and relational difficulties in the workplace, I attempt to define the construct space, identify the core features of these relationships, and highlight what we know about how they develop, are sustained, and resolved. Throughout, I identify issues that research needs to address in order to enhance our understanding of these relationships, and hence, their prevention, management, and amelioration.

The Construct Space: Oh, the Things We Do

In every relationship, there will be behaviors that are negative (even hostile), but in most relationships, these behaviors occur in a broader relational context characterized as constructive or positive (Folger, 1993). As such, they are experienced as blips on the overall screen of the relationship. We can get into a heated disagreement with a coworker around a specific issue yet still experience the coworker as a good person and the relationship as a positive one (i.e., the hostile behavior is perceived as occasional or episodic; Aquino & Lamertz, 2004).

Very different in nature are hostile relationships—those ongoing relationships that demonstrate sustained patterns of negative and often aggressive interaction between the parties. In these relationships, the destructive or negative character of the interaction defines the gestalt meaning of the relationship. The umbrella term for behaviors in these relationships is best captured by the term "workplace aggression," which can be defined as "any negative act, which may be committed towards an individual within the workplace, or the workplace itself, in ways the target is motivated to avoid" (Hershcovis & Barling, 2007, p. 271).

This definition of workplace aggression captures an enormous behavioral domain, and Buss's (1961) dimensional framework is useful in mapping the content of this domain (Baron & Neuman, 1996). Buss argued that aggressive behavior (regardless of context) can be characterized along three dimensions: physical (deeds)–verbal (words, tone), active (actions)–passive (withholding, fails to do), and direct (at the target)–indirect (at something or someone the target values). This framework captures all manner of behavior ranging from the more overt physical violence (e.g., assault) as physical, active, and direct, to yelling and cursing as verbal, active, and direct, to the silent treatment as verbal, passive, and direct. Interestingly, while public attention is often focused on more visible acts of physical violence and harm, by far the majority of aggression in workplaces is covert and nonphysical in nature, earning the name of psychological aggression (Baron & Neuman, 1996; Schat, Frone, & Kelloway, 2006). In addition, these types of behaviors are often perceived as more severe by recipients than physical action or criticisms directed at task competency (e.g., Escartin, Rodriguex-Carballeira, Zapf, Porrua, & Martin-Pena, 2009; Meglich-Sespico, 2006).

While useful in defining the behavioral space, this definition of workplace aggression is limited as it focuses only on behaviors rather than the context of those behaviors. Up until recently, the broader workplace aggression literature (unlike the workplace abuse and relational difficulties literatures) has tended to focus implicitly, if not explicitly, on understanding single aggressive encounters or aggregate levels of aggression, without consideration of who was being aggressive to whom (Glomb, 2002; Neuman & Baron, 1997; O'Leary-Kelly, Griffin, & Glew, 1996). Accumulating evidence, however, demonstrates that the types of behaviors used and the nature and extent of impact on the parties are conditioned by the nature of the relationship between the parties as defined by organizational position such as superior-subordinate, peer-peer, or employee-client. That is, workplace aggression has a relational face (Hershcovis & Barling, 2007). Looking at behavior, Neuman and Keashly (2010) argued that the nature of the relationship between parties provided a context within which certain behaviors were more or less likely on the basis of available means and opportunity to utilize these means. For example, supervisors engaged in aggressive actions reflective of their control over employee activities, such as withholding praise, failing to provide feedback, unfairly denying a raise, and putting someone down in front of others. Peers were more likely to engage in behaviors reflecting the sources of their influence, including information and relationships (e.g., interrupt, take credit for others' work, fail to defend a colleague's plan to others, and refuse requests for assistance). Subordinates engaged in more covert behaviors as is reflective of their position (e.g., consistently being late to meetings and turning other people against the boss). In terms of impact, Keashly and Neuman (2002) found that, even after controlling for types of behavior used, aggression from supervisors was more strongly associated with negative outcomes than similar aggression coming from peers or clients.

This conceptualization of the relational nature of aggression and hostility encompasses relationships that have occasional aggressive acts and those relationships whose character is hostile (Aquino & Lamertz, 2004). In this chapter, I focus on relationships characterized by sustained patterns of hostile and aggressive interaction. Under this umbrella resides a collection of constructs that explicitly captures persistent or enduring forms of hostility (i.e., hostile relationships; Keashly & Jagatic, 2003). These constructs include workplace bullying (Einarsen, 1999) or mobbing (Leymann, 1990, 1996), generalized workplace harassment (Richman, Rospenda, Nawyn, Flaherty, Fendrich, Drum, & Johnson, 1999), social undermining (Duffy, Ganster, & Pagon, 2002), abusive supervision (Tepper, 2000), petty tyranny (Ashforth, 1997), emotional tyranny (Waldron, 2009), interpersonal conflict (Spector & Jex, 1998), interpersonal mistreatment (Price Spratlen, 1995), psychological abuse (Sheehan, White, Liebowitz, & Baldwin, 1990), emotional abuse (Keashly, Trott, & MacLean, 1994) or simply abuse (Ryan & Oestreich, 1991), harassment (Brodsky, 1976), workplace harassment (Björkqvist, Österman, & Hjelt-Back, 1994; Bowling & Beehr, 2006), status-blind harassment (Yamada, 2000), workplace victimization (Aquino et al., 1999), and problematic work relationships (Fritz & Omdahl, 2006). While such construct profusion can be frustrating because it makes consolidation difficult, it does reflect the interest in exploring broadly how we interact at work, particularly when these interactions are characterized by hostile and aggressive behaviors.

So what distinguishes hostile work relationships from relationships with occasional hostile episodes? It is the element of time. Specifically, hostile work relationships are characterized by repetition, duration, and the patterning of behaviors (Keashly & Jagatic, 2011).

Persistence: Repetition and Duration

Regardless of which of the hostile-work-relationship constructs are studied, the frequency of occurrence of negative behaviors is an important variable (Keashly & Jagatic, 2003). Not surprisingly, the evidence is consistent that the greater the frequency of exposure, the greater the negative impact on the target. In addition, the length of time over which a person is exposed to such behaviors from a particular actor or within a specific relationship (i.e., the duration) has been linked to the range and severity of impact. Specifically, research has consistently found that the longer the exposure, the greater the harm (e.g., Rospenda, Richman, & Shannon, 2006, 2008; Rospenda, Richman, Wislar, & Flaherty, 2000). Longer exposure has also been associated with increasing involvement of others in the situation, often negatively as people choose sides or "gang up" (Zapf & Gross, 2001). The significance of duration of exposure is highlighted by evidence from the broader workplace abuse literature reporting experiences ranging from one month to 10 years in the United States with an average of over two years (e.g., Burnazi, Keashly, & Neuman, 2005; Namie & Lutgen-Sandvik, 2010) and an average of 15 to 46 months in European research (Zapf & Gross, 2001). Indeed, it is the enduring nature of many of these hostile relationships that has resulted in their characterization as "chronic" workplace stressors (Keashly & Harvey, 2005; Rospenda et al., 2000).

The combination of repetition and duration is the quality of **persistence** that is most implicated in the range and nature of negative effects. Persistence of these behaviors has been linked to the inability to respond and cope effectively, thereby increasing the effects on the individuals to the point of trauma (e.g., Glomb & Cortina, 2006; Janson & Hazler, 2004) and contributing to the devolution of the relationship. The persistence of the interactions in these relationships raises the question about how people endure under such hostile treatment. This issue is discussed in a later section.

Patterning and Sequencing: The Whole Is More Than the Sum of Its Parts

Hostile relationships are not typically characterized by repeated engagement in single behaviors; rather, they are notable for the variety of behaviors utilized (Keashly & Jagatic, 2010). Drawing from interviews with those who self-identified as having interpersonal difficulties at work, Keashly (2001) noted that respondents found that describing the specific behaviors of the actor did not capture the totality of their experience. Respondents needed to talk about the interrelationships among the behaviors and the process of their development. This notion of connection across behaviors is supported by research assessing a variety of forms of harassment (e.g., incivility, sexual harassment, racial discrimination), which has found that these behaviors co-occur rather than happen independently or in isolation (e.g., Glomb, 2002; Lim & Cortina, 2005; Raver & Nishii, 2010; Richman et al., 1999; Rospenda et al., 2000). While this co-occurrence speaks to larger issues of hostile work environment, when applied to specific relationships, it focuses attention on moving beyond aggregating across behaviors for mean frequency to patterning of behaviors over time (Glomb, 2002; Keashly et al., 1994). In fact, hostile relationships may become apparent only when whole patterns of behavior are examined (Bassman, 1992). The overall patterning of the interaction is also critical to people's judgments of the type of treatment they are receiving and the types of responses that are viable (Lind, 1997). Patterning over time highlights the importance of the dynamics and processes involved in the evolution of the relationship.

The number, nature, and sequencing of behaviors over time are important to the discernment of patterning. Keashly, Harvey, and Hunter (1997), in their study of resident assistants' exposure to hostile behavior from residents, found that the number of different behaviors utilized accounted for variance in job tension above and beyond the variance explained by frequency of behaviors. This study was cross-sectional and did not permit an exploration of whether number and nature of behaviors changed over time and whether these behavioral changes occurred in identifiable sequences. Both the conflict (Keashly & Nowell, 2003) and aggression (e.g., Barling, 1996; Glomb, 2002; Glomb & Miner, 2002) literatures provide evidence that subtle, covert, and more psychological forms of aggressive behavior precede more overt and direct forms of hostility, including physical violence. This sequencing reflects a progression of increasing severity and frequency of behaviors overall (Andersson & Pearson, 1999; Glomb, 2002). This description of sequenced and increasingly severe actions is characteristic of the European research on the evolving process of workplace bullying, which involves an escalation of a bully's behaviors from indirect and subtle behaviors to more direct psychologically aggressive acts and ultimately to severe psychological and physical violence (e.g., Einarsen, 1999). Thus, hostile relationships are characterized by a variety of hostile behaviors that, over time, may increase in frequency and severity if the trajectory is not changed.

This articulation of sequenced and progressive aggression describes one direction that a hostile relationship may follow (i.e., an escalatory spiral that, if left unchecked, will result in damage to, and potential "destruction" of, one or both parties and those around them; see Keashly & Nowell, 2011, for a fuller discussion of escalatory processes). Yet, not all hostile relationships devolve to such destruction. This raises the question of how a relationship moves in one direction or another, which, in turn, draws our attention to the roles of both parties in relationship character and trajectory (Aquino & Lamertz, 2004). Andersson and Pearson (1999), in their description of an "incivility spiral," focused on the actions and reactions of both parties and suggested that reciprocating rude or uncivil behavior can escalate to more severe and coercive action if a "tipping point" has been reached such as one or the other experiencing actions as a threat to identity. How do some of these relationships avoid reaching the tipping point? Rainivaara (2009) described strategies both parties use in bullying relationships to continue working even when the relationship is painful. Thus, this discussion of overall patterning raises the bigger question of how these relationships develop, are sustained, and resolve. I now turn attention to what we know about the dynamics and processes involved in the development and maintenance of these relationships.

Development and Maintenance of Hostile Relationships

To this point, I have discussed that the frequency, duration, and patterning of hostile and aggressive behaviors are important markers in defining a relationship as hostile. This discussion, though, begs the question of how the relationship arrived at the point of hostility in the first place. Research on the factors that "set the stage" is extensive, so detailed discussion is beyond the scope of this chapter (see Aquino & Thau, 2009; Barling, Dupre, & Kelloway, 2009; Bowling & Beehr, 2006; Einarsen et al., 2011; and Fritz & Omdahl, 2006, for detailed discussion). However, there are two recent frameworks that are useful in considering relational development. Specifically, I discuss Aquino and Lamertz's (2004) dyadic role relations model of workplace victimization and Baillien, Neyens, DeWitte, and De Cuyper's (2009) pathways to bullying framework.

Aquino and Lamertz (2004) theorized about the nature and impact of the social roles of partners in the dyad on the evolution of behaviors and the relationship. Specifically they sought to understand the relational dynamics that would lead to two different forms of workplace victimization, episodic (discrete incidents of harmful interaction) and institutionalized (persistent and habitual patterns of harmful interaction) aggression. The distinction centers around whether the actors in the dyad "view aggression, exploitation, coercion or any combination thereof as the core of their relationship" (p. 1027). Thus, institutionalized victimization is what we are considering here as hostile relationships. Drawing on role relations theory, Aquino and Lamertz (2004) argued that employees enact various social roles as reflected in the social system of the organization. Noting that hostile or conflictual interactions are created and maintained through the actions of both actors and that people move back and forth between being "victims" and "perpetrators" (e.g., Glomb, 2002), they proposed the notion of relational roles as a way to understand hostile relationships. Briefly, relational roles are ones that are enacted only in connection with a counter-role (e.g., in order for there to be a victim, there needs to be a perpetrator). Building from there, they identified four "archetypal" relational roles defined by actor status (victim and perpetrator) and specific behavioral styles. There are two types of perpetrator roles. The **dominating perpetrator role** is characterized by attempts to maintain control of, or superiority over, others through coercive and hostile behavior. This role is often how the bully is characterized in the workplace bullying literature, that is, the predatory bully (e.g. Einarsen, 1999). It also conforms to the construct of instrumental aggression articulated in the workplace aggression literature (e.g., Tedeschi & Felson, 1994). The **reactive perpetrator role** is characterized by responding in a hostile manner to some perceived transgression, such as norm violation or threat to identity. Thus, the motive is a desire to redress perceived unfairness. This type of response is often referred to as reactive, reciprocal, or affective aggression (Glomb, 2002). Similarly, there are two victim roles: provocative victim and submissive victim. The **provocative victim role** is characterized by negative affectivity and aggressive and irritating behaviors. These behaviors are often directed at social control. The **submissive victim role** is characterized by socially awkward, anxious behaviors and avoidance of negative interactions. Such behavior has been characterized as signaling vulnerability and less likelihood of retaliating.

In the pairing of these roles, episodic or institutionalized hostility becomes more or less likely to occur. Specifically, Aquino and Lamertz (2004) proposed that the pairing of a dominant perpetrator with a submissive victim and a reactive perpetrator with a provocative victim would result in sustained patterning of hostile behavior. While these dyadic combinations may lay the groundwork for hostile relationships, the (im)balance of social power in the dyad and the presence and involvement of others who have relationships to both parties can influence whether and how the hostility and aggression actually occurs (Aquino & Lamertz, 2004; Lamertz & Aquino, 2004).

What is valuable about the role relations perspective is that it draws attention to how hostile work relationships are molded by both parties and those around them (Hodson, Roscigno, & Lopez, 2006; Namie & Lutgen-Sandvik, 2010; Venkataramani & Dalal, 2007). However, it leaves open the question about what might trigger these roles to be engaged and enacted. To provide some insight into this question, I now turn attention to the work of Baillien, et al. (2009), who identified three pathways by which hostile relationships can develop and be maintained: intrapersonal, interpersonal, and intragroup/organizational. Individual and work-related antecedents are implicated in either being the source of these processes or influencing how employees cope with the challenges created by these processes.

The **intrapersonal** pathway focuses on workplace stressors and frustrations as key influences on how employees may come to enact the victim and perpetrator roles that Aquino and Lamertz (2004) identified. A basic premise of their argument is that research on victim and perpetrator characteristics reveals that at the core of both roles are negative affect and anxiety. These characteristics have their influence by either affecting how an employee perceives an ambiguous event (e.g., hostile attribution bias) or by conditioning the employee's affective and behavioral responding. So the question becomes what may explain an employees becoming either a victim or a perpetrator. Baillien et al. (2009) suggest that it is ineffective coping behavior in response to stressors and frustrations (such as lack of autonomy and decision control, poor communication, role overload, conflict and ambiguity, and uncomfortable physical environments, Neuman & Baron, 1997) that may provide the key. Specifically, in their analysis of 87 cases of workplace bullying, they found that an employee might become vulnerable to victimization by others when the employee copes with frustrations in a passive-inefficient way (e.g., by withdrawing, becoming helpless, or reducing productivity). Such behavior may be perceived as violating existing norms (not carrying one's load) and result in other workers' responding negatively towards the employee. When an employee copes with an experienced frustration in an active-ineffective way, the employee may displace frustration onto an "innocent" coworker (e.g. Tepper, Duffy, Henle, & Lambert, 2006). There is evidence to suggest that prior experience as a target/victim of hostile relationships influences the likelihood of the actor's choosing aggressive behavior as a strategy (Hauge et al., 2009; Glomb and Liao, 2003). This pathway is reminiscent of the dominant perpetrator and submissive victim pairing predicted by Aquino and Lamertz (2004).

The **interpersonal** pathway describes how some hostile relationships develop as a result of interpersonal conflict that is ineffectively managed and escalates (Keashly & Nowell, 2003; Zapf & Gross, 2001). In escalated conflicts, everyone engages in increasingly hostile and damaging actions. Parties may be able to maintain equal abilities to reciprocate in an ever-escalating sequence, and the result is increasing damage to both. However, in many situations, one party becomes notably unable to defend himself or herself, yet the other continues on an increasingly punitive path (i.e., a power imbalance occurs). This imbalance may be present initially as a result of formal organizational power (e.g., supervisor-subordinate) or differential access to sources of social power such as centrality of social network or control of critical information (Keashly & Jagatic, 2003; Lamertz & Aquino, 2004). This imbalance may also develop over time as a result of the increasingly hostile interaction and an inability to cope. In terms of coping, there is evidence that attempts by the target to actively address hostile behaviors from the other are often unsuccessful, and such failure is often tied to increasingly negative impact on the target (Richman, Rospenda, Flaherty, & Freels, 2001; Zapf & Gross, 2001). In this process, the more powerful employee becomes the actor, and the less powerful employee becomes the target. Thus, however it develops, the power imbalance affects both the ability of the target to respond and defend and the means and opportunities available to an actor to mistreat (Neuman & Keashly, 2010). Einarsen (1999) argued that conflictual and hostile interactions between parties equally able to defend themselves are not bullying situations but conflicts. In Aquino and Lamertz's (2004) language, the interpersonal pathway may reflect the pairing of reactive perpetrator and provocative victim. These situations can be challenging to assess and address because their genesis may have been mutually determined, but the balance has swung.

This perspective on the interpersonal pathway could be enriched by a consideration of the literature on relational difficulties, specifically the work on turning points in relationships. Hess, Omdahl, and Fritz (2006) set out to assess whether relationships with disliked coworkers were always difficult or whether these were relationships that became negative. They found that the majority of the problematic relationships examined in their study started out as positive. They identified several types of turning points, including task issues, such as job ineptitude or unreasonable demands, social/interpersonal issues, such as attack on someone like face threat or malicious treatment, and combination of task and social issues, including conflict and unsupportive or obstructive behaviors. Interestingly, many of the negative and positive turning points were mirror images, which could be interpreted as reflective of dimensions or standards of behavior that people expect to be met in the workplace. The concept and empirical documentation of turning points in relationship trajectory helps explain the finding in the hostile work relationships literature that assessment of a relationship as abusive or harassing is tied to perceived violations of norms of respect and fairness and standards of appropriate conduct (Keashly, 1998, 2001). In the context of interpersonal dynamics, such perceived relational transgressions have been linked to aggressive responding on the part of the perceived target, and thus, the evolution of a hostile relationship. This work highlights the importance of identifying these standards or expectations, empirically assessing their link to interactions, and targeting them for intervention (Hess et al., 2006; Keashly & Jagatic, 2010).

The **intragroup/organizational** pathway reflects the understanding that all work relationships are embedded in the organizational context, and therefore, are influenced by organizational structures and dynamics. This embeddedness is a feature of hostile work relationships. While a full discussion of the nature and impact of these various factors is beyond the scope of this chapter (see Aquino & Thau, 2009, and Einarsen et al., 2011, for reviews), I briefly highlight Salin's (2003) model of enabling, motivating, and precipitating organizational features as it helps clarify how organizational and group factors may influence the development and maintenance of hostile work relationships. Briefly, **enabling** features are structures and processes whose existence or nonexistence affects whether sustained hostile interactions are even possible. These features include power imbalance (as discussed earlier), low perceived costs and risks for engaging in aggressive behaviors, as reflected in organizational cultures in which harassment is equated with the "way to do business," controlling (authoritarian) and uninvolved (laissez-faire) leadership, lack of clear and enforceable policies, which suggests that these behaviors are not problematic, and qualities of the working environment that create stress and frustration for employees. As noted earlier, some hostile relationships may be the result of inefficient coping with these stressors. **Motivating** features are structures and processes that "make it rewarding to harass others" (Salin, 2003, p. 1222). These are conditions that promote the functionality of bullying (i.e., as a rational response to those employees perceived as "threats" or "burdens"; Hoel & Salin, 2003). One such feature is an internally competitive environment, where employees are promoted or rewarded for outperforming other coworkers, so it could be construed to be in an employee's interest to undermine or sabotage another, that is, micropolitical behavior (Zapf & Einarsen, 2003). As noted above, hostility and aggression can be a response to perceived norm violation or other relational transgression on the part of a coworker (such as a "rate buster") in an effort to bring the person "back into line" with production norms. As described with the dominating perpetrator role, hostile and coercive action can also be a way of establishing social dominance or a form of constructive dismissal, making the environment uncomfortable enough so that the other leaves. Westhues (2004) talked about mobbing by a group of professors against another professor as just such a strategy. Finally, **precipitating factors** are organizational structures and processes that may actually trigger an episode of hostility and aggression, assuming that other factors as noted above are in place. These factors are typically associated with some types of organizational change, such as changes in management or work group, restructuring, downsizing, and increasing diversity (Baillien & De Witte, 2009; Neuman & Baron, 2010). The argument is that these changes create stress, anxiety, and frustration, which can lead to aggressive responding as discussed earlier. Salin (2003) argued that sustained hostile relationships are a result of an interaction among at least two factors, if not all three factors.

These frameworks, while focusing on different aspects of the relational context, provide a comprehensive picture of the variety of mechanisms that enable, motivate, and precipitate these relationships. What they do not articulate is what happens "on the ground" in these relationships. For this level of detail, I now turn attention to the literature on coping and responding to aggression. Specifically, I focus on research on target coping and research on maintenance strategies, such as distancing.

Responding, Coping, and Resolution

The evidence on target coping with persistent hostility from another is discouraging. Strategies characterized as active and problem-focused forms of coping have been found to be relatively ineffective in changing the trajectory of an established hostile relationship, and when they fail, they put the parties at increased risk for escalation and increasing damage (Cortina & Magley, 2003; Rospenda, 2002; Tepper, Moss, Lockhart, & Carr, 2007; Zapf & Gross, 2001). For example, Cortina and Magley (2003) have documented the increased risk to targets of persistent incivility of utilizing voice to challenge the situation.

Retaliation often was the response, with impact on both work and personal indicators of well-being. Keashly and Neuman (in press) found that active strategies such as telling the actor to stop or reporting to management resulted in a worsening of the situation. More successful responses (at least in the immediate term) tended to be more passive, and in some cases, they took the form of avoidant strategies of seeking support, comfort, and help from those in the immediate environment. Zapf and Gross (2001) examined the conflict management approaches of "successful" and "unsuccessful" targets and found that those who were successful refrained from active engagement (confrontation) and problem solving with the actor and sought more passive ways of responding, such as accommodating or reducing contact. In many cases, the most "successful" form of coping was to exit literally (leave the organization) and, when a literal exit was not possible, to leave figuratively (e.g., neglect, work withdrawal). Even with leaving the organization, the individuals continued to bear the scars of the relationship.

Looking at responding from a coping framework may position the person experiencing the hostility as a victim, suggesting a certain passivity and lack of ability to influence the situation. Another way of considering the issue of responding is to view the target, in this case, as being agentic in choice of action (i.e., an actor in his or her own right; Lutgen-Sandvik, 2006; Rainivaara, 2009; Skarlicki & Folger, 1997). The target may engage in actions characterized as resistance and retaliation in an effort to modify the interaction to be more balanced and perhaps constructive. For example, Lee and Brotheridge (2006) found that recipients of verbal abuse or undermining of work from a coworker would respond with the same type of aggression. Yet, as agentic as these responses are, they carry risks of escalation and further damage.

As noted earlier, while some of these hostile relationships devolve into actual removal or figurative destruction of one or the other or may turn in more constructive directions, many of them endure for extended periods of time at a "moderate" level of hostility. This possibility suggests that parties are engaging in other kinds of behavior that allow the relationship to continue and work to be accomplished. On some level, the parties have to "cooperate" to accomplish the work of the organization (Rainivaara, 2009). Therefore, the perspective of relational maintenance strategies becomes important in understanding the dynamics of these relationships (e.g., Tepper et al., 2007). Of particular relevance is theorizing on relational distancing strategies in the context of undesired relationships (Hess, 2002, 2006). Based on interviews with self-identified victims and those who had been identified as bullies by others, Rainivaara

(2009) identified deliberative and strategic planning on the part of both parties to maintain the undesirable, yet inescapable, relationship. Strategies included utilizing carefully planned interaction to avoid contact, limiting the amount and personal nature of the interaction so as to limit negative impact on quality of work and the individuals themselves, doing work flawlessly to avoid opportunities for negative feedback, utilizing "silent contracts" between the parties regarding safe or allowed topics, holding fast to norms of polite and professionally civil discourse, and other preventative actions. What is enlightening about this perspective is that it highlights strategic and constructive action on the part of parties to do work productively while the relationship itself remains interpersonally hostile and harmful.

Yet such strategies are inherently problematic over the long haul. They neither stop nor reduce the hostile aspects of the relationship that wear down the parties and increase the possibility of sustained damage (Tepper et al., 2007). Also, displaying such "productivity" and politeness may underplay the problematic and severe nature of the relationship to third parties who could potentially intervene to change the situation (Richman et al., 1999; Tracy, Alberts, & Rivera, 2007).

To this point, the actions discussed have focused on what could be characterized broadly as retaliation/revenge or avoidance. Another approach that responds to norm violation in particular is forgiveness (emotional transformation) and reconciliation (behavioral action) (Aquino, Tripp, & Bies, 2006; Metts, Cupach, & Lippert, 2006). For example, Crossley (2009) examined how perceived motive of the actor (malice or greed) for undermining the target was linked to choice of response: revenge, avoidance, and reconciliation. He found that the effect of perceived motive was mediated through emotional reactions such as anger or sympathy. Anger was strongly associated with revenge and avoidance, while sympathy was most strongly associated with reconciliation. Identifying the types of strategies that people engage in response to transgression or aggressive action highlights the importance of understanding how people perceive and experience behaviors. The perceptions and experience of the behaviors influence choices of responding, which have implications for the trajectory of the relationship. It is clear that the people in these relationships make choices in acting and reacting to each other and thus influence the direction of the relationship. However, at some point, the sustained and often escalated pattern of interaction that characterizes these hostile relationships locks parties into a dynamic that is hard to break free from without external assistance.

Involvement of Others

In many ways, these hostile relationships, once established, are resistant to change in more constructive directions by the parties themselves. This recognition highlights the importance of other parties in the maintenance and management of these relationships. One thing that is clear about hostile work relationships is that others are aware of them, because they either witness the interactions or become part of them (Namie & Lutgen-Sandvik, 2010; Rayner & Keashly, 2005).

What do they do? How do those actions influence the trajectory of these hostile relationships? As noted in the discussion of duration, these witnesses can be drawn into the interactions in ways that increase the destructiveness of the relationship, for example, by becoming active accomplices or through their failure to become engaged (e.g., Namie & Lutgen-Sandvik, 2010; Westhues, 2004). Witnesses can also become involved in ways that can change the relationships in more constructive directions. In addition to managers, human resources personnel, and others who are formally empowered to intervene, coworkers can undertake informal actions that can be helpful to the parties (e.g., Keashly & Neuman, 2007; Scully & Rowe, 2009). Unfortunately, there is little in the workplace aggression and abuse literatures about what witnesses actually do with respect to responding to what they see or hear. In our study on faculty hostility (Keashly & Neuman, in press), those who identified themselves as witnessing such interactions indicated what actions they took and how effective they perceived these actions to be. The majority of witnesses indicated that they were unsure about what to do. However, many did take action. The most frequent responses involved talking with others in the workplace, such as other coworkers, and also with the target about what they had observed, possibly in an effort to understand what was happening. This discussion with the target and coworkers can be important in terms of legitimizing and validating the target's experiences and providing him or her with emotional, and possibly instrumental, support (Lewis, 2001; Schat & Kelloway, 2003). The discussions among coworkers could be particularly helpful to witnesses as a basis for considering subsequent action, including a collective response. Some relatively successful actions on the part of witnesses involved buffering the victim by advising him or her to avoid the bully or keep the bully away. These actions appear to be what Bowes-Sperry and O'Leary-Kelly (2005) characterized as low involvement strategies (i.e., the witness is not putting himself or herself out publicly and potentially risking retaliation). However, these strategies can be useful by reducing the opportunity for hostility to occur (Neuman & Keashly, 2010). Finally, some witnesses did become more directly involved by either confronting the other party or reporting to management, actions that appeared to worsen the situation. We also found that targets perceived the action of reporting as worsening the situation. This finding is very disturbing, given that organizational policies encourage formal reporting for mistreatment and harassment. To the extent that witnesses and targets worry about possible escalation, underreporting may result, culminating in the organization's lack of awareness of the severity and impact of hostile work relationships. The good news about these preliminary data on witness actions is that such actions can have a positive effect on the experience of the relational partners and possibly on the overall trajectory and tenor of the relationship. The challenge is to facilitate coworkers' efficacy regarding what they can do to enhance their capacity and willingness to engage (Ashburn-Nardo, Morris, & Goodwin, 2008; Keashly & Neuman, 2007). An interesting empirical question is how witnesses become involved (i.e., their decision-making process, nature of connection to the parties) and, when they do, how these various actions actually influence the parties, their behaviors, and the resultant trajectory of the relationship.

Another set of "others" who could become engaged in the management and alteration of the relationship is dispute resolution practitioners (Fox & Stallworth, 2009). While these practitioners could be organizational members or come from outside the organization, the application of dispute resolution processes to these hostile relationships, particularly mediation, has been controversial. The argument in favor of the role of alternative dispute resolution (ADR) is grounded in the characterization of these sustained hostile relationships as intractable, escalated conflicts (Keashly & Nowell, 2011). To the extent that this analogy is appropriate, there is solid theorizing to support exploring the possibilities for these processes. The concern is that these strategies will, at the very least, be unsuccessful or, even worse, may result in further victimization. While there are many facets to this criticism, the main one is that ADR processes in general, and mediation in particular, assume equal ability and motivation on the part of the parties to participate actively in the conversation as well as the ability of the mediator to "balance power." The evidence that these enduring relationships can result in psychological, emotional, and physical deterioration of the parties involved (see Keashly & Jagatic, 2011, for a review) suggests that at least one, if not both parties, may not be able to uphold their perspective in such processes.

While this suggests that mediation may not be appropriate or effective when these hostile relationships have become established, other processes may be (see Keashly & Nowell, 2011, and Zapf & Gross, 2001, for further discussion). Most recently, work has begun to appear on the utilization of processes grounded in restorative justice principles that seems promising for possible rebuilding of relationships characterized by severe harm and damage (e.g., Davey, 2007). Like the work on witness action, the application of ADR to these relationships and the articulation of how it influences the parties, and ultimately, the relationship, remains an empirical question. Finally, the discussion of the limitations of ADR highlights the importance of strategies and actions to prevent hostility from becoming entrenched in work relationships.

Opportunities for Change: An Ounce of Prevention Is Worth a Pound of Cure

The damage inherent in prolonged hostile relationships limits the means of handling such situations. Long-term involvement in hostile relationships effectively disables and damages the parties so that a "return to normal" is highly unlikely. This point highlights the importance of preventive measures addressing harmful interactions early, before the patterned interaction becomes entrenched and more damage occurs. Further, early on is when there is a chance for (re)building productive relationships. Individual skill development, such as communication, anger management, stress management, perspective taking, and conflict management skills, may be relevant in these relationships and prevent hostility from becoming entrenched (e.g., Avtgis & Chory, 2010; Schat & Kelloway, 2000).

While enhancing individual skills is important, as noted in the discussion of Salin's (2003) work, the organizational context can either support or undermine them. Therefore, any efforts that require acknowledging organizational culpability and focusing efforts at this level become important. Types of efforts would include the development, and consistent and effective implementation, of policies and associated procedures in consultation with organizational employees (e.g., Rayner, Hoel, & Cooper, 2002; Schat & Kelloway, 2000). More broadly, theorizing and research considering organizational tolerances and discourses and their role in creating and sustaining such relationships (e.g., Lutgen-Sandvik & Davenport Sypher, 2009) highlight the need in some organizations for cultural change. Systematic cultural change efforts undertaken in the Veterans Administration focusing on altering the norms of engagement and nature of the conversations (communicative climate) among organizational members have produced positive changes in the quality of work relationships, and as a result, organizational outcomes (e.g., Keashly & Neuman, 2009; Osatuke, Ward, Dyrenforth, & Belton, 2009).

In Sum: More Remains to Be Done

Hostile work relationships are a very real and damaging part of people's experiences. They are shaped and maintained through a variety of mechanisms, including the parties themselves, dynamic relational processes, the parties around them, and the organizational context in which they are embedded. While there is considerable research and theorizing that is relevant to understanding and ameliorating these relationships, this work is done under different names with extremely limited cross-disciplinary uses. In this chapter, I shared the variety of constructs and literatures and identified how their collective findings inform both our understanding of and need for further work on hostile relationships.

Having provided a backdrop of theory and research, I would like to draw attention to two areas I find particularly intriguing. One fundamental question to explore further focuses on the role of identity in the development and maintenance of these relationships. For example, in the case of institutionalized victimization (Aquino & Lamertz, 2004) and intractable, escalated conflict (Keashly & Nowell, 2011), the hostile relationship has become a core organizing principle of parties' identities. Hess et al. (2006) identified face threat as a key turning point in relationships. Andersson and Pearson (1999) identified threat to identity as a tipping point for moving from uncivil to coercive and hostile behavior. Lutgen-Sandvik and Foss (in press) took the notion of hostile relationships and identity to another level by exploring how women-bullying-women is a structure within the larger construction of professional identity. Understanding how identity connects to and is transformed in these relationships opens up spaces for actions to prevent and manage their development and impact.

The other intriguing area is methodology. The bulk of the research tends to be cross-sectional, retrospective, and often from the perspective of only one party to the relationship. Given that these relationships develop over time, there is a need to examine the dynamics and processes of development, maintenance, and resolution. This need calls for prospective, longitudinal studies that include the voices, thoughts, emotions, and actions of both members of the dyad as well as those that surround them. Such research is characteristic of research in other relational contexts, so there are places from which we can draw inspiration (e.g., Frederickson, 2009; Gottman, 1995).

References

Andersson, L. M., & Pearson, C. M. (1999). Tit for tat? The spiraling effect of incivility in the workplace. *Academy of Management Review, 24,* 452–471.

Aquino, K., & Lamertz, K. (2004). Relational model of workplace victimization: Social roles and patterns of victimization in dyadic relationships. *Journal of Applied Psychology, 89,* 1023–1034.

Aquino, K., & Thau, S. (2009). Workplace victimization: Aggression from the target's perspective. *Annual Review of Psychology, 60,* 717–741.

Aquino, K., Tripp, T. M., & Bies, R. J. (2006). Getting even or moving on? Power, procedural justice, and offense as predictors of revenge, forgiveness, reconciliation and avoidance in organizations. *Journal of Applied Psychology, 91,* 653–668.

Ashburn-Nardo, L., Morris, K. A., & Goodwin, S. A. (2008). The Confronting Prejudiced Responses (CPR) model: Applying CPR in organizations. *Academy of Management Learning & Education, 7,* 332–342.

Ashforth, B. (1997). Petty tyranny in organizations: A preliminary examination of antecedents and consequences. *Canadian Journal of Administrative Sciences, 14,* 126–140.

Avtgis, T. A., & Chory, R. M. (2010). The dark side of organizational life: Aggressive expression in the workplace. In T. A. Avtgis & A. S. Rancer (Eds.), *Arguments, aggression, and conflict: New directions in theory* (pp. 285–304). Hoboken, NJ: Routledge.

Baillien, E., & De Witte, H. (2009). Why is organizational change related to workplace bullying: Role conflict and job insecurity as mediators. *Economic and Industrial Democracy, 30,* 348–371.

Baillien, E., Neyens I., De Witte, H., & De Cuyper, N. A. (2009). A qualitative study on the development of workplace bullying: Towards a three way model. *Journal of Community and Applied Social Psychology, 19,* 1–16.

Barling, J. (1996). The prediction, psychological experience, and consequences of workplace violence. In G. VandenBos & E. Q. Bulatao (Eds.), *Violence on the job: Identifying risks and developing solutions* (pp. 29–50). Washington, DC: American Psychological Association.

Barling, J., Dupre, K. E., & Kelloway, E. K. (2009). Predicting workplace aggression and violence. *Annual Review of Psychology, 60,* 671–692.

Baron, R. A., & Neuman, J. H. (1996). Workplace violence and workplace aggression: Evidence on their relative frequency and potential causes. *Aggressive Behavior, 22,* 161–173.

Bassman, E. (1992). *Abuse in the workplace.* Westport, CT: Quorum Books.

Baumeister, R. F., Bratslavsky, E., Finkenauer, C., & Vohs, K. D. (2001). Bad is stronger than good. *Review of General Psychology, 5,* 323–370.

Björkqvist, K., Österman, K., & Hjelt-Back, M. (1994). Aggression among university employees. *Aggressive Behavior, 20,* 173–184.

Blustein, D. L. (2010). A relational theory of working. *Journal of Vocational Behavior, 79,* 1–17.

doi:10.1016/j.jvb.2010.10.004
Bowes-Sperry, L., & O'Leary-Kelly, A. M. (2005). To act or not to act: The dilemma faced by sexual harassment observers. *Academy of Management Review, 30,* 288–306.
Bowling, N. A., & Beehr, T. A. (2006). Workplace harassment from the victim's perspective: A theoretical model and meta-analysis. *Journal of Applied Psychology, 91,* 997–1012.
Brodsky, C. M. (1976). *The harassed worker.* Lexington, MA: Lexington Books.
Burnazi, L., Keashly, L., & Neuman, J. H. (2005, August). *Aggression revisited: Prevalence, antecedents, and outcomes.* Paper presented at the annual meeting of the Academy of Management, Oahu, HI.
Burnazi, L., Keashly, L., & Neuman, J. H. (2005, August). *Aggression revisited: Prevalence, antecedents, and outcomes.* Paper presented at the annual conference of the Academy of Management Annual Conference, Honolulu, HI.
Buss, A. H. (1961). *The psychology of aggression.* New York: Wiley
Crossley, C. D. (2009). Emotional and behavioral reactions to social undermining: A closer look at perceived offender motives. *Organizational Behavior and Human Decision Processes, 108,* 14–24.
Cortina, L. M., & Magley, V. J. (2003). Raising voice, risking retaliation: Events following interpersonal mistreatment in the workplace. *Journal of Occupational Health Psychology, 8,* 247–265.
Davey, L. (2007, November). *Restorative practices in workplaces.* Paper presented at the 10th International Institute for Restorative Practices World Conference, "Improving citizenship and restoring community," Budapest, Hungary.
Duffy, M. K., Ganster, D. C., & Pagon, M. (2002). Social undermining in the workplace. *Academy of Management Journal, 45,* 331–351.
Dutton, J. (2003). *Energizing your workplace: How to create and sustain high quality connections at work.* San Francisco, CA: Jossey-Bass.
Einarsen, S. (1999). The nature and causes of bullying at work. *International Journal of Manpower, 20,* 16–27.
Einarsen, S., Hoel, H., Zapf, D., & Cooper, C. L. (Eds.). (2011). *Bullying and harassment in the workplace: Developments in theory, research, and practice* (2nd ed.). Boca Raton, FL: CRC Press/Taylor & Francis.
Escartin, J., Rodriguex-Carballeira, A., Zapf, D., Porrua, C., & Martin-Pena, J. (2009). Perceived severity of various bullying behaviors at work and the relevance of exposure to bullying. *Work & Stress, 23,* 191–205.
Folger, R. (1993). Reactions to mistreatment at work. In K. Murnighan (Ed.), *Social psychology in organizations: Advances in theory and research* (pp. 161–183). Englewood Cliffs, NJ: Prentice Hall.
Fox, S., & Stallworth, L. (2009). Building a framework for two internal organizational approaches to resolving and preventing workplace bullying: Alternative dispute resolution and training. *Consulting Psychology Journal: Practice and Research, 61,* 220–241.
Frederickson, B. (2009). *Positivity: Groundbreaking research reveals how to embrace the hidden strength of positive emotions, overcome negativity, and thrive.* New York, NY: Crown Archetype.
Fritz, J. M. H., & Omdahl, B. L. (Eds.). (2006). *Problematic relationships in the workplace.* New York, NY: Peter Lang.

Glomb, T. M. (2002) Workplace aggression: Informing conceptual models with data from specific encounters. *Journal of Occupational Health Psychology, 7,* 1, 20–36.

Glomb, T. M., & Cortina, L. M. (2006). The experience of victims: Using theories of traumatic and chronic stress to understand individual outcomes of workplace abuse. In E. K. Kelloway, J. Barling, & J. Hurrell (Eds.), *Handbook of workplace violence* (pp. 517–534). Thousand Oaks, CA: Sage.

Glomb, T. M., & Liao, H. (2003). Interpersonal aggression in work groups: Social influences, reciprocal and individual effects. *Academy of Management Journal, 46,* 486–496.

Glomb, T. M., & Miner, A. G. (2002). Exploring patterns of aggressive behaviors in organizations: Assessing model-data fit. In J. M. Brett & F. Drasgow (Eds.), *The psychology of work: Theoretically based empirical research* (pp. 235–252). Mahwah, NJ: Lawrence Erlbaum.

Gottman, J. (1995). *Why marriages succeed or fail: And how you can make yours last.* New York, NY: Simon & Schuster.

Hauge, L. J., Skogstad, A., & Einarsen, S. (2009). Individual and situational predictors of workplace bullying: Why do perpetrators engage in the bullying of others? *Work & Stress, 23,* 349–358.

Hershcovis, M. S., & Barling, J. (2007). Towards a relational model of workplace aggression. In J. Langan-Fox, C. L. Cooper, & R. J. Klimoski (Eds.), *Research companion to the dysfunctional workplace: Management challenges and symptoms* (pp. 268–284). Northampton, MA: Edward Elgar Publishing

Hess, J. A. (2002). Distance regulation in personal relationships: The development of a conceptual model and a test of representational validity. *Journal of Personal and Social Relationships, 19,* 663–683.

Hess, J. A. (2006). Distancing from problematic coworkers. In J. M. H. Fritz & B. L. Omdahl (Eds.), *Problematic relationships in the workplace* (pp. 205–232). New York, NY: Peter Lang.

Hess, J. A, Omdahl, B. L., & Fritz, J. M. H. (2006). Turning points in relationships with disliked coworkers. In J. M. H. Fritz & B. L. Omdahl (Eds.), *Problematic relationships in the workplace* (pp. 89–108). New York, NY: Peter Lang.

Hodson, R., Roscigno, V. J., & Lopez, S. H. (2006). Chaos and the abuse of power: Workplace bullying in organizational and interactional context. *Work and Occupations, 33,* 382–416.

Hoel, H., & Salin, D. (2003). Organizational antecedents of workplace bullying. In S. Einarsen, H. Hoel, D. Zapf, & C. Cooper (Eds.), *Bullying and emotional abuse in the workplace: International perspectives in research and practice* (pp. 203–218). London, England: Taylor & Francis.

Janson, G. R., & Hazler, R. J. (2004). Trauma reactions of bystanders and victims to repetitive abuse experiences. *Violence and Victims, 19,* 239–255.

Keashly, L. (1998). Emotional abuse in the workplace: Conceptual and empirical issues. *Journal of Emotional Abuse, 1,* 85–117.

Keashly, L. (2001). Interpersonal and systemic aspects of emotional abuse at work: The target's perspective. *Violence and Victims, 16,* 233–268.

Keashly, L., & Harvey, S. (2005). Emotional abuse in the workplace. In S. Fox & P. Spector (Eds.), *Counterproductive work behavior: Investigations of actors and targets* (pp. 201–236). Washington, DC: American Psychological Association.

Keashly, L., Harvey, S., & Hunter, S. (1997). Abusive interaction and role state stressors: Relative impact on student resident assistant stress and work attitudes. *Work and Stress, 11,*

175–185.

Keashly, L., & Jagatic, K. (2003). By any other name: American perspectives on workplace bullying. In S. Einarsen, H. Hoel, D. Zapf, & C. L. Cooper (Eds.), *Bullying and emotional abuse in the workplace: International perspectives in research and practice* (pp. 31–91). London, England: Taylor & Francis.

Keashly, L., & Jagatic, K. (2011). North American perspectives on hostile behaviors and bullying at work. In S. Einarsen, H. Hoel, D. Zapf, & C. L. Cooper (Eds.), *Bullying and harassment in the workplace: Developments in theory, research, and practice* (2nd ed., pp. 41–71). Boca Raton, FL: CRC Press/Taylor & Francis.

Keashly, L., & Neuman, J. H. (2002, August). *Exploring persistent patterns of workplace aggression.* Paper presented at the annual meeting of the Academy of Management, Denver, CO.

Keashly, L., & Neuman, J. H. (2007, November). Stepping up: Developing peer strategies for managing bullying at work. In S. Dickmeyer (Chair), *Building workplace bullying seminars: Grounding training and development in strong communication scholarship.* Symposium conducted at the annual conference of the National Communication Association, Chicago, IL.

Keashly, L., & Neuman, J.H. (2009). Building a constructive communication climate: The Workplace Stress and Aggression Project. In P. Lutgen-Sandvik & B. Davenport Sypher (Eds.), *Destructive organizational communication: Processes, consequences and constructive ways of organizing* (pp. 339–362). New York, NY: Routledge.

Keashly, L., & Neuman, J. H. (in press). Bullying in higher education: What current research, theorizing and practice tell us. In J. Lester (Ed.), *Workplace bullying in higher education.* New York, NY: Routledge.

Keashly, L., & Nowell, B. (2003). Conflict, conflict resolution and bullying. In S. Einarsen, H. Hoel, D. Zapf, & C. Cooper (Eds.), *Bullying and emotional abuse in the workplace: International research and practice perspectives* (pp. 339–358). London, England: Taylor & Francis.

Keashly, L., & Nowell, B. L. (2011). Conflict, conflict resolution, and bullying. In S. Einarsen, H. Hoel, & D. Zapf, & C. L. Cooper (Eds.), *Workplace bullying: Developments in theory, research, and practice* (2nd ed., pp. 423–455). Boca Raton, FL: CRC Press/Taylor & Francis.

Keashly, L., Trott, V., & MacLean, L. M. (1994). Abusive behavior in the workplace: A preliminary investigation. *Violence and Victims, 9,* 125–141.

Lamertz, K., & Aquino, K. (2004). Social power, social status and perceptual similarity of workplace victimization: A social network analysis of stratification. *Human Relations, 57,* 795–822.

Lee, R. T., & Brotheridge, C. M. (2006). When prey turns predatory: Workplace bullying as a predictor of counteraggression/bullying, coping, and well-being. *European Journal of Work and Organizational Psychology, 15,* 352–377.

Lewis, D. (2001). Perceptions of bullying in organizations. *International Journal of Management and Decision Making, 2,* 48–63.

Leymann, H. (1990). Mobbing and psychological terror at workplaces. *Violence and Victims, 5,* 119–126.

Leymann, H. (1996). The content and development of mobbing at work. *European Journal of Work and Organizational Psychology, 5,* 165–184.

Lim, S., & Cortina, L. M. (2005). Interpersonal mistreatment in the workplace: The interface and impact of general incivility and sexual harassment. *Journal of Applied Psychology, 90,*

483–496.
Lind, T. (1997) Litigation and claiming in organizations: Antisocial behavior or quest for justice? In R. A. Giacalone & J. Greenberg (Eds.), *Antisocial behavior in organizations* (pp. 150–171). Thousand Oaks, CA: Sage.
Lutgen-Sandvik, P. (2006). Take this job and . . . : Quitting and other forms of resistance to workplace bullying. *Communication Monographs, 73*, 406–433.
Lutgen-Sandvik, P., & Davenport Sypher, B. (Eds.). (2009). *Destructive organizational communication: Processes, consequences, and constructive ways of organizing.* New York, NY: Routledge.
Lutgen-Sandvik, P., & Foss, K. A. (in press). Priming, painting, peeling and polishing: Constructing and deconstructing the woman-bullying-woman identity at work. In S. Fox & T. Lituchy (Eds.), *Gender and the dysfunctional workplace* (pp. 61–77). Northampton, MA: Edward Elgar.
Meglich-Sespico, P. A. (2006). *Perceived severity of interpersonal workplace harassment behaviors* (Unpublished doctoral dissertation). Kent State University, Kent, OH.
Metts, S., Cupach, W. R., & Lippert, L. (2006). Forgiveness in the workplace. In J. M. H. Fritz & B. L. Omdahl (Eds.), *Problematic relationships in the workplace* (pp. 249–278). New York, NY: Peter Lang,
Namie, G., & Lutgen-Sandvik, P. (2010). Active and passive accomplices: The communal character of workplace bullying. *International Journal of Communication, 4*, 343–373.
Neuman, J. H., & Baron, R. A. (1997). Aggression in the workplace. In R. A. Giacalone & J. Greenberg (Eds.), *Antisocial behavior in organizations* (pp. 37–67). Thousand Oaks, CA: Sage.
Neuman, J. H., & Keashly, L. (2010). The means, motive, and opportunity framework and insidious workplace behavior. In J. Greenberg (Ed.), *Insidious workplace behavior* (pp. 31–76). Hillsdale, NJ: Lawrence Erlbaum.
O'Leary-Kelly, A. M., Griffin, R. W., & Glew, D. J. (1996). Organization-motivated aggression: A research framework. *Academy of Management Review, 21*, 225–253.
Osatuke, K., Ward, C., Dyrenforth, S. R., & Belton, L. W. (2009). Civility, respect, engagement in the workforce (CREW): Nationwide organization development intervention at Veterans Health Administration. *The Journal of Applied Behavioral Science, 45*, 384–410.
Price Spratlen, L. (1995). Interpersonal conflict, which includes mistreatment in a university workplace. *Violence and Victims, 10*, 285–297.
Rainivaara, S. (2009). Workplace bullying relationships. In T. A. Kinney & M. Pörhölä (Eds.), *Anti and pro-social communication: Theories, methods, and applications* (pp. 59–70). New York, NY: Peter Lang.
Raver, J. L., & Nishii, L. H. (2010). Once, twice, or three times as harmful? Ethnic harassment, gender harassment, and generalized workplace harassment. *Journal of Applied Psychology, 95*, 236–254.
Rayner, C., Hoel, H., & Cooper, C. (2002). *Workplace bullying: What we know, who is to blame and what can we do?* London, England: Taylor & Francis.
Rayner, C., & Keashly, L. (2005). Bullying at work: A Perspective from Britain and and North America. In S. Fox & P. Spector (Eds.), *Counterproductive workplace behavior: Investigations of actors and targets* (pp. 271–296). Washington, DC: American Psychological Association
Richman, J. A., Rospenda, K., Flaherty, J. A., & Freels, S. (2001). Workplace harassment, active coping and alcohol-related outcomes. *Journal of Substance Abuse, 13*, 347–366.
Richman, J. A., Rospenda, K. M., Nawyn, S. J., Flaherty, J. A., Fendrich, M., Drum, M. L., &

Johnson, T. P. (1999). Sexual harassment and generalized workplace abuse among university employees: Prevalence and mental health correlates. *American Journal of Public Health*, 89, 358–363.

Rospenda, K. M. (2002). Workplace harassment, services utilization, and drinking outcomes. *Journal of Occupational Health Psychology*, 7, 141–155.

Rospenda, K., Richman, J. A., & Shannon, C. A. (2006). Patterns of workplace harassment, gender, and use of services: An update. *Journal of Occupational Health Psychology*, 11, 379–393.

Rospenda, K., Richman, J. A., & Shannon, C. A. (2008). Prevalence and mental health correlates of harassment and discrimination in the workplace: Results from a national study. *Journal of Interpersonal Violence*, 24, 819–843.

Rospenda, K., Richman, J. A.., Wislar, J. S., & Flaherty, J. A.(2000). Chronicity of sexual harassment and generalized workplace abuse: Effects on drinking outcomes. *Addiction*, 95, 1805–1820.

Ryan, K. D., & Oestreich, D. K. (1991). *Driving fear out of the workplace: How to overcome the invisible barriers to quality, productivity, and innovation*. San Francisco, CA: Jossey-Bass.

Salin, D. (2003). Ways of explaining workplace bullying: A review of enabling, motivating and precipitating structures and processes in the work environment. *Human Relations*, 56, 1213–1232.

Schat, A. C. H., Frone, M. R., & Kelloway, E. K. (2006). Prevalence of workplace aggression in the US workforce: Findings from a national study. In E. K. Kelloway, J. Barling, & J. J. Hurrell (Eds.), *Handbook of workplace violence* (pp. 47–90). Thousand Oaks, CA: Sage.

Schat, A. C. H., & Kelloway, E. K. (2000). Effects of perceived control on the outcomes of workplace aggression and violence. *Journal of Occupational Health Psychology*, 5, 386–402.

Schat, A. C. H., & Kelloway, E. K. (2003). Reducing the adverse consequences of workplace aggression and violence: The buffering effects of organizational support. *Journal of Occupational Health Psychology*, 8, 110–122.

Scully, M., & Rowe, M. (2009). Bystander training within organizations. *Journal of the International Ombudsman Association*, 2(1), 1–9.

Sheehan, K. H., Sheehan, D. V., White, K., Leibowitz, A., & Baldwin, D. C. (1990). A pilot study of medical student abuse and student perception of mistreatment and misconduct in medical school. *Journal of the American Medical Association*, 263, 533–537.

Skarlicki, D. P., & Folger, R. (1997). Retaliation in the workplace: The roles of distributive, procedural, and interactional justice. *Journal of Applied Psychology*, 82, 434–443.

Spector, P. E., & Jex, S. M. (1998). Development of four self-report measures of job stressors and strain: Interpersonal Conflict at Work Scale, Organizational Constraints Scale, Quantitative Workload Inventory, and Physical Symptoms Inventory. *Journal of Occupational Health Psychology*, 3, 356–367.

Tedeschi, J. T., & Felson, R. B. (1994). *Violence, aggression, and coercive actions*. Washington, DC: American Psychological Association.

Tepper, B. J. (2000). Consequences of abusive supervision. *Academy of Management Journal*, 43, 178–190.

Tepper, B. J., Duffy, M. K., Henle, C. A., & Lambert, L. S. (2006). Procedural injustice, victim precipitation, and abusive supervision. *Personnel Psychology*, 59, 101–123.

Tepper, B. J., Moss, S. E., Lockhart, D. E., & Carr, J. C. (2007). Abusive supervision, upward maintenance communication, and subordinates' psychological distress. *Academy of Management Journal, 50,* 1169–1180.

Totterdell, P., Hershcovis, S., Niven, K., Reich, T., & Stride, C. (in press). Induced emotional regulation: How employees can be emotionally drained by interactions between coworkers. *Work & Stress.*

Tracy, S. J., Alberts, J. K., & Rivera, K. D. (2007). *How to bust the office bully: Eight tactics for explaining workplace abuse to decision-makers* (Report No. 0701, The Project for Wellness and Work-Life). Tucson, AZ: Arizona State University Press.

Venkataramani, V., & Dalal, R. S. (2007). Who helps and harms whom? Relational antecedents of interpersonal helping and harming in organizations. *Journal of Applied Psychology, 92,* 952–966.

Waldron, V. (2009). Emotional tyranny at work: Suppressing the moral emotions. In P. Lutgen-Sandvik & B. Davenport Sypher (Eds.), *Destructive organizational communication: Processes, consequences and constructive ways of organizing* (pp. 7–26). New York, NY: Routledge.

Westhues, K. (2004). *Workplace mobbing in academe: Reports from twenty universities.* Lewiston, NY: The Edwin Mellen Press.

Yamada, D. (2000). The phenomenon of "workplace bullying" and the need for status-blind hostile work environment protection. *Georgetown Law Journal, 88,* 475–536.

Zapf, D., & Einarsen, S. (2005). Mobbing at work: Escalated conflicts in organizations. In S. Fox & P. E. Spector (Eds.), *Counterproductive work behavior: Investigations of actors and targets* (pp. 237–270). Washington, DC: American Psychological Association.

Zapf, D., & Gross, C. (2001). Conflict escalation and coping with workplace bullying: A replication and extension. *European Journal of Work and Organizational Psychology, 10,* 497–523.

· 4 ·

WORKPLACE BULLYING AS INTERPERSONAL VIOLENCE?

A Reconceptualization in Progress

Terry A. Kinney

Are vicious gossip, slander, demeaning statements, sabotage, insults, and social exclusion forms of violence? This question is currently being debated as more and more states adopt anti-bullying legislation and consider taking legal action against those who bully. Due to our increased awareness of the effects of bullying, bullying is being reconceptualized from a childhood or office nuisance to a criminal offense that holds prosecutable punishments. This reconceptualization requires aligning acts of bullying with specific forms of violence in order to determine appropriate punishments, and it means that organizations such as schools and workplaces must develop new policies and procedures that define acceptable and unacceptable behavior. These organizations must then grapple with enforcement. This process of clarifying harms, realigning actions with forms of violence, drafting policy, and enforcing policy parallels the processes countries, states, and organizations undertook in addressing the harms of racism, discrimination, and harassment.

This chapter seeks to explicate the components of workplace bullying in order to understand why bullying, as a form of interpersonal violence, is so pervasive. Despite its ill effects on individual and relational well-being, bullying behavior continues to exist not only in private relationships, but also in public spheres. In order to understand this complicated behavior and review promising remedies, I address six themes: (1) bullying as interpersonal violence, (2) the conceptualization of workplace violence, (3) workplace bullying as a serious social problem, (4) the effects of workplace bullying, (5) coping with workplace bullying, and (6) thoughts on prevention and intervention strategies.

Bullying as Interpersonal Violence

In 2002, the World Health Organization (WHO; Butchart, Cerda, Villaveces, & Sminkey, 2002; Krug, Dahlberg, Mercy, Zwi, & Lozano, 2002) published two comprehensive reports on the state of interpersonal violence across the world. Among the many important conclusions advanced in the WHO reports is the claim that interpersonal violence is a pan-cultural epidemic. This conclusion holds several important implications for violence prevention and intervention efforts in general and for interpersonal interactions, especially workplace bullying.

The first implication of the WHO reports is that the nature of interpersonal interactions and relationships in all environments, including workplaces, is important. Given the long hours spent working and importance of work, the sense of self and self-worth are heavily influenced by the workplace. Self and self-worth are concepts that have tremendous impact on the sense of well-being. In asserting that interpersonal violence is a pan-cultural epidemic, the WHO reports raise awareness of a cascading sequence of harm from interpersonal violence. As individuals experience harm, they commonly develop denigrated perceptions of self, self-worth, and well-being. These effects, in turn, lead to strains in productivity and interpersonal relationships, which have a high capacity to reduce worker morale further (Ilgen, Mitchell, & Fredrickson, 1981; Niedl, 1996; Wilson, 1991; Zapf & Gross, 2001).

A second implication of the WHO reports is that interpersonal violence is placed in a spotlight. The light functions to elevate the driving forces behind acts formerly dismissed as schoolyard or workplace nuisance to social process worthy of careful attention and management. The WHO reports pull bullying from the shadows into the limelight of record keeping and reform on par with sexual harassment, racism, and discrimination.

Claiming that workplace bullying is a form of interpersonal violence is warranted because of its goals and consequences. Olweus (1993a) argued that bullying in general is abusive as it seeks to hurt individuals through repeated name-calling, direct physical assaults, negative gossip, and social isolation/exclusion. Olweus (1993a) further defined bullying as encompassing four components: (1) hostile, abusive, and unethical communication or behavior or intentional harm-doing, (2) which is carried out repeatedly and over time, (3) in an interpersonal relationship characterized by an imbalance of power, and (4) resulting in hurt to the victim, often leading to decreased motivation and reduced levels of well-being. These events are considered violence because they are abusive and hold the potential to harm individuals psychologically, physically, economically, and socially (de Pedro, Sanchez, Navarro, & Izquierdo, 2008; Hawker & Boulton, 2000; Niedl, 1995; Olweus, 1993b, 2003). As a result, workplace bullying needs to be managed just as harassment, racism, and discrimination are through various social and legal procedures and sanctions.

Conceptual Foundations of Workplace Bullying

The WHO reports and others document that interpersonal violence can be subtle, long term, and damaging to both the perpetrators and the victims (e.g., Cupach & Spitzberg, 1994; Kowalski, 2001; Spitzberg & Cupach, 1998). These researchers further argue that interpersonal violence is driven by a complex set of psychological, social, and cultural phenomena.

Underlying these driving forces is a conceptual foundation: The establishment and maintenance of interpersonal relationships involve influence, and people engage in a wide array of methods for influencing one another on a regular basis in relationships (Canary & Stafford, 1994; Dindia & Baxter, 1987; Lee & Jablin, 1995). Linking bullying to social influence processes permits an explanation for why bullying is so pervasive across workplaces.

As the voluminous literature on social influence reveals, we can influence others in many ways, including via persuasion, compliance gaining, and aggression (see Dillard, Anderson, & Knobloch, 2002, for a review). These three types of social influence can be arrayed along moral/ethical and politeness dimensions, making the use of many forms of compliance gaining falling on the less ethical, less polite side of the array problematic for the maintenance of healthy workplace relationships. The following social influence methods are examples of forms falling on the less ethical and less polite side of the continuum: coercion, intimidation, harassment, and aggression in the form of hitting, kicking, insults, and sabotage. Despite the unethical and abusive nature of these forms, they occur with notable frequency in many types of interpersonal relationships (Spitzberg & Cupach, 1998), including relationships in the workplace (Fritz & Omdahl, 2006; Pryor & Fitzgerald, 2003; Rayner, 1997; Salin, 2001).

The use of strong forms of compliance gaining and most forms of aggression in the workplace suggests being impolite and inflicting harm on coworkers is, at times, perceived as necessary. Given the keen awareness most people have of workplace rules, the use of these forms also suggests that they are viewed by some as appropriate or, at the very least, tolerated in the workplace. Dillard, Segrin, and Harden's (1989) original finding that people choose influence strategies based on goals and their associated outcomes indicates that at least some workers are deciding that persuasion and the use of reason, arguments, politeness, respect, and civility will not meet the outcome they identify as most important (e.g., effectiveness in accomplishing the goal). Believing they are choosing influence methods which will get them to top goals enables individuals to justify their use of harsher compliance gaining strategies and use of aggression. Furthermore, the existence of these forms of social influence in the workplace suggests the presence of structural factors in the workplace (e.g., competition, lack of support) that foster the use of these negative social influence tactics.

The influence of structural factors in the workplace such as competition and lack of support suggests that individuals who desire to achieve their goals and tasks in the workplace may perceive that they are on their own and need to disadvantage their coworkers to get ahead or to maintain their social standing. This approach may lead individuals to become strategic, manipulative, and secretive in how they interact with coworkers. Dillard's (1990) work on the goals-plan-action model of social influence message production holds value as one way to explain why individuals may use anti-social influence strategies such as bullying to achieve outcomes in the workplace rather than more pro-social strategies such as politeness and persuasion (see also Pörhölä & Kinney, 2010). At its core, the goals-plan-action model holds that social actors are driven by primary and secondary goals, which bring about specific plans that drive actions. If the original goals are "tainted" by the structural factors of the workplace, such as believing that the workplace is hostile and operates on a win-lose model and that there is little to no support, individuals are likely to generate goals that are self-preserving and self-promoting, which can manifest as bullying (harassment, manipulation, intimidation, coercion) as a way to gain an upper hand and disadvantage others.

In addition to individual justifications for rude and hurtful behavior in the workplace, organizational factors also allow for or contribute to bullying behavior. Organizational factors that have been found to be important antecedents of workplace bullying include stressful and competitive work environments, failure to establish a supportive atmosphere, excessive organizational changes, authoritarian ways of settling differences in opinions, and ineffective leadership and management styles (Hoel, Cooper, & Faragher, 2001; Hoel & Salin, 2003;

Meares, Oetzel, Torres, Derkacs, & Ginossar, 2004; Vartia, 1996). Each of these factors affects various components of the workplace environment and holds the potential to shift the environment (and the culture) toward acceptance and/or tolerance of bullying. However, these factors hold in common the ability to affect how individuals approach interpersonal influence situations in the workplace by affecting goals and associated plans through the beliefs that individuals develop as they come to understand the culture of the workplace. As stated earlier, if individuals believe that the workplace is operating on a win-lose model with little to no social support, perceptual biases are set in place that can shift interpersonal interactions toward anti-social approaches. Adding other factors to the mix, such as ineffective leadership and management styles, can amplify these anti-social biases, leading to destructive social practices, tolerance of such behavior, and, over time, expectations that individuals will act in these ways while at work.

As the research indicates, when the workplace culture is perceived as competitive or cutthroat, and/or if incivility is commonplace and tolerated, then the use of intimidation, harassment, coercion, and aggression (all forms of bullying) are more likely to manifest as individuals are more likely to use these forms of social influence to get what they want, need, or desire. Additionally, as antecedents to workplace bullying, these organizational factors set in place a structure into which personalities and interpersonal interactions can play themselves out, adding to the potential that workplace bullying will occur (Hoel & Salin, 2003; Leymann, 1990; Lutgen-Sandvik, 2003; Vartia, 1996).

Given that workplace bullying can be characterized as a form of social influence, its use in the workplace is not unexpected, despite its negative consequences and cultural expectations not to harm others. At times getting what we want, need, or deserve from others supersedes or interferes with notions of politeness, ethics, and morality, especially when interpersonal relationships are strained, which may occur when we are distressed (Latane & Darley, 1970) or when we dislike another person (Hess, 2000). As a result, as we choose to use compliance gaining and aggression rather than persuasion, our verbalizations and interpersonal interactions become less moral/ethical, less polite, and more hurtful, and they take the form of exerting power over others and/or hurting others. Additionally, victims of workplace bullying may lack sensitivity to the implicit rules and norms of the working community (see Kramer & Hess, 2002), and this insensitivity might lead to their irritating others and becoming the target for negativity (Einarsen, 1999, 2000; Einarsen & Raknes, 1997; Einarsen & Skogstad, 1996).

For example, Einarsen (1999) found two types of bullying in the workplace: dispute related and predatory. Dispute-related bullying is driven by unresolved conflicts, which can be a function of ineffective organizational policy and practice and/or a function of individuals not managing their interpersonal relationships well. Predatory bullying comes about because the bully seeks to achieve some personal advantage or to right a perceived wrong at the victim's expense without direct provocation by the victim, suggesting again that the culture of the organization may interact with personal traits and qualities to drive this type of bullying. These two motivations for bullying suggest that the victims of workplace bullying may have prompted the negative response. The point here is not to suggest that the negative response is justified but to illustrate that it may be explained by reference to some attribute or behavior of the target.

Workplace Bullying as a Serious Social Problem

Workplace bullying is a serious and widespread problem. Several studies show that a large number of individuals have been exposed (as victim or observer) to various forms of workplace bullying (e.g., Pryor & Fitzgerald, 2003; Rayner, 1997; Salin, 2001; Woodman & Kumar, 2008). These studies indicate that bullying is a prevalent and persistent problem emerging in workplaces of different kinds and that a substantial number of people are affected by this social problem.

Workplace bullying is often categorized into two general types that provide insight into its nature: direct and indirect. In direct forms of bullying, a bully targets a victim in face-to-face or face-to-face-like (e-mail, phone) contexts, and the victim can identify the bully. Alternatively, indirect forms of bullying (e.g., exclusion, sabotage, the withholding of information, the silent treatment) are often hidden and occur outside of the knowledge of the victim (behind his or her back, behind closed doors). Indirect forms of bullying are designed to obscure and protect the identity of the bully. Both forms are hurtful, serve to point out deficits, and may hamper the victim in the performance of his or her duties or the achievement of his or her goals while at work.

Given that most individuals in the workplace are socially sophisticated and driven to protect their own status, the types of bullying that occur at work tend to be complex and subtle, operating within a framework of "plausible deniability," which allows perpetrators to deny wrongdoing or claim misunderstanding of intent if they are asked to explain their behavior (see Pearson & Porath,

2005). Concern for self-protection may prompt individuals to generate indirect bullying messages and behaviors such as social isolation, exclusion, sabotage, gossip, or the blocking or interfering with promotions or training opportunities that would allow victims to advance in the workplace (Einarsen, 1999; Einarsen & Raknes, 1997; Salin, 2001).

Indirect bullying is insidious in that victims have limited opportunities to express themselves or to influence the situation. They often are not aware of the original bullying, and they may realize its existence only through indirect means such as not being invited to participate in work tasks or social events, by missed promotion opportunities, or through shunning by coworkers. In essence, due to the nature of indirect bullying, its effects may persist for years and across contexts. These tactics suggest that workplace bullies desire to cover their tracks as they disadvantage and hurt others and at the same time protect (or elevate) their social status in the workplace hierarchy, which is a social influence strategy most easily used by supervisors as they protect and promote themselves (Ilgen et al., 1981; Lutgen-Sandvik, 2003; Meares et al., 2004; Sias & Jablin, 1995).

The Effects of Workplace Bullying

Given the importance of the workplace to a sense of self, social status, and connections with our coworkers, it is not surprising that when the social atmosphere at work turns negative, the negativity affects various aspects of our health and well-being (de Pedro et al., 2008; Einarsen & Skogstad, 1996; Hawker & Boulton, 2000; Kinney, 2006; Leymann, 1990; Niedl, 1996). The distress caused by being exposed to workplace bullying (or general negativity at work) manifests in several ways and may be characterized as having two distinct types: hurt (direct, immediate effects) and harm (indirect, long-term effects). Both hurt and harm can be subdivided further into categories of effects on specific areas significant to individual identity, including psychological/emotional, social/relational, behavioral, and professional domains.

Consistent with the literature on stress and well-being, hurt is typically defined as an immediate outcome that surfaces in direct response to a negative or aversive event, while harm is typically defined as a longer-term consequence that surfaces over time (Friedman, 1992; Herbert & Cohen, 1993; Keller, Shiflett, Schleifer, & Bartlett, 1994; O'Leary, 1990). Given that research on workplace bullying has found that being bullied at work by supervisors, bosses, and coworkers exacts a toll on victims, understanding the nature of the potential outcomes of exposure to workplace bullying is important as a first step toward casting workplace bullying as a form of interpersonal violence.

Various forms of hurt are the most commonly recognized outcomes of workplace bullying (Hawker & Boulton, 2000). Many research studies measure the effects of bullying by asking individuals how they felt, what they thought, and if they experienced any ill effects (Hawker & Boulton, 2000). Researchers favor the reporting of direct and immediate effects because longer-term consequences are harder to track. However, if the immediate effects are not resolved, it is likely that they will develop into longer-term harms. For example, the anxiety and fear that may come about from workplace bullying may develop into a depressive or anxiety disorder if the bullying persists and/or if the original anxiety and fear do not subside (de Pedro et al., 2008; Einarsen & Skogstad, 1996; Hawker & Boulton, 2000; Leymann, 1990). Further, depressive and anxiety disorders hold significant consequences for physical, social, and relational health and well-being (e.g., Herbert & Cohen, 1993; Keller et al., 1994; O'Leary, 1990).

In terms of direct, immediate effects, research finds that thoughts and emotions are often affected negatively by exposure to workplace bullying (Baron, 1988; de Pedro et al., 2008; Kinney, 2003, 2006; Leymann, 1990; Lutgen-Sandvik, 2003; Niedl, 1996). Instances of workplace bullying often manifest as destructive criticism, insults, coercion, demeaning comments, and forms of harassment (Leymann, 1990, 1996), all of which attack or call into question various aspects of an individual's perceptions of self-esteem and self-worth, independence and autonomy, and social standing (Kinney, 1994, 2003, 2006).

Several psychological and communication-based theories hold that receiving negative information about one's self is threatening because it forces comparison and evaluation (e.g., Bruch, Rivet, & Laurenti, 2000; Higgins, 1987, 1989; Gonnerman, Parker, Lavine, & Huff, 2000). This process often results in the activation of negative emotions and moods as a way to signal that a threat has been encountered that needs to be dealt with to protect the integrity of the self (see Kinney, 2009). As a result, fear, anxiety, anger, resentment, and rage are common emotional states experienced by individuals who have been bullied. If not dealt with effectively, these emotional states can develop into harms or long-term outcomes such as depressed mood and loss of concentration, which may affect one's sense of self-worth and life satisfaction, leading to alcoholism, depression, anxiety disorders, and problems with emotional, psychological, and physical health and well-being (Cohen, Tyrrell, & Smith, 1993; Friedman, 1992; Herbert & Cohen, 1993; Higgins, Klein, & Strauman, 1985; Keller et al., 1994; O' Leary, 1990).

In terms of indirect, long-term effects, the cascade of direct, immediate effects brought about by exposure to workplace bullying may contribute to longer-term outcomes that may become divorced from the original bullying incidents or amplified due to repeated exposure to bullying incidents. These effects center on psychological, emotional, and behavioral reactions and hold importance for overall health and well-being, professional advancement, and social status. Repeated exposure to workplace bullying often wears individuals down due to the distress that it produces in part from the anxiety, fear, anger, and resentment that it elicits and due to the amount of attention and energy that must be devoted to manage these emotional states. These types of states may lead to insomnia, melancholy, apathy, social isolation, feelings of stigmatization, helplessness, shame, paranoia, and suspiciousness (Cohen et al., 1993; Friedman, 1992; Herbert & Cohen, 1993; Higgins et al., 1985; Keller et al., 1994; O' Leary, 1990). As a result, the eventual wearing down can result in poor psychosomatic functioning, opening individuals up to increased potential to become physically ill and weak.

In addition, managing intense negative emotional states takes a toll on the mental acuity of individuals, producing confusion, lack of organizational skill, and overall lower ability to function at high levels, which may be problematic in a highly demanding work environment. These states may lead to lower job satisfaction, despair, lower productivity, absenteeism, and eventually leaving one's job to escape the turmoil that has been created by the bullying, all of which affect one's social status and professional development (Niedl, 1996; Wilson, 1991). In addition, the literature on coping with negativity (see Friedman, 1992) shows that the stress produced by the original event may linger for extended periods as individuals cope with the issue. These findings suggest that employees exposed to bullying at work may experience stress outside of the workplace as they think about the issues surrounding the bullying episode and its implications, enhancing the potential for harm.

Thus, exposure to workplace bullying can hurt individuals, which may lead to harm. Specifically, if the direct, immediate effects of workplace bullying are not dealt with adequately, they may develop into forms of harm, which hold an array of negative consequences, including affecting aspects of one's health and well-being and aspects of one's professional, relational, and personal well-being.

Coping with Workplace Bullying

Rainivaara (2009) showed that workplace bullying is an interpersonal process which evolves into a permanent way of interacting. Rainivaara examined the coping strategies used by victims of workplace bullying and found that victims maintained their relationship with bullies by distancing themselves, much like the process that Hess (2000) uncovered with responses to disliked coworkers. Various distancing behaviors were reported, including avoiding face-to-face interaction, changing working hours and shifts, taking sick leave and leaves of absence, using non-face-to-face communication channels (e.g., e-mail), using third parties as messengers, restricting communication with the bully only to necessary and formal situations, avoiding self-disclosure and problematic topics, showing exaggerated politeness and formality, and managing the display of negative emotions. In addition, study participants reported that they had used strategies such as seeking social support, telling themselves that they were free from blame, forcing themselves to avoid thinking about the issue, trying not to be affected by using humor, and feeling pity toward the bully.

Rainivaara's (2009) findings indicated that maintaining a relationship with a workplace bully is a complex and demanding communication process requiring a host of coping strategies that can change depending on the context. Attempts to maintain the relationship seem to require creative ways in which to interact as simple avoidance is not always possible. However, avoidance appears to be a significant factor in the maintenance of the bullying relationship, which suggests an absence of features of relational communication that would be likely to help the relationship develop in a positive, constructive manner. These findings also suggest that bullied individuals define the bullying experience as a form of conflict and not as violence, which provides insight into how individuals cope with the situation.

Casting workplace bullying in terms of conflict situates it as a process of disagreement between individuals (Sias & Jablin, 1995; Spratlen, 1995). Zapf and Gross (2001) argued that conflict management strategies can be used to cope with the stress of workplace bullying. They claimed that individuals who are able to activate conflict management strategies are better able to manage workplace bullying situations. Their four strategies included Exit (quitting), Voice (active, constructive problem solving), Loyalty (hoping the problem will resolve itself), and Neglect (changing one's orientation to the workplace and becoming less committed, more apathetic). While each of these four strategies may work to some extent, only Voice is pro-social/pro-active. However, the main problem with the Voice strategy is that it assumes the victim knows the bully or knows that he or she is being degraded/derided by another and that the victim has the will and skill to address the issue with the bully. As Sillars's (1980) original work on conflict shows, conflict management strategies are communicatively complex, and the workplace bullying literature will need to situate itself within this long-standing literature base to examine more comprehensively how individuals cope with workplace bullying as a form of conflict (see also Roloff & Soule, 2002, for a review). As important, shifting the definition of bullying from interpersonal conflict to interpersonal violence will help move the conceptualization of bullying as "disagreement" toward bullying as a form of violence, and as a result, will make more relevant specific prevention and intervention strategies that aim to reduce interpersonal violence.

Thoughts on Prevention and Intervention Strategies

Extensive media coverage of several high profile cases of school bullying that resulted in suicides in the United States (e.g., Phoebe Prince, Tyler Clementi) have raised awareness of the contexts, types, and effects of bullying. We now know that bullying does not stop at the schoolyard but follows us into our neighborhoods, homes, and workplaces. One of the results of this enhanced awareness has been the passage of anti-bullying legislation aimed to protect children while at school, with at least two of these cases of bullying resulting in criminal prosecutions (see Phoebe Prince's and Tyler Clementi's cases). As demonstrated in the criminal cases prompted by Phoebe Prince's and Tyler Clementi's suicides, there is a shift toward thinking about bullying as a prosecutable offense along the lines of criminal harassment, stalking, civil rights violations, intentional infliction of emotional distress, defamation, intimidation, invasion of privacy, and discrimination. Anti-bullying legislation and a willingness to prosecute signal an important reconceptualization of bullying, moving it from a schoolyard event between children to a crime that holds potentially severe sanctions.

As Pörhölä and Kinney (2010) reported, the concern over bullying has led to the development of prevention and intervention programs (Baron, 1990; Hogh & Dofradottir, 2001; Olweus, 2003; Osatuke, Moore, Ward, Dyrenforth, & Belton, 2009), which tend to target attitudes, values, and beliefs to raise awareness of bullying and to teach those involved that there are policies and procedures designed to aid in the reporting of bullying. However, when bullying is aligned with criminal harassment, stalking, civil rights violations, intentional infliction of emotional distress, defamation, and discrimination, not only has it been linked to violence, but it becomes a form of violence. As a result, prevention and intervention programs designed to reduce incidents of bullying and help those who have been exposed to it need to move beyond targeting attitudes, values, and beliefs to include specific guidelines that outline clearly what is likely to happen if individuals bully another person. This move entails the adoption of conceptualizations of bullying as a form of interpersonal violence and linking official sanctions to specific aspects of bullying.

Consistent with the WHO reports, there are several meaningful ways to define and cast interpersonal violence. How workplace bullying is defined holds important implications for prevention and intervention strategies. For example, if workplace bullying is defined as a psychological trait, prevention and intervention programs need to be designed to influence and modify perpetrators' ethics, values, attitudes, beliefs, norms, and emotional states. If workplace bullying is defined as a product of social contexts and dynamics, prevention and intervention programs need to be designed to influence and modify aspects of interpersonal relationships and social groups in the workplace. If workplace bullying is defined as a result of environmental structures and situations, prevention and intervention programs need to be designed to influence and modify aspects of the workplace environment, atmosphere, and culture. In reality, workplace bullying spans all three of these perspectives, so effective prevention and intervention programs need to be designed to influence and modify associated psychological, social, and environmental perspectives, preferably simultaneously. As such, prevention and intervention programs that aim to reduce workplace bullying need to adopt the same principles that drive violence prevention and intervention programs. Violence prevention and intervention strategies normally develop along two distinct lines that can be characterized as formal and informal strategies.

At the formal and legal levels, workplace rules, guidelines, and policies often serve to give individuals guidance in terms of what is acceptable and unacceptable behavior in the workplace, as has been done with harassment and discrimination policies. Rules, guidelines, and policies serve an important first step in altering the overall workplace environment because they can be widely disseminated and promoted and can be enforced through official venues. As a result, these official stances are a vital component that can contribute to reducing instances of workplace bullying because they function to help set the tone of the workplace environment, put potential offenders on notice, and promote increased awareness of the instances that constitute unacceptable behavior. Additionally, developing anti-bullying legislation and aligning bullying with criminal harassment, stalking, civil rights violations, infliction of emotional distress, defamation, and discrimination provide legal tools and sanctions for violations. Formal rules, guidelines, and policies are an important way to address workplace bullying as they can effectively curb instances of it. In addition, forming and enacting policy that addresses workplace bullying serves to shift the issue from a disagreement among coworkers to actions that are taken seriously by the administration and not tolerated in the workplace, as has happened with sexual harassment, racism, and discrimination.

At the informal level, workplaces that promote tolerance and diversity of thought can foster a social environment that does not accept instances of bullying. Individuals who perceive that they are supported, valued, and an important part of the work process often treat their coworkers with respect and empathy (Baron, 1990; Butchart et al., 2002; Olweus, 2003; Osatuke et al., 2009; Pearson & Porath, 2005). In essence, if the workplace takes care of its employees, those employees often will take care of each other. This framework of mutual care situates managers and supervisors as vital in terms of implementing and modeling informal strategies in the workplace. In addition, individual employees also hold a great deal of power over the workplace environment. Employees who participate in diversity and sensitivity training are able to model pro-social behavior in the workplace, understand that their actions affect their colleagues, and are able to take the perspective of others and show empathy and tolerance (Baron, 1990; Osatuke et al., 2009).

Formal and informal prevention and intervention strategies are generally designed to promote an ethic of personal responsibility and tolerance in the workplace, while at the same time serving to define the types of behaviors that are not acceptable in the workplace (Baron, 1990; Olweus, 2003; Osatuke et al., 2009). In addition, the overall themes of these prevention and intervention strategies must include promoting a healthy and safe work environment in which all employees believe that they are important and valued. As Pörhölä and Kinney (2010) outlined, prevention and intervention efforts should be developed with four guidelines in mind: (1) developing a plan that addresses the issue(s) with implementation via clear and public practices and policies, (2) evaluating and monitoring the plan for effectiveness, (3) implementing an incident reporting and tracking system, and (4) developing continuing education programs for employees on issues that are addressed by the plan. Adoption and implementation of these four guidelines, along with the shift in thinking about bullying that defines bullying as a form of violence, will give anti-bullying efforts currency, holding the potential to reduce workplace bullying significantly.

References

Baron, R. A. (1988). Negative effects of destructive criticism: Impact on conflict, self-efficacy, and task performance. *Journal of Applied Psychology, 73*, 199–207.

Baron, R. A. (1990). Countering the effects of destructive criticism: The relative efficacy of four interventions. *Journal of Applied Psychology, 75*, 235–245.

Bruch, M. A., Rivet, K. M., & Laurenti, H. J. (2000). Type of self-discrepancy and relationships to components of the tripartite model of emotional distress. *Personality and Individual Differences, 29*, 37–44.

Butchart, A., Cerda, M., Villaveces, A., & Sminkey, L. (2002). *Framework for interpersonal violence prevention: Framework development document.* Geneva, Switzerland: World Health Organization.

Canary, D. J., & Stafford, L. (1994). Maintaining relationships through strategic and routine interaction. In D. J. Canary & L. Stafford (Eds.), *Communication and relational maintenance* (pp. 3–22). New York, NY: Academic Press.

Cohen, S., Tyrrell, D. A. J., & Smith, A. P. (1993). Negative life events, perceived stress, negative affect, and susceptibility to the common cold. *Journal of Personality and Social Psychology, 64*, 131–140.

Cupach, W. R., & Spitzberg, B. H. (Eds.). (1994). *The dark side of interpersonal communication.* Hillsdale, NJ: Lawrence Erlbaum.

de Pedro, M. M., Sanchez, M. I. S., Navarro, M. C. S., & Izquierdo, M. G. (2008). Workplace mobbing and effects on workers' health. *The Spanish Journal of Psychology, 11*, 219–227.

Dillard, J. P. (1990). A goal-driven model of interpersonal influence. In J. P. Dillard (Ed.), *Seeking compliance: The production of interpersonal influence messages* (pp. 41–56). Scottsdale, AZ: Gorsuch Scarisbrick.

Dillard, J. P., Anderson, J. W., & Knobloch, L. K. (2002). Interpersonal influence. In M. L. Knapp & J. A. Daly (Eds.), *Handbook of interpersonal communication* (pp. 423–474). Thousand Oaks, CA: Sage.

Dillard, J. P., Segrin, C., & Harden, J. M. (1989). Primary and secondary goals in the production of interpersonal influence messages. *Communication Monographs, 56*, 19–38.

Dindia, K., & Baxter, L. A. (1987). Strategies for maintaining and repairing marital relationships. *Journal of Social and Personal Relationships, 4*, 143–158.

Einarsen, S. (1999). The nature and causes of bullying at work. *International Journal of Manpower, 20*, 16–27.

Einarsen, S. (2000). Harassment and bullying at work: A review of the Scandinavian approach. *Aggression and Violent Behavior, 5*, 379–401.

Einarsen, S., & Raknes, B. I. (1997). Harassment in the workplace and the victimization of men. *Violence and Victims, 12*, 247–263.

Einarsen, S., & Skogstad, A. (1996). Bullying at work: Epidemiological findings in public and private organizations. *European Journal of Work and Organizational Psychology, 5*, 185–201.

Friedman, H. S. (Ed.). (1992). *Hostility, coping, and health.* Washington, DC: American Psychological Association.

Fritz, J. M. H., & Omdahl, B. L. (Eds.). (2006). *Problematic relationships in the workplace.* New York, NY: Peter Lang.

Gonnerman, M. E., Jr., Parker, C. P., Lavine, H., & Huff, J. (2000). The relationship between self-discrepancies and affective states: The moderating roles of self-monitoring and standpoints on the self. *Personality and Social Psychology Bulletin, 26*, 810–819.

Hawker, D. S. J., & Boulton, M. J. (2000). Twenty years' research on peer victimization and psychosocial maladjustment: A meta-analytic review of cross-sectional studies. *Journal of Child Psychology and Psychiatry and Allied Disciplines, 41*, 441–455.

Herbert, T. B., & Cohen, S. (1993). Depression and immunity: A meta-analytic review. *Psychological Bulletin, 113*, 472–486.

Hess, J. A. (2000). Maintaining nonvoluntary relationships with disliked partners: An investigation into the use of distancing behaviors. *Human Communication Research, 26*, 458–488.

Higgins, E. T. (1987). Self-discrepancy: A theory relating self and affect. *Psychological Review, 94*, 319–340.

Higgins, E. T. (1989). Self-discrepancy theory: What patterns of self-beliefs cause people to suffer? *Advances in Experimental Social Psychology, 22*, 93–136.

Higgins, E. T., Klein, R., & Strauman, T. (1985). Self-concept discrepancy theory: A psychological model for distinguishing among different aspects of depression and anxiety. *Social Cognition, 3*, 51–76.

Hoel, H., Cooper, C. L., & Faragher, B. (2001). The experience of bullying in Great Britain: The impact of organizational status. *European Journal of Work and Organizational Psychology, 10*, 443–465.

Hoel, H., & Salin, D. (2003). Organizational antecedents of workplace bullying. In S. Einarsen, H. Hoel, D. Zapf, & C. Cooper (Eds.), *Bullying and emotional abuse in the workplace: International perspectives in research and practice* (pp. 203–218). London, England: Taylor & Francis.

Hogh, A., & Dofradottir, A. (2001). Coping with bullying in the workplace. *European Journal of Work and Organizational Psychology, 10*, 485–495.

Ilgen, D. R., Mitchell, T. R., & Fredrickson, J. W. (1981). Poor performers: Supervisors' and subordinates' responses. *Organizational Behavior and Human Performance, 27*, 386–410.

Keller, S. E., Shiflett, S. C., Schleifer, S. J., & Bartlett, J. A. (1994). Stress, immunity, and health. In R. Glaser & J. Kiecolt-Glaser (Eds.), *Handbook of human stress and immunity* (pp. 217–244). San Diego, CA: Academic Press.

Kinney, T. A. (1994). An inductively derived typology of verbal aggression and its association to distress. *Human Communication Research, 21*, 183–222.

Kinney, T. A. (2003). Themes and perceptions of written sexually harassing messages and their link to distress. *Journal of Language and Social Psychology, 22*, 8–28.

Kinney, T. A. (2006). Should I stay or should I go now? The role of negative communication and relational maintenance in distress and well-being. In J. M. H. Fritz & B. L. Omdahl (Eds.), *Problematic relationships in the workplace* (pp. 179–201). New York, NY: Peter Lang.

Kinney, T. A. (2009). Toward understanding anti-social communication: A theoretical model. In T. A. Kinney & M. Pörhölä (Eds.), *Anti and pro-social communication: Theories, methods, and applications* (pp. 3–14). New York, NY: Peter Lang.

Kinney, T. A., & Pörhölä, M. (Eds.). (2009). *Anti and pro-social communication: Theories, methods, and applications*. New York, NY: Peter Lang.

Kowalski, R. M. (Ed.). (2001). *Behaving badly: Aversive behaviors in interpersonal relationships*. Washington, DC: American Psychological Association.
Kramer, M. W., & Hess, J. A. (2002). Communication rules for the display of emotions in organizational settings. *Management Communication Quarterly, 16*, 66–80.
Krug, E. G., Dahlberg, L. L., Mercy, J. A., Zwi, A. B., & Lozano, R. (Eds.). (2002). *World report on violence and health*. Geneva, Switzerland: World Health Organization.
Latane, B., & Darley, J. (1970). *The unresponsive bystander: Why doesn't he help?* Englewood Cliffs, NJ: Prentice Hall.
Lee, J., & Jablin, F. M. (1995). Maintenance communication in superior-subordinate work relationships. *Human Communication Research, 22*, 220–257.
Leymann, H. (1990). Mobbing and psychological terror at workplaces. *Violence and Victims, 5*, 119–126.
Leymann, H. (1996). The content and the development of mobbing at work. *European Journal of Work and Organizational Psychology, 5*, 165–184.
Lutgen-Sandvik, P. (2003). The communicative cycle of employee emotional abuse: Generation and regeneration of workplace mistreatment. *Management Communication Quarterly, 16*, 471–501.
Meares, M. M., Oetzel, J. G., Torres, A., Derkacs, D., & Ginossar, T. (2004). Employee mistreatment and muted voices in the culturally diverse workplace. *Journal of Applied Communication Research, 32*, 4–27.
Niedl, K. (1995). *Mobbing/bullying am arbeitsplatz* [Mobbing/bullying at the workplace]. München, Germany: Rainer Hampp Verlag.
Niedl, K. (1996). Mobbing and well-being: Economic and personnel development implications. *European Journal of Work and Organizational Psychology, 5*, 239–249.
O'Leary, A. (1990). Stress, emotion, and human immune function. *Psychological Bulletin, 108*, 363–382.
Olweus, D. (1993a). *Bullying at school: What do we know and what can we do?* Oxford, England: Blackwell.
Olweus, D. (1993b). Victimization by peers: Antecedents and long-term outcomes. In K. H. Rubin & J. B. Asendorf (Eds.), *Social withdrawal, inhibition, and shyness in childhood* (pp. 315–341). Hillsdale, NJ: Lawrence Erlbaum.
Olweus, D. (2003). Bully/victim problems in school: Basic facts and an intervention programme. In S. Einarsen, H. Hoel, D. Zapf, & C. L. Cooper (Eds.), *Bullying and emotional abuse in the workplace: International perspectives in research and practice* (pp. 62–78). London, England: Taylor & Francis.
Osatuke, K., Moore, S. C., Ward, C., Dyrenforth, S. R., & Belton, L. (2009). Civility, respect, engagement in the workforce (CREW): Nationwide organization development intervention at Veterans Health Administration. *The Journal of Applied Behavioral Science, 45*, 384–410.
Pearson, C. M., & Porath, C. L. (2005). On the nature, consequences, and remedies of workplace incivility: No time for "nice"? Think again. *Academy of Management Executive, 19*, 7–18.
Pörhölä, M., & Kinney, T. A. (2010). *Bullying: Contexts, consequences, and control*. Barcelona, Spain: Editorial Aresta.

Pryor, J. B., & Fitzgerald, L. F. (2003). Sexual harassment research in the United States. In S. Einarsen, H. Hoel, D. Zapf, & C. L. Cooper (Eds.), *Bullying and emotional abuse in the workplace: International perspectives in research and practice* (pp. 79–100). London, England: Taylor & Francis.

Rainivaara, S. (2009). Workplace bullying relationships. In T. A. Kinney & M. Pörhölä (Eds.), *Anti and pro-social communication: Theories, methods, and applications* (Vol. 6., pp. 59-69). New York, NY: Peter Lang.

Rayner, C. (1997). The incidence of workplace bullying. *Journal of Community and Applied Social Psychology, 7*, 173–256.

Roloff, M. E., & Soule, K. P. (2002). Interpersonal conflict: A review. In M. L. Knapp & J. A. Daly (Eds.), *Handbook of interpersonal communication* (3rd ed., pp. 475–528). Thousand Oaks, CA: Sage.

Salin, D. (2001). Prevalence and forms of bullying among business professionals: A comparison of two different strategies for measuring bullying. *European Journal of Work and Organizational Psychology, 10*, 425–441.

Sias, P. M., & Jablin, F. M. (1995). Differential superior-subordinate relations, perceptions of fairness, and coworker communication. *Human Communication Research, 22*, 5–38.

Sillars, A. L. (1980). Attributions and communication in roommate conflicts. *Communication Monographs, 47*, 180–200.

Spitzberg, B. H., & Cupach, W. R. (Eds.). (1998). *The dark side of close relationships*. Mahwah, NJ: Lawrence Erlbaum.

Spratlen, L. P. (1995). Interpersonal conflict which includes mistreatment in a university workplace. *Violence and Victims, 10*, 285–297.

Vartia, M. (1996). The sources of bullying—psychological work environment and organizational climate. *European Journal of Work and Organizational Psychology, 5*, 203–214.

Wilson, C. B. (1991). U.S. businesses suffer from workplace trauma. *Personnel Journal, 70*, 47–50.

Woodman, P., & Kumar, V. (2008). *Bullying at work 2008: The experience of managers*. London, England: Chartered Management Institute.

Zapf, D., & Gross, C. (2001). Conflict escalation and coping with workplace bullying: A replication and extension. *European Journal of Work and Organizational Psychology, 10*, 497–522.

· 5 ·

THE RELATIVE PREDICTABILITY OF INCIVILITY ON INTERPERSONAL AND ORGANIZATIONAL TRUST

BEVERLY DAVENPORT SYPHER & MATTHEW J. GILL

Trust at both the interpersonal and organizational levels is fundamental to building the relationships necessary to make organized action possible. It is built upon basic human values including honesty, openness, reliability, and competence. Trust predicts both job satisfaction and perceptions of organizational effectiveness, and conversely, low levels of organizational trust are linked to a variety of negative consequences including lost productivity, inefficiency, reduced profits, damaged social identities, and diminished effectiveness (Bies & Tripp, 1996; Ellis & Shockley-Zalabak, 1999; Kramer & Cook, 2004; Shockley-Zalabak, Ellis, & Cesaria, 2000). Low levels of interpersonal trust have another set of negative consequences. In addition to dissatisfaction and damaged social identities, low levels of interpersonal trust also diminish organizational identification, commitment, and a positive sense of self while increasing dislike and discontent with what employees spend the better part of every day doing.

Interestingly, the literature suggests that humans can develop trust fairly quickly. Messick and Kramer (2001) coined the term "swift trust" to describe what appears to be a fundamental need humans have to connect with others and rely on their reciprocated trust. Heimer (2001) explained that trust resides in our inherent vulnerabilities. Social action is inherently risky because individual interests do not perfectly coincide with one another. Individuals feel at risk of being taken advantage of and therefore invest in trust as a sort of protective mechanism (Rousseau, Sitkin, Burt, & Camerer, 1998). In effect, uncertainty creates a kind of vulnerability that makes people dependent upon one another, and therefore trust becomes a requirement of social interactions. While people implicitly accept the possibility of being taken advantage of, trusting means those violations are not expected. Still, "for trust to be relevant, there must be the possibility of *exit*, betrayal, defection" (Gambetta, 1988, pp. 218–219) by the trusted. So just as repeated instances of open, honest, and respectful communication coupled with reliability and perceived competence build trust, instances of betrayal, exit, and defection damage trust. Incivility, broadly construed, may very well be the perceived betrayal that leads to exits, defections, or perceived trust violations.

In an earlier study, we describe the increased attention on workplace incivility and the more extreme bullying and verbal aggression linked to a growing list of serious negative outcomes associated with these anti-social behaviors (see Gill & Davenport Sypher, 2009). Among those outcomes is diminished trust. In effect, incivility can be recast as a trust violation that plays on people's vulnerabilities. The study reported here builds on our earlier work and provides the findings from an empirical investigation of organizational trust and workplace incivility.

Despite a growing literature on both organizational trust and workplace incivility, there appears to be little, if any, empirical research that examines this potential relationship. Many of the acts that are considered uncivil at work, such as talking about someone behind his or her back, being condescending, or belittling others, appear consistent with the behaviors described by Bies and Tripp (1996) as "trust violations" that may damage relationships and divide organizational members. Given that trust is fundamental to social action and employee and organizational well-being, recognizing and appreciating potential trust violations is central to understanding organizational life. This chapter provides a brief review of the salient literature on trust and incivility and posits the research questions that guided the study reported here. The chapter concludes with a discussion of the implications of the study findings that confirm a significant negative relationship between incivility and individual and organizational trust.

Trust

In organizational settings, interpersonal trust is considered to have both cognitive and affective foundations (Lewis & Weigert, 1985; McAllister, 1995) that address the vulnerability and risk associated with trust. Trust has cognitive foundations because "we choose whom we will trust in which respects and under what circumstances, and we base the choice on what we take to be 'good reasons,' constituting evidence of trustworthiness" (Lewis & Weigert, 1985, p. 970). Research demonstrates that competence, dependability, and reliability are central to the cognitive aspect of trust in organizational settings (Butler, 1991; Zucker, 1986).

The cognitive aspect of trust can also arise from the organizational role an individual holds. Such trust develops from people's perceptions of accountability, training, and knowledge that accompany organizational roles and reduce uncertainty about such roles (Kramer, 1999). This type of trust is also based on organizational norms regarding appropriate behavior (Kramer, 1999). Incivility, therefore, may be seen as an inappropriate behavior that damages trust. March and Olsen (1989) argued that socialization processes maintain this dimension of trust because they allow for the continued acceptance of and adherence to current norms about appropriate behavior, which reinforces expectations about trust, providing a socially constructed and self-reinforcing dynamic (March, 1994).

Organizational members also use third parties as conduits of trust. Burt and Knez (1995) argued that third parties are important agents in the trust building (or diminishing) process because of their ability to provide information to people about others through personal experience and gossip, although the information may be skewed and biased. Still, third parties provide useful information and perspective in organizations, particularly for new employees or employees who are engaging in new relationships (Uzzi, 1997).

Trust also has affective foundations because there are bonds created between people that lead to care, concern, and emotional investments that affect trust (Lewis & Weigert, 1985; McAllister, 1995). Research reveals that the willingness to engage in trusting behaviors is largely dependent upon relational history (Boon & Holmes, 1991; Deutsch, 1958) and that trust is fostered or damaged depending upon cumulative interaction (Kramer, 1999), which provides evidence of intentions and motivations that can be used to determine trustworthiness. People are also more likely to trust those who share membership in a given category because it "bypasses the need for personal knowledge and the costs of negotiating reciprocity" (Brewer, 1981, p. 356) and because people tend to ascribe positive characteristics to those in the same group.

While interpersonal trust exists between organizational members, organizational trust refers to the level of trust between organizational members and the organization itself. This trust is fostered through interaction among coworkers, supervisors, and organizational leadership. Shockley-Zalabak, Ellis, and Cesaria (2000) argued for a multidimensional conception of organizational trust based on Mishra's (1996) four-factor model. The first factor is competence or the perceptions of organizational members that the leadership is effective and the organization can survive in the marketplace. The second is openness or the honest and transparent sharing of information. The third factor is concern or the degree to which the organization worries about employees' well-being. The fourth factor is reliability or the expectation of consistent and dependable behavior based on information received by organizational members. Shockley-Zalabak, Ellis, and Cesaria (2000) added identification or the degree to which organizational members are connected to the organization's goals, values, norms, and beliefs as a fifth dimension to Mishra's (1996) model because Ellis and Shockley-Zalabak (1999) found that the more organizational members identify with their organization, the more likely they are to trust the organization.

On an individual level, people judge the competence and reliability of others to determine whether they will trust them. Emotional bonds often develop between people who foster care and concern because such behaviors reduce perceived risk and vulnerability. Clearly, what one knows about others, how one treats and is treated by others, and how one relates to others have significant consequences for the development of trust. The perceived levels of competence, openness, concern, reliability, and identification create and build organizational trust. Therefore, negative communicative behaviors perceived to permeate the workplace would likely have a harmful impact on organizational trust. In summary, both cognitive and affective foundations of trust are based on behavioral patterns that reduce uncertainty and increase positive perceptions of the person and organization. It stands to reason, then, that behavioral variances resulting from both the cognitive and affective dimensions of trust lead directly to questions of how we treat each other in the workplace and the resulting outcomes.

Workplace Incivility

Andersson and Pearson (1999) defined workplace incivility as "acting rudely or discourteously without regard for others, in violation of norms of respect in social interaction" (p. 455). They defined this kind of incivility in terms of subtle, deviant behaviors. Level of intensity and intent to harm are the two dimensions that distinguish workplace incivility from workplace aggression (Lim, Cortina, & Magley, 2008). Workplace aggression generally includes a clear intent to harm the target physically or psychologically (Neuman & Baron, 1997), but incivility does not necessarily have an obvious intent. Uncivil behaviors are also less intense than behaviors classified as workplace aggression (Pearson, Andersson, & Wegner, 2001).

However, unlike Cortina, Magley, Williams, and Langhout (2001), who argued that subtle, ambiguous, and less intentional and intense forms of incivility are a milder form of psychological mistreatment, Davenport Sypher (2004) contended that these forms are just as harmful as more intense, intentional, and aggressive behaviors in the workplace. She argued that

> Repeated instances of disregard, exclusion, interrupted talk and insults are no less troublesome and no less likely to escalate and lead to feelings of isolation, anxiety and lowered self esteem than more intense and intentional forms of name calling, profanity, put downs and other more verbally aggressive displays considered deviant, unjust, and harassing. (Davenport Sypher, 2004, p. 260)

Baron and Neuman (1996) likewise concluded that covert forms of aggression at work occur more frequently and to more people than overt forms of aggression, and therefore they are potentially more harmful because of their breadth and depth than isolated and uncommon instances of workplace violence. Many studies have focused on workplace violence because of its high-profile nature, and we hope this focus continues. While the phenomenon is alarming and certainly deserves our attention, other, less intense, behaviors should not be ignored, downplayed, or forgotten, because of their potentially cumulative negative effect.

There is a great deal of evidence about the damage associated with incivility at work. Einarsen and Raknes (1997), for example, found a positive correlation between workplace harassment and poorer psychological well-being, while Leymann (1992) linked experiences of bullying to posttraumatic stress disorder. Matthiesen, Raknes, and Rokkum (1989) discovered more psychological complaints and greater physical health complaints among people who have been bullied at work. Bjorkqvist, Osterman, and Hjelt-Back (1994) also found that victims of harassment had higher levels of anxiety and depression. Cortina et al. (2001) concluded that stress, depression, and anxiety could hurt productivity, decrease job involvement, job satisfaction, and organizational commitment, and increase work absences, tardiness, and turnover.

Baron and Neuman (1996) called for a focus on verbal and passive forms of workplace aggression because they appear considerably more frequently in many organizations and carry with them serious consequences, such as damaged reputations and careers. Davenport Sypher (2004) concluded that incivility may be related to a number of physical health issues such as stress, insomnia, anxiety, poor eating habits, increased smoking and drinking, and psychological issues such as decreased self-esteem, withdrawal, and depression. Workplace incivility can take on a variety of forms that are worthy of concern because they all can damage organizational participation and efficiency while causing harm to the individuals who are involved.

Most existing research has focused on individuals as instigators and targets of workplace incivility, providing data on a single level of analysis (Lim, Cortina, & Magley, 2008). However, if we expand our level of analysis to include data at the group level, we can explore how experiencing incivility in the workplace without being its target is related to perceptions of organizational trust. Lim et al. (2008) argued that while incivility is most often thought of as an experience on the personal level, it can also be conceptualized as a characteristic of the work environment. "Given that most organizations do not prohibit incivility, it is perhaps more likely that such conduct would occur in the public work space . . . thus increasing the probability that fellow group members would witness it" (Lim et al., 2008, p. 96). Andersson and Pearson (1999) argued that witnessing incivility could lead to uncivil behavior becoming a characteristic of the work climate, something they referred to as an "incivility spiral." Therefore, even when organizational members are not direct targets of workplace incivility, it can define the workplace climate and have a negative effect on the individuals and organization.

Workplace incivility is a communication phenomenon that clearly has many negative and destructive consequences for organizational members. Incivility may also damage trust on the interpersonal and organizational levels. Understanding if, and how strongly, incivility and trust are related will help us understand each phenomenon more clearly and provide new avenues of potentially beneficial research on how to overcome these obstacles. Therefore, the following research questions were posited for this study:

RQ1: Is incivility negatively correlated with interpersonal trust?

RQ2: Is incivility differentially correlated with affective and cognitive trust?

RQ3: To what extent does incivility predict interpersonal trust in one's supervisor?

RQ4: Is incivility negatively correlated with organizational trust?

RQ5: Is incivility differentially correlated with the multiple dimensions of organizational trust?

RQ6: To what extent does incivility predict organizational trust?

Method

Participants

Information Technology Solutions[1] (ITS) is a medium-sized, Midwestern organization consisting of 468 employees. It is responsible for planning and coordinating central computing and telecommunication services, which are organized around five major business units and two strategic support units. ITS is mostly male; women make up only about 35% of the workforce. The employees are highly educated; almost all of the employees hold a college degree, and many of them have advanced degrees. They describe their workplace as competitive, fast-paced, stressful, and constantly changing.

Data were collected through an organizational survey distributed electronically to all employees ($N = 468$). A response rate of 67% yielded a final sample of 315 complete and usable surveys. The gender makeup of the respondents mirrored that of the organization, with a little over 37% female and just over 56% male; less than 6% (5.71%) chose not to disclose their gender. The survey was built with Zoomerang,[2] an online survey software company that leases secure server space for launching and storing survey data. Confidentiality and anonymity were guaranteed to those who participated in the survey.

Measures

Survey items captured interpersonal and organizational levels of workplace incivility. At the interpersonal level, trust and incivility were measured with regard to the relationship respondents had with their immediate supervisors. Organizational trust and incivility were measured as general perceptions of the organizational environment.

Workplace incivility. To measure workplace incivility, we used the Workplace Incivility Scale (WIS; Cortina et al., 2001). The WIS measures the frequency of a participant's experiences of disrespectful, rude, or condescending behaviors. There are seven items, which require respondents to rate their level of agreement or disagreement using a five-point Likert-type scale. Goldhaber, Yates, Porter, and Lesniak (1978) suggested that one of the most important relationships at work is the one an employee develops with his or her supervisor. Therefore, to measure incivility at the interpersonal level, the wording of the scale was modified to focus only on the relationship between employees and their supervisors. Cortina et al. (2001) reported high inter-item reliability using Cronbach's alpha ($\alpha = .89$). The reliability in this study was even higher ($\alpha = .94$).

A second modified form of the WIS was used to measure perceptions of organizational incivility. The wording was altered to focus on employees' observations of incivility in the organization. As such, respondents were reporting on how they had seen others at ITS treated rather than how they had been treated themselves. This version of the WIS demonstrated high reliability, generating a Cronbach's alpha of .93.

Trust. Creed and Miles (1996) highlighted the central role managers play in determining the overall level of trust within organizations. The relationship one has with one's supervisor was consistently found to be the strongest predictor of job satisfaction (for a review, see Jablin, 1979). Therefore, at the interpersonal level, trust was measured with respect to immediate supervisors using McAllister's (1995) 11-item trust scale, which requires respondents to rate their level of agreement or disagreement using a five-point Likert-type scale. McAllister's scale is made up of two subscales: affect-based trust (five items) and cognitive-based trust (six items). McAllister reported a reliability coefficient of .91 for the cognitive-based subscale of the trust measure, and this study produced the same reliability coefficient. McAllister reported a .89 reliability coefficient for the affect-based subscale while the reliability in this study was .94. The two subscales create an overall measure of interpersonal trust between employees and supervisors for which Cronbach's alpha yielded a .95 reliability coefficient.

To measure trust at the organizational level, Shockley-Zalabak, Ellis, and Cesaria's (2000) Organizational Trust Index (OTI) was used. The OTI has 29 items that require respondents to rate their level of agreement or disagreement with each item using a five-point Likert-type scale. The OTI includes five different subscales of organizational trust: concern for employees, openness and honesty, reliability, identification, and competence. The five subscales are summative in nature and are combined and averaged to create an overall measure of organizational trust. Shockley-Zalabak, Ellis, and Cesaria (2000) reported an overall reliability for the OTI of .95 and reported the reliabilities of the subscales as ranging from .85 to .90. For this study, the OTI produced a reliability of .96, and the reliabilities for the subscales were similar to those from the original study (competence α = .84, openness and honesty α = .87, concern for employees α = .87, reliability α = .80, and identification α = .78).

Results

Employees reported having trusting relationships with their immediate supervisors when there were low levels of reported incivility. In fact, as seen in Table 1, the average level of interpersonal trust and its dimensions were above the midpoint, and the average levels of subtle and intense incivility were well below the midpoint. Fully 84.4% of respondents indicated that they had a trusting relationship with their supervisor, and only 11.7% indicated experiencing incivility from their supervisors, with only 0.3% indicating that it occurred often or always. Cortina et al. (2001) reported that 71% of the respondents in their study reported experiencing incivility in the previous five years. So although this study focused only on the previous year and only with immediate supervisors, it is encouraging to see that the percentage of respondents reporting incivility in this study is substantially lower than that of the Cortina et al. study.

Table 1. Descriptive Statistics for Variables at the Interpersonal Level

Variable	Mean	SD	Skewness	Kurtosis
Workplace incivility	1.55	.839	2.04	3.89
Interpersonal trust	3.83	.912	-1.20	1.06
Affect-based trust	3.75	1.010	-0.96	.34
Cognitive-based trust	3.90	.914	-1.28	1.42

Note. Scales for the variables range from 5 (strongly agree) to 1 (strongly disagree).

Pearson correlations were used to examine the relationship between interpersonal trust in one's immediate supervisor and the incivility one experiences from one's immediate supervisor. Workplace incivility evidenced a strong negative correlation with overall interpersonal trust ($r = -0.773, p < 0.001$). Simply stated, increased supervisor incivility was strongly associated with lower levels of trust. The interpersonal trust subscales were also negatively correlated with workplace incivility (affect-based trust, $r = -0.713, p < 0.001$; cognitive-based trust, $r = -0.764, p < 0.001$). Table 2 rank orders each uncivil act represented in this study according to its correlation strength with overall interpersonal trust.

Regression analyses were used to determine the extent to which workplace incivility predicted interpersonal trust. Table 3 provides the results of the regression analyses. The analysis revealed that 53% of the variance associated with interpersonal trust was explained ($R = .728, R^2 = 0.53$) by workplace incivility. Using workplace incivility as a predictor of interpersonal trust resulted in a significant prediction model, $F(1, 313) = 352.941, p < 0.001$. A high negative B value for incivility indicates that for every one unit increase in incivility,

Table 2. Uncivil Acts Correlated with Interpersonal Trust and Sub-Scales

Uncivil act	Interpersonal trust	Affect-based trust	Cognitive-based trust
Paid little attention to statements or showed little interest in subordinate's opinions	-.776**	-.695**	-.686**
Doubted subordinate's judgment on a matter over which he or she has responsibility	-.698**	-.618**	-.614**
Made demeaning or derogatory remarks about subordinate	-.678**	-.566**	-.636**
Put subordinate down or was condescending	-.662**	-.564**	-.591**
Addressed subordinate in unprofessional terms	-.661**	-.546**	-.621**
Ignored or excluded subordinate from professional camaraderie	-.628**	-.547**	-.539**
Made unwanted attempts to draw subordinate into a discussion of personal matters	-.557**	-.413**	-.530**

**Significant at the $p < .001$ level.

employees reported a 0.791 decrease in levels of interpersonal trust, and the high absolute value of the beta coefficient (0.728) demonstrates the high level of importance of incivility in predicting interpersonal trust.

Two other regression analyses examined the extent to which workplace incivility predicted affect-based and cognitive-based trust. The analyses revealed that almost 51% of the variance associated with affect-based trust ($R = 0.713$, $R^2 = 0.508$) and over 58% of the variance associated with cognitive-based trust ($R = 0.764$, $R^2 = 0.584$) was explained by workplace incivility. Using workplace incivility as a predictor of affect-based trust, $F(1, 313) = 323.525$, $p < 0.001$, and cognitive-based trust, $F(1, 313) = 438.970$, $p < 0.001$, resulted in signifi-

Table 3. Regression Analysis Results for Supervisor Incivility

	R	R^2	B	Std. Error	Beta	Sig.	F	Sig.
Overall interpersonal trust	0.728	0.530	-0.791	0.042	-0.728	0.000	352.941	0.000
Affect-based trust	0.713	0.508	-0.858	0.048	-0.713	0.000	323.525	0.000
Cognitive-based trust	0.764	0.584	-0.833	0.040	-0.764	0.000	438.970	0.000

cant prediction models. The high negative B values for incivility indicate that for every one unit increase in incivility, employees reported a 0.858 decrease in levels of affect-based trust and a 0.833 decrease in levels of cognitive-based trust. The high absolute values of the beta coefficients (0.713 for affect-based trust and 0.764 for cognitive-based trust) evidence a strong relationship between incivility and perceptions of interpersonal trust, with a slightly lower level of affect-based trust, which is based on the care and concern and emotional bond a person has with another.

At the organizational level, 42.5% of employees reported observing incivility in the organization. Employees reported observing incivility at ITS substantially more than they experienced it with their immediate supervisors. Employees reported slightly positive responses concerning organizational trust. The average level of organizational trust and almost all of its dimensions were above the midpoint, and 73% of employees reported trusting ITS (see Table 4).

Pearson correlations were used to examine the relationship between organizational trust and the perception of incivility in the organization. Workplace incivility evidenced a strong negative correlation with organizational trust (r = -0.525, $p < 0.001$). Workplace incivility was also negatively correlated with the dimensions of organizational trust (see Table 5). Perceptions of incivility at work were negatively correlated with organizational trust; simply stated, as the level of incivility employees perceived at work increased, their trust in the organization decreased.

Table 4. Employee Means on the Organizational Trust Index (OTI)

Dimension of organizational trust	Mean
Competence	2.83
Openness	3.26
Concern for employees	3.50
Reliability	3.53
Identification	3.33
Overall OTI	3.31

Table 5. Pearson R Coefficients for Incivility and the Dimensions of Organizational Trust

	Competence	Openness	Concern	Reliability	Identification
Workplace incivility	-.414**	-.487**	-.483**	-.459**	-.466**

**Significant at the $p < .001$ level.

Regression analyses were used to determine the extent to which workplace incivility predicted organizational trust. The analysis revealed that almost 28% of the variance was explained ($R = 0.525$, $R^2 = 0.276$). Workplace incivility appeared as a significant predictor of organizational trust, $F(1,313) = 119.024$, $p < 0.001$. The negative B value indicates that for every one unit increase in perceived workplace incivility, employees reported a 0.369 decrease in organizational trust, and the absolute value of the beta coefficient (0.525) demonstrates the high level of importance of incivility in predicting organizational trust. Table 6 displays the results of the regression analyses examining the relative predictability of workplace incivility on the dimensions of organizational trust. The perception of incivility in the workplace best predicted the subscales of openness and concern for employees.

Discussion

This study suggests that workplace incivility from supervisors is negatively correlated with overall interpersonal trust. This finding may mean that trust in

Table 6. Regression Analysis Results for Incivility at the Organizational Level

	R	R^2	B	Std. Error	Beta	Sig.	F	Sig.
Organizational trust	0.525	0.276	-0.369	0.034	-0.525	0.000	119.024	0.000
Competence	0.414	0.172	-0.366	0.045	-0.414	0.000	64.882	0.000
Openness	0.487	0.237	-0.314	0.032	-0.487	0.000	97.161	0.000
Concern for employees	0.482	0.234	-0.405	0.041	-0.483	0.000	95.426	0.000
Reliability	0.459	0.211	-0.413	0.045	-0.459	0.000	83.697	0.000
Identification	0.466	0.217	-0.387	0.042	-0.466	0.000	86.899	0.000

a supervisory relationship is largely defined by the everyday, repeated interactions in the relationship rather than distinctive and infrequent events. Both the cognitive and affective foundations of trust appear to have been damaged by incivility, with cognitive-based trust suffering slightly more.

The results of the regressions provided even stronger evidence that workplace incivility is a strong predictor of the overall interpersonal trust employees have with their immediate supervisors. The prediction model accounted for 53% (R^2 = 0.530) of the variance in overall interpersonal trust. These findings suggest that uncivil supervisors are not likely to be trusted by their subordinates.

Workplace incivility was also found to predict lower levels of cognitive versus affect-based trust. This finding seems to indicate that workplace incivility is potentially more damaging to the cognitive foundations of interpersonal trust employees have with their immediate supervisors. In short, while incivility appears to diminish the likeability or emotional connection a person has with his or her supervisor (affective basis of trust), it appears to affect the cognitive basis of trust somewhat more. That is, perceptions of the competence, dependability, and reliability of one's supervisor are diminished even more than likeability when he or she is seen as uncivil. Incivility thus appears to provide what Lewis and Weigert (1985) consider a "good reason" or evidence for deeming a supervisor untrustworthy.

Past research on incivility, and interpersonal communication more generally, suggests that high levels of interpersonal insensitivity reduce degrees of liking, and these findings bear out much of the same in that incivility predicted low levels of affect-based trust and even lower levels of cognitive-based trust. These findings suggest that when supervisors are uncivil and/or disrespectful, even in subtle ways, their employees do not see them as open, supportive, or caring. However, our study found that uncivil supervisors even more strongly damaged the cognitive foundations of interpersonal trust. Uncivil bosses were considered less competent, professional, dedicated, and reliable than civil bosses. So not only do these findings suggest that employees dislike and feel emotionally disconnected from uncivil supervisors, they also suggest that employees question the managerial competency of uncivil supervisors. Position does not excuse incivility or prevent employees from doubting another's competence or ability. Indeed, we may have less patience and tolerance for "preying bosses" (Hornstein, 1997) than we do for uncivil peers, and we need to acknowledge the harm that even their subtle incivilities can do to the organization and employees.

Another explanation for why incivility is more strongly related to cognitive rather than affective bases of trust could be the trend to more transactional and market-like relationships in American workplaces that some argue have left workers less emotionally attached to their coworkers and supervisors (Pfeffer, 2006). As a result, employees may be hurt less emotionally by incivility from their supervisors because they are not emotionally invested in the relationship to begin with. Transactional organizational relationships have led workers to base more work decisions, particularly where to work and for how long, on money rather than the type of organization, the meaningfulness of the work, and the treatment of employees (Pfeffer, 2006). People may be more concerned with their ability to advance and make more money than with more existential aspects of the job, such as meaningful work and satisfying relationships. Since high levels of incivility were shown to result in lower levels of cognitive-based trust, people may be concerned more with a supervisor's ability to lead them or do his or her job well, especially in a competitive, fast changing, high-tech company, than with the supervisor's ability or willingness to develop an emotional connection with employees. However, it is clear that incivility jeopardizes both. Since judgments of competence are at stake, uncivil supervisors may potentially damage their own career opportunities while also damaging their employees' quality of work life. In short, these findings position workplace incivility, and the way we treat others at work, at the center of explanations of organizational trust (and, potentially, distrust).

The data collected at the interpersonal level support the notion that trust and incivility are related. Experiencing incivility from supervisors damaged trust, and the data revealed that incivility proved to be correlated with and acted as a predictor of trust. Incivility was a significant predictor of interpersonal trust and accounted for 53% of the variance associated with trust.

On the organizational level, this study was primarily concerned with employee perceptions of incivility in the organization as a whole and how those perceptions may or may not have influenced organizational trust. At the interpersonal level, incivility was a stronger predictor of cognitive-based aspects of trust. At the organizational level, incivility demonstrated stronger correlations with what would be considered the more affect-based subscales. Incivility was most strongly correlated with openness/honesty and concern for employees, while it was least correlated with competence.

One potential explanation for the differential effects of the different kinds of trust may be the specificity of the target in the perceptions of interpersonal trust. On the interpersonal level, respondents were answering questions regarding a very specific and important organizational relationship. On the organizational level, respondents answered questions about a generalized group of others. Perhaps when we are emotionally invested in relationships, we are willing to explain away incivility to develop and/or maintain an emotional and professional connection with someone of such direct importance and control over our own work lives. In this way, the data may support Robinson, Dirks, and Ozcelik's (2004) "love is blind" hypothesis. The "love is blind" hypothesis argues that prior trust would soften the blow of betrayal and that people are therefore granted the benefit of the doubt because of an accumulated history of otherwise benign and positive experiences. Or, maybe it's a "love is forgiveness" hypothesis. Even though we recognize incivility for what it is, we tolerate it because we have little choice or because we want to maintain a level of decorum with our bosses and coworkers.

In sum, the data collected at the organizational level support the notion that organizational trust and incivility are related. Consistent with the results on the interpersonal level, perceiving incivility in the organization damaged trust, and the data revealed that incivility proved to be correlated with and acted as a predictor of organizational trust. However, the amount of variance accounted for in organizational trust by the perceived amount of incivility in the organization was not as high as that for the interpersonal level. Still, incivility was a significant predictor of organizational trust, and it did account for almost 28% of the variance. Overall, the data support the idea that perceptions of incivility in an organization are related to organizational trust.

Understanding the relationship between trust and incivility may benefit the ways in which Americans choose to manage employees. Research suggests that the negative ways we treat others in the workplace can have serious and harmful effects on our relationships and ourselves. Trust has been identified as a fundamental part of social interaction (Gambetta, 1988), and by damaging trust, we damage the complex web of relationships that make up an organization. We also harm the possibility of cooperating and collaborating, making our interactions at work less efficient, more time consuming, and, ultimately, more difficult.

This study makes it clear that if an organization wants to build trust, then it cannot create a culture where treating others uncivilly is acceptable or even tolerated. Repeated instances of disregard and disrespect significantly damage trust. One potential solution for minimizing workplace incivility is to manage organizations as communities where we help employees in need, promote long-term employment, work to resolve work-family issues, and cultivate high levels of trust and stability while moving away from the market-like, transactional relationships to which American workplaces are becoming accustomed (Pfeffer, 2006).

Moving toward more communal organizations may enable the creation of stronger social relationships at work, making people less likely to treat others in uncivil ways. The data examined here suggest that levels of trust will increase as incivility decreases. As trust increases, organizational members will be able to avoid the consequences of low levels of trust such as lost productivity, inefficiency, reduced profits, damaged social identities, and diminished effectiveness (Bies & Tripp, 1996; Ellis & Shockley-Zalabak, 1999; Kramer & Cook, 2004; Shockley-Zalabak, Ellis, & Cesaria, 2000). The data examined here demonstrate that acts of incivility do, indeed, significantly damage trust. The relationship between incivility and trust adds to the explanation of how workplace incivility can be harmful to organizations. By continuing to tolerate incivility in the workplace, we are damaging our organizational relationships and, ultimately, the organization as a whole. Although trust is only one aspect of a social relationship, it is an extremely important one.

Conclusion

Pfeffer (2006) argued that decreased trust and increased incivility are two consequences of the move away from communal organizations toward more market-like and transactional relationships. He calls for actions and behaviors that protect and enhance community, that create social identities, and that help fill the existential void that Fineman (2000) says people are looking to the workplace to fill. Such actions and behaviors must include civility and respect for the other. People need emotional connections with the people they work with, and it is especially important that one trust and feel valued by one's boss. The studies that reveal lost productivity, inefficiencies, reduced profits and diminished effectiveness associated with low levels of trust are now punctuated by the findings from this study that show trust is diminished at both the interpersonal and organizational levels when others are perceived as uncivil.

Civility alone may not produce the trust necessary for effective organizations and meaningful work relationships, but these data suggest that perceived incivility certainly reduces trust and thus damages the potential for healthy, constructive work relationships. The data presented here suggest that treating others with respect and regard, in effect, more civilly, can increase the trust necessary for building communal organizations that provide the comfort, joy, and meaning that humans seek. However, the nature of the relationships among trust, civility and organizational meaningfulness are complex. For example, does workplace civility mean organizations are more communal in nature? Can civility also be a norm in less meaningful workplaces? We expect the answer is "yes."

We know that the presence of incivility is damaging, but it may very well be that the presence of civility is not enough. People need more than simple politeness. As Brown and Levinson (1987/1978) argued in their now famous explication of universal politeness, we have both positive and negative face needs or wants. We need to mitigate face threats by avoiding insults, belittling comments, and humiliation, but we also need to be liked, affirmed, supported, encouraged, and acknowledged. So while we conclude that face threatening, uncivil acts can damage the very fabric of who we are and damage possibilities that make work and life meaningful and organizations successful, we acknowledge that civility alone is not the simple path to existential or organizational well-being.

As demonstrated by this study, trust and incivility are connected in important ways, and the rise of incivility in an organization will damage and diminish trust. If left unchecked, incivility can potentially create a workplace in which people are unable or unwilling to cooperate or work together. Managing damaged relationships that result from incivility also takes time away from the work itself and potentially damages productivity as well as organizational and worker identity. Incivility damages the emotional bond employees should share, and it damages the very foundation of relationships. In short, incivility damages interpersonal trust. If we can answer Pfeffer's (2006) call for the reemergence of organizations as communities by practicing meaningful civility and avoiding incivility, we may help stem the tide of decreasing trust and soulless organizations.

Clearly, we need to focus efforts on raising worker awareness of the impact of their words. What we say matters. How we say it matters. At the same time, what we do not say matters, as well. Communicative choices, especially respectful, trust building comments and behaviors, connect and bind employees to one another in ways that reaffirm their sense of self, their sense of belonging, their feelings of commitment and satisfaction, and their overall disposition and commitment to the work itself.

In short, civil discourse engenders trust at both the individual and organizational levels. By reducing or eliminating incivility from work settings, we increase the likelihood of more satisfied and committed workers. By engaging in more civil and caring behaviors, we can potentially increase trust, worker satisfaction and well-being, and organizational commitment. Unchecked incivility will continue to damage perceptions of self worth and relationships that are essential for both employee and organizational well-being, Moreover, as this study evidences, uncivil communication at work is a striking predictor of jeopardized trust among coworkers and reduced trust with the organization. Meaningful civility as a norm gets us closer to the sense of community work can and should invoke. It can build trust, respect, enhanced self worth and social identities and, by definition, healthier communities and people.

Notes

1. Information Technology Solutions is a pseudonym for the real organization.
2. Zoomerang is owned by MarketTools, Inc., a leading provider of full-service, online market research services. Founded in 1997, MarketTools, Inc., is a privately held company, headquartered in Mill Valley, California, with offices in New York, Minneapolis, Cincinnati, Chicago, London, and Sydney.

References

Andersson, L. M., & Pearson, C. M. (1999). Tit for tat? The spiraling effect of incivility in the workplace. *Academy of Management Review, 24*, 452–471.

Baron, R. A., & Neuman, J. H. (1996). Workplace violence and workplace aggression: Evidence on their relative frequency and potential causes. *Aggressive Behavior, 22*, 161–173.

Bies, R. J., & Tripp, T. M. (1996). Beyond distrust: "Getting even" and the need for revenge. In R. M. Kramer & T. R. Tyler (Eds.), *Trust in organizations: Frontiers of theory and research* (pp. 246–260). Thousand Oaks, CA: Sage.

Bjorkqvist, K., Osterman, K., & Hjelt-Back, M. (1994). Aggression among university employees. *Aggressive Behavior, 20*, 173–184.

Boon, S. D., & Holmes, J. G. (1991). The dynamics of interpersonal trust: Resolving uncertainty in the face of risk. In R. A. Hinde & J. Groebel (Eds.), *Cooperation and prosocial behavior* (pp. 167–182). New York, NY: Cambridge University Press.
Brewer, M. B. (1981). Ethnocentrism and its role in interpersonal trust. In M. B. Brewer & B. E. Collins (Eds.), *Scientific inquiry and the social sciences* (pp. 345–359). San Francisco, CA: Jossey-Bass.
Brown, P., & Levinson, S. (1987). *Politeness: Some universals in language use.* New York, NY: Cambridge University Press. (Original work published 1978).
Burt, R. S., & Knez, M. (1995). Kinds of third party effects on trust. *Rationality and Society, 7,* 255–292.
Butler, J. K. J. (1991). Toward understanding and measuring conditions of trust: Evolution of a conditions of trust inventory. *Journal of Management, 17,* 643–663.
Cortina, L. M., Magley, V. J., Williams, J. H., & Langhout, R. D. (2001). Incivility in the workplace: Incidence and impact. *Journal of Occupational Health Psychology, 6,* 64–80.
Creed, W. E. D., & Miles, R. E. (1996). Trust in organizations: A conceptual framework linking organizational forms, managerial philosophies, and the opportunity costs of control. In K. L. Kraemer & T. R. Tyler (Eds.), *Trust in organizations: Frontiers of theory and research* (pp. 16–38). Thousand Oaks, CA: Sage.
Davenport Sypher, B. (2004). Reclaiming civil discourse in the workplace. *The Southern Communication Journal, 69,* 257–269.
Deutsch, M. (1958). Trust and suspicion. *Journal of Conflict Resolution, 2,* 265–279.
Einarsen, S., & Raknes, B. I. (1997). Harassment in the workplace and the victimization of men. *Violence and Victims, 12,* 247–263.
Ellis, K., & Shockley-Zalabak, P. (1999, November). *Communicating with management: Relating trust to job satisfaction and organizational effectiveness.* Paper presented at the meeting of the National Communication Association Convention, Chicago, IL.
Fineman, S. (2000). Emotional arenas revisited. In S. Fineman (Ed.), *Emotion in organizations* (2nd ed) (pp. 1–24). London: Sage.
Gambetta, D. (1988). Can we trust trust? In D. Gambetta (Ed.), *Trust: Making and breaking cooperative relationships* (pp. 231–237). Cambridge, MA: Blackwell.
Gill, M. J., & Davenport Sypher, B. (2009). Rising concerns about workplace incivility and interpersonal trust. In P. Lutgen-Sandvik & B. Davenport Sypher (Eds.), *Destructive organizational communication: Processes, consequences and constructive ways of organizing* (pp. 53–73). New York, NY: Routledge.
Goldhaber, G. M., Yates, M. P., Porter, D. T., & Lesniak, R. (1978). Organizational communication: 1978. *Human Communication Research, 5,* 76–96.
Heimer, C. A. (2001). Solving the problem of trust. In K. S. Cook (Ed.), *Trust in society* (pp. 40–88). New York, NY: Russell Sage Foundation.
Hornstein, H. A. (1997). *Brutal bosses and their prey.* New York, NY: Riverhead Trade.
Jablin, F. M. (1979). Superior-subordinate communication: The state of the art. *Psychological Bulletin, 86,* 1201–1222.
Kramer, R. M. (1999). Trust and distrust in organizations: Emerging perspectives, enduring questions. *Annual Review of Psychology, 50,* 569–598.
Kramer, R. M., & Cook, K. S. (Eds.). (2004). *Trust and distrust in organizations: Dilemmas and*

approaches. New York, NY: Russell Sage Foundation.

Lewis, D. J., & Weigert, A. (1985). Trust as a social reality. *Social Forces, 63*, 967–985.

Leymann, H. (1992). *From bullying to exclusion from working life*. Stockholm, Sweden: Publica.

Lim, S., Cortina, L. M., & Magley, V. J. (2008). Personal and workgroup incivility: Impact on work and health outcomes. *Journal of Applied Psychology, 93*, 95–107.

Lutgen-Sandvik, P., & Davenport Sypher, B. (Eds.). (2009). *Destructive organizational communication: Processes, consequences, and constructive ways of organizing*. New York, NY: Routledge.

March, J. G. (1994). *A primer on decision making*. New York, NY: Free Press.

March, J. G., & Olsen, J. P. (1989). *Rediscovering institutions: The organizational basis of politics*. New York, NY: Free Press.

Matthiesen, S. B., Raknes, B. I., & Rokkum, O. (1989). Bullying at work. *Tidsskrift for Norsk Psykologforening, 26*, 761–774.

McAllister, D. J. (1995). Affect- and cognition-based trust as foundations for interpersonal cooperation in organizations. *The Academy of Management Journal, 38*, 24–59.

Messick, D. M., & Kramer, R. M. (2001). Trust as a form of shallow morality. In K. S. Cook (Ed.), *Trust in society* (pp. 89–118). New York: Russell Sage Foundation.

Mishra, A. K. (1996). Organizational response to crisis: The centrality of trust. In R. M. Kramer & T. R. Tyler (Eds.), *Trust in organizations: Frontiers of theory and research* (pp. 261–287). Thousand Oaks, CA: Sage.

Neuman, J. H., & Baron, R. A. (1997). Aggression in the workplace. In J. Greenberg (Ed.), *Antisocial behavior in organizations* (pp. 37–67). Thousand Oaks, CA: Sage.

Pearson, C. M., Andersson, L. M., & Wegner, J. W. (2001). When workers flout convention: A study of workplace incivility. *Human Relations, 54*, 1387–1419.

Pfeffer, J. (2006). Working alone: What ever happened to the idea of organizations as communities? In J. O'Toole & E. E. Lawler (Eds.), *The new American workplace* (Vol. 1, pp. 3–21). New York, NY: Palgrave Macmillan.

Robinson, S. L., Dirks, K. T., & Ozcelik, H. (2004). Untangling the knot of trust and betrayal. In R. M. Kramer & K. S. Cook (Eds.), *Trust and distrust in organizations: Dilemmas and approaches* (pp. 327–341). New York, NY: Russell Sage Foundation.

Rousseau, D. M., Sitkin, S. B., Burt, R. S., & Camerer, C. (1998). Not so different after all: A cross-discipline view of trust. *Academy of Management Review, 23*(3), 393–404.

Shockley-Zalabak, P., Ellis, K., & Cesaria, R. (2000). *Measuring organizational trust: Trust and distrust across cultures: The organizational trust index*. San Francisco, CA: IABC Research Foundation.

Uzzi, B. (1997). Social structure and competition in interfirm networks: The paradox of embeddedness. *Administration Science Quarterly, 42*, 35–67.

Zucker, L. G. (1986). Production of trust: Institutional sources of economic structure (1840–1920). In B. M. Staw & L. L. Cummings (Eds.), *Research in organizational behavior* (pp. 53–111). Greenwich, CT: JAI Press.

· 6 ·

EXCLUSIVE OR EXCLUSORY

Workplace Relationships, Ostracism, and Isolation

PATRICIA M. SIAS

Research and the popular press frequently herald the benefits of engaging in high quality workplace relationships. Having a good relationship with your supervisor, for example, is associated with being better informed, having more autonomy, and experiencing faster career progression than engaging in a low-quality relationship (Gagnon & Michael, 2004; Graen, Liden, & Hoel, 1982; Sias, 2005). Being friends with peer coworkers is associated with having job satisfaction, being well-informed, and exerting influence (Sias, 2005; Sias & Cahill, 1998). Given these benefits, it is not surprising that the bulk of workplace relationship research has focused on the perspective of those included in various relationships. The excluded are largely ignored. Yet exclusion is inherent to workplace relationships and social networks. If some employees are members of the leader's "in-group" (Graen & Cashman, 1975), others, by implication, must be in the "out-group." Similarly, there are different levels of inclusion among peer relationships as well. The closest and most rare peer relationship is labeled a "special peer" relationship (Kram & Isabella, 1985), expressing the exclusive nature of that bond. This chapter addresses those left out of high quality workplace relationships. Specifically, I discuss the nature and consequences of exclusion, the processes by which employees are excluded from relationships, personal and contextual factors that contribute to relational exclusion, and the consequences of relational exclusion for employees and organizations.

Workplace Relationships

Although organizations of various types produce goods, provide services, and accomplish a variety of goals, they are all essentially systems of interpersonal relationships. Organizations are social collectivities comprising people and the links or relationships among those people enabling organizing (Sias, 2009; Wheatley, 2001). Workplace relationships are, therefore, central to workplace functioning. Workplace relationships differ from workplace acquaintanceships. Interpersonal relationships are ongoing entities characterized by, and constituted in, regular patterned interaction. As Sias (in press) noted, employees who interact only occasionally with one another engage in coworker communication, but they are not engaged in a coworker relationship.

Because workplace relationships are substantive and effectual entities (Sias, Krone, & Jablin, 2002), inclusion in, or exclusion from, such dyads has important consequences for organizational members. As noted earlier, inclusion is linked to being better informed, increased levels of support and latitude, better performance, faster career progression, and a host of other attractive outcomes (e.g., Sias, 2005; Sias & Cahill, 1998). Exclusion is linked to the opposite. It is important to understand why and how some employees are excluded from important workplace relationships. A simple approach to addressing this issue is to consider the processes of inclusion and reason that exclusion involves opposing dynamics. Such an approach would provide partial insights but would ignore the complexity of relational exclusion. In this chapter, I draw upon existing research from a variety of fields to outline processes of exclusion, antecedents to exclusion processes, and relational and other consequences of exclusion.

Processes of Relational Exclusion

Relationships are dynamic entities, and therefore, relationship initiation, development, and maintenance are dynamic social processes. More specifically, they are *communicative* processes. As employees begin a relationship such as a workplace friendship, the employees interact with one another more frequently and discuss work as well as personal topics in a more intimate and less guarded fashion (Sias & Cahill, 1998). Inclusion in workplace relationships, therefore, is accomplished by frequent, regular interaction. Inclusion in "exclusive" (e.g., friendships) or high quality relationships (e.g., high quality leader-member exchanges) is accomplished via frequent, intimate, and less cautious interaction about work, non-work, and personal topics.

In contrast, exclusion from workplace relationships is generally accomplished via no or infrequent, superficial, and cautious communication limited primarily to task-related needs and concerns (Sias, 2009). Thus, relational exclusion is often marked by a noticeable lack or absence of verbal communication. This absence, paradoxically, speaks volumes to an employee about his or her role in the social network. As mentioned earlier, however, exclusion is not simply the lack of inclusion. It is important to note that exclusion can also be accomplished by frequent, but hostile, communication such as harassment and bullying. Thus, relational exclusion can also occur via the noticeable *presence* of verbal communication.

Relational exclusion takes many forms and occurs via a variety of processes including ostracism, shunning, depersonalization, and ignoring (Sias, 2009). Although these processes all result in an employee's exclusion from important workplace relationships, they vary in the extent to which they are done mindfully and with intent.

Ostracism refers to the physical and/or social "act of banishing or excluding" from a relationship or group (The Free Dictionary, 2007a). Physical ostracism refers to placing the target in an isolated or solitary location; social ostracism refers to instances in which an individual is " . . . ignored by others who are in [the individual's] presence" (Williams & Sommer, 1997, p. 693). Similarly, *shunning* refers to "*purposely* cutting off all interaction with the target individual" (Sias, 2009, p. 148, emphasis added), and therefore reflects mindful intent. Like shunning, *depersonalization* involves intentional changes in communication. However, depersonalization refers only to discontinuing communication with the target employee regarding non-work-related and personal topics; interaction required for task accomplishment continues (Sias, 2009; Sias & Cahill, 1998). In contrast to ostracism, shunning, and depersonalization, *ignoring* may be carried out with intent or in a relatively mindless fashion. Defined as "to be ignorant of or not acquainted with" or "to refuse to take notice of" (The Free Dictionary, 2007b), an employee may be ignored by others either because of intentional refusal to acknowledge him or her or because others are unaware of his or her presence or existence.

To date, most research examining exclusion processes has focused on the network level, identifying the processes via which individuals are excluded from the larger social network. That social network, however, is a network of dyadic social relationships. Thus, social network isolation essentially represents the aggregate of isolation from various interpersonal relationships. Accordingly, the remainder of this chapter addresses how and why certain employees are excluded from high quality peer and supervisor-subordinate interpersonal relationships.

Factors Influencing Exclusion

In general, all new employees are technically "isolates" the moment they join an organization (Sias, 2009). Their new workplace relationships are characterized by superficial communication regarding a narrow range of work-related topics (Graen & Uhl-Bien, 1995; Kram & Isabella, 1985; Sias & Cahill, 1998). Over time, as newcomers settle into their new positions and engage in conversation with coworkers and supervisors, their workplace relationships begin to take form. Research indicates several factors associated with workplace relationship development and the extent to which an employee is included in or excluded from high quality workplace relationships. These factors include both personal characteristics of the isolated individual and characteristics of the work environment.

Personal Characteristics

Dissimilarity. Interpersonal and organizational research consistently shows that people tend to form interpersonal relationships with similar others (Sherif, 1958; Sias & Cahill, 1998; Turner & Oakes, 1986). Accordingly, excluded employees are often those other employees perceived to be dissimilar. In particular, individuals are often excluded from workplace relationships because of *demographic dissimilarity*. Studies consistently demonstrate, for example, that in-group LMX (leader-member exchange) relationships are more likely to develop between supervisors and subordinate employees of the same sex, race, ethnicity, and generational cohort (Foley, Linnehan, Greenhaus, & Weer, 2006; Pelled & Xin, 2000). Similar dynamics manifest in peer and workplace friendships, with employees who are demographically similar being more likely to develop special peer relationships and close or very close friendships (Fritz, 1997; Odden & Sias, 1997).

This type of exclusion can occur with more or less intent. Employees may purposely avoid those who are different from them to avoid discomfort or conflict. Demographic exclusion can also result from a lack of access to similar others. Women and minority employees who obtain positions high in the organizational hierarchy often find themselves as "outsiders within" a male-dominated environment, making it difficult to form close relationships with colleagues who are demographically dissimilar. For example, Ibarra (1995) found that minority managers had fewer intimate relationships than did majority managers. Thus, even when minority and women employees break the "glass ceiling" and are promoted, they become essential "outsiders on the inside" due to exclusion from important social relationships at their new levels (Gray, Kurihara, Hommen, & Feldman, 2007). Research indicates that *sexual orientation* is also linked to relational exclusion, particularly targeted exclusion. Specifically, homosexual employees are among the more likely targets of ostracism. Because of the possibility of such treatment, such employees experience a great deal of anxiety regarding whether or not to "come out" at work (Day & Schoenrade, 1997; Embrick, Walther, & Wickens, 2007; Lewis, 2009).

Employees from *ethnic and racial minority* groups are also more vulnerable to ostracism than are majority employees "because these workers already face a certain degree of isolation from majority groups" (Hodson, Roscigno, & Lopez, 2006, p. 386). For similar reasons, employees are often ostracized because of a *physical disability* (Zapf, 1999). Such exclusion may also be less intentional than other forms of exclusion. Along these lines, Steinburg, Sullivan, and Montoya (1999) found that deaf individuals reported being socially excluded at work because of the difficulties they had participating in communication with their coworkers. Again, this type of exclusion could result from coworkers' intentional avoidance of an uncomfortable situation or could occur unintentionally via the general absence of the deaf coworker from oral communication processes.

Personality. Employees may also be excluded from workplace relationships due to their *personality* traits. Shy employees, for example, can effectively exclude themselves from workplace relationships by avoiding communication, thereby avoiding opportunities to develop relationships (McDaniel, 2003). Likewise, studies indicate that employees who suffer communication apprehension (i.e., anxiety about communicating with others) are more likely to be isolated from workplace relationships. Along these lines, Cole and McCroskey (2003) found that although supervisors suffering from communication anxiety do communicate with employees, their apparent discomfort with doing so makes them less likable to employees, influencing their ability to form in-group exchanges with employees. Similarly, Reinking and Bell (1991) found that individuals with lower levels of communication competence were more likely to be lonely at work than their more competent colleagues, indicating a link between lack of communication ability and relational exclusion.

Language. The continuing increase in a diverse, multicultural, and multilingual workforce has introduced another relational exclusion factor to contemporary organizations—language. Studies indicate that employees use language to exclude others who do not speak the same language. Hitlan, Kelly,

Schepman, Schneider, and Zarate (2006), for example, found employees in the United States effectively excluding immigrant employees by speaking English only in the workplace. The immigrant employees reported feeling marginalized and isolated by their coworkers because they could not share in conversation. Dotan, Rubin, and Sommer (2004) found similar processes occurring when bilingual employees in the United States spoke in a language other than English. In these cases, the English-speaking employees were excluded. They also found that excluded employees reported a decrease in liking for their coworkers who spoke in another language. Such exclusion may be done intentionally or somewhat mindlessly when an individual reverts to his or her native language because of comfort and ease of doing so.

In sum, employees are excluded from high quality workplace relationships because of a variety of personal factors. They may be excluded because they are different from others with respect to sex, age, race, ethnicity, sexual orientation, or any number of other characteristics. They may be excluded because they do not speak the preferred or proprietary language of coworkers. They may also functionally exclude themselves because of their own desire to disassociate or because of their discomfort with communicating with others. The important role of personal factors in the exclusion process sheds light on the unique nature of relational exclusion; in other words, it goes a long way toward explaining why certain people, or types of people, are excluded while others are not. The following section details the impact of factors related not to specific individuals but to the organizational context itself.

Workplace Context

Workplace relationships are defined by the social context in which they exist—the workplace. It is not surprising, then, that relationship exclusion is associated with a variety of workplace contextual elements.

Proximity. With respect to mindless or unintentional exclusion, perhaps the most powerful contextual factor is *physical proximity*. Workplace relationships tend to develop among employees who work in the same physical location, and informal relationships (e.g., friendships) are likely to develop among coworkers who work near one another (Hodson, 1996; Sias & Cahill, 1998). Physical proximity provides opportunities for communication that physical distance can deny. As a consequence, those who are physically isolated from others at work suffer from an "out of sight, out of mind" effect, resulting in their relatively mindless exclusion.

Certain types of employees, such as boundary spanners (e.g., those whose jobs require much time away from work, such as salespeople and recruiters) and telecommuters (i.e., employees who accomplish much, or all, of their tasks away from a central workplace), are particularly at risk of becoming excluded from workplace relationships (Dubinsky, Yammarino, Jolson, & Spangler, 1995; Marshall, Michaels, & Mulki, 2007; see also Fay, this volume). This isolation results primarily from a largely mindless process—other employees are simply unaware of, or generally forget about, more remote employees. Along these lines, telecommuters often report feelings of isolation as a consequence of their distant and "virtual" employment status (Brake, 2006; Crandall & Gao, 2005).

Tasks and position. The nature and requirements of an employee's *tasks and position* also have important consequences for that employee's work experiences, including his or her workplace relationships. As noted earlier, certain types of tasks impair an employee's ability to move about the organization in ways that will enable engagement in communication with coworkers. Jobs that require employees to work in solitary environments, such as annexes, or that require a great deal of travel and time away from the primary workplace, remove or significantly reduce the opportunities for physical proximity required for relational development.

One's position in the organizational hierarchy can also influence relational exclusion. Despite the common stereotype that life is "lonely at the top," most studies examining managerial loneliness have failed to find empirical evidence that those at the upper levels of the corporate hierarchy tend to be more isolated and lonely than other employees. Instead, research indicates employees at the *lower* levels are more likely to report feeling lonely (Bell, Roloff, Van Camp, & Karol, 1990; Reinking & Bell, 1991). The authors explained that this result may reflect greater social and interaction skills typically required to move into positions of leadership; that is, socially competent employees are more likely to develop high quality interpersonal relationships and more likely to be promoted to leadership roles.

Supervision and leadership. The quality of leadership in a particular unit can also affect relational exclusion. For example, supervisors who are "out of the loop" or disconnected from the social nature of the work environment are likely to be unaware of exclusory processes that may be occurring. Thus, if an employee is being ostracized, shunned, depersonalized, or ignored, a neglectful, disconnected supervisor enables such treatment to continue and perhaps even escalate. This lack of attention may also send an implicit message to employees that exclusory practices are permitted, thus exacerbating the problem (Sias, 2009).

The relationships a supervisor has with his or her various employees can also result in relational exclusion among those employees. Along these lines, research indicates that differential treatment (favorable or unfavorable) from a supervisor to a particular employee can harm that employee's relationships with his or her coworkers (Sias, 1996; Sias & Jablin, 1995). These relational effects depend largely on the extent to which the coworkers perceive the differential treatment as fair. For example, if coworkers perceive that an employee is receiving favorable treatment from the supervisor that is undeserved and unfair, they tend to ostracize that employee (whom they consider the "boss's pet") through exclusion from coworker relationships. Similar effects result from situations in which an employee receives unfavorable differential treatment (e.g., a reprimand) and the coworkers think that employee deserved such treatment (e.g., the treatment resulted from the target's poor job performance). These "boss's victims" tend to be ostracized because the other employees fear guilt by association.

Climate. The general workplace climate also influences employee relationships in a number of ways. Odden and Sias (1997), for example, found that employees were more likely to develop friendships at work when they worked in a cohesive workplace in which employees tended to support one another and help each other out. In contrast, work environments that reward individual success and competition over group success and collaboration can harm collegiality and employee relationships (Seidenberg, 1980).

In sum, in addition to a host of personal factors, the work environment also plays a role in relational exclusion processes. Where an employee works, what the employee does, and at what hierarchical level, the supervisor's management style and relationships with others, and the overall workplace climate all have important implications for that employee's workplace relationships.

Consequences of Exclusion

Although the processes of exclusion differ, their consequences are largely the same and are substantial and important for both the excluded employees and the larger organization. This section addresses the various psychological and behavioral consequences of exclusion.

Psychological Consequences

Excluded employees often take it personally. Being excluded from social relationships inclusive of other employees likely creates uncertainty for the excluded employee, harming his or her self-esteem and leading to a host of other psychological and even physiological consequences. It is important to note at this point, however, that not all people mind being excluded. Some, such as those individuals who are shy or apprehensive about communicating with others, may even prefer it. Therefore, the psychological consequences discussed in this section are relevant to individuals who unsuccessfully seek inclusion.

Loneliness. Employees who report being excluded or isolated from social relationships at work also tend to report experiencing loneliness (Sommer, Williams, Ciarocco, & Baumeister, 2001). Workplace loneliness is a subjective perceptual construct reflecting an individual's perceived deficiency in social relationships. Wright (2009) defined workplace loneliness as "the distress caused by the perceived lack of good quality interpersonal relationships between employees in a work environment" (p. 13). Hence, individuals who desire high quality interpersonal relationships at work and are excluded from them experience loneliness. As mentioned earlier, an individual who lacks high quality relationships but does not want such relationships is unlikely to feel lonely. In general, however, research indicates that workplace loneliness is a common experience for many employees (Wright, 2009).

Alienation. Distinct from loneliness, alienation refers to a feeling of disconnection and separation. Alienated individuals feel cut off from their social environment and from others in that environment. As Erickson (1986) noted, "People can also be said to be alienated when they become estranged from their fellow creatures" (p. 2). Alienation involves a sense of powerlessness. Wright (2009) noted, "When people are alienated, they feel like they don't belong to the social world. Alienation is the separation from social institutions and feeling powerless and normless" (p. 14). More specifically, alienation reflects the separation from social relationships that can result from relational exclusion (Wright, 2009).

Stress and anxiety. Relational exclusion creates stress and anxiety for isolated employees in a number of ways. First, exclusion, whether intentional or not, provides a blow to the isolated individual's self-concept and self-esteem (Sommer et al., 2001). The exclusion process can create a great deal of uncertainty and self-doubt, which are linked to anxiety and stress (Sommer et al., 2001). Second, excluded employees also experience stress and anxiety because of fears that their isolation may affect their performance and career goals. As Sias (2009) explained, isolated employees " . . . may fear that being out of the loop will harm their task performance or may result in their being overlooked for rewards such as promotions, bonuses, training, and social rewards such as high-quality relationships with their supervisor and coworkers" (p. 157).

Finally, and somewhat paradoxically, relational exclusion is linked to stress and anxiety due to the important social support function of high quality workplace relationships. Much research demonstrates the important, valuable social support provided by peers, workplace friends, and supervisors (Cahill & Sias, 1997; Ray, 1991). The closer and more intimate these relationships, the more high quality and substantive support they provide (Sias & Cahill, 1998). Hence, individuals can count on coworkers they perceive to be close friends for both instrumental support (i.e., tangible help) and emotional support. Both forms of support are crucial in helping individuals navigate and negotiate the many stressors that accompany organizational life. Employees who are excluded from such relationships lack an effective social support network, leaving them prey to such stressors and more likely to experience high levels of anxiety as a result of those stressors. In other words, exclusion from high quality workplace relationships creates stress and anxiety for employees, and the lack of such relationships leaves them with few or no sources of social support to help them deal with that and other forms of workplace stress.

In sum, workplace relational exclusion creates a number of psychological consequences for excluded employees, including loneliness, feelings of alienation, stress, and anxiety. Psychology and behavior are closely linked, and as the following section demonstrates, exclusion leads to a number of important behavioral consequences.

Behavioral Consequences

Given the preceding psychological impacts of exclusion, it is not surprising that relational exclusion results in a number of behavioral consequences that have important implications for employees and the larger organization.

Tardiness and absenteeism. The psychological consequences of relational exclusion take a toll on the excluded employee's health, which affects tardiness and absenteeism. Much research indicates that stress and anxiety can disturb sleep patterns, compromise one's immune system, and increase the likelihood of illness in a variety of forms (Taylor, Klein, Lewis, Gruenewald, Gurung, & Updegraff, 2000). Interestingly, research also indicates that the social support derived from high quality interpersonal relationships, such as friendships, can provide significant relief from stress and anxiety and improve an individual's mental and physical health (Raymond, 1999; Taylor et al., 2000). Thus, as discussed earlier, relational exclusion can harm one's mental and physical health, and relational exclusion withholds key sources of support necessary for maintaining mental and physical health.

Impaired performance. Relational exclusion negatively influences employee job performance in a number of ways. First, isolated employees who miss work due to stress, anxiety, and health problems fall behind in their work (which, paradoxically, increases their stress and anxiety). Thus, their inability to keep up with other workers detracts from their job performance. Missing work also means missing opportunities to interact with coworkers and to obtain information that can contribute to job performance. Therefore, exclusion affects employee performance via its impact on information exchange.

Along these lines, research indicates that information exchange is linked to interpersonal relationship quality. Brass and Burkhardt (1993), for example, found that isolated employees received significantly less information than others. They also received lower quality information. As Sias (2005) found, employees with high quality relationships with their supervisors and peer coworkers received more accurate and useful information in a timelier manner than did those excluded from such relationships.

With respect to specific kinds of information, research indicates that isolated employees are particularly likely to miss out on information carried by rumors (e.g., messages addressing topics of general uncertainty such as layoffs or mergers) and gossip (informal talk typically about an individual). Both rumors and gossip are useful sources of information. As Sias (2009) explained, "Receiving a 'heads up' via the rumor mill, for example, can help an individual prepare for potential organizational problems. In contrast, employees excluded from the rumor mill will be caught by surprise and slower to react and adjust to such events [and] although gossip is often 'trivial,' it can also be useful…" (p. 155).

Aggression and sabotage. Isolated employees sometimes respond to exclusion with acts of aggression and sabotage. Research indicates that individuals who are socially excluded can become increasingly aggressive and decreasingly pro-social (Twenge, Zhang, Catanese, Dolan-Pascoe, Lyche, & Baumeister, 2007). Unfortunately, such behavior tends only to increase their exclusion (Coie, 1990). Thau, Aquino, and Poortvilet (2007) explained this process by using belongingness theory (Baumeister & Leary, 1995). According to belongingness theory, individuals have strong needs to engage in high quality interpersonal relationships, and when those needs go unfulfilled, they react negatively. In particular, they experience ego depletion and a threat to their identity, which, in turn, motivates negative reactions (Baumeister & Leary, 1995). Along these lines, Thau et al. (2007) found that "thwarted belonging was associated with certain forms of self-defeating behaviors" (p. 844), including interpersonally harmful behaviors such as aggression and sabotage. Unfortunately, such behaviors tend to exacerbate rather than mitigate relational exclusion and are, therefore, self-defeating (Thau et al., 2007).

Relational exclusion is also linked to aggression and sabotage via alienation. Specifically, alienated individuals can become so disconnected from the social environment that they are essentially "norm-less." This normlessness makes it more likely that they will violate norms via acts of aggression (Argyris, 1973; Giesberg, 2001). In a broad examination of corporate sabotage incidents, Giesberg (2001) concluded that "a lack of effective employer/employee exchange of communication is the primary cause for corporate sabotage" (p. 2439). Similar to Argyris (1973), Giesberg (2001) related this effect to alienation and lack of belongingness as well as to a lack of communication that could preclude violence and sabotage when employees' behaviors signal potential problems.

In sum, relational exclusion leads to a host of behavioral consequences, including tardiness, absenteeism, and poor performance as well as more extreme consequences such as aggression and sabotage.

Future Research

As the preceding sections indicate, research has contributed a great deal of knowledge regarding why employees may be excluded from workplace relationships, how the exclusion is accomplished, and the consequences of relational exclusion for employees and the larger organization. There is still much to learn about workplace relational exclusion, however. In this section, I briefly highlight some areas for future research that would help scholars and practitioners better understand and manage this damaging process.

Future research should examine in greater detail the concept of intent. As noted earlier, employees exclude coworkers with more or less intent, but we know little about how the excluded employee interprets or attributes intentionality to relational exclusion. Such interpretations likely influence cognitive and behavioral outcomes. One can imagine a situation in which employees, for example, exclude a coworker unintentionally because of lack of proximity but the target perceives the exclusion to be intentional. Such an interpretation likely triggers many of the cognitive and behavioral outcomes discussed earlier. The excluding employees, however, may be caught by surprise by the target's behavior, unaware that they prompted the same. These employees likely then make faulty attributions about the target employee that can lead to further *inten-*

tional exclusion. Research examining how excluded employees interpret and attribute intentionality would provide important insights into such processes.

Research to date tends to conceptualize the excluded employee, at least implicitly, as a passive participant in the exclusion process. As noted earlier, organizations and relationships are dynamic social creations, yet existing research largely ignores the excluded employee's role in that dynamism. For example, although we know much about how employees exclude coworkers, we know nothing about how the excluded employees may attempt to include themselves communicatively or engage in workplace relationships. Research examining the methods by which isolated employees attempt to engage in workplace relations, and the relative effectiveness of those engagement processes, would provide many important and useful insights into how excluded employees experience, react to, and attempt to mitigate or rectify their social exclusion.

Existing research has largely ignored the interdependent nature of the various consequences of workplace relational exclusion. Instead, such consequences are generally examined in isolation from one another. Yet it is likely that certain consequences influence others. It is possible, for example, that sabotage and aggression are preceded by more benign behaviors such as absenteeism and impaired performance. Future research examining the interdependence of consequences could provide important insights into indicators of potential behavioral escalation and "tipping points" at which relatively minor consequences can become more serious.

Concluding Comments

As this chapter demonstrates, relational exclusion is a common, but unfortunate, aspect of the workplace social environment. Individuals are excluded from important, high quality workplace relationships for a variety of reasons and via processes that are carried out with more or less intent. Regardless of the reasons for the exclusion, exclusionary processes bring a host of negative consequences for the excluded employees as well as for the larger department and the organization as a whole.

Understanding relational exclusion is important for developing organizational practices that mitigate or prevent employees from becoming isolated. Such understanding suggests a number of things practitioners can do to encourage high quality relationships among all employees. First, managers should study their employee social networks to discover who, if anyone, is suffering from relational exclusion. Once exclusion is identified, these managers should examine the work environment for clues about the reasons for the exclusion and potential solutions. For example, if the excluded employee works in a physically isolated environment, management should develop processes (such as regular on-site meetings, teleconferences, collaborative assignments with other employees) to create opportunities for communication and connection. If the exclusion may result from the isolated employee's shyness or social anxiety, managers should consider developing other, less anxiety-inducing, ways for the employee to communicate and connect with others, such as via computer-mediated communication methods. In cases of demographic dissimilarity, practitioners should consider ways to integrate the workgroup more effectively via collaborative tasks, increased proximity, and the like. This approach is more difficult, of course, if the exclusion results from intentional ostracism. In such cases, managers must address the perpetrators by implementing training and perhaps disciplinary remedies.

In all instances of relational exclusion, however, the first step toward mitigation is management's awareness of the situation. Accordingly, managers must ensure that they are themselves connected to, rather than isolated from, the workplace social milieu. As noted earlier, isolated managers are not only unable to prevent relational exclusion, but they may actually exacerbate the problem.

References

Argyris, C. (1973). *On organizations of the future*. Beverly Hills, CA: Sage.
Baumeister, R. F., & Leary, M. R. (1995). The need to belong: Desire for interpersonal attachments as fundamental human motivation. *Psychological Bulletin, 117*, 497–529.
Bell, R. A., Roloff, M. E., Van Camp, K., & Karol, S. H. (1990). Is it lonely at the top?: Career success and personal relationships. *Communication Research, 40*, 9–23.
Brake, T. (2006). Leading global virtual teams. *Industrial and Commercial Training, 38(3)*, 116–121.
Brass, D. J., & Burkhardt, M. S. (1993). Potential power and power use: An investigation of structure and behavior. *Academy of Management Journal, 36*, 441–472.
Cahill, D. J., & Sias, P. M. (1997). The perceived social costs and importance of seeking emotional support in the workplace: Gender differences and similarities. *Communication Research Reports, 14*, 231–240.
Coie, J. D. (1990). Toward a theory of peer rejection. In S. R. Asher & J. D. Coie (Eds.), *Peer rejection in childhood* (pp. 365–401). New York, NY: Cambridge University Press.
Cole, J. G., & McCroskey, J. C. (2003). The association of perceived communication apprehension, shyness, and verbal aggression with perceptions of source credibility and affect in organizational and interpersonal contexts. *Communication Quarterly, 51*, 101–110.

Crandall, W., & Gao, L. (2005). An update on telecommuting: Review and prospects for emerging issues. *S.A.M. Advanced Management Journal, 70,* 30–38.

Day, N. E., & Schoenrade, P. (1997). Staying in the closet versus coming out: Relationships between communication about sexual orientation and work attitudes. *Personnel Psychology, 50,* 147–163.

Dotan, O., Rubin, Y., & Sommer, K. L. (2004, April). *Impact of language diversity on team-members' self-feelings, team-perceptions, and individual-performance.* Paper presented at the annual conference of the Society for Industrial and Organizational Psychology, Chicago, IL.

Dubinsky, A. J., Yammarino, F. J., Jolson, M. A., & Spangler, W. D. (1995). Transformational leadership: An initial investigation in sales management. *Journal of Personal Selling & Sales Management, 15,* 17–32.

Embrick, D. G., Walther, C. S., & Wickens, C. M. (2007). Working class masculinity: Keeping gay men and lesbians out of the workplace. *Sex Roles, 56,* 757–766.

Erickson, K. (1986). On work and alienation: American Sociological Association, 1985 presidential address. *American Sociological Review, 51,* 1–8.

Foley, S., Linnehan, F., Greenhaus, J. H., & Weer, C. H. (2006). The impact of gender similarity, racial similarity and work culture on family supportive supervision. *Group & Organization Management, 31,* 420–441.

The Free Dictionary. (2007a). "Ostracism." Retrieved from http://www.thefreedictionary.com/ostracism.

The Free Dictionary. (2007b). "Ignoring." Retrieved from http://www.thefreedictionary.com/ignoring.

Fritz, J. H. (1997). Men's and women's organizational peer relationships: A comparison. *Journal of Business Communication, 34,* 27–46.

Gagnon, M. A., & Michael, J. H. (2004). Outcomes of perceived supervisor support for wood production employees. *Forest Products Journal, 54,* 172–177.

Giesberg, J. (2001). The role of communication in preventing workplace sabotage. *Journal of Applied Social Psychology, 31,* 2439–2461.

Graen, G., & Cashman, J. F. (1975). A role-making model of leadership in formal organizations: A developmental approach. In J. G. Hunt & L. L. Hunt (Eds.), *Leadership frontiers* (pp. 143–165). Kent, OH: Kent State University Press.

Graen, G. B., Liden, R., & Hoel, W. (1982). Role of leadership in the employee withdrawal process. *Journal of Applied Psychology, 67,* 868–872.

Graen, G. B., & Uhl-Bien, M. (1995). Development of leader-member exchange theory of leadership over 25 years: Applying a multi-level multi-domain perspective. *Leadership Quarterly, 6,* 219–247.

Gray, J., Kurihara, T., Hommen, L., & Feldman, J. (2007). Networks of exclusion: Job segmentation and social networks in the knowledge economy. *Equal Opportunities International, 26,* 144–160.

Hitlan, R. T., Kelly, K. M., Schepman, S., Schneider, K. T., & Zarate, M. A. (2006). Language exclusion and the consequences of perceived ostracism in the workplace. *Group Dynamics: Theory, Research, and Practice, 10,* 56–70.

Hodson, R. (1996). Dignity in the workplace under participative management: Alienation and freedom revisited. *American Sociological Review, 61,* 719–738.

Hodson, R., Roscigno, V. J., & Lopez, S. H. (2006). Chaos and the abuse of power. *Work and Occupations, 33*, 382–416.

Ibarra, H. (1995). Race, opportunity, and diversity of social circles in managerial networks. *Academy of Management Journal, 38*, 673–703.

Kram, K. E., & Isabella, L. A. (1985). Mentoring alternatives: The role of peer relationships in career development. *Academy of Management Journal, 28*, 110–132.

Lewis, A. P. (2009). Destructive organizational communication and LGBT workers' experiences. In P. Lutgen-Sandvik & B. Davenport Sypher (Eds.), *Destructive organizational communication: Processes, consequences, and constructive ways of organizing* (pp. 184–202). New York, NY: Routledge.

Marshall, G. W., Michaels, C. E., & Mulki, J. P. (2007). Workplace isolation: Exploring the construct and its measurement. *Psychology & Marketing, 24*, 195–233.

McDaniel, P. A. (2003). *Shrinking violets and Caspar Milquetoasts: Shyness, power, and intimacy in the United States, 1950 to 1995*. New York, NY: New York University Press.

Odden, C. M., & Sias, P. M. (1997). Peer communication relationships and psychological climate. *Communication Quarterly, 45*, 153–166.

Pelled, L. H., & Xin, K. R. (2000). Relational demography and relationship quality in two cultures. *Organization Studies, 21*, 1077–1094.

Ray, E. B. (1991). The relationship among communication network roles, job stress, and burnout in educational organizations. *Communication Quarterly, 39*, 91–102.

Raymond, N. (1999, November 1). The hug drug. *Psychology Today, 32*, 17.

Reinking, K., & Bell, R. (1991). Relationships among loneliness, communication competence, and career success in a state bureaucracy: A field study of the "lonely at the top" maxim. *Communication Quarterly, 39*, 358–373.

Seidenberg, R. (1980). The lonely marriage in corporate America. In J. Hartog, J. R. Audy, & Y. A. Cohen (Eds.), *The anatomy of loneliness* (pp. 186–203). New York, NY: International Universities Press.

Sherif, M. (1958). Superordinate goals in the reduction of intergroup conflicts. *American Journal of Sociology, 63*, 349–356.

Sias, P. M. (1996). Constructing perceptions of differential treatment: An analysis of coworker discourse. *Communication Monographs, 63*, 171–187.

Sias, P. M. (2005). Workplace relationship quality and employee information experiences. *Communication Studies, 56*, 375–396.

Sias, P. M. (2009). Social ostracism, cliques, and outcasts. In P. Lutgen-Sandvik & B. Davenport Sypher (Eds.), *Destructive organizational communication: Processes, consequences, & constructive ways of organizing* (pp. 145–163). New York, NY: Routledge.

Sias, P. M. (in press). Workplace relationships. In L. L. Putnam & D. K. Mumby (Eds.). *Handbook of organizational communication* (3rd ed.). Thousand Oaks, CA: Sage.

Sias, P. M., & Cahill, D. J. (1998). From coworkers to friends: The development of peer friendships in the workplace. *Western Journal of Communication, 62*, 273–299.

Sias, P. M., & Jablin, F. M. (1995). Differential superior-subordinate relations, perceptions of fairness, and coworker communication. *Human Communication Research, 22*, 5–38.

Sias, P. M., Krone, K. J., & Jablin, F. M. (2002). An ecological systems perspective on workplace relationships. In M. L. Knapp & J. Daly (Eds.), *Handbook of interpersonal communication* (3rd ed., pp. 615–642). Newbury Park, CA: Sage.

Sommer, K. L., Williams, K. D., Ciarocco, N. J., & Baumeister, R. F. (2001). When silence speaks louder than words: Explorations into the intrapsychic and interpersonal consequences of social ostracism. *Basic and Applied Social Psychology, 23*, 225–243.

Steinburg, A., Sullivan, V. J., & Montoya, L. A. (1999). Loneliness and social isolation in the workplace for deaf individuals during the transition years. *Journal of Applied Rehabilitation Counseling, 30(1)*, 22–30.

Taylor, S. E., Klein, L. C., Lewis, B. P., Gruenewald, T. L., Gurung, R. A. R., & Updegraff, J. A. (2000). Biobehavioral responses to stress in females: Tend-and-befriend, not fight-or-flight. *Psychology Review, 107*, 411–429.

Thau, S., Aquino, K., & Poortvilet, M. (2007). Self-defeating behaviors in organizations: The relationship between thwarted belonging and interpersonal work behaviors. *Journal of Applied Psychology, 92*, 840–847.

Turner, J. C., & Oakes, P. J. (1986). The significance of the social identity concept for social psychology with reference to individualism, interactionism, and social influence. *British Journal of Social Psychology, 25*, 237–252.

Twenge, J.M., Zhang, L., Catanese, K. R., Dolan-Pascoe, B., Lyche, L. F., & Baumeister, R. F. (2007). Replenishing connectedness: Reminders of social activity reduce aggression after social exclusion. *British Journal of Social Psychology, 46*, 205–224.

Wheatley, M. (2001). *Leadership and the new science: Discovering order in a chaotic world.* San Francisco, CA: Jossey-Bass.

Williams, K. D., & Sommer, K. L. (1997). Social ostracism by coworkers: Does rejection lead to loafing or compensation? *Personality and Social Psychology Bulletin, 23*, 693–706.

Wright, S. L. (2009). In a lonely place: The experience of loneliness in the workplace. In R. L. Morrison & S. L. Wright (Eds.), *Friends and enemies in organizations: A work psychology perspective* (pp. 10–31). London, England: Palgrave MacMillan.

Zapf, D. (1999). Organizational, work group related and personal causes of mobbing/bullying at work. *International Journal of Manpower, 20*, 70–85.

PART II

Frameworks for Understanding Problematic Relationships in the Workplace

· 7 ·

OUT OF SIGHT, OUT OF...THE LOOP?

Relationship Challenges for Teleworkers and Their Co-Located Peers, Managers, and Organizations

Martha J. Fay

Coworker relationships have been an increasing focus for organizational communication researchers. Characterized by higher levels of interaction, trust, and self-disclosure, coworker friendships function to mentor, exchange information, influence, facilitate innovation, and provide social support (McManus & Russell, 2007; Sias, 2009). One meta-analysis found that high quality coworker relationships in co-located contexts are associated with positive work attitudes and job performance (Winstead, Derlega, Montgomery, & Pilkington, 1995). Conversely, workplace isolation and problematic coworker relationships in co-located contexts are associated with greater job stress and burnout and less job satisfaction and commitment (Marshall, Michaels, & Mulki, 2007). Unfortunately, many employees report not having strong ties with their coworkers (Dahlin, Kelly, & Moen, 2008), despite the positive buffering effects of such connections.

Social ties with coworkers may be particularly limited for teleworking employees (i.e., those working remotely using technology). Although teleworkers typically adopt flexible practices to coordinate their work flow activities (Ballard & Gossett, 2007), studies indicate that they struggle with their work relationships (McDonald, Bradley, & Brown, 2008; Tietze & Musson, 2010). To explain these struggles, researchers have theorized that temporal and spatial distance reduces opportunities for teleworkers to interact with their colleagues, which produces less engagement in the organizational routines that provide connection and understanding (DeSanctis & Monge, 1998). The face-to-face encounters that characterize co-located settings are less available for remote employees and their colleagues but are nevertheless important for developing common ground and building interpersonal bonds (Feldman & Rafaeli, 2002). Moreover, telework researchers have noted that communication in a reduced-cue media environment may require more effort, compounding the time and energy required to develop relationships with coworkers (Morgan & Symon, 2002). In light of these obstacles to building good working relationships, it is not surprising that teleworkers who work outside of the office more than three days a week (high-intensity) report more negative coworker relationships and more negative effects on job performance than colleagues who are working on-site to a greater degree.

These challenges to the development and maintenance of workplace relationships warrant concern. Remote workers with fewer spontaneous (and fewer face-to-face) opportunities for interacting are likely to experience isolation (Wiesenfeld, Raghuram, & Garud, 2001), loss and detachment (Hylmo & Buzzanell, 2002), reduced visibility (Reinsch, 1997), especially as it relates to promotion opportunities (Olson, 1987), and compromised feelings of belonging (Morgan & Symon, 2002). In addition, when workplace relationships become problematic for co-located employees, people employ distancing strategies to remove themselves from the other either physically or emotionally, or both (Hess, 2009). The distancing strategy options are reduced for teleworkers, and given that some teleworkers choose this type of work for the freedom it affords from office politics and stress (Leonardi, Treem, & Jackson, 2010), they may be even more likely to choose strategies that further reduce their connection to others. Finally, researchers have found that problematic relationships in the workplace are associated with reduced job satisfaction and organizational commitment, and increased cynicism, burnout, depression, anxiety, and physical symptoms (Fritz & Omdahl, 2006; Omdahl & Fritz, 2006).

Therefore, there are many reasons to be concerned about the relational challenges and potential costs of working remotely. This chapter is devoted to explicating the relational issues faced by this rapidly growing segment of workers, with an eye toward providing information needed to develop methods of managing the fallout. The sections that follow address four issues: (1) the prevalence and nature of telework, (2) relationship building and maintenance when teleworkers are involved, (3) communication related to individual and organizational processes and outcomes, and (4) management challenges.

The Prevalence and Nature of Telework

The number of people teleworking was estimated at 26.2 million in 2010, or almost 20% of the U.S. adult working population; between 2008 and 2010, the percentage of teleworkers who work remotely more than once a week increased, going from 72% to 84% (WorldatWork, 2011). While many companies remain exclusively either site-based or telestructured, there are many companies with both site workers and teleworkers (sometimes trading roles depending on the day of the week or assigned tasks).

Researchers have defined telework in many different ways (Qvortrup, 1998) and used a variety of terms to address the core concept (e.g., telecommuter, teleworker, distributed worker, open-collar worker, distance worker, and remote worker). Some describe telework as a social innovation and a form of organizational change (Aichholzer, 1998), as work done outside a central office in which other employees are co-located (Ellison, 1999), and as work performed by people whose connection to the central office is primarily via mediated communication (Gainey, Kelley, & Hill, 1999). For this chapter, telework is considered work that involves employees performing at least part of their responsibilities remotely, outside their central organization's physical boundaries, using technology to interact (Gajendran & Harrison, 2007).

Some distinctive features of this arrangement help to explain its attractiveness to both employees and organizations. Organizations realize the benefits of expanded geographic representation, cost savings (overhead) due to the reduction in owned or leased space, and higher productivity (Mallia & Ferris, 2000). Remote work programs also broaden companies' access to talented people who may be disabled or otherwise unable or unwilling to work from the central office location. Employees gain control over their working arrangements, flexibility, and autonomy, as well as savings in time (traveling to and from work) and money (usually no-cost parking, fewer restaurant and fuel bills, and reduced clothing expenditures).

The advantages of telework for both companies and individuals give reason to believe the projections for steady growth in the number of teleworkers. However, the qualities of teleworking also pose unique challenges. As the next section explores, these challenges are practical as well as personal and exist on corporate, managerial, and individual levels. In a unique way, telework highlights the interdependence of individuals and the organizations of which they are a part. The next section takes a deeper look at how relationships are constructed and maintained and how informal and formal structures influence and are influenced by these unique relationships.

Relationship Building and Maintenance, Informal Communication, and Organizational Processes and Outcomes

Workplace relationships may be especially important in the remote context where one's sense of belonging to the collective is compromised. Using a constructivist theoretical perspective, I frame these relationships as instantiated in talk and as playing an important role in both individual and organizational processes. This section first covers informal communication and relationships in general and moves then to integrate findings on specific types of informal talk and how these forms of talk relate to organizational outcomes, specifically, organizational identification, organizational commitment, and job satisfaction; the role of coworker liking and relationship quality in all of these areas is further examined.

Informal Communication and Relationships

> I have no interaction with peers. Sometimes it is isolating and I do not feel a part of the company.—Anonymous Research Participant

Informal communication in work settings has been defined as interpersonal, social, or small talk that is not solely work-task focused (Holmes, 2000); informal relations constitute an important integrating process in the organization (Blau, 2000) and an interactional region in which employees' needs are met, social identities formed, commonalities established, and meaningful relationships generated (DeSanctis & Monge, 1998; Sias & Cahill, 1998). Informal communication has been linked to workplace friendships (Sias & Perry, 2004), social capital (Knoke, 1999), and instrumental support directly related to accomplishing tasks (Albrecht, Burleson, & Goldsmith, 1994). Recent research shows that informal communication between teleworkers and their co-located peers plays a particularly important role in integrating individual and organizational goals and that such relationships have both direct and buffering effects (Fay, 2011; Fay & Kline, 2011).

By its nature, informal communication is not, however, obligatory, and it becomes a more conscious effort in the remote context. The visual cues, rituals, traditions, and opportunities for casual talk that co-located employees share are not readily available to remote employees. These opportunities provide the means for interacting through which common ground is established and friendships are formed and maintained.

Informal communication creates opportunities for teleworkers to present themselves as credible actors who want interpersonal relationships with coworkers (Thatcher & Zhu, 2006), but remote workers exchange information less frequently than their co-located peers (Fonner & Roloff, 2010). For teleworkers who do not communicate at all, there is no chance to build the trust necessary to form interpersonal relationships. One teleworker reported the following experience:

> I have no communication with coworkers. It would be nice.—Anonymous Research Participant

However, worse than no interaction is a negatively phrased or intentioned response to efforts to communicate with peers by remote employees. One teleworker reported responding to a series of e-mails looking for members for an employee bowling league and receiving a message of apathy in return:

> I offered to join if they made it a traveling league. I knew this wouldn't happen but responded just to get some dialogue going. I got a short response telling [me] thanks for the offer but that it wasn't possible.—Anonymous Research Participant

As this quotation highlights, *how* informal communication works to facilitate individual and organizational goals is very important and has only recently emerged as a focus of scholars. In a recent thematic analysis of teleworkers' reported informal interactions with co-located colleagues, the key themes identified—personal disclosure, sociality, support giving and getting, commiserating and complaining, and business updates and exchanges—provide some specific evidence of how teleworkers attempt to develop friendships (Fay, 2011).

Informal Communication, Processes and Outcomes, and Relationships

> There are plenty of occasions where I feel secluded from our group and out of the loop.—Anonymous Research Participant

The separation from other employees and from the physical plant affects processes instantiated through communication, including organizational identification, organizational commitment, and job satisfaction (Fay & Kline, 2011; Golden, 2007). Thatcher and Zhu (2006) have contended that teleworkers' work-related identities are challenged because their reduced visibility and face-to-face communication opportunities affect the way they develop and verify the work self-concepts involved in organizational identification and organizational commitment. With remote workers physically and sometimes psychologically removed from the usual visual cues, rituals, and spontaneous opportunities for the social interactions that facilitate these outcomes, telecommuting arrangements pose an inherent risk of fragmenting organizations (Wiesenfeld et al., 2001).

Early teleworker studies linked higher frequency of teleworkers' informal e-mail interactions with higher levels of organizational identification (Wiesenfeld et al., 2001), and satisfaction with informal communication in general has been positively associated with teleworkers' organizational commitment (Fay & Kline, 2011). Only recently have specific types of messages from interactions between teleworkers and co-located peers been associated with organizational identification, organizational commitment, and job satisfaction; relationship quality has also recently been shown to moderate some of these relationships (Fay & Kline, 2012). Further, informal communication that results in teleworkers experiencing greater embeddedness in their organizations has been associated with meeting multiple relational and organizational goals. As one teleworker explained, "I felt valued that he asked my opinion." Other teleworkers have described mutual collaboration, recognition of ideas, involvement in planning, and compliments as talk types that help to bind them to their organizations (Fay & Kline, 2012).

Recalled teleworker interactions have also revealed empirical links between messages of inclusion and higher organizational identification and organizational commitment, and between messages of exclusion and lower organizational identification, organizational commitment, and job satisfaction. However, teleworkers with high coworker relationship quality were more identified with their organizations regardless of the level of exclusion messages they had experienced, and those with low coworker relationship quality who experienced exclusion messages were less identified with their organizations. Teleworkers with high coworker relationship quality were also more highly committed to their organizations, regardless of the level of exclusion messages they had experienced. Hence, having a trusted coworker to offer social validation for one's identity and membership may play a key role in developing feelings of organizational identification and organizational commitment (Fay & Kline, 2011).

Other specific types of informal communication examined in related studies include coworker social support, collegial talk, and complaining talk. When high-intensity teleworkers experienced collegial talk and social support, they identified more strongly with their organizations; supportive communication was also associated with higher organizational commitment (Fay & Kline, 2012).

Coworker liking appears to play an important buffering role for teleworkers. For example, liking for coworkers has been shown to play a moderating role in the effect of complaining talk on organizational commitment (Fay & Kline, 2011). Liking has also been positively related to teleworkers' informal communication satisfaction with coworkers and with their organizational commitment and job satisfaction (Fay & Kline, 2011). Teleworkers with a liked coworker have also demonstrated higher levels of commitment toward their organizations regardless of the amount of complaining talk in which they engaged with co-located peers; by contrast, those with low coworker liking who experienced more complaining talk reported less commitment to their organizations (Fay & Kline, 2012). Thus, coworker liking may buffer the effects of complaining talk on organizational commitment. Informal complaining may actually generate commitment because it brings employees together and helps them clarify and manage their work roles. More so than other forms of informal interaction, complaining may offer a bonding experience that helps teleworkers solidify their membership claims to the organization and their feelings of connection. However, it appears that complaining must be done with a colleague who is well liked in order to generate commitment (Fay & Kline, 2012).

Workplace relationships are not possible without interaction and are integrally involved in organizational processes and outcomes, so challenges related to building and maintaining workplace relationships imply similar difficulties for organizational identification, organizational commitment, and job satisfaction. Some remote workers report self-disclosing with co-located peers in ways that demonstrate trust and a desire to develop personal relationships and manage impressions but also reflect identity construction efforts (Fay, 2011), as in this example of an interaction between a teleworker and central office colleague at a trade show:

> "I am learning a lot from you as well. I like to hear the different statistics that you quote as well as hear the questions you ask as you prospect a customer." We both agreed that day that we were helping one another sell the services better.—Anonymous Research Participant

Impression Management

People actively work to manage impressions others have of them while interacting (Goffman, 1959), using an array of self-presentation tactics. Studies on impression management behaviors in the workplace tend to focus on the use of tactics for career enhancement rather than for interpersonal purposes, but teleworkers struggle with both. Choosing self-presentation tactics is complex for teleworkers who need to appear to coworkers as simultaneously desiring personal relationships and working hard and who wish to make a favorable impression on managers for career purposes.

Face-to-face interaction exerts social force through empathy, avoidance of conflict, and other face concerns (Bimber, 1998). Tanis and Postmes (2003) found that even minimal physical cues (e.g., photos) affect the ambiguity and positivity of impressions, and Hancock and Dunham (2001) demonstrated that impressions formed in computer-mediated communication (CMC) were less detailed but more intense (e.g., ratings on personal attractiveness and affection for interactional partner were higher) than impressions formed in face-to-face interaction.

Walther's (1996) hyper-personal model suggests CMC interactants engage in selective self-presentation, make overattributions, and create trust that can result in relational closeness. However, teleworkers may deliberately avoid the informal contact necessary for building common ground and developing friendships *because* they are working to manage impressions. Specifically, the autonomy that remote workers enjoy can foster coworkers' perceptions that their remote colleagues' context confers special privilege or permits slacking (Baruch, 2000), which can put remote workers in a defensive position. Teleworkers report feeling that they must establish legitimacy with co-located peers (Hylmo, 2006), who may view them as working less diligently (Thatcher & Zhu, 2006). Brocklehurst (2001) found that, rather than reveling in their "freedom" from constraint, teleworking employees attempted to construct a convincing work identity for themselves and others. Hence, impression management is also a management concern as it relates to harmonious relations among all employees.

The processes by which people gauge similarities and manage impressions, a factor associated with those with whom people seek relationships, are facilitated by observation of others' behavior (Bradac, 2001) and by nonverbal communication. Physical separation and reliance on technology create difficulties in these areas for both teleworkers and the central office employees who may need or want to form relationships.

Reliance on Computer-Mediated Communication (CMC)

Informal and formal interaction in the remote context is more dependent on mediated channels than in the co-located setting. Early CMC research concentrated on pressing technology into service for organizational goals in co-located contexts, on the use of technology to connect groups for temporary projects or meetings (see Baltes, Dickson, Sherman, Bauer, & LaGanke, 2002), and on group productivity (DeSanctis & Monge, 1998). People who rely more heavily on CMC may develop skills that assist in harnessing resources through networking and in transferring knowledge (Tretheway & Corman, 2001).

Early studies on electronic mail in personal relationships and in co-located organizational settings suggested that e-mail can remove not only geographic barriers to communication in order to develop relationships (Stafford, Kline, & Dimmick, 1999) but temporal, departmental, and hierarchical barriers as well (Sproull & Kiesler, 1986). However, Waldron (2003) suggested that electronic networks may magnify the effects of small talk and of destructive relational behaviors. Additionally, he speculated that maintaining relationships in the absence of unplanned, unscripted opportunities for interaction may make relationship maintenance a "more deliberate and mindful process" (p. 180).

The effects of distance on personal relationships, and the use of technology to bridge the gap, have been contested among scholars. Nie (2001) argued that "telecommuting will have consequences for the sociability of the workplace" (p. 430); however, Morgan and Symon (2002) suggested that the appropriate use of technologies "can facilitate shared understanding and help remote staff to view their company as alive and exciting" (p. 302).

One central theme of these early findings was that CMC involved a reduction in nonverbal social and relational cues, resulting in depersonalized communication to the detriment of interpersonal relations (for reviews, see Parks & Floyd, 1996, and Walther, 1996). A second general theme was that the trust necessary to form interpersonal relationships (Roloff & Anastasiou, 2001) can develop via CMC (Jarvenpaa & Leidner, 1999). However, the adoption of communication technology requires attention to interpersonal, as well as technological and organizational, practices and processes.

Management Challenges

Teleworking poses many management challenges. First, managers must learn to manage without the traditional cues related to control and authority. Second, different management skills are needed to design and maintain processes that ensure information flow and appropriate and timely content selections. Third, management must uncover and correct biases favoring observable performance. Fourth, instilling an appreciation for the organization's culture is another challenge for managers of teleworkers. Finally, management must adjust to how knowledge is shared and compromised when informal communication between coworkers is weak or non-existent. How management responds to these challenges directly influences relationships teleworkers have with coworkers, managers, and the company as a whole.

Control and Authority

Because remote workers are physically distanced from the parent organization, they operate with little supervision, increased autonomy, and greater control over their own time and schedules. Research from a critical perspective suggests that the unobtrusive control desired by organizations (e.g., Gossett & Tompkins, 2001) may be at risk because visual status cues and rituals used by management to reinforce existing power structures are missing in non-traditional contexts. In organizations with tightly structured hierarchies, managers may also experience perceived loss of control and may struggle to maintain a coherent identity for the group (DeSanctis & Monge, 1998; Wiesenfeld et al., 2001). Such contexts require different management (including communication) skills and practices, the ability to exert authority without the use of visual cues, and the ability to discern the appropriate amount of communication (Morgan & Symon, 2002).

Supervisors must be more explicit in dealing with teleworkers due to the lack of nonverbal and status cues traditionally used to exert influence. Some supervisors prefer to rely more heavily on visual cues for asserting their power (Morgan & Symon, 2002). The absence of visual cues and/or too little contact with remote employees may suggest lack of effort on the manager's part and a resulting increase in pressure on teleworkers to do more, as in this teleworker's comment:

> We were talking about how our supervisors basically don't do anything so what we do in a typical day is important, because no one is watching to make sure we don't make mistakes.—Anonymous Research Participant

Early research on managing teleworkers focused on the impact an existing employee/supervisor relationship had on the decision to telecommute. For example, Reinsch (1997) found that people believed that the longer a relationship between employee and manager existed prior to telecommuting, the less likely an employee would be to choose to work remotely, presumably because of a desire to maintain the relationship as it was. In another study, Reinsch (1999) found that teleworkers and their managers enjoyed an initial happy (honeymoon) phase, after which some relationships tended to deteriorate;

these teleworkers complained that managers became difficult to reach and that they perceived teleworkers as not working hard. For teleworkers who have no pre-existing relationship with supervisors, or who have never worked face-to-face with their supervisors, these problems may be exacerbated.

Information Provision

Morgan and Symon (2002) have noted information problems from the remote worker's point of view, including overload (management sent too much) and lack of thought (with how messages were constructed). Determining how much, and what kind of, information teleworkers need, and which media to use for different purposes, are additional management challenges that ultimately influence relationships between teleworkers and their managers and coworkers. One teleworker commented as follows:

> We receive e-mails from our large corporate headquarters say 6–8/week that rarely relate to anything that our part of the company is involved in.—Anonymous Research Participant

This teleworker further noted that he would rather receive no information than continuing unrelated communication because the effect was feeling as if no thought was given to him at all. Too much supervisor contact is also problematic for teleworkers. Hartman, Stoner, and Arora (1992) found that too much supervisor contact was interpreted as a lack of trust. Quality of communication and content is important in how teleworkers evaluate their relationship with managers and/or the company. In at least one study, teleworkers reported that they would rather receive no information at all than regular information about people and events that have nothing to do with them (Fay, 2007). Finally, communication adequacy tends to decrease as horizontal complexity increases; companies with extensive telework programs are usually horizontally complex by nature. Rosenfeld, Richmind, and May (2004) found that the amount of information needed and the amount received differed for office and field personnel, in support of this contention.

In the remote work literature, support from management has been reported as a major challenge (Hill, Hawkins, & Miller, 1996). For example, teleworkers have reported an inability to reach their managers and other employees when they needed information. This teleworker reported as follows:

> My other manager told me that she is in a big project and very busy. But still it was very discouraging to have no answer back. It is very hard to feel like I am part of the

company working remotely at home or (at the) client's site and it makes it feel worse to have such a breakdown in communication.—Anonymous Research Participant

Managers and supervisors may duck conflict or difficult situations by choosing media that provide limited information and/or permit little or no feedback. This strategy is inappropriate and damaging to relationships. One teleworker reported as follows:

> I told my colleague that she had been switched to another team per an e-mail sent out by our regional manager. She was unaware of this, and looked up the e-mail as we spoke. She said she was shocked. Later, she said she had e-mailed the manager and confirmed that transfer. She said she was devastated.—Anonymous Research Participant

In a similar instance, another teleworker recounted a lengthy series of e-mails between him and his boss, in which his boss showed complete disregard for this employee's dignity and feelings, and the teleworker expressed great dismay. The first e-mail sets the tone, demonstrating an inappropriate choice of media for the task at hand:

> I was asked by my boss to go into a website and look at my performance review and electronically acknowledge it.—Anonymous Research Participant

Performance Bias

Finally, a managerial bias toward observed versus reported performance when rating teleworkers has been documented. Golden, Barnes-Farrell, and Mascharka (2009) found that teleworking supervisors biased their performance ratings of office-based subordinates toward information they observed directly in the office rather than information that was virtually received. Teleworkers' reported concerns over others' perceptions of effort and productivity appear to be warranted. To eliminate these biases, management needs to grapple with how effort and productivity can be reported or evidenced in ways that are accepted as valid indicators of performance.

Instilling an Appreciation for the Organizational Culture

Management also faces a challenge in helping teleworkers connect to organizational culture. Teleworkers often feel excluded from informal opportunities to interact with others and get to know people embedded in the culture of the organization. One teleworker reported as follows when asked what made him or her feel more or less included in the organization:

> Hearing about things that other people are doing together, such as going to lunch.—Anonymous Research Participant

Doing things together as a work team is usually encouraged by co-located managers, but managers are not trained to find ways to bring the teleworker into that culture. More often, they fail to consider the effect that small talk has on those who are not able to join the group, even for mundane events.

Connections to organizational culture may be even more difficult to forge in cases in which remote workers have self-selected because they do not desire relational closeness with others through their work. For example, one teleworker reported as follows:

> I have no desire to communicate with coworkers.—Anonymous Research Participant

Managers must assess such situations to determine whether relational benefits outweigh potential negative consequences.

Culture Representation

Helping teleworkers establish a sense of belonging and identity with the organization and creating a sense of culture are two additional challenges identified by managers. Scholars have shown that storytelling and discussion of stories (Eisenberg & Riley, 2001), socialized language practices (Robichaud, Giroux, & Taylor, 2004), and rituals (Feldman & Rafaeli, 2002) reinforce corporate culture, but, as traditionally practiced, these opportunities are largely inaccessible to teleworkers. For example, the simple display of information through artifacts and visual cues can symbolize culture and important values in organizations (Feldman & March, 1981), but remote workers don't see them unless they physically visit the office. Thatcher and Zhu (2006) contended that teleworkers need to develop interaction routines to sustain their identities with supervisors and coworkers in light of teleworkers' feelings of isolation from others and relational uncertainty.

Knowledge Sharing

A final management concern, knowledge sharing, also depends on successfully building relationships between teleworkers and their managers and coworkers. The leveraging of intellectual and learning capabilities has been widely studied in the co-located context (e.g., Weick & Ashford, 2001), and interest has grown given the general increased use of technology. However, this line of study has not been pursued in the remote context. Tretheway and Corman (2001) argued that virtual environments *encourage* development of knowledge resources, which are in turn a primary resource for virtual organizations. They suggested that virtual workers may be most expert at locating, developing, and using knowledge processes as a result. However, knowledge resources must be shared to be of value, and teleworkers are less likely to share knowledge with those with whom they have no relationship.

Future Research and Implications for Practitioners

Ultimately, the success or failure of teleworking arrangements rests on how spatial and temporal distance is managed, and there is a wide range of "things" to be managed, from the organizational culture reflected in policies, processes, and symbolic communication to teleworker, supervisor, and co-located employee interaction. Most research to date has examined ways that perceptions of distance might be reduced (Fonner & Roloff, 2010).

The relationship between teleworkers and their peers and supervisors is critical to understand and requires continuing effort to build and maintain. Relationships that take place over space and time require extra care to accomplish important goals both organizationally and individually. One of the most challenging tasks is to develop ways to legitimize and clarify roles of both remote and co-located employees and to help establish a new paradigm among management regarding the importance of informal communication to both employee satisfaction and important organizational outcomes, such as organizational identification and organizational commitment. Managers must also be prepared to position and sometimes defend the role of remote workers to their co-located peers, who sometimes perceive that their remote colleagues enjoy special privileges. Changing such perceptions will also help promote trusting coworker relationships within which all employees feel free to communicate informally about concerns.

More research on coworker relationship quality and on specific types of informal communication will provide future guidance on specific methods for meeting interpersonal needs of both teleworkers and their central office peers. Interpersonal trust and liking in specific relationships appear to have structuring qualities that affect individual employees' organizational experiences, and these structuring qualities are yet to be completely understood. Findings on teleworker feelings of inclusion and exclusion and the relationship between these feelings and organizational identification further suggest that recognition of teleworkers' contributions at the organizational level (e.g., publishing results achieved or ideas presented by teleworkers in a company newsletter) may help build teleworkers' sense of belonging. More research on specific message features and talk types that may be closely associated with teleworkers feelings of inclusion and exclusion will also help guide efforts to strengthen organizational identification, organizational commitment, and job satisfaction and to build relationships.

With recent data to support the importance of coworker relationships and informal communication for teleworkers and their organizations, the argument for training managers in how to encourage peer liking and trust, and how to develop opportunities for the kinds of informal talk identified here, is compelling. These results point to a need to move from casting as insignificant informal talk and friendships at work to committing resources to their practice and development and for shifting existing mindsets from a focus on formal communication and recognition programs to a more holistic perspective that considers employees' relationship and communication needs.

Communication scholars should provide results of their work to practitioners in a way that underscores the interdependence of communication processes and individual and organizational outcomes such that appropriate resources will be devoted to issues of informal as well as formal communication. Practitioners have suggested that teleworkers participate more in face-to-face meetings, chat rooms, and other online arenas (Jacobs, 2008), but the effectiveness of these recommendations has not yet been tested. Teleworkers and co-located employees may also be exposed to a conception of boundaries that gives everyone a higher degree of control in managing interpersonal processes such as impressions and identities; Panteli (2003) argued that such boundaries in virtual organizations should be dynamic and actively defined by the people in the context themselves.

Efforts to foster relationships and a sense of belonging must be well-informed and based on needs articulated by teleworkers and co-located peers and managers. An article in the *Wall Street Journal* includes a description of CUNA Mutual's practices designed to bridge the physical distance between teleworkers, who comprise 36% of its workforce. In comment posts that followed, teleworkers expressed a need to connect more fully than a one-dimensional virtual party allows. Such assessments tend to boil down to authenticity—that is, efforts to help teleworkers and their co-located colleagues interact and develop relationships must be perceived as "real" or sincere if anyone is to benefit from them.

Teleworker relationships do not have to be any more problematic than any other workplace relationships. Indeed, the very distance that is associated with relational challenges is sometimes sought when dealing with difficult coworkers who are proximally located. Although it is possible that telework may appeal more to people who prefer to be alone, most employees who work remotely still have to interact with others to do their jobs and welcome that interaction, and, for some, working remotely may not be their choice.

As technology continues to advance and new ways of managing work processes enable higher levels of productivity, the physical challenges of teleworking have also continued to improve. But the human elements of interpersonal relationships and interaction, whether work-related or social, will be ongoing and essential challenges to address.

References

Aichholzer, G. (1998). A social innovation in its infancy. In P. Jackson & J. M. van der Wielen (Eds.), *Teleworking: International perspectives* (pp. 292–302). London, England: Routledge.

Albrecht, T. L., Burleson, B. R., & Goldsmith, D. (1994). Supportive communication. In M. L. Knapp & G. R. Miller (Eds.), *Handbook of interpersonal communication* (pp. 419–449). Thousand Oaks, CA: Sage.

Ballard, D. I., & Gossett, L. M. (2007). Alternative times: Temporal perceptions, processes, and practices defining the nonstandard work relationship. In C. S. Beck (Ed.), *Communication yearbook 31* (pp. 274–320). Mahwah, NJ: Lawrence Erlbaum.

Baltes, B. B., Dickson, M. W., Sherman, M. P., Bauer, C. C., & LaGanke, J. S. (2002). Computer-mediated communication and group decision-making: A meta-analysis. *Organizational Behavior and Human Decision Processes, 87*, 156–179.

Baruch, Y. (2000). Teleworking: Benefits and pitfalls as perceived by professionals and managers. *New Technology, Work and Employment, 15*, 34–50.

Bimber, B. (1998). The internet and political transformation: Populism, community, and accelerated pluralism. *Polity, XXXI* (1), 133–160.

Blau, P. (2000). The structure of social associations. In J. Fargaris (Ed.), *Readings in social theory* (pp. 297–310). Boston, MA: McGraw-Hill.

Bradac, J. J. (2001). Theory comparison: Uncertainty reduction, problematic integration, uncertainty management and other curious constructs. *Journal of Communication, 51*, 459–475.

Brocklehurst, M. (2001). Power, identity and new technology homework: Implications for "new forms" of organizing. *Organization Studies, 22*, 445–466.

Dahlin, E., Kelly, E., & Moen, P. (2008). Is work the new neighborhood? Social ties in the workplace, family, and neighborhood. *Sociological Quarterly, 49*, 719–736.

DeSanctis, G., & Monge, P. (1998). Communication processes for virtual organizations. *Journal of Computer-Mediated Communication, 3*, 1–23.

Eisenberg, E. M., & Riley, P. (2001). Organizational culture. In F. M. Jablin & L. L. Putnam (Eds.), *The new handbook of organizational communication: Advances in theory, research, and methods*

(pp. 291–322). Thousand Oaks, CA: Sage.
Ellison, N. B. (1999). Social impacts: New perspectives on telework. *Social Science Computer Review, 17*, 338–356.
Fay, M. J. (2007). *Informal communication practices between peers in the remote work context* (Doctoral dissertation). Available from Dissertation Abstracts International. (UMI No. AA13246110)
Fay, M. J. (2011). Informal communication of coworkers: A thematic analysis of messages. *Qualitative Research in Organizations and Management, 6*, 212–229.
Fay, M. J., & Kline, S. L. (2011). Coworker relationships in high-intensity telecommuting. *Journal of Applied Communication Research, 39*, 144–163.
Fay, M. J., & Kline, S. L. (2012). The influence of informal communication on organizational identification and commitment in the context of high-intensity telecommuting. *Southern Communication Journal, 77*, 61–76.
Feldman, M. S., & March, J. G. (1981). Information in organizations as signal and symbol. *Administrative Science Quarterly, 26*, 171–187.
Feldman, M. S., & Rafaeli, A. (2002). Organizational routines as sources of connections and understandings. *Journal of Management Studies, 39*, 309–323.
Fonner, K. L., & Roloff, M. E. (2010). Why teleworkers are more satisfied with their jobs than are office-based workers: When less contact is beneficial. *Journal of Applied Communication Research, 38*, 336–361.
Fritz, J. M. H., & Omdahl, B. L. (2006). Reduced job satisfaction, diminished commitment, and workplace cynicism as outcomes of negative work relationships. In J. M. H. Fritz & B. L. Omdahl (Eds.), *Problematic relationships in the workplace* (pp. 131–151). New York, NY: Peter Lang.
Gainey, T. W., Kelley, D. E., & Hill, J. A. (1999). Telecommuting's impact on corporate culture and individual workers: Examining the effect of employee isolation. *SAM Advanced Management Journal, 64*(4), 4–10.
Gajendran, R. S., & Harrison, D. A. (2007). The good, the bad, and the unknown about telecommuting: Meta-analysis of psychological mediators and individual consequences. *Journal of Applied Psychology, 92*, 1524–1541.
Goffman, E. (1959). *The presentation of self in everyday life*. London, England: Penguin.
Golden, T. D. (2007). Coworkers who telework and the impact on those in the office: Understanding the implications of virtual work for coworker satisfaction and turnover intentions. *Human Relations, 60*, 1641–1667.
Golden, T. D., Barnes-Farrell, J. L., & Mascharka, P. B. (2009). Implications of virtual management for subordinate performance appraisals: A pair of simulation studies. *Journal of Applied Social Psychology, 39*, 1589–1608.
Gossett, L. M., & Tompkins, P. K. (2001). Community as a means of organizational control. In G. Shepherd & E. W. Rothenbuhler (Eds.), *Communication and community* (pp. 111–133). Mahwah, NJ: Lawrence Erlbaum.
Hancock, J., & Dunham, P. (2001). Impression formation in computer-mediated communication revisited: An analysis of the breadth and intensity of impressions. *Communication Research, 28*, 325–347.
Hartman, R. C., Stoner, C. R., & Arora, R. (1992). Developing successful organizational telecommuting arrangements: Worker perceptions and managerial prescriptions. *SAM*

Advanced Management Journal, 57(3), 35–42.
Hess, J. A. (2009). Distancing from problematic coworkers. In J. M. H. Fritz & B. L. Omdahl (Eds.), Problematic relationships in the workplace (pp. 205–232). New York, NY: Peter Lang.
Hill, E. J., Hawkins, A., & Miller, B. (1996). Work and family ties in the virtual office: Perceived influence of mobile telework. Family Relations, 45, 293–301.
Holmes, J. (2000). Victoria University's language in the workplace project: An overview (Language in the Workplace Occasional Papers). Wellington, New Zealand: Victoria University. http://www.victoria.ac.nz/luls/lwp/docs/ops/op.htm
Hylmo, A. (2006). Telecommuting and the contestability of choice: Employee strategies to legitimize personal decisions to work in a preferred location. Management Communication Quarterly, 19, 541–569.
Hylmo, A., & Buzzanell, P. M. (2002). Telecommuting as viewed through cultural lenses: An empirical investigation of the discourses of utopia, identity, and mystery. Communication Monographs, 69, 329–356.
Jacobs, G. (2008). Constructing corporate commitment amongst remote employees. Corporate Communications: An International Journal, 13, 42–55.
Jarvenpaa, S. L., & Leidner, D. E. (1999). Communication and trust in virtual teams. Organization Science, 10, 791–815.
Knoke, D. (1999). Organizational networks and corporate social capital. In R. Leenders & S. Gabbay (Eds.), Corporate social capital and liability (pp. 17–42). Boston, MA: Kluwer Academic.
Leonardi, P. M., Treem, J. W., & Jackson, M. H. (2010). The connectivity paradox: Using technology to both decrease and increase perceptions of distance in distributed work arrangements. Journal of Applied Communication Research, 38, 85–105.
Mallia, K. L., & Ferris, S. P. (2000). Telework: A consideration of its impact on individuals and organizations. Electronic Journal of Communication, 10, 1–12.
Marshall, G. W., Michaels, C. E., & Mulki, J. P. (2007). Workplace isolation: Exploring the construct and its measurements. Psychology & Marketing, 24, 195–223.
McDonald, P., Bradley, L., & Brown, K. (2008). Visibility in the workplace: Still an essential ingredient for career success? The International Journal of Human Resource Management, 19, 2198–2215.
McManus, S. E., & Russell, J. E. A. (2007). Peer mentoring relationships. In B. R. Ragins & K. E. Kram (Eds.), The handbook of mentoring at work: Theory, research, and practice (pp. 273–298). Thousand Oaks, CA: Sage.
Morgan, S. J., & Symon, G. (2002). Computer-mediated communication and remote management. Social Science Computer Review, 20, 302–311.
Nie, N. (2001). Sociability, interpersonal relations and the internet. American Behavioral Scientist, 45, 420–435.
Olson, M. H. (1987). Telework: Practical experience and future prospects. In R. E. Kraut (Ed.), Technology and the transformation of white collar work (pp. 135–152). Hillsdale, NJ: Lawrence Erlbaum.
Omdahl, B. L., & Fritz, J. M. H. (2006). Stress, burnout, and impaired mental health: Consequences of problematic work relationships. In J. M. H. Fritz & B. L. Omdahl (Eds.), Problematic relationships in the workplace (pp. 109–130). New York, NY: Peter Lang.

Panteli, N. (2003). Virtual interactions: Creating impressions of boundaries. In N. Paulsen & T. Hernes (Eds.), *Managing boundaries in organizations: Multiple perspectives* (pp. 76–92). New York, NY: Macmillan.
Parks, M. R., & Floyd, K. (1996). Making friends in cyberspace. *Journal of Communication, 46*, 80–97.
Qvortrup, L. (1998). From teleworking to networking: Definitions and trends. In P. Jackson & J. M. van der Wielen (Eds.), *Teleworking: International perspectives* (pp. 21–29). London, England: Routledge.
Reinsch, Jr., N. L. (1997). Relationships between telecommuting workers and their managers: An exploratory study. *Journal of Business Communication, 34*, 343–369.
Reinsch, N. L. (1999). Selected communication variables and telecommuting participation decisions: Data from telecommuting workers. *Journal of Business Communication, 36*, 247–254.
Robichaud, D., Giroux, H., & Taylor, J. R. (2004). The metaconversation: The recursive property of language as a key to organizing. *Academy of Management Review, 29*, 617–634.
Roloff, M., & Anastasiou, L. (2001). Interpersonal communication research: An overview. In W. B. Gundykunst (Ed.), *Communication yearbook 24* (pp. 51–70). Thousand Oaks, CA: Sage.
Rosenfeld, L. B., Richman, J. M., & May, S. K. (2004). Information adequacy, job satisfaction and organizational culture in a dispersed-network organization. *Journal of Applied Communication Research, 32*, 28–54.
Sias, P. M. (2009). *Organizing relationships: Traditional and emerging perspectives on workplace relationships*. Thousand Oaks, CA: Sage.
Sias, P. M., & Cahill, D. J. (1998). From coworkers to friends: The development of peer relationships in the workplace. *Western Journal of Commmunication, 62*, 273–299.
Sias, P. M., & Perry, T. (2004). Disengaging from workplace relationships: A research note. *Human Communication Research, 30*, 589–602.
Sproull, L., & Kiesler, S. (1986). Reducing social context cues: Electronic mail in organizational communications. *Management Science, 32*, 1492–1512.
Stafford, L., Kline, S. L., & Dimmick, J. (1999). Home e-mail: Relational maintenance and gratification opportunities. *Journal of Broadcasting & Electronic Media, 43*, 659–669.
Tanis, M., & Postmes, T. (2003). Social cues and impression formation in CMC. *Journal of Communication, 53*, 676–693.
Thatcher, S. M., & Zhu, X. (2006). Changing identities in a changing workplace: Identification, identity enactment, self-verification, and telecommuting. *Academy of Management Review, 31*, 1076–1088.
Tietze, S., & Musson, G. (2010). Identity, identity work, and the experience of working from home. *Journal of Management Development, 29*, 148–156.
Tretheway, A., & Corman, S. R. (2001). Anticipating K-Commerce. *Management Communication Quarterly, 14*, 619–628.
Waldron, V. (2003). Relationship maintenance in organizational settings. In D. J. Canary & M. Dainton (Eds.), *Maintaining relationships through communication: Relational, contextual, and cultural variations* (pp. 163–184). Mahwah, NJ: Lawrence Erlbaum.
Walther, J. B. (1996). Computer-mediated commuication: Impersonal, interpersonal and hyper-

personal interaction. *Communication Research, 23,* 3–43.
Weick, K. E., & Ashford, S. J. (2001). Learning in organizations. In F. M. Jablin & L. L. Putnam (Eds.), *The new handbook of organizational communication: Advances in theory, research, and methods* (pp. 704–731). Thousand Oaks, CA: Sage.
Wiesenfeld, B. M., Raghuram, S., & Garud, R. (2001). Organizational identification among virtual workers: The role of need for affiliation and perceived work-based social support. *Journal of Management, 27,* 213–229.
Winstead, B. A., Derlega, V. J., Montgomery, M. J., & Pilkington, C. (1995). The quality of friendships at work and job satisfaction. *Journal of Social and Personal Relationships, 12,* 199–215.
WorldatWork. (2011). Telework 2011: A special report from WorldatWork. Retrieved from http://www.worldatwork.org/waw/adimLink?id=53034

· 8 ·

THE BUREAUCRAT AS PROBLEMATIC OTHER

Arendt's Warning

RONALD C. ARNETT

> But the concern about levelling, the end of heroism, of greatness, has also been turned into a fierce denunciation of the modern moral order, and everything it stands for, as we see with Nietzsche. Attempts to build a polity around a rival notion of order in the very heart of modern civilization, most notably the various forms of fascism and related authoritarianism, have failed. But the continued popularity of Nietzsche shows that his devastating critique still speaks to many people today. The modern order, though entrenched—perhaps even because entrenched—still awakens much resistance. (Taylor, 2007, p. 185)

The bureaucrat is the key character type in contemporary organizational life. This essay follows the lead of Hannah Arendt in her deconstruction of this central role within modernity. This essay explores taken-for-granted problematic communicative practices forming the moral topology of organizations. Working within a critical framework established by Hannah Arendt (1906–1975), I join this conversation about "troublesome others" (Fritz, 2002) with a communication description of the bureaucrat as a "problematic Other." I link the terms "bureaucrat" and "problematic Other" in an intentionally depreciatory fashion, following Arendt's lead. She named the bureaucrat as the problematic character within modernity, a role that functions in a stealth-like fashion, socially cloaked and simultaneously immersed in practices that give definition to the "banality of evil" (Arendt, 1963/2006). This essay revisits Arendt's pejorative deconstruction of this modern role of the bureaucrat.

Introduction

This essay underscores the all-too-often dangerous consequences of communicative practices exhibited by the bureaucrat, who exemplifies a lack of rootedness and connection to a given place or set of practices. Arendt's (1963/2006) legendary derogatory description of this role fills the pages of one of her most controversial books, *Eichmann in Jerusalem: A Report on the Banality of Evil*, where her principal target was not Eichmann but rather the role of the modern bureaucrat. Arendt detailed the communicative attributes of the bureaucrat, framing this role as a modern negative icon that offers one of the identifying, and mistaken, coordinates of modernity. She underscores the bureaucrat as a problematic Other engaged in communicative practices that take place within the shadows of responsibility; the actions are sustained by routine communicative machinations and by the cunning of blame, shifting responsibility for mistakes to another. Following Arendt's negative portrayal, this essay unmasks the modus operandi of the bureaucrat, which consists of communicative practices that eschew responsibility and hide the perpetrator behind processes and procedures that influence the lives of many. The stealth nature of these communicative actions too often makes them unnoticed, untraceable, devoid of personal fingerprints—yet of significant consequence for many who are under their supposed "care."

This deconstructive portrait consists of four sections, each offering an impressionistic picture of a single central thesis—the bureaucrat is an archetype for communicative practices that nourish a "banality of evil" (Arendt, 1963/2006). First, "Arendt's Project—Banality and Modernity" outlines the principal object of her criticism, modernity, with the bureaucrat playing a central role in this drama. Second, I examine background nutrients that give rise to the "Soil for the Problematic Other," examining the communicative background that permits bureaucratic action to garner support with little challenge. Third, I turn to "Arendt's Argument," centered on Eichmann as an exemplar of the danger of bureaucratic communicative practices in action. In Arendt's (1963/2006) *Eichmann in Jerusalem: A Report on the Banality of Evil*, she interprets and reports otherwise than expected; instead of focusing on Eichmann, she underscores the role of the bureaucrat as the heartbeat of growth and strength in modernity's war against human connection and roots. The final section of this essay, "Ignored Learning," examines the consequences of ignoring Arendt's warning about communicative practices void of personal responsibility.

Arendt's project connects the role of the bureaucrat with career advancement rather than concern for a given task, a set of labor practices, or a community of persons. The communicative practices of the bureaucrat give rise to a narrow and limited world marked by concern about consequences tied solely to personal advancement. This pejorative retelling of Arendt's essay stresses the vital importance of one's particular communicative focus of attention—that which gathers our attention matters. We are shaped by the focus of our attention and the practices that constitute our daily lives. Arendt offers a harsh critique. She would have agreed with my father, a decorated military veteran. He had a succinct way of describing how one should pick out a friend—find someone you would trust to protect your back in a foxhole under fire. The bureaucrat did not fool my father, the owner of a small company that never employed more than two workers at a given time. To protect himself, his friends, and his country, my father would not have issued an invitation to a bureaucrat to join him in the foxhole when under fire.

Arendt's Project—Banality and Modernity

This essay follows Arendt's negative assessment of the bureaucrat and relies upon a fuller treatment of Arendt's deconstructive engagement with modernity. Before I commence further, I must offer a warning. The bureaucrat's particular manner—self-obsession related to career advancement—is void of sincere consideration for the institution, individual, and environment that makes a meaningful livelihood possible. However, it is important not to confuse this negative rendering of the term "bureaucrat" with leadership and managers who caringly attend to institutions, people, and the local and larger environment that nourishes a given place. Leaders meet the unexpected and the bureaucrat's sanctioned commonality.

I frame Arendt's contentious battle in *Communication Ethics in Dark Times: Hannah Arendt's Rhetoric of Warning and Hope* (Arnett, in press). In that work, I define Arendt's lifelong project as a deconstruction of modernity, asserting that modernity lives by coordinates that put one's faith in the routine of method and process. Arendt rejected the optimism of modernity and its fascination with progress. Modernity embraces the myth that one can stand above sociality and the ties of community. Modernity invites us to assume a nomad-like existence that takes us into a world of "existential homelessness" (Arnett, 1994).

I contend that there is a secular trinity that sustains modernity composed of efficiency, individual autonomy, and progress. This sacred set of coordinates entices us to remove the ground from under our feet. We are falsely convinced that genuine roots are not necessary as we adopt these abstract assurances: (1)

efficiency, which misses the unscripted creativity and give and take of real living; (2) individual autonomy, which attempts to forgo the burden and the joy of community and sociality with others; and (3) progress, which embraces "bad faith" of lying to ourselves (Sartre, 1943/1957, p. 48), missing the reality of crooked lines that define a life. Existence in today's world reminds us that these coordinates cannot be trusted long term. Both Eric Voegelin (1901–1985; 1956) and Kenneth Burke (1897–1993; 1941/1973) repeatedly stated that existence cannot be ignored. Just ask someone who is part of the Occupy Wall Street Movement (2011–present), someone unemployed for over a year, a family unable to pay the mortgage, or employees whose company just moved to another city, state, or country without them. When existence attacks the fantasies of our time, the mythology of modernity begins to appear as an upper class lie offered as an "opium of the people" (Marx, 1927/1982, p. 131). To those suffering, modernity resembles "dark times" (Arendt, 1955/1995). Ironically, this conception of darkness emerges from modernity's love of artificial light that eclipses both genuine darkness and authentic light.

Modernity does not elicit genuine light. Witness, for example, commercial enterprises like Motel 6 portraying themselves as someone's familial home, offering artificial light—"We'll leave the light on for you." Artificial light confuses; it makes use of words in such a manner that their original semiotic implications are lost, robbing us of authentic meaning—leaving us with slogans clothed in crass banality. Arendt's project unmasked banality; she exposed problematic taken-for-granted assumptions of commonplace routines that constitute modernity.

Within any modern human community, there is, all too often, a temptation to confuse genuine light with artificial light. We use words like community, friend, and love ever so glibly, forgetting profound differences between those terms and words such as aggregate, acquaintance, and liking. In everyday discourse, we lose the semantic distinctions between complex and difficult, lazy and bored, and leisure and recreation (Holba, 2007); these everyday acts of discursive banality are cloaked within the facileness of taking terms as synonymous when to do so ignores important distinctions. Not noticing dissimilarities between the genuine and the contrived results in placing trust in artificial light, a phoniness that disconnects word from deed and attacks the human spirit, giving rise to unadulterated darkness that is ultimately more devastating to the human condition than the natural absence of light. Arendt sought to counter a banality of artificial optics that blinds us, making it difficult, if not impossible, to distinguish between ground that supports us and quicksand that can claim a life—artificial light engenders darkness.

There have been only 17 total eclipses of the sun visible in the United States since 1851. It has been 21 years since our last total solar eclipse, which was only visible in parts of Hawaii, and 45 years since there was one observed by the continental states. Another is not anticipated until August 21, 2017. According to B. Ralph Chou of the School of Optometry at the University of Waterloo, "The only time that the Sun can be viewed safely with the naked eye is during a total eclipse" (1997, p. 19). Total solar eclipses, however, are rare. One painful fact about the more frequent partial and annular eclipses is that if one gazes at them directly, the result can be dreadful eye damage. The threat of improper viewing of eclipses is significant not only because it can cause "'eclipse blindness' or retinal burns" but also because the eyes become damaged without the viewer feeling anything due to a lack of pain receptors in the retina (Chou, 1997, p. 19). Modernity is like a partial eclipse; its fascination brings injury and suffering in the long run, with the immediate moment being one of interest and assurance. The tragedy of the artificial light of modernity is that it is akin to an eclipse that captivates our attention without our knowledge of its danger. Such light is seductive, this faux light, just as an eclipse brings damage by falsifying the reality of genuine darkness.

Soil for the Problematic Other

The soil that nourishes the problematic Other via the role of the bureaucrat is announced by Alexis de Tocqueville (1805–1859); he offers a warning to early Americans about the dangers of "individualism." Arendt writes about Tocqueville in at least nine of her books. Tocqueville's (1835/1963a, 1840/1963b) *Democracy in America* is known for the dialectical definition of the American Dream, which includes both individual achievement and concern for the community. Tocqueville (1840/1963b) was the first to coin the term "individualism" (p. 98), which he distinguished from selfishness; Tocqueville considered selfishness much more likely to benefit the human condition than the notion of individualism. I contend that the soil for the problematic Other comes from the development of individualism[1]—what I consider the fundamental sin of the West.

The connection of the bureaucrat with individualism seems counterintuitive. The common link is rootlessness, which permits the bureaucrat to become forgetful of institutions. At first blush, one ponders an obvious point of disconnection—"Is not the bureaucrat synonymous with institutions?" The answer is "no" in the larger sense, and the answer is "yes" to those accepting the premises of modern institutions that disavow roots, connections, ties, and loyalty to local soil.

Individualism, as a myth about the possibility of disconnecting from others, makes the communicative practices of the bureaucrat inevitable. The bureaucrat is the modern organization's extension of individualistic communicative practices, cloaked by official detachment from the roots of a given place. Individualism is a modern manifestation of earlier historical efforts at discounting practices of a local place. Conquerors have historically disregarded their subjugated prey. What is novel about modernity is the overlooking of the significance of a particular place, making organizational identity problematic.

Tocqueville's individualism was offered as a warning about the desire to stand above social restraints, attempting to rise above the hubbub of human sociality. A culture defined by obsession with self-advancement with little attachment to genuine roots of a place and a people required an official role that sanctioned lack of care about others. Such a role depends upon a modern individualist myth in which attachment is disavowed; the goal of such a role is to be objective and remain untouched, beyond all human associations, constraints, and burdens, while seeking to achieve individually.

This desire to rise above all human connections, no longer limited by the needs and hopes of another, leads the bureaucrat into an official modern role that carries out the sin of individualism in a manner that generally goes undetected and is officially sanctioned. As stated earlier, it is the stealth-like character of the bureaucrat, who disregards all close acquaintances unless they functionally benefit a career, that permits this role to be worthy of Arendt's (1963/2006) deconstructive label, the "banality of evil." Individualism gives rise to a modern official role that mechanically attaches people and operations without being attached to or with the local soil of a particular organization and its surrounding commitments.

The soil for the problematic Other in the role of the bureaucrat is not only nourished by individualism but fertilized by monad-like disregard for others. Negative nutrients are added to this soil that refuses to nourish roots through self-absorption, self-advancement, and self-protection. In each case, the concerns of the Other and the environment of a given place are ignored and quietly abused as one seeks to discount concern for the welfare of anyone other than oneself. The soil is tilled with a benign neglect of others through abuse of community, forgetfulness of institutions, and rejection of human roots.

Abuse of community is played out in the appearance of belonging without any real investment in concern for the growth of a given place and the human beings who are dependent upon that community for part of their sense of meaning and purpose. This self-serving view of community was the negative thesis in *Communication and Community: Implications of Martin Buber's Dialogue* (Arnett, 1986), where I discussed persons who do not contribute to a community but rather use the community with a single-minded objective—tapping the resources of the community for their own personal good. These persons are members of a community without any investment in anyone or anything beyond themselves. This soil does not give support to a person of service but rather offers shelter for a self-protective user of the community. As Bellah, Madsen, Sullivan, Swidler, and Tipton (1991) stated in *The Good Society*, we need to reclaim our commitment to institutions; they are the carriers of much of the meaning of our lives. The soil of a problematic Other without roots of sociality provides a fulcrum point for institutional forgetfulness. The dwelling is unimportant unless participation there offers career advantage.

Rejection of human roots is a principal definition of the modern project of individual autonomy, efficiency, and progress (Arnett, in press). Both MacIntyre (1981) and Bellah et al. (1991) described the role of bureaucrat as a weak substitute who tries to stand in for the loss of traditional characters who defined a different historical moment tied to a craftsman and a gray collar worker/owner. Instead, we discover power within the hands of characters that find pride in not getting their hands dirty, literally and figuratively.

The bureaucrat, understood as a problematic Other, gives shape to communication practices that constitute the identity and the character of a historical juncture termed modernity, a central conceptual foe in Arendt's scholarly life. Arendt deconstructed the surreptitiousness and cold-blooded calculation of the bureaucrat. I now turn directly to Hannah Arendt's pejorative argument against the bureaucrat, an exemplar of modernity's unexamined characters and practices of disconnection.

Arendt's Argument

Without question, the most controversial book of Hannah Arendt's career was *Eichmann in Jerusalem: A Report on the Banality of Evil* (Arendt, 1963/2006; Benhabib, 2000). This work continues to attract critics who question Arendt's objective in writing the Eichmann book (McHale & Stevenson, 2006, p. 162; see also Foer, 2011). With genuine wonder, opponents aggressively pose the question, "What did she think she was doing?" Arendt is no longer here for us to ask, and I am wary of speculating about "authorial intent" (Arnett, Fritz, & Holba, 2007, p. 118). I do, however, have a hermeneutic thesis, a determined conviction about Arendt's larger project; she sought to warn the West about the dangers of modernity—ideas and practices that disconnect us from one another in a manner that invites no thoughtful reflection. The precepts of modernity often go unquestioned because at face value, they simply look banal, so common that they could do no harm. However, for Arendt (1963/2006), extreme commonness when associated with modernity is better understood as a cluster of unexamined assumptions and practices that give rise to a "banality of evil." Arendt's assertive position against modernity displays her rationale and determination for not wanting to attribute all evil to a single man, Eichmann. In my retelling of Arendt's condemnation of the bureaucrat, I underscore the metaphors she used to describe the role of the bureaucrat and Eichmann as a representative. Additionally, I render direct quotes that provide an imaginative vision of Arendt's disgust for the role and her contention that there are grave dangers invited by a culture when the rootless are the empowered decision makers.

The role of bureaucrat permitted Eichmann to hide from responsibility while he simultaneously tried to take credit for actions that were outside of his domain of influence. The worst grievance was his defense. He sent millions to their death while he cited the obligation of "duty." Eichmann felt pride in his manipulations of the Jewish population he supervised (Arendt, 1963/2006, p. 135).

> He did his *duty*, as he told the police and the court over and over again; he not only obeyed *orders*, he also obeyed the *law*. Eichmann had a muddled inkling that this could be an important distinction, but neither the defense nor the judges ever took him up on it. The well-worn coins of "superior orders" versus "acts of state" were handed back and forth; they had governed the whole discussion of these matters during the Nuremberg Trials....(Arendt, 1963/2006, p. 135)

Eichmann was fond of citing Kant, over and over, about the necessity of duty. This constant referencing was both philosophically and pragmatically inaccurate (Arendt, 1963/2006, pp. 135–136). Kant's understanding of duty is in direct opposition to the practice of "blind obedience" (Arendt, 1963/2006, p. 136). Eichmann's confused understanding of duty placed blind obedience higher than the obligation and responsibility to make personal judgments (Arendt, 1963/2006, p. 137). In what Arendt understood as a caricature role of the problematic nature of the bureaucrat, Eichmann simply followed personal sentiments of career advancement. The rootless nature of the role of bureaucrat makes the office a parody—a warning sign which suggests that the banality of evil in modernity has a communicative agent.

Arendt's (1963/2006) *Eichmann in Jerusalem: A Report on the Banality of Evil* framed her case against the bureaucrat nearly fifty years ago. In fact, I argue that we have actually expanded the bureaucratic communicative practices that offer self-defense into public spheres of controversy where the self-serving objective is single-minded—remove oneself from the realm of responsibility and find another to blame.[2]

As Arendt covered the Eichmann trial, she recorded not just Eichmann's communicative gestures but, more specifically and generally, the problematic nature of communicative practices associated with the role of the bureaucrat. Amos Elon wrote the introduction to *Eichmann in Jerusalem: A Report on the Banality of Evil*. The title of his leading essay indicates the powerful negative reaction to the book—"The Excommunication of Hannah Arendt." The first page discusses the story of Isaiah Berlin getting out-of-control angry whenever he discussed Arendt or her book; the problem was that he had not read the book (Elon, 2006, p. vii). Elonthen stated Arendt's thesis: "Eichmann's alleged banality was the main reason the book provoked such a storm. Most people still assumed that murder was committed by monsters or demons" (Elon, 2006, p. xiv). One need not use standpoint theory to understand a portion of the anger aroused in the Jewish community. Good people reacted to Arendt's finished product as a betrayal of the Jewish population. One can make a case that this book was not Arendt's finest moment in terms of sensitivity to persons. Yet, on the other hand, in Arendt's defense, she was on a mission to deconstruct the foundation that made this horrible era possible; she sought to unmask modernity itself. Arendt, knowingly or otherwise, removed Eichmann from the center and placed the notion of bureaucrat at center stage long before many could understand the "why" of her story. At that juncture in modernity, when those alive felt enormous responsibility to witness for the dead, there was a legitimate demand for revenge, punishment, and justice. However, Arendt discovered a greater evil within modernity itself:

> Her private letters from Jerusalem enable us to trace the slow development of her thesis. She plowed through the 3,000-page transcript of Eichmann's pretrial interrogation by the Israeli police captain Avner Less and gradually came to think that it was mostly, as she first put it, a kind of brainlessness on Eichmann's part that had predisposed him to becoming the faceless bureaucrat of death and one of the worst criminals of all time. (Elon, 2006, p. xiii)

Arendt's target became the face of modernity, with the faceless bureaucrat functioning as one exemplar of modernity in action.

A description of Eichmann begins Arendt's story. She informs her readers about an ordinary man who used a position for personal gain that resulted in great evil. She unmasks him—painting a picture of a pathetic creature.

> Justice insists on the importance of Adolf Eichmann, son of Karl Adolf Eichmann, the man in the glass booth built for his protection: medium-sized, slender, middle-aged, with receding hair, ill-fitting teeth, and nearsighted eyes, who throughout the trial keeps craning his scraggy neck toward the bench (not once does he face the audience)....(Arendt, 1963/2006, p. 5)

Arendt's suggestion is that justice is tied to the trial of a man, but her description intends to remind us of a basic fact—pathetic little men can hide within the role of the bureaucrat and inflict great harm and suffering.

Eichmann's defense was simple—it "was his duty to obey" (Arendt, 1963/2006, p. 21). This line of defense defines the bureaucrat, who uses allegiance to an organization or a government as a shield to cover an intense commitment to self-promotion. The psychiatrists, about a dozen, all testified in agreement to one basic fact—Eichmann was not insane. Arendt informs the reader of the details of Eichmann's unemployment, dependence upon others for a job, and desire for relationships of convenience. He "gave the impression of a typical member of the lower middle classes, and this impression was more than borne out by every sentence he spoke or wrote while in prison" (Arendt, 1963/2006, p. 31). Eichmann was actually a member of the middle class; the performativity aspects of his life led him to degenerate in social status. Arendt (1963/2006) described Eichmann as a man without a vision, a man without a life before him; he even viewed himself as living a "leaderless" life (p. 32). Yet, it was clear in Eichmann's telling of his own story that he was "ambitious" (Arendt, 1963/2006, p. 33). With this combination of a leaderless life and raw ambition, Eichmann announced his own formation, which molded him into the role of bureaucrat. Also, Eichmann's own story often used the phrase "bored to distraction" (Arendt, 1963/2006, p. 35). Eichmann understood his life as a consumer, not a producer; he viewed excitement and meaning as the task of existence, not his own responsibility. He wanted joy to be given to him, not found in the meaningful roots of work and interaction with others. Eichmann moved from one job to another when he was bored. Without roots or commitments to make each day worthy of work and labor, he looked to others for excitement. One is bored whenever others are no longer able to provide the necessary stimulation for a life; such a life uses others.

Eichmann stumbled into his role with supervision of the "Jewish Question" (Arendt, 1963/2006, p. 40). He did so because he had one gift—the ability to "organize" and "negotiate" (Arendt, 1963/2006, p. 45). Perhaps the skill of negotiation comes from lack of attachment to anything except one's own advancement:

> Eichmann was troubled by no questions of conscience. His thoughts were entirely taken up with the staggering job of organization and administration in the midst not only of a world war but, more important for him, of innumerable intrigues and fights over spheres of authority among the various State and Party offices that were busy "solving the Jewish question." (Arendt, 1963/2006, p. 151)

Arendt (1963/2006) repeatedly stated that the personal vice that defined him was "bragging" about himself (p. 46).

What propels the impulse to brag? Arendt stated that he actually made the case against himself as he bragged about decisions and responsibilities that were beyond his scope of influence:

> His role in the Final Solution, it now turned out, had been wildly exaggerated—partly because of his own boasting, partly because the defendants at Nuremberg and in other postwar trials had tried to exculpate themselves at his expense.... (Arendt, 1963/2006, p. 210)

Eichmann personified the hope of bureaucrats—for all "opponents [to] disappear in silent anonymity" (Arendt, 1963/2006, p. 232). An enemy is anyone getting in the way of one's advancement. Therefore, as Eichmann hid away in Argentina, he made no contact with his family or wife. His wife was in Germany, "penniless"; the actions registered loudly about who mattered and the hope of self-preservation to the point of using personal secrecy with the objective of hiding from the consequences of his own actions. This communicative practice of blaming is at the center of the bureaucratic ethic—take credit, but if something goes wrong, find another to bear the fault and the penalties. One might speculate that the use of such communicative practices makes it unlikely that accomplishment is appropriately attributed. Eichmann personified the bureaucrat in his consistent display of "bad memory" unless there was a direct benefit in the memory (Arendt, 1963/2006, p. 49). "Eichmann's memory functioned only in respect to things that had had a direct bearing upon his career" (Arendt, 1963/2006, p. 62). The other side of bragging brought defensiveness; Eichmann claimed that all mistakes were those made by others:

> Thus, confronted for eight months with the reality of being examined by a Jewish policeman, Eichmann did not have the slightest hesitation in explaining to him at considerable length, and repeatedly, why he had been unable to attain a higher grade in the S.S., that this was not his fault. (Arendt, 1963/2006, p. 49)

Arendt (1963/2006) gave us a number of descriptive metaphors that lend insight into Eichmann's functioning as a little man: "undeniable ludicrousness of the man," "clever, calculating liar," "worst clowneries," unknowing "inconsistencies," and conversation riddled with "clichés" (pp. 54–55). This man lacked "taste" and "education" and was in description a "small fry" (Arendt, 1963/2006, p. 145). Without question, Arendt's self-appointed task was to move our imaginations from a monstrous little man to a role that pervades modernity and permits the limited intelligence to do so many wicked acts. She wanted her readers to understand the "ruthless toughness" that the role of the bureaucrat permitted; the actions were largely supported under the sanctuary of an official office (Arendt, 1963/2006, p. 162).

Eichmann was consistently interested in promotions. Between 1937 and 1941, he had four of them. He did what he had to do to gather new responsibilities—this was his real definition of duty. His specialty was the "Jewish Question," and he was the bureaucratic expert. All the concentration camps were under the responsibility of the W.V.H.A., *Wirtschafts-Verwaltungshaumptmt*; only the Theresienstadt camp, in present-day Terezín, Czech Republic, was under the sole control of Eichmann. This camp was the only one for which Eichmann had the kind of power that was attributed to him by others and by himself. The camp was a showcase for the International Red Cross. He ran the camp well; the bureaucrat knows the value of image over the real.

Eichmann was superb at delivering a message that portrayed the organization in a favorable light; his actions worked to cloak truth. His role required him to be the "bearer of secrets" and lies, and he was more than up to the requisites of the task (Arendt, 1963/2006, p. 85). Eichmann covered the intentions of his actions with clichés, "stock phrases," and "catch words"; he was seemingly unable to speak in "ordinary speech" (Arendt, 1963/2006, p. 86). Eichmann also kept himself from seeing too much, as if he shaped his bureaucratic sensibilities with "hear no evil, see no evil, speak no evil," which he legitimized with his perverted view of duty. He never personally witnessed a mass execution; he worked at giving the appearance of clean hands as he zealously assisted the Nazi cause. Eichmann was an energetic, enthusiastic, and self-promoting bureaucrat within a system that had no soul. For instance, toward the end of the war, a female "leader" for the Reich offered "consolation" to some German people who stated that Hitler would not let them suffer and would find a way to gas all the German citizens, keeping them from the domination of an adversary. "Oh, no, I'm not imagining things, this lovely lady is not a mirage, I saw her with my own eyes…" (Arendt, 1963/2006, p. 110). The bureaucratic mentality of self-promotion, cloaked with other language, pervaded the Nazi regime. Arendt stated that the war did not stop the precision of the bureaucratic system; if anything, such rootless precision was enhanced. Eichmann had been "overawed" with the personal benefits of a bureaucratic society (Arendt, 1963/2006, p. 126). In such an environment, Arendt (1963/2006) contended, the bureaucrat, like Eichmann, naturally took on the role of Pontius Pilate (p. 112), of washing one's hands of consequences associated with decisions.

The bureaucrat, however, finds a life of support—the amenities of the job provide a sense of significance:

> The prosecution, though it could not prove that Eichmann had profited financially while on the job, stressed rightly his high standard of living in Budapest, where he could afford to stay at one of the best hotels, was driven around by a chauffeur in an amphibious car, an unforgettable gift from his later enemy Kurt Becher, went hunting and horseback riding, and enjoyed all sorts of previously unknown luxuries under the tutelage of his new friends in the Hungarian government. (Arendt, 1963/2006, pp. 197–198)

The amenities function as visual clichés of life without depth, roots, conviction, or passion for others. In his final moments before being hanged, Eichmann uttered one cliché after another, demonstrating the art of the bureaucrat—the ability to offer copious comments without saying much of value: "It was as though in those last minutes he was summing up the lesson that this long course in human wickedness had taught us—the lesson of the fearsome, word-and-thought-defying *banality of evil*" (Arendt, 1963/2006, p. 252). Arendt ends her disgust with Eichmann and his role by reminding us that obedience and official support are all too often politically isomorphic. To fail to use genuine Kantian judgment that demands accountability for one's own actions makes the earth a place no longer a home for the evader of responsibility. The trial determined that a share of the space on the planet we inhabit should not be allotted to Eichmann for the crimes of self-advancement without concern for the Other. He took human lives to advance his own career. The bureaucratic defense of blind duty permits one to participate in atrocities; such a reality called for Eichmann's removal from the earth—a place in which he really had no genuine roots.

Ignored Learning

This lack of regard for Otherness and disdain for roots makes the role of the bureaucrat a fitting recipient of the problematic Other award in this historical moment. The critical assertions that guided Arendt against the role of the bureaucrat point to communicative practices played out in the realm of career advancement, loyalty to no one but oneself, constant hiding in "red tape," committees, processes, and procedures that protect one from taking personal decision-making responsibilities. As stated earlier, Arendt made a case in *Eichmann in Jerusalem: A Report on the Banality of Evil* (1963) that has been energetically rejected by many (Benhabib, 2000, p. 65). In a 1965 "Postscript," Arendt (1963/2006) informed readers that the controversy surrounding this book began prior to its publication (p. 282). Her response essay was an opportunity to resurrect her warning about the bureaucrat within the West and modernity.

As we enter the second decade of the 21st century, the human landscape within the United States and the West demands a reevaluation of previously held assumptions—we need persons in official roles who assume responsibility for the soil that makes their work and that of so many others possible. For instance, we have countries near bankruptcy, high rates of unemployment, and little confidence in government. Where is the concern for the Other and care for the local soil? In Levinasian (1991/1998) terms, where is justice (p. 19)? Where is the ongoing concern for those not at the table of decision making? The implicit power of the bureaucrat rests within the modern belief/conviction that the next generation will do better than this one, with the current trend suggesting that this assumption is no longer viable (Uchitelle, 2010).

This essay did not attend to the development of the construct or a review of the lineage of the bureaucrat. One can discover the development of bureaucracy through the insights of Max Weber (1924/2008). This essay joins the critical stories offered by Alasdair MacIntyre (1981), a philosopher of ethics, and Robert Bellah (Bellah et al., 1991), a sociologist. The role of the bureaucrat as a character type was unmasked through the deconstructive insights of Hannah Arendt. She did not give us historical lineage of the term, just repeated warnings about the danger of action that is cloaked in the garb of process with a vigorous "responsibility refusal" about the consequences. Arendt offers us a picture of a modern and socially sanctioned Pontius Pilate who displays the impression of being pressured to put a religious leader to death and, at the end, washes his hands of all responsibility. As the connection suggests, this character type is not new. What is novel is not that this evasion of responsibility was given an official role in modernity; there has long been an active sanctioning of the evasion of responsibility in decision making. Rootlessness and "responsibility refusal" propel the communicative evil that Arendt attached to the role of the bureaucrat.

When bureaucratic career obsession enters one's life, one can no longer discern why one should have an obligation to others. Awareness of such persons, however, brings a new consciousness about the death of progress announced in questions such as, "Is it any longer possible for the next generation to do better than this one?" (Uchitelle, 2010). Such statements would have been unheard of a generation ago in the United States, but they now announce an increasing lack of confidence in the coordinates of modernity. With rising experiential dissatisfaction with core beliefs that sustain modernity, Arendt's critique of the bureaucrat looks more like the insights of a communicative prophet than those of a disgruntled academic.

The contention of this essay is that we have ignored Arendt's warning about the danger of an official role that has no roots and finds its identity, ironically, through individualism, feigning loyalty to a given people and place at the expense of those supposedly under one's realm of responsibility. Arendt's bureaucrat is a "problematic Other," a counterknight who works within the shadows of the power of an organization, giving loyalty solely for one purpose—advancing and maintaining a career. The bureaucrat's existence does not center on a life composed of multiple persons and obligations, just a single-minded, quiet intensity for self-protection and self-advancement.

As a teacher, I am attentive to another cliché of modernity: "Those who cannot, teach." The hope of education is not only in the gathering of knowledge but also in the discovery of resources that give one an "enlarged mentality" (Arendt, 1977/1992; Kant, 1781/1855) in the making of decisions. The Nazi machine was tied to education with a "limited mentality," the dwelling place of the bureaucrat. Such a danger lurks anywhere education loses its ability to expand the horizons of students, teachers, and societal leaders. In the United States today, we live in an era that may someday be described as a loss of commitment to education and to the importance of an enlarged mentality. Bureaucratic calls for one cut in educational budgets after another as well as for the closing of libraries eclipse the pragmatic and symbolic importance of libraries as sacred spaces in a secular culture (Kristof, 2011) and create the soil that gives rise to more bureaucrats.

Tocqueville (1835/1963a, 1840/1963b) warned about emerging anti-intellectualism in early 19th-century America. My contention in this essay is that this anti-intellectualism is housed in the role of a bureaucrat who relies upon process, procedure, and an impersonal sense of distance that makes a banality of evil possible and inevitable. Relying upon clichés such as "It is only business," "Do not take this personally," "It is not my opinion—we are just following the data," and "I cannot help; your concern is outside my domain" is alive and well in modern life. The bureaucrat hides under the claim, "I was only doing my job." The Nuremburg Trials demanded justice and punishment for those who refused to use their own sense of responsibility and judgment.

Indeed, today there is increasingly less tolerance on the part of a democratic audience when a bureaucrat resorts to clichés such as "I was just doing my job;

I was just doing as I was required; I just did not know." In the case of Eichmann, the response to his use of such clichés for a defense was a verdict of death. He was hanged at Ramleh Prison on May 31, 1962. One wonders if the depth of anger unleashed in the French Revolution came from the utter disgust for those maintaining amenities while watching the masses starve and die. The French Revolution was not Arendt's model for protest, but she had a similar impulse—she raged against the purveyors of decision making who forget and eclipse the existential importance of roots and our connectedness to the Other. Justice does not live in self-advancement, only in concern for those unable to join the table of decision making. It is the forgotten Other that defines a world without justice; such was the source of the rage that Arendt brought to the task of unmasking the extreme commonness of the bureaucrat. Arendt's warning is not about the danger of roles in organizations but forgotten connections to persons, places, and events. The hypocrisy of engaging in individualistic self-concern under the guise of a major organizational structure offers the soil for a banality of evil. As I conclude, I suggest that the executive director of Goldman Sachs, Greg Smith (2012), in his public resignation, continues to echo Arendt's cry in the wilderness:

> My proudest moments in life—getting a full scholarship to go from South Africa to Stanford University, being selected as a Rhodes Scholar national finalist, winning a bronze medal for table tennis at the Maccabiah Games in Israel, known as the Jewish Olympics—have all come through hard work, with no shortcuts. Goldman Sachs today has become too much about shortcuts and not enough about achievement. It just doesn't feel right to me anymore. (para. 15)

Smith, like Arendt, reminds us how naturally modernity seems to cloak a banality of evil, life without roots void of personal responsibility.

Notes

1. Individualism is not to be confused with individual, self, enlightened self-interest, or selfishness. The entity of individualism is in a category all by itself, working to ignore the constraints and restraints of social obligation and responsibility.
2. Some contemporary examples of bureaucratic communicative practices include the involvement of Rupert Murdoch and the editors of the *News of the World* in the phone hacking scandal (2009–present), the business leaders involved in the collapse of Enron in 2001, the automotive CEOs which led to the need for a governmental bailout (2008–2010), and the managers of Lehmann Brothers (2008).

References

Arendt, H. (1992). *Lectures on Kant's political philosophy.* Chicago, IL: University of Chicago Press. (Original work published 1977)

Arendt, H. (1995). *Men in dark times.* San Diego, CA: Harcourt Brace. (Original work published 1955)

Arendt, H. (2006). *Eichmann in Jerusalem: A report on the banality of evil.* New York, NY: Penguin Books. (Original work published 1963)

Arnett, R. C. (1986). *Communication and community: Implications of Martin Buber's dialogue.* Carbondale, IL: Southern Illinois University Press.

Arnett, R. C. (1994). Existential homelessness: A contemporary case for dialogue. In R. Anderson, K. N. Cissna, & R. C. Arnett (Eds.), *The reach of dialogue: Confirmation voice and community* (pp. 229–244). Hampton, NJ: Hampton Press.

Arnett, R. C. (in press). *Communication ethics in dark times: Hannah Arendt's rhetoric of warning and hope.* Carbondale, IL: Southern Illinois University Press.

Arnett, R. C., Fritz, J. M. H., & Holba, A. M. (2007). The rhetorical turn to otherness: Otherwise than humanism. *Cosmos and History: The Journal of Natural and Social Philosophy, 3,* 115–133.

Bellah, R. N., Madsen, R., Sullivan, W. M., Swidler, A., & Tipton, S. M. (1991). *The good society.* New York, NY: Vintage Books.

Benhabib, S. (2000). Arendt's *Eichmann in Jerusalem.* In D. R. Villa (Ed.), *The Cambridge companion to Hannah Arendt* (pp. 65–85). Cambridge, England: Cambridge University Press.

Burke, K. (1973). *Philosophy of literary form: Studies in symbolic action.* Berkeley, CA: University of California Press. (Original work published 1941)

Chou, B. R. (1997). Eye safety during solar eclipses. Retrieved from http://eclipse.gsfc.nasa.gov

Elon, A. (2006). The excommunication of Hannah Arendt. In H. Arendt (Ed.), *Eichmann in Jerusalem: A report on the banality of evil* (pp. vii–xxiii). New York, NY: Penguin Books.

Foer, F. (2011, April 8). Why the Eichmann trial really mattered. *The New York Times.* Retrieved from http://www.nytimes.com

Fritz, J. M. H. (2002). How do I dislike thee? Let me count the ways: Constructing impressions of troublesome others at work. *Management Communication Quarterly, 15,* 410–438.

Holba, A. (2007). *Philosophical leisure: Recuperative practice for human communication.* Milwaukee, WI: Marquette University Press.

Kant, I. (1855). *Critique of pure reason* (J. M. D. Meiklejohn, Trans.). London, England: Henry G. Bohn. (Original work published 1781)

Kristoff, N. D. (2011, July 16). Our broken escalator. *New York Times.* Retrieved from http://www.nytimes.com

Levinas, E. (1998). *Entre nous: Thinking-of-the-other* (M. B. Smith & B. Harshav, Trans.). New York, NY: Columbia University Press. (Original work published 1991)

MacIntyre, A. C. (1981). *After virtue: A study in moral theory.* Notre Dame, IN: University of Notre Dame Press.

Marx, K. (1982). *Critique of Hegel's "philosophy of right."* Cambridge, England: Cambridge University Press. (Original work published 1927)

McHale, B., & Stevenson, R. (2006). *The Edinburgh companion to twentieth-century literatures in English*. Edinburgh, Scotland: Edinburgh University Press.

Sartre, J. P. (1957). *Being and nothingness: An essay in phenomemological ontology* (H. E. Barnes, Trans.). Oxford, England: Taylor & Francis. (Original work published 1943)

Smith, G. (2012, March 14). Why I am leaving Goldman Sachs. *The New York Times*. Retrieved from http://www.nytimes.com

Taylor, C. (2007). *A secular age*. Cambridge, MA: Belknap Press.

Tocqueville, A. de (1963a). *Democracy in America*. New York, NY: Alfred Knopf. (Original work published 1835, Vol. 1)

Tocqueville, A. de (1963b). *Democracy in America*. New York, NY: Alfred Knopf. (Original work published 1840, Vol. 2.)

Uchitelle, L. (2010, July 6). American dream is elusive for new generation. *The New York Times*. Retrieved from http://www.nytimes.com

Voegelin, E. (1956). *Order and history: The ecumenic age*. Baton Rouge, LA: Louisiana State University Press.

Weber, M., & Whimster, S. (2008). *Economy and society: The final version by Max Weber*. Oxford, England: Taylor & Francis. (Original work published 1924)

· 9 ·

CONTEMPLATING AN UPWARD SPIRAL

When Cultural Diversity Emerges in Problematic Workplace Relationships

Lisa M. Millhous

Differences matter in work relationships—specifically because they cause problems. Fritz (2002, 2006) derived a typology of troublesome people at work using two separate samples with cluster analyses of emergent factors. For each of the troublesome profiles of boss, peer, and subordinate, the factor titled "different from me" emerged as important in both samples. Although cultural difference was not measured in the study, clearly, when troublesome others are identified, people distinguish them as "different." Within an organization, people who are different may be stigmatized or victimized; they may receive preferential treatment, causing jealousy, perceptions of inequity, and reduced morale. Further, differences in goals, resources, or processes can become the source of destructive conflict. Clearly, differences matter at work.

At the same time, differences can also have benefits for work relationships. There is a rich literature on multicultural education that begins with the assumption that heterogeneity is a strength for larger social groups (Alred, Byram, and Fleming, 2006, offered an interesting global review of education practices for intercultural sensitivity across 16 national groups). Diversity can be a source of creativity in groups (see Oetzel, 2005, for a review), and a large network of weak relationships that links one to diverse groups can increase power (Granovetter, 1983).

Nonetheless, I set aside the benefits of intercultural contact for the moment to focus on the problems associated with diversity.

The spotlight of this chapter is on the *problematic work relationship* as it is intersected by the issue of *cultural difference*. After defining these core concepts, I consider the intersection as it spirals upward from individual-level issues, to dyad-level issues, and finally to issues emerging from broader social structures. This approach follows a similar logic to Oetzel, Dhar, and Kirschbaum's (2007) multilevel review of intercultural conflict research and is consistent with Hecht's (1993) layered identity theory, reflecting a more complex integration of context.

The notion of cultural difference calls into question the ways that scholars have considered and framed the problematic work relationship, because culture is not a characteristic of an individual. Situating the relational problem in the workplace and within a juxtaposition of cultures reveals a more complex vision of relational problems. Simply by considering the social construct of cultural difference as a factor in work relationships, we have broadened our lens beyond the problem individual, a problematic relationship, or even the toxic corporate culture that might foster such negativity.

Defining Theoretical Frameworks

Before considering how the dynamics of culture intersect problematic workplace relationships, it is important to establish what is meant by *culture* and *cultural difference* as well as the idea of *problematic work relationships*. Introductory textbooks on intercultural communication routinely note that the term culture has been used by scholars in a variety of different ways, many of which are complementary but not identical. Typically, culture is not considered a problem until it is juxtaposed against a different culture, so the idea that cultures are different is at the core of our understanding. In the following section, I define the scope of the term culture, consider how individuals perceive cultural differences, and consider the dynamics of the problematic work relationship. With this theoretical grounding, I then outline a spiraling approach to considering problematic workplace relationships where culture is a factor.

Theoretically Grounding Cultural Difference

Hofstede's (1991) metaphor for culture as the "software of the mind" succinctly captures the cognitive and perceptual nature of the phenomenon as I will be using it. National cultures, or what might be termed *macro-cultures*, were more homogenous in an earlier historical time, and it was possible for individuals to be encapsulated in a worldview that was defined by language, physical geography, normative behavior, historical narrative, and core values that were passed on through generations. The residual effects of national cultures are still visible, but culture and communication scholars have suggested that individuals' identification with national cultures are fragmented by other, more global, identities (Barber, 1995; Buell, 1994; Hall, 1991). The powerful globalizing effects of the media highlight the current tendency to identify beyond national boundaries while engaging in ethnic strife within those boundaries (Gilboa, 2000, 2005, 2009).

Despite the fragmentation of national cultures, it is possible to use nationally based, cross-cultural research as a starting point to identify how cultures vary. Dimensions of cultural difference as defined by Kluckhohn and Strodtbeck (1961; Hills, 2002), Hofstede (1984, 1991), Trompenaars (1997, 2003), and others reveal significant, deeply ingrained differences in how human beings evaluate their behavior and interaction in the world.

Scholars have also considered how micro-cultures of shared understanding and commonly held assumptions occur, for example, in organizations (Martin, 1992; Schein, 1985). Using a recent sample of non-managerial Mexican workers employed in Mexican organizations, Madlock (2012) demonstrated that the macro-level value of power distance (see Hofstede, 1991) was reflected in the micro-level practices of the organizations. Further, communication that was consistent with the cultural values was positively associated with job satisfaction and organizational commitment. Madlock's findings suggest that national dimensions of culture continue to be relevant in a fragmented world structured by global corporations.

Given the fundamental differences between cultures (both macro- and micro-), the negative consequences of intercultural interaction are hardly unexpected. Research has shown that the greater the cultural difference between participants, the more challenges they experience. Ward, Bochner, and Furnham (2001) referred to this phenomenon as the *culture-difference hypothesis*, and it undergirds much intercultural and cross-cultural research.

In fact, the fields of intercultural communication and cross-cultural psychology evolved in response to the significant challenges that cultural differences create. After World War II, the expanding influence of an emerging U.S. superpower brought scholars together at the Foreign Service Institute to lay the groundwork for how American diplomats and overseas sojourners could exert influence in a conflict-filled world (Leeds-Hurwitz, 1990; Rogers, Hart, & Miike, 2002). Gilboa (2009) similarly concluded that in the field of mass communication, scholars have tended to focus on the negative role that the media plays in exacerbating violent conflict. In this way, the scholarly literature on cultural problems in micro- and macro-level work relationships differs from the interpersonal communication literature addressing similar problems. Hess, Omdahl, and Fritz (2006) have suggested that the scholarly treatment of negative relationships by interpersonal communication scholars is "long overdue" (p. 89), whereas intercultural scholars generally begin with the premise that overcoming relational obstacles is the substance of intercultural work.

As globalization brings people closer together, it raises the question of whether national differences, or even organizational differences, are still significant in a postmodern age. Organizational culture research suggests the answer is yes. One visible example of failure to affirm the importance of cultural difference can be seen in the 2001 collapse of the DaimlerChrysler merger (Finkelstein, 2002). To re-affirm the importance of cultural difference, Weber and Camerer (2003) demonstrated through an experimental study that even simplistic cultural differences that were artificially induced in subject groups could result in visible productivity decreases and interpersonal conflict. Webster and White's (2010) study involving actual service organizations in the United States and Japan revealed significant interaction effects between organizational and national cultures on outcome variables such as financial performance and customer satisfaction. Webster and White concluded that cultural differences will continue to be an important factor in a globalizing work environment.

In fact, it is amazing that positive cross-cultural interactions occur at all. Culture is rooted in behavioral sequences that evolve idiosyncratically in a group over time, and these behaviors are connected with meaning for the group. Because the routine performance of these behaviors is meaningful, cultural difference interferes in key attribution processes (cognitive) that are normally outside of awareness.

Attribution refers to the causes that an individual perceives and assigns to another person's behavior and to the individual's own behavior. Scholars have identified systematic differences in attribution that can easily result in misunderstanding and conflict, particularly in the case of cross-cultural relations (see Brislin, 1981). Kelley and Michela's (1980) review identified the antecedents of attribution in information, beliefs, and motivation, while the consequents of attribution emerge in behavior, affect, and expectancy.[1]

Culture (information, beliefs, values) provides the framework for making attributions that in turn may produce incorrect understanding, unexpected behavior, and negative affect when people from different cultures interact. In fact, one successful training model for intercultural communication relies exclusively on attribution theory for preventing intercultural conflict. Albert's (1996) review of the theory and research behind the intercultural sensitizer suggested that teaching intercultural sojourners to pause before attributing meaning or causality helps prevent misunderstandings in cross-cultural dialogue.

In summary, culture (as I am using it) is a cognitive construct that frames our thinking, with strong ties to affect through beliefs and values. Further, cultural programming patterns human behavior in ways that are largely outside of awareness. When cultures come into contact, the differences become more visible, and scholars have identified systematic variations in culture using dimensions of cultural difference. An underlying theme of the culture research is the identification of conflict or problems when cultures come into contact. In the next section, I explore the nature of work relationships.

Framing the Problematic Work Relationship

Conceptually, the problematic work relationship involves three theoretical elements: (a) the discursive nature of relationships, (b) the mechanics of identity management, and (c) a specified frame of reference. To clarify my perspective, I address each of these elements in turn.

In approaching involuntary workplace relationships, I take a discursive approach to view the relationship as enacted by conversation and existing through talk. Similarly, Taylor (2003) identified organizations as existing through talk (social acts), and Lauring (2011) identified culture as created in communication, with cultural differences negotiated in conversation. The existence of such discursive entities is both constrained and enabled by the social structure of organizing. I have intentionally used the term *perception* to implicate the constructive, discursive meaning-building that surrounds a problematic work relationship. There is no simple causal chain of events where A does something that causes something in B (e.g., A wears perfume to work; B gets a rash). Instead, A makes a statement that B interprets in light of a historical narrative; A responds in ways that confirm/disconfirm B's interpretation; others weigh in on the interpretation, and so forth. It is not simple behavior that is the problem but the discursive process. To illustrate, U.S. television shows like *Hell's Kitchen* or *The Apprentice* might justify the inference that yelling, swearing, and otherwise humiliating a subordinate is a reasonable managerial style choice in U.S. culture (cause-effect). However, we can recognize that the layers of larger social discussion enable audience members to take away different interpretations of the narratives presented in these television series.

Following the lead of Duck, Foley, and Kirkpatrick (2006), I identify a second dynamic of the problematic workplace relationship within the process of identity management. Duck and colleagues suggested that the reason certain people are identified as a problem at work is because "they impose undesired social identities on others" (p. 7). Interaction with the problem individual gives the other a negative self-image that does not go away. Rather, the negative self-image is discursively enacted through every conversation.

The advantage of situating problem relationships as a challenge of identity management is that it invites us to interrogate cultural difference within an identity framework, a move that is consistent with a variety of approaches to understanding cross-cultural difference (Collier & Thomas, 1988; Cupach & Imahori, 1993; Hecht, 1993; Ting-Toomey, 1999). Collier and Thomas (1988) envisioned successful intercultural communication as occurring when, in the course of conversation, speakers negotiate their identities so that the cultural identity they ascribe to the other person comes into synchrony with the avowed cultural identity of that person. This conceptualization of identity focuses on the individual's self-concept in relation to a group, which is appropriate for considering cultural identities enacted in organizations.

Finally, it is important to note that the identification of a problem requires a particular frame of reference that implies a value judgment. Whether or not a particular relationship qualifies as a "problematic" workplace relationship depends on who gets to define the problem. The same relationship may be valued differently by each person in the relationship and valued alternatively by outside stakeholders in the relationship. For example, Pat may view a relationship with coworker Erin to be a problem, or, conversely, Erin may view it as a problem, but they may not mutually view it as a problem. Alternatively, neither Pat nor Erin might see the problem, but a supervisor or colleague may consider their relationship to be a problem.

In order to analyze problematic relationships, it is critical to determine who is valuing the relationship and what criteria are being used for judgment. Rather than taking a managerial bias or a marginalized perspective, I have considered multiple perspectives in writing this manuscript. Nonetheless, it is critical to note that for any problematic relationship to be identified, a particular frame of reference must also be identified.

The pairing of the terms *work* and *relationship* expands the notion of an interacting dyad to implicate a larger social group. A collectivist scholar might not see the need to pair these terms, but from an individualist perspective it is important to specifically invoke the group context for individuals' behavior as relevant to the inquiry. Cultural groups have been found to favor varying degrees of (a) private, independent visions of identity (individualism) or (b) group-oriented, relational visions of identity (collectivism), but Triandis (1994) explored individual-level manifestations of individualism and collectivism and cited evidence that these operate on separate dimensions and are stored in different places in the brain. Thus it makes sense to explicitly mark the individual's social relationship as existing within the group work context.

In American English, the construction of a problematic work relationship specifically focuses on the task element, which is culturally an individual achievement (individualism). In a different culture, where ascription or "being" is valued over "doing," the importance of preserving the relationship (at work) might be foregrounded (collectivism). U.S. Americans compartmentalize work and privilege work achievements in a way that masks the overlap between task and relationship.

As a counter-example, consider the traditional Hawaiian approach to conflict resolution, where family members, friends, and elders are systematically involved to resolve relational disputes (Shook, 2002). In modern-day Hawaiian culture, where work relationships often overlap with family and friend relationships, (Ka'imikaua, 2009) indicated this practice has been effective to resolve social problems such as prison reform, mental illness, and drug abuse. Hosmanek (2005) further applied the approach to the context of criminal law. When relationships become a problem in the workplace, not every culture will focus on the interruption of work over the disruption in the relational (often extended-family) network.

In the previous section I have considered the theoretical definitions that inform my approach, including the constructs of cultural difference and the problematic workplace relationship. Cultural differences emerge when individuals do not share basic assumptions about the world and are thus rooted in the cognitive process of perception. Perception also plays a role in the naming of workplace relationships as problematic. As work colleagues discursively negotiate their identities in relation to the workgroup (and other groups), those identities affect the evaluation of a work relationship. When cultural differences emerge as salient in problematic work relationships, they play out on multiple levels. In the next section I develop a spiraling approach to consider how culture intersects work relationships at the individual, dyadic, and societal levels.

A Spiraling Approach to the Problematic Impact of Cultural Difference on Work Relationships

The literature addressing the intersection of intercultural communication with problematic workplace relationships can be organized in several ways. As Schein (1985) has pointed out, culture is a property of groups, not of individuals, so the effects of culture on interpersonal relationships operate at multiple levels. To unpack this phenomenon, I begin with attributes of the individual that may be conflated with the issue of culture. Next, I address obstacles to relationships that can emerge in dyadic interaction, in particular during the initial phases of a relationship. Finally, I consider the ways that the larger social context is appropriated by individuals through discourse to highlight that even non-problematic relationships may be fraught with cultural challenges, depending on the normative standards that are being used to evaluate the relationship. For each of these levels, I consider prototypical case examples that illustrate the scholarly research in that area.

A Person as "the Problem"

The first level of analysis for problematic workplace relationships involving cultural difference is a misattribution of the concept of culture. People tend to identify an individual as the problem at work, and if cultural difference is salient, the problem may be misattributed to culture. Cultural misattribution is the culprit when stereotypes bias an individual's behavior and when negative personality traits coincide with visible cultural differences.

The case of the prejudiced individual. Cultural differences tend to be salient markers for individuals and are frequently the locus for stereotypes, resulting in unjust attributions. In the situation where a cultural Other is employed and a colleague is biased or prejudiced against that person purely as a result of a cultural stereotype, the relationship is fraught with problems. The problem might be identified as the bigoted employee or, alternatively, the cultural Other may be targeted. In either case, *culture* or behavioral and cognitive expectations that make up the "software of the mind" (Hofstede, 1991) are not really the problem. Employees' *ability to handle difference* is the problem.

A great deal has been written about how stereotypes are formed and stored in the mind, as well as the resulting prejudiced behavior that comes from such cognitive heuristics (for reviews, see Dovidio, Glick, & Rudman, 2005; Nelson,

2009). This psychological phenomenon creates significant challenges for cross-cultural workplace relationships. Bennett (1993) suggested that it is not merely the tendency to act on prejudice that is a problem, but an individual's ability to handle difference (intercultural sensitivity[2]) can mediate the way stereotypes inform behavior. Individuals who are comfortable with difference may become curious, whereas those who are uncomfortable may become hostile. Furthermore, there may be times when it is difficult to disentangle stereotypes from real cultural differences. For example, Ellis and Maoz (2009) described real differences in the speech codes of Israeli Jews and Palestinians. Those real differences feed antagonistic perceptions of the Other and reinforce stereotypes. Given cultural behavior and expectations for both the Israeli Jewish and Palestinian groups, it might be expected that each would see the Other as a problem in the workplace.

In short, the existence of stereotypes and prejudicial attitudes can create problematic relationships at work. These problems are marked by cultural difference but can be resolved through education to increase intercultural sensitivity. As Sha (2006) has pointed out, culture is not always used as a descriptive or objective category, and when it is invoked for political (evaluative) reasons, it may disguise an otherwise non-cultural dynamic.

For the moment, I set this particular case aside because the remedy is relatively clear (although less easy to enact): If the bigoted individuals can be educated to correct inaccurate stereotypes and raise their comfort level with difference, and if the relationship can be built at an interpersonal level, rather than an intergroup level, then the problem can be resolved. Next I turn to a second type of individual-level problem for intercultural workplace relationships.

The case of the problem personality. An alternative situation is when an individual sees the use of power and inflicting pain on others as appropriate within a work relationship. A variety of problem personalities might be identified, although I limit myself to authoritarian and sadistic personalities as particularly problematic for intercultural relationships. Similar to the case of the prejudiced individual, a problem personality is only tangentially about cultural difference, although culture may be salient in the interaction.

The concept of an *authoritarian personality* has a long history and a wealth of scholarly research, but it is mired in significant critique consisting of both theoretical and methodological challenges (Adorno, Frenkel-Brunswik, Levinson, & Sanford, 1950; Altemeyer, 1981; Martin, 2001; Oesterreich, 2005). Nonetheless, research does suggest that certain individuals are quick to feel attacked and threatened when their norms and expectations are violated and may therefore respond aggressively toward peer, unconventional, and low-status targets (for an extensive review, see Altemeyer, 1981).

Sadistic personality tendencies represent a similar problem, where an individual "humiliates others, shows a longstanding pattern of cruel or demeaning behavior to others, or intentionally inflicts . . . pain or suffering on others in order to assert power and dominance or for pleasure and enjoyment" (definition from O'Meara, Davies, & Hammond, 2011, p. 523). Neither sadistic nor authoritarian personalities are included as disorders in the latest edition of the *Diagnostic and Statistical Manual of Mental Disorders* (*DSM-IV-TR;* American Psychiatric Association, 2000), but both have received attention as personality traits that drive negative behavior.[3]

A work relationship may be problematic due to the personality of one or more individuals, and their cultural differences may be less relevant to the problem. Research on bullying suggests that bullies might hail from any culture (Craig, Harel-Fisch, Fogel-Grinvald, Dostaler, Hetland, Simons-Morton, & Pickett, 2009), and there is cross-cultural evidence for authoritarian personality syndrome (Duriez, Van Hiel, & Kossowska, 2005; Kemmelmeier, Burnstein, Krumov, Genkova, Kanagawa, Hershberg, & Noels, 2003; McFarland, Ageyev, & Abalkina, 1993; Rubinstein, 1996). The social dynamics of bullying indicate that marginalized cultural minority groups may be frequent targets of aggression because of their low status.

Authoritarian personalities were identified by the U.S. Peace Corps and the Foreign Service Institute as having difficulty when adapting to deployment abroad (see Brislin, 1981). Although there is less empirical evidence that individuals can be sorted by personality type (Altemeyer, 1981; Martin, 2001), an authoritarian behavior pattern can be discerned. Varying definitions of the authoritarian personality exist, but the general concept describes an individual who has such a strong, inflexible adherence to a particular value system that he or she may try to eliminate perceived threats to please a legitimate authority figure.

Whether or not an individual is the problem at work depends on the perspective of the evaluator. A victim or a human resources professional may identify the authoritarian personality as problematic, while those in the chain of command who get results from the authoritarian behavior may see the problem as residing in the individual who does not acquiesce to authority. Either of these individuals might be marked by a cultural difference.

In short, some work relationships that involve authoritarian personalities (or any difficult personality) may seem to involve cultural difference. However, I suggest that culture is secondary in this case. The resolution needs to address the personality rather than the cultural difference. Research on authoritarian personality suggests that situational factors may mediate the negative behavior (see Oesterreich, 2005, for review and explanation). Therefore, it might be possible to reduce the level of threat in the situation or for legitimate authorities explicitly to advocate collaboration with cultural Others (or reject violence) as possible solutions to the problem.

Although personality may be at the core of the problem, cultural differences can make the resolution more challenging. For example, firing a minority employee for abuse of power or silencing minority victims carries an added layer because of U.S. legal protections for minority groups. Similarly, a manager with a culturally different background may not understand his or her own behavior to be an abuse of power, although it may be driven by personality. For example, managers from cultures with a high power distance might be comfortable operating in "a society [that] accepts the fact that power in institutions and organizations is distributed unequally" (Hofstede, 1980, p. 45). In spite of these cultural caveats, I set the case of the problem personality aside as a separate type of problem for work relationships.

In the preceding paragraphs, I have considered how a problem individual might create challenging, negative work relationships. This approach is appealing because individuals have a tendency to focus on the Other and frame the Other as the problem in a relationship. There is no doubt that these cases pose significant challenges at work; however, attributing the difficulty to culture is an error that masks the real cause. In the following section, I consider relational challenges that do arise from cultural differences.

The Problem Relationship

When an individual from a different culture is embedded in a homogenous cultural milieu, it is easy to locate the cultural problem in the head of the individual. This is the case when an individual interprets a situation with prejudice or if the problem is a personality trait (such as authoritarianism). However, cultural problems at work also emerge from interaction where the problems are co-created by the participants. This interactive emergence is more visible when we consider the unfolding process of acculturation or the relational negotiation that occurs to establish work roles. In the following cases, the focus of the problem is interactional, but in all likelihood, issues of prejudice or personality may also be present when the interactants work in tandem to generate a negative situation in the workplace.

The case of stressful cultural contact. Several permutations are possible when individuals are *acculturating*, or learning a new cultural system. First, a culturally different individual may be overwhelmed by the cultural differences and experience work relationships as problematic (i.e., culture shock). A second possibility is that employees who feel at home in the cultural environment may perceive that the culturally different person is unable to function or is a problem to work with. Finally, native employees may experience *intercultural communication apprehension* or high anxiety aroused by interacting with culturally dissimilar individuals (Gudykunst, 1995; Neuliep & Ryan, 1998). In these situations, attribution biases associated with in-group and out-group status operate, but the repeated failure to meet cultural expectations produces acculturation stress for the culturally different person that is mediated by factors in the situation.

Ward et al. (2001) reviewed the research on culture shock, concluding that cultural contact is a stressful life event and that people adjust to cultural contact with varying degrees of competence. Ward and colleagues identified three possible mechanisms in the literature to explain the stressful experience. First, the culture-learning approach suggests that lack of knowledge about the cultural Other (appropriate behaviors, value differences, etc.) creates a steep learning curve that is perpetuated in every interaction. It is not unusual for individuals with high interpersonal skills in their home culture to be particularly frustrated by their lack of social competence in a new cultural context (Ward et al., 2001, p. 52).

A second mechanism identified by Ward et al. (2001) uses a stress-coping framework to consider how intercultural contact coincides with life changes identified by Holmes and Rahe's (1967) social readjustment rating scale. High levels of life change are reliably associated with increased physical and mental distress, which explains negative affect changes often associated with cultural contact. Ward and colleagues suggested a third mechanism in the literature, derived from social identity theory (Tajfel, 1982; Tajfel & Turner, 1986). Social identity theory considers how individuals must create a new understanding of themselves as cultural individuals within a new cultural context.

Ward et al. (2001) reviewed scholarship that supported each of these approaches and suggested that the approaches explained different parts of the acculturation process. They identified the following factors as explaining the varying experiences of acculturating persons: cultural distance, the availability of social support, the individual's style for coping with stress, and the individual's expectations of the situation. Other people within the situation and the organizational structure surrounding the interaction contribute to these factors by offering coping strategies and social support networks, helping people to frame their expectations, and adding or subtracting from the degree of cultural difference.

Adapting to cultural difference takes time and multiple interactions before it plays out to a successful or problematic outcome. Ward et al. (2001) suggested that the stage models of culture shock have been less fruitful because of variation across situations. Still, there is empirical evidence to suggest that positive affect is higher prior to cultural contact, takes a significant dip initially, and follows a steep learning curve to taper off after approximately one year (see review in Ward et al., 2001).

Hess et al. (2006) found that most of the negative relationships in their U.S. study were evaluated positively at the start but then turned negative. A different study on negative relationships by Sias, Heath, Perry, Silva, and Fix (2004) found that some U.S. respondents reported an initially attractive, endearing behavior that ultimately became annoying and unbearable. Neither of these studies looked at cultural difference as a factor, but both might be describing a new work relationship with a cultural Other that initially seemed promising but over time generated stress and negative affect for the participants. The process of culture shock can take a year for the stress level to normalize, and not all individuals achieve high levels of competence. Heuristically, the concept of acculturation stress may be useful to explain problematic work relationships where micro-cultural differences are present.

Fortunately, the acculturation process is time-bound and has received a great deal of research. Educational programs and intentional support systems can assist individuals significantly as they cope with the initial stress of cultural contact. The *Handbook of Intercultural Training* is now in its third edition (Landis, Bennett, & Bennett, 2003), providing a wealth of resources for acculturative stress management. In the next section I consider role conflict, which is related to the social identity explanation for acculturation but may extend beyond the time boundaries of the preceding processes.

The case of incompatible role expectations. Role conflict can occur when two individuals are asked to play particular, culturally defined roles, but they do not agree on the role definitions. When individuals have interdependent roles, it is nearly impossible for them to feel competent in their role without the counterpart fulfilling a complementary role. Essentially, the role of *boss* (or sales associate, receptionist, nurse, student, lawyer, dean, etc.) is enacted when others treat the individual in interaction according to expectations for how persons in that role should be treated. Such treatment becomes a problem if the boss does not behave as expected; in addition, the boss will not feel competent if employees do not behave as expected. Business scholars such as Harris and Moran (1993), Hofstede (1991), Huijser (2006), and Lewis (2003, 2006) described significant differences among cultures with respect to leadership and the impact these differences have on organizations in a global economy.

Concerning the performance of one's cultural identity, scholars have distinguished between the identity an individual claims and the identity that is ascribed to that person by others (Grotevant, 1992; Hecht, Collier, & Ribeau, 1993). Conflict between the avowed and ascribed identities may be implicated when naïve stereotypes are used as part of ascription, but Collier (1994) suggested that even people who claim the same national heritage may disagree about how it is enacted. In that case, more complex understandings of culture are in play but the ascribed and avowed identities still do not match. For example, second-generation immigrants may identify their cultural heritage differently than first-generation immigrants from the same nation. In fact, Collier (2009) found that individuals working to reduce ethnic conflict in Israel experienced tension among multiple group identities because there were layers of disagreement about the respective identities and appropriate role enactment (such as which language should be spoken, etc.).

Role conflict can occur in situations like South Africa, Northern Ireland, or Israel where intergroup identifications are evolving and in conflict, but this is only one possible area where role conflict might occur. New cultural transients might experience role incompatibility as a part of culture shock, and many veteran sojourners with significant intercultural competence may experience incongruity when they move into a new role. Therefore, I have separated the case of role incompatibility from the larger process of acculturation. In fact, it is likely just a continuing part of cultural learning. Conflicting role expectations may also occur in multicultural groups, where culture shock is somewhat masked if there is no dominant cultural milieu. Oetzel (2005) reviewed the research on cross-cultural teams, suggesting that diverse groups may take longer to establish roles as a result of the role negotiation process (see also Huijser, 2006).

All members of an organization must find a way to perform their individual identities through role behavior and to juggle multiple roles in complex ways. The emergent, negotiated identities are constituted in discourse, but they are mutually dependent, and conflict can create problematic workplace relationships. To illustrate, Foster (1992, p. 226) and others reported that non-Americans often have a negative attitude toward the consultative style favored by U.S. managers. In many countries, subordinates expect to be told what to do, and the American tendency to ask for input may be seen as stupid. If subordinates are unprepared to speak openly, there can be great dissatisfaction in the work relationship when an American manager uses a consultative style. Subordinates may not trust the manager, who appears to lack authority and take action based on poor advice (from subordinates). The manager may come to evaluate subordinates negatively because they do not tell the truth, and when the manager makes decisions on their recommendations, the implementation fails.

When managers and subordinates do not have a shared understanding of their respective roles, workplace relations become strained, and negative evaluations of both self and other are likely. In fact, Madlock's (2012) research on Mexican employees in Mexican organizations found that managerial behaviors based on high power distance were associated with significant increases in communication apprehension and avoidance communication strategies. Counter-intuitively (for American managers), communication apprehension and avoidance communication were *positively* associated with communication satisfaction. This finding illustrates how role expectations are culturally defined and reside largely out of awareness.

Resolution of incompatible roles can take several possible trajectories. In some cases, it makes the most sense for an individual to assimilate to the cultural expectations of the majority. Training an employee to understand the new expectations and perform associated behaviors is relatively well established in the field of human resources training.

An alternative solution to role conflict is engaging both sides in a meta-conversation to agree on mutually acceptable role definitions. These might combine the cultural expectations or be completely unique to the dyad or context. Gudykunst, Chua, and Gray (1987) concluded that cultural differences had a reduced effect on communication when relationships were more personally tailored. Millhous (1999) cautioned, however, that the parties involved may come to understand one another using their group's unique norms and values, but they risk negative evaluation by outside stakeholders who use cultural assumptions in judging the work performed by the group.

Marginalized or minority groups may encounter an additional layer to role conflict. As identified by Jamieson (1995), women may encounter a dilemma because the role expectations for women run counter to role expectations for leaders. This idea is further developed in a research study that focused specifically on women leaders of U.S. corporations (The double-bind, 2007). In fact, any minority group may encounter such incompatible role expectations. Imagine the issues for African American managers who may work in Spain or South Africa where African ethnicity is salient but different from the expectations of Americans or native managers. How does the African American manager in this cultural context demonstrate competence as a manager?

The double-bind dilemma brings into focus the confluence of individual-level stereotypes with dyad-level role expectations. I have considered how the problems of an individual (who may be bigoted or have certain personality predispositions) can be amplified in interaction with another person to create acculturation stress or incompatible role performance. The double-bind issue also draws attention to broader social factors that may become problematic in workplace relationships where culture is salient.

The Problem Social Structure

The discursive practice of communication defines how a relationship deteriorates (or is positively negotiated). The dyadic outcome may include acculturation stress or evaluations of low competence, but the larger social structure may further affect workplace relationships to create problems. I address two cases where the challenge for a workplace relationship is situated in the broader social structure rather than within the dyad.

The case of oppositional roles. In the preceding section, I considered the workplace situation where an individual manager (or doctor, teacher, sales associate, etc.) is unable to perform a role because a subordinate (or nurse, student, customer, etc.) does not have the same definition for the role due to cultural differences. In this case, there is a localized negotiation of roles where both parties realize the incompatibility is a problem. However, it is possible that the role conflict is not localized and cultural differences are more systematically distributed. Cultural differences, in other words, are likely to operate at the organizational level. This phenomenon becomes visible when double-bind situations are considered. In Jamieson's (1995) analysis, it was not that one woman struggled to perform expected leadership behaviors, but that at the broader level of the organization itself, men were leaders and women struggled to be judged competent when they performed the role.

Consider the situation in maquiladoras on the U.S.–Mexican border, in which Mexican women workers are supervised by non-Mexican (frequently American) managers. For the Mexican women employed in these factories, the struggle to play the role of competent employee clashes with the non-Mexican upper management expectations of how work should be performed. While Pena (1997) described the exploitation of Mexican women, Sable (1989) explored the U.S. managerial struggles to make a corporation thrive in this cross-cultural economic environment. In fact, these role expectations are not solely the result of cultural programming, since U.S. corporate watch groups have called for U.S. companies to improve working conditions using U.S. cultural expectations of employment (e.g., activist group Women on the Border). Activist accounts report that Mexican employees evaluate their maquiladora workplace relationships with supervisors as problematic (see Brickner, 2010; Pena, 1997). Employee unrest and activism creates problematic relationships for managers, regardless of cultural differences. The systematic cultural barrier between management and workers is conflated with cultural barriers that include systematic differences in language, economic resources, and values.

Similar role opposition with systematic cultural differences occurs regularly in the United States at hotels, restaurants, and other work environments where lower paid workers come from resident immigrant groups. The situation is played out on a larger stage when work is outsourced by a U.S. firm to India, China, or other countries, and employees in the international subsidiary are expected to produce for the American management and customer base. At Indian call centers, where U.S. customer service calls are routed, American customers expect a particular role enacted by the operator. Indian employees are trained to approximate these roles, but do they experience conflict in this situation? Do they experience their work relationships as problematic?

Collier, Hegde, Lee, Nakayama, and Yep (2002) reminded us that intercultural contact is historicized and politicized, a notion Collier (2009) built on to explore the intersections of culture, context, history, gender, age, and class. These larger social dynamics affect discourse in dyadic work relationships and may reflect a work relationship problem that is larger than the dyad.

Lauring (2011) offered a rich ethnography of relationships in a multinational organization where intercultural interaction was systematized. His account of a Danish subsidiary located in Saudi Arabia reveals cultural segregation among multiple expatriate groups, including Danes, Egyptians, Indians, and Filipinos. In that organization, organizational roles became conflated with ethnicity to facilitate better communication. Thus Danes were managers, Egyptians were supervisors, Philippine employees tended to be technicians, while Indians worked in production or sales. This allowed employees to communicate more effectively within their own cultural group but also had the effect of imposing a status hierarchy on the ethnic differences. Participant observation and interview data suggested that the employees had negative evaluations of their intercultural relationships.

In the case of Lauring (2011), participants may have experienced their relationships as problematic, but what if the participants in the relationships do *not* perceive systematic cultural conflict as problematic? What if a U.S. hotel manager accepts that a particular immigrant group needs to be "slapped around" before it will conform to expected U.S. norms? What if the immigrant employee accepts that this is what U.S. managers are like, and to keep a job in the United States one must tolerate or accept the behavior? What if these individual views are shared more broadly? This situation may occur in well-established cross-cultural environments and, ironically, is implicated in one solution for addressing systematic cultural differences.

One remedy for addressing cultural diversity is for the organization to separate from the larger social fabric, with the individuals involved working together to create a *third culture* that bridges the cultural background of the people involved (see Casmir, 1999). This process might also be termed *symbolic convergence* for a group (Bormann, Cragan, & Shields, 2001). For example, there are particular norms and expectations that make up the culture of the United Nations that allow participants from a multiplicity of cultures to work together (see Alger, 1965). Casmir (1999) pointed out that many of our assumptions about culture are uniquely modern, and the third culture concept allows us to adapt to a postmodern reality.

Multinational teams may benefit greatly from the third culture remedy, but caution is in order. Millhous (1999) concluded that culture was most visible in long-term, cross-national teams as an external factor—that is, outside agents imposed norms and expectations on the group. Groups in that study were able to develop internal norms that facilitated group work but sometimes found that external stakeholders did not value their work because these external stakeholders did not maintain the same cultural expectations. Lest we forget, the many expatriate cultures that exist around the globe are a form of third culture that often accepts the tyranny of colonial domination.

The preceding section describes problem social structures where cultural differences are systematically interwoven with organizational roles. From this description emerges the final category of problematic work relationships that involve cultural difference—a situation that is not considered a problem.

The exploding case of non-problems in intercultural work relationships. The insertion of cultural difference as a factor in problematic workplace relationships draws attention to the cases where cross-cultural relationships are NOT considered problematic—these cases may turn out to be the greatest problem after all. On how many pre-Civil War plantations were there slave-master relationships that were functional? It seems reasonable to believe that some African slaves may not have seen their workplace relationships as problematic. Certainly many white slave owners did not see that their relationships to slaves were a problem. Our human ability to normalize relationships in the face of systematic cultural differences may be functional, but it draws attention to the implicit criteria for evaluation in the concept of the problematic workplace relationship. If everyone involved considers the relationship to be "normal" and "functional," does that mean the relationship is not a problem? I argue that the acceptance of the relationship may, itself, be problematic.

Previously, I described a strategy for reducing cultural differences through interpersonal (rather than intergroup) relationship building. This approach influences normative cultural procedures so that they can accommodate diverse individuals in a particular workplace, building a shared micro-culture that deviates from the broader cultural norm. In fact, the processes of globalization and postmodernism may fracture the apparent pervasiveness of agreement in a national culture, making micro-cultural accommodation a factor in many more work relationships in the future. The problem is not our ability to build working relationships but our tendency to focus on the individual rather than the systemic.

Ashcraft and Allen (2003) reviewed organizational communication textbooks to consider how race and cultural difference were treated in the field. They concluded that tactics for managing diversity (such as sensitivity training) focused on cultural differences that operate at the individual level. Their analysis pointed out that the premise of cultural difference is systemic—culture is not an attribute of an individual. By reducing cultural difference to an individual problem, or even a relational problem, it belies structural power imbalances that feed problematic organizational or workplace relationships.

Martin (1992) used the concepts of postmodernism to conceptualize the increasing fragmentation of our cultural milieu. She built on Derrida's notion of *differance* to point out that creating oppositional binaries to understand cultural differences conceals the fact that there is only one way to be the same but there are many ways to be different (see Martin, 1992, p. 138). In a complex, multicultural workplace there may not appear to be cultural difficulties when the focus is on dyadic pairs because of the variety of difference in the workplace. Problem relationships can be attributed to unique factors associated with the individual or the dyad.

A number of scholars, such as Agathangelou and Ling (2002), have suggested that the first members of a minority group to achieve positions of power often become gatekeepers to maintain the dominant values system against other members of the same minority group. Thus, the organization could not be called discriminatory because one member of the minority group was visible in a power position. Agathangelou and Ling's analysis of U.S. institutions of higher education suggested that minority members paradoxically helped to represent the "universal standards" of white, male, heterosexual, upwardly mobile class values in the organization. In this case, systematic cultural differences were normalized and not seen as a problem factor in workplace relationships, but this is because the organization worked to prevent those cultural differences from crossing certain relational boundaries.

Scholars of intercultural and cross-cultural communication have typically analyzed relational problems, but perhaps they need to consider the interpersonal communication bias for reconstructing positive relationships. In fact, by considering the social structures that allow positive relationships in a multicultural workplace, we may gain new insight into problematic workplace relationships. Warmington (2008) advocated the use of "sociocultural theories of mediation, wherein societies, groups and individuals alter the world through the production and appropriation of cultural artifacts and are themselves altered by developing and using those artifacts" (p. 146). He used Latour's (1999) ideas about subject-tool-object relationships to consider action as a feature not of individuals but emergent from a complex network of people, concepts, tools, and technologies.

Culture is a feature of every workplace relationship. Given the problematic nature of culture, it behooves us to consider how a workplace relationship appropriates values from systemic cultures that make the relationship functional. Scholarly maps of cultural difference can assist us to some degree to identify the mechanisms used when various artifacts are appropriated. For example, how does the acceptance of power differentials facilitate the boss-subordinate relationship? How are assumptions of individuality and group identity used to frame a particular relationship? How are assertiveness/nurturing values enacted and validated in the relationship, and to what extent is tolerance for ambiguity a facilitating factor?

The challenge in locating interpersonal relationships at work in a larger sociocultural framework is that it exposes the values that are being used to evaluate the relationship as themselves problematic. If we accept that at least some non-problematic relationships at work are actually problems that have become normalized, it raises the question of what standard to use in evaluating the workplace relationship. Perhaps a better approach is to consider multiple standards in order to recognize that in a postmodern society, our workplace relationships are embedded in multiple social structures and fractured cultural structures that should be explored.

A layered or multifaceted view of intercultural relationships is supported by other scholars (Gilboa, 2009; Hecht, 1993; Oetzel et al., 2007) and works well with the organizational perspective. In addition, Toffolo (2003) suggested that we should begin with the assumption that the natural state is one of tension and conflict and see as suspect those relationships that are not a site for conflict. Collier, Parsons, Hadeed, and Nathaniel (2011) challenged the notion of bipolar dimensions of cultural difference and replaced them with multidirectional dialectic tensions that are negotiated in conversation. By considering workplace problems from the individual, dyadic, and social context, the role of culture is more richly explored and understood.

Conclusion

The preceding review of the literature brings together different perspectives to consider how culture may be involved in problematic workplace relationships. After defining the core terms (cultural difference and problematic workplace relationship), I have considered the exploration of this topic in a spiraling fashion to expose the nature of a problematic intercultural workplace relationship as the intersection of multiple conflicting tensions. Whereas ordinarily, a relationship is understood in a dyadic framework and typical approaches to problems are individually rooted, situating those relations at work invokes a larger social structure framing the relationship. To implicate culture as a problem in the relationship is to acknowledge that our dyadic relationships function within much larger social networks.

Typical solutions for workplace diversity problems are based at the individual level to address stereotypes or personality traits. A novel approach is to educate people so that they are better able to assimilate or adapt to mutually functional expectations. However, the third culture solution exposes a much larger network of social expectations because the good office relationship is evaluated from multiple perspectives. The third culture approach not only coordinates the participants' value systems but permits external stakeholders to impose their own value systems on the relationship. In this case, even relationships that are evaluated positively may still be problematic.

As a result, the inclusion of culture as a factor in research on problematic workplace relationships offers insight into the complexity of dyadic interaction and the ways that our discourse draws on larger social structures to create understanding. It also encourages us to look more closely at what are considered to be non-problematic relationships to understand how the participants have adapted to one another and appropriated value standards from a variety of social structures. It may well be that resolving an overt conflict institutionalizes a much deeper concern as a result of building a functional third culture.

Notes

1. More recent work on attribution has been in applied areas and offers promising foundations for resolving relationship problems. One such field is sports psychology, where attribution processes are considered a resource for handling stress (see Biddle, Hanrahan, & Sellars, 2001, and Coffee, 2010).
2. Bennett's (1993) construct of "intercultural sensitivity" is measured by the Intercultural Development Inventory (IDI; see Hammer, Bennett, & Wiseman, 2003). See Hammer (2008) and Paige (2003) for reviews.
3. Sadistic Personality Disorder was included in the previous version (*DSM-III-TR*; American Psychiatric Association, 1987). Authoritarian Personality has never been classified as a disorder.

References

Adorno, T. W., Frenkel-Brunswik, E., Levinson, D. J., & Sanford, R. N. (1950). *The authoritarian personality*. New York, NY: Norton.

Agathangelou, A. M., & Ling, L. M. H. (2002). An unten(ur)able position: The politics of teaching for women of color in the U.S. *International Feminist Journal of Politics, 4*, 368–398.

Albert, R. (1996). The intercultural sensitizer. In R. S. Bhagat & D. Landis (Eds.), *Handbook for intercultural training* (2nd ed., pp. 185–202). Thousand Oaks, CA: Sage.

Alger, C. F. (1965). Personal contact in intergovernmental organizations. In H. C. Kelman (Ed.), *International behavior: A social-psychological analysis* (pp. 523–547). New York, NY: Holt, Rinehart & Winston.

Alred, G., Byram, M., & Fleming, M. (Eds.). (2006). *Education for intercultural citizenship: Concepts and comparisons*. Bristol, England: Multilingual Matters.

Altemeyer, B. (1981). *Right-wing authoritarianism*. Winnipeg, MB, Canada: University of Manitoba Press.

American Psychiatric Association. (1987). *Diagnostic and statistical manual of mental disorders* (3rd ed., rev.). Washington, DC: Author.

American Psychiatric Association. (2000). *Diagnostic and statistical manual of mental disorders* (4th ed., text rev.). Washington, DC: Author.

Ashcraft, K. L., & Allen, B. J. (2003). The racial foundation of organizational communication. *Communication Theory, 13*, 5–38.

Barber, B. (1995). *Jihad vs. McWorld*. New York, NY: Times Books

Bennett, M. J. (1993). Towards ethnorelativism: A developmental model of intercultural sensitivity. In R. M. Paige (Ed.), *Education for the intercultural experience* (2nd ed., pp. 21–71). Yarmouth, ME: Intercultural Press.

Biddle, S. J. H., Hanrahan, S. J., & Sellars, C. N. (2001). Attributions: Past, present, and future. In R. N. Singer, H. A. Hausenblas, & C. M. Janelle (Eds.), *Handbook of sport psychology* (2nd ed., pp. 444-471). New York, NY: Wiley.

Bormann, E. G., Cragan, J. F., & Shields, D. C. (2001). Three decades of developing, grounding, and using symbolic convergence theory. In W. B. Gudykunst (Ed.), *Communication Yearbook 25* (pp. 271-313). Mahwah, NJ: Erlbaum.

Brickner, R. K. (September 2010). *Why bother with the state?: Transnational activism, local activism, and lessons for a women workers' movement in Mexico* (Gendered Perspectives on International Development, Working Paper No. 298). Retrieved from Michigan State University, Center for Gender in Global Context website: http://gencen.isp.msu.edu/documents/Working_Papers/WP298.pdf

Brislin, R. W. (1981). *Cross-cultural encounters: Face-to-face interaction*. Elmsford, NY: Pergamon.

Buell, F. (1994). *National culture and the new global system*. Baltimore, MD: Johns Hopkins University Press.

Casmir, F. L. (1999). Foundations for the study of intercultural communication based on a third-culture building model. *International Journal of Intercultural Relations, 23*, 91-116.

Coffee, P. (2010). Attributions: Contemporary research and future directions. *Sport & Exercise Psychology Review, 6*(2), 6-18.

Collier, M., & Thomas, M. (1988). Cultural identity. In Y. Y. Kim & W. B. Gudykunst (Eds.), *Theories of intercultural communication* (pp. 99-120). Newbury Park, CA: Sage.

Collier, M. J. (1994). Cultural identity and intercultural communication. In L. A. Samovar & R. E. Porter (Eds.), *Intercultural communication: A reader* (7th ed., pp. 36-45). Belmont, CA: Wadsworth.

Collier, M. J. (2009). Contextual negotiation of cultural identifications and relationships: Interview discourse with Palestinian, Israeli, and Palestinian/Israeli young women in a U.S. peace-building program. *Journal of International and Intercultural Communication, 2*, 344-368.

Collier, M. J., Hegde, R. S., Lee, W., Nakayama, T. K. & Yep, G. A. (2002). Dialogue on the edges: Ferment in communication and culture. In M. J. Collier (Ed.), *Transforming communication about culture* (International and Intercultural Communication Annual, Vol. 24, pp. 219-280). Thousand Oaks, CA: Sage.

Collier, M. J., Parsons, R. J., Hadeed, L., & Nathaniel, K. (2011). Problematizing national dimensions: Community members' views of conflict management in Trinidad and Tobago West Indies. *Howard Journal of Communications, 22*, 140-162.

Craig, W., Harel-Fisch, Y., Fogel-Grinvald, H., Dostaler, S., Hetland, J., Simons-Morton, B., & Pickett, W. (2009). A cross-national profile of bullying and victimization among adolescents in 40 countries. *International Journal of Public Health, 54* (Supplement 2), 216-224.

Cupach, W. R., & Imahori, T. T. (1993). Identity management theory: Communication competence in intercultural episodes and relationships. In R. L. Wiseman & J. Koester (Eds.), *Intercultural communication competence* (pp. 112-131). Newbury Park, CA: Sage.

The double-bind dilemma for women in leadership: Damned if you do, doomed if you don't. (2007). New York, NY: Catalyst. Retrieved from http://www.catalyst.org/publication/83/the-double-bind-dilemma-for-women-in-leadership-damned-if-you-do-doomed-if-you-dont

Dovidio, J. F., Glick, P. S., & Rudman, L. A. (2005). *On the nature of prejudice: Fifty years after Allport*. Chichester, England: John Wiley & Sons.

Duck, S., Foley, M. K., & Kirkpatrick, D. C. (2006). Uncovering the complex roles behind the "difficult" coworker. In J. M. H. Fritz & B. Omdahl (Eds.), *Problematic relationships in the workplace* (pp. 3–20). New York, NY: Peter Lang.

Duriez, B., Van Hiel, A., & Kossowska, M. (2005). Authoritarian and social dominance in western and eastern Europe: The importance of the sociopolitical context and of political interest and involvement. *Political Psychology, 26,* 299–320.

Ellis, D. G., & Maoz, I. (2009). Dialogue, argument, and cultural communication codes between Israeli-Jews and Palestinians. In L. A. Samovar, R. E. Porter, & E. R. McDaniel (Eds.), *Intercultural communication: A reader* (12th ed., pp. 244–250). Boston, MA: Wadsworth Cengage Learning.

Finkelstein, S. (2002). *The DaimlerChrysler merger.* Hanover, NH: Dartmouth College, Tuck School of Business. Retrieved from http://mba.tuck.dartmouth.edu/pdf/2002-1-0071.pdf

Foster, D. A. (1992). *Bargaining across borders: How to negotiate business successfully anywhere in the world.* New York, NY: McGraw-Hill.

Fritz, J. M. H. (2002). How do I dislike thee? Let me count the ways: Constructing impressions of troublesome others at work. *Management Communication Quarterly, 15,* 410–438.

Fritz, J. M. H. (2006). Typology of troublesome others at work: A follow-up investigation. In J. M. H. Fritz & B. Omdahl (Eds.), *Problematic relationships in the workplace* (pp. 21–46). New York, NY: Peter Lang.

Gilboa, E. (2000). Mass communication and diplomacy: A theoretical framework. *Communication Theory, 10,* 275–309.

Gilboa, E. (2005). The CNN effect: The search for a communication theory of international relations. *Political Communication, 22,* 27–44.

Gilboa, E. (2009). Media and conflict resolution: A framework for analysis. *Marquette Law Review, 93,* 87–111.

Granovetter, M. (1983). The strength of weak ties: a network theory revisited. *Sociological Theory, 1,* 201–233.

Grotevant, H. D. (1992). Assigned and chosen identity components: A process perspective on their integration. In G. R. Adams, T. P. Gullotta, & R. Montemayor (Eds.), *Adolescent identity formation* (pp. 73–90). Newbury Park, CA: Sage.

Gudykunst, W. B. (1995). Anxiety/uncertainty management (AUM) theory. In R. L. Weisman (Ed.), *Intercultural communication theory* (pp. 8–58). Thousand Oaks, CA: Sage.

Gudykunst, W. B., Chua, E., & Gray, A. (1987). Culture dissimilarities and uncertainty reduction processes. In M. McLaughlin (Ed.), *Communication yearbook 10* (pp. 456–469). Newbury Park, CA: Sage

Hall, S. (1991). The local and the global: Globalization and ethnicity. In A. D. King (Ed.), *Culture, globalization and the world system* (pp. 19–39). Minneapolis, MN: University of Minnesota Press.

Hammer, M. R. (2008). The Intercultural Development Inventory (IDI): An approach for assessing and building intercultural competence. In M. A. Moodian (Ed.), *Contemporary leadership and intercultural competence: Understanding and utilizing cultural diversity to build successful organizations* (pp. 245–259). Thousand Oaks, CA: Sage.

Hammer, M. R., Bennett, M. J., & Wiseman, R. (2003). Measuring intercultural sensitivity: The intercultural development inventory. *International Journal of Intercultural Relations, 27,*

421–443. doi:10.1016/S0147-1767(03)00032-4
Harris, P. R., & Moran, R. T. (1993). *Managing cultural differences: High performance strategies for a new world of business* (3rd ed.). Houston, TX: Gulf Publishing Company.
Hecht, M., Collier, M. J., & Ribeau, S. (1993). *African-American communication.* Newbury Park, CA: Sage.
Hecht, M. L. (1993). 2002—A research odyssey toward the development of a communication theory of identity. *Communication Monographs, 60,* 76–82.
Hess, J., Omdahl, B. L., & Fritz, J. M. H. (2006). Turning points in relationships with disliked coworkers. In J. M. H. Fritz & B. L. Omdahl (Eds.), *Problematic relationships in the workplace* (pp. 89–108). New York, NY: Peter Lang.
Hills, M. D. (2002, August). Kluckhohn and Strodtbeck's values orientation theory. *Online Readings in Psychology and Culture* (Unit 6, Chapter 3). International Association for Cross-Cultural Psychology. Retrieved from http://www.wwu.edu/culture/Hills.htm
Hofstede, G. (1980). *Culture's consequences: International differences in work-related values.* Beverly Hills, CA: Sage.
Hofstede, G. (1984). *Culture's consequences: International differences in work-related values* (abridged ed.). Newbury Park, CA: Sage.
Hofstede, G. (1991). *Cultures and organizations: Software of the mind; intercultural cooperation and its importance for survival.* New York, NY: McGraw-Hill.
Holmes, T. H., & Rahe, R. H. (1967). The social readjustment rating scale. *Journal of Psychosomatic Research, 11,* 213–218.
Hosmanek, A. J. (2005). Cutting the cord: Ho'oponopono and Hawaiian restorative justice in the criminal law context. *Pepperdine Dispute Resolution Law Journal, 5,* 359–376.
Huijser, M. (2006). *The cultural advantage: A new model for succeeding with global teams.* London, England: Nicholas Brealey.
Jamieson, K. H. (1995). *Beyond the double bind: Women and leadership.* New York, NY: Oxford University Press.
Ka'imikaua, C. I. (2009). Ho'oponopono: A Hawaiian cultural process to conflict resolution. In L. A. Samovar, R. E. Porter, & E. R. McDaniel (Eds.), *Intercultural communication: A reader* (12th ed., pp. 197–199). Boston, MA: Wadsworth Cengage Learning.
Kelley, H. H., & Michela, J. L. (1980). Attribution theory and research. *Annual Review of Psychology, 31,* 457–501.
Kemmelmeier, M., Burnstein, E., Krumov, K., Genkova, P., Kanagawa, C., Hirshberg, M., & Noels, K. A. (2003). Individualism, collectivism, and authoritarianism in seven societies. *Journal of Cross-Cultural Psychology, 34,* 304–322.
Kluckhohn, F. R., & Strodtbeck, F. L. (1961). *Variations in value orientations.* Evanston, IL: Row, Peterson & Co.
Landis, D., Bennett, J. M., & Bennett, M. J. (2003). *Handbook of intercultural training* (3rd ed.). Thousand Oaks, CA: Sage.
Latour, B. (1999). *Pandora's hope: Essays on the reality of science studies.* London, England: Harvard University Press.
Lauring, J. (2011). Intercultural organizational communication: The social organizing of interaction in international encounters. *Journal of Business Communication, 48,* 231–255. doi:10.1177/0021943611406500

Leeds-Hurwitz, W. (1990). Notes in the history of intercultural communication: The Foreign Service Institute and the mandate for intercultural training. *Quarterly Journal of Speech, 76,* 262–281.

Lewis, R. D. (2003). *The cultural imperative: Global trends in the 21st century.* Boston, MA: Intercultural Press.

Lewis, R. D. (2006). *When cultures collide: Leading across cultures* (3rd ed.). London, England: Nicholas Brealey.

Madlock, P. E. (2012). The influence of power distance and communication on Mexican workers. *Journal of Business Communication, 49,* 169–184.

Martin, J. (1992). *Cultures in organizations: Three perspectives.* New York, NY: Oxford University Press.

Martin, J. L. (2001). "The authoritarian personality" 50 years later: What lessons are there for political psychology? *Political Psychology, 22,* 1–26.

McFarland, S. G., Ageyev, V. S., & Abalkina, M. (1993). The authoritarian personality in the United States and the former Soviet Union: Comparative studies. In W. F. Stone, G. Lederer, & R. Christie (Eds.), *Strength and weakness: The authoritarian personality today* (pp. 199–225). New York: Springer-Verlag.

Millhous, L. M. (1999). The experience of culture in multicultural groups: Case studies of Russian-American collaboration in business. *Small Group Research, 30,* 280–308.

Nelson, T. D. (2009). *Handbook of prejudice, stereotyping, and discrimination.* New York, NY: Taylor & Francis.

Neuliep, J. W., & Ryan, D. J. (1998). The influence of intercultural communication apprehension and socio-communicative orientation on uncertainty reduction during initial cross-cultural interaction. *Communication Quarterly, 46,* 88–99.

Oesterreich, D. (2005). Flight into security: A new approach and measure of the authoritarian personality. *Political Psychology, 26,* 275–297.

Oetzel, J. (2005). Effective intercultural workgroup communication theory. In W. B. Gudykunst (Ed.), *Theorizing about intercultural communication* (pp. 351–372). Thousand Oaks, CA: Sage.

Oetzel, J., Dhar, S., & Kirschbaum, K. (2007). Intercultural conflict from a multilevel perspective: Trends, possibilities, and future directions. *Journal of Intercultural Communication Research, 36,* 138–204.

O'Meara, A., Davies, J., & Hammond, S. (2011). The psychometric properties and utility of the Short Sadistic Impulse Scale (SSIS). *Psychological Assessment, 23,* 523–531. doi:10.1037/a0022400

Paige, R. M. (2003). The Intercultural Development Inventory: A critical review of the research literature. *Journal of Intercultural Communication, 6,* 53–61.

Pena, D. C. (1997). *The terror of the machine: Technology, work, gender, and ecology on the U.S.-Mexico border.* Austin, TX: University of Texas at Austin, Center for Mexican American Studies.

Rogers, E. M., Hart, W. B., & Miike, Y. (2002). Edward T. Hall and the history of intercultural communication: The United States and Japan. *Keio Communication Review, 24,* 3–26. Retrieved from http://www.mediacom.keio.ac.jp/publication/pdf2002/review24/2.pdf

Rubinstein, G. (1996). Two peoples in one land: A validation study of Altemeyer's right-wing authoritarianism scale in the Palestinian and Jewish societies in Israel. *Journal of Cross-Cultural Psychology, 27,* 216–230.

Sable, M. (1989). *Las maquiladoras: Assembly and manufacturing plants on the United States-Mexico border: An international guide*. New York, NY: Routledge.
Schein, E. H. (1985). *Organizational culture and leadership: A dynamic view*. San Francisco, CA: Jossey-Bass.
Sha, B. (2006). Cultural identity in the segmentation of publics: An emerging theory of public relations. *Journal of Public Relations Research, 18*, 45–65.
Shook, V. E. (2002). *Ho'oponopono: Contemporary uses of a Hawaiian problem-solving process*. Honolulu, HI: University of Hawaii Press.
Sias, P. M., Heath, R. G., Perry, T., Silva, D., & Fix, B. (2004). Narratives of workplace friendship deterioration. *Journal of Social and Personal Relationships, 21*, 321–340.
Tajfel, H. (Ed.). (1982). *Social identity and intergroup relations*. Cambridge, England: Cambridge University Press.
Tajfel, H., & Turner, J. C. (1986). The social identity theory of inter-group behavior. In S. Worchel & L. W. Austin (Eds.), *Psychology of intergroup relations* (pp. 7–24). Chicago, IL: Nelson-Hall.
Taylor, J. R. (2003). Dialogue as the search for sustainable organizational co-orientation. In R. Anderson, L. A. Baxter, & K. N. Cissna (Eds.), *Dialogue: Theorizing difference in communication studies* (pp. 125–140). Thousand Oaks, CA: Sage.
Ting-Toomey, S. (1999). *Communicating across cultures*. New York, NY: Guilford Press.
Toffolo, C. E. (2003). Overview and critique of the present research into the politics of cultural pluralism. In C. E. Toffolo (Ed.), *Emancipating cultural pluralism* (pp. 1–22). Albany, NY: SUNY Press. Retrieved from http://www.sunypress.edu/pdf/60683.pdf
Triandis, H. C. (1994). Theoretical and methodological approaches to the study of collectivism and individualism. In U. Kim, H. C. Triandis, C. Kagitcibasi, S. Choi, & G. Yoon (Eds.), *Individualism and collectivism: Theory, method and applications* (pp. 41–51). Newbury Park, CA: Sage.
Trompenaars, F. (1997). *Riding the waves of culture: Understanding cultural diversity in business*. New York, NY: McGraw-Hill.
Trompenaars, F. (2003). *Business across cultures*. New York, NY: Capstone.
Ward, C., Bochner, S., & Furnham, A. (2001). *The psychology of culture shock*. London, England: Routledge.
Warmington, P. (2008). The "R" word: Voicing race as a critical problem and not just a problem of practice. In J. Satterthwaite, M. Watts, & H. Piper (Eds.), *Talking truth, confronting power* (pp. 143–157). Sterling, VA: Trentham Books.
Weber, R. A., & Camerer, C. F. (2003). Cultural conflict and merger failure: An experimental approach. *Management Science, 49*, 400–415. Retrieved from http://www.hss.caltech.edu/~camerer/mgtsci03.pdf
Webster, C., & White, A. (2010). Exploring the national and organizational culture mix in service firms. *Journal of the Academy of Marketing Science, 38*, 691–703.

· 1 0 ·

EXPLAINING TENSIONS IN WORKPLACE RELATIONSHIPS

Toward a Communicative and Situated Understanding of Tokenism

BRITTANY L. COLLINS, REBECCA GILL, & JENNIFER J. MEASE

For over a quarter of a century, organizational communication scholars have taken up issues of difference in a number of contexts such as shop floors (Collinson, 1988), academia (Allen, 1996; Ashcraft & Allen, 2003), and human service organizations (Trethewey, 1997). Additionally, critical and feminist scholars have drawn our attention to organizational processes that sustain gender and racial inequality. Some of the key issues that have been explored include organizational socialization processes (Allen, 1996), maternity leave practices (Buzzanell & Liu, 2005), and informal rules surrounding emotions in organizations (Martin, Knopoff, & Beckman, 1998; Mumby & Putnam, 1992). More recently, scholars have taken seriously how multiple social differences connect and interact in organizational contexts. The types of issues revealed in the critical and feminist organizational communication literature often seem to speak to a particular sociological theory that has garnered decades of attention in related fields: tokenism theory. Since its inception, tokenism theory has been investigated in sociology (Scott, 2005; Turco, 2010; Wingfield, 2010), social psychology (Danaher & Branscombe, 2010), management (King, Hebl, George, & Matusik, 2010; Simpson, 1997), and education (Bank, 2009; Kelly, 2007). Despite this attention from other fields, communication scholars—with the exception of Allen (2000) and Cloud (1996)—have not explicitly connected our research to the tenets of tokenism theory.

In this chapter, we explore if and why organizational communication scholarship has overlooked tokenism theory and advocate that we more explicitly, and critically, embrace tokenism as a theoretical and practical lens. In making our argument, we direct our comments to two audiences. First, we intend for this chapter to be of interest to scholars in organizational communication and related fields who are engaging research at the level of critical and feminist studies of difference, intersectionality, and tokenism. Second, our chapter is aimed at practitioners and people who may be observing or navigating token dynamics in their own workplace relationships. Therefore, in addition to addressing theoretical issues, we also pay attention to the situated and practical concerns that practitioners face when addressing token dynamics. At the end of the essay, we offer a model of tokenizing processes as a tool to help understand how token dynamics might function in workplaces and individual interactions.

A tokenism lens represents a necessary approach that benefits greatly from the theoretical and practical tools brought to the table by critical and feminist communication scholars. Our chapter is structured to explore this claim. First, we identify key themes across the current body of tokenism literature. These themes are delineated into macro-level and micro-level issues. Second, we introduce and identify how an organizational communication perspective changes the study of tokenism and creates possibilities for in-depth, revolutionary understandings. Finally, we offer theoretical observations and practical strategies designed to aid both individuals and organizations to recognize, negotiate, and, ideally, change the nature of token dynamics.

Tokenism: Where Have We Been?

The tradition of studying token dynamics in the workplace can be traced back to the work of Rosabeth Moss Kanter (1977), who identified minority individuals in dominant workplace situations as "tokens." Kanter's intention was to demonstrate how the increase of women in managerial positions in the 1960s and 1970s was not a revolutionary result of gender equality but a way to proffer "representatives" of marginalized groups as evidence of the organization's commitment to equality. Arguably, studies on tokenism have not changed much since Kanter's groundbreaking work, and as we argue later, tokenism theory's adherence to functional, managerialist approaches to the workplace have caused this theory and its usefulness to stagnate. As a way to set the stage for our later arguments, we first discuss how tokenism has been addressed as a macro-level issue and then move to address tokenism as a micro-level experience.

Tokenism as a Macro-Level Issue

We begin by discussing how scholars link macro-level issues to token dynamics, demonstrating how broad ideologies are at play in tokenizing processes. In this arena of research, many scholars map out the ways broad assumptions about race and/or gender inform meso-level organizational processes and constrain individuals' micro-level subject positions (Kanter, 1977; Kelly, 2007). Thus, arguments along these lines suggest that one factor of token dynamics is societal conceptualizations of difference or stereotypes. These stereotypes become embedded in organizational practices such as hiring, firing, and promoting. For instance, Kanter's research identified the way that social stereotypes about women led to fewer opportunities for women to be hired into particular positions or receive promotions within an organization (see also Ferguson, 1984). Women who are in positions of upper management are then further marginalized, given their rarity in that context. This, in turn, sustains broad-scale assumptions of the group's ineptitude. Thus, because of who they are, women are assumed not to belong, and the fact that they continue to be rare is taken as evidence that they *should not* belong. For researchers, a macro-level perspective suggests that in order to understand employees' individual experiences, we must start with broad stereotypes about the group.

From this perspective, however, token dynamics are not solely attributed to stereotypes of identity-based differences (i.e., gender, race, sexual orientation, etc.). A second element of token dynamics includes broad discourses and assumptions about particular job titles, job rankings, and industries. For instance, we have particular assumptions about how an MBA graduate (Simpson, 1997), a teacher (Bank, 2009; Kelly, 2007), or a flight attendant (Young & James, 2001) *should* look, behave, or even show emotion (Wingfield, 2010). In many cases, stereotypes of the "ideal worker" (Acker, 1990), or who belongs in which workplace roles, can provide a "particularly powerful schema" that "shapes processes of evaluation and exclusion" (Turco, 2010, p. 904). These assumptions can lead to the prevalence—and absence—of people of certain social groups in certain job roles. For instance, evaluations of a presidential nominee by U.S. citizens are shaped by patterns and images of presidential hopefuls (Squires & Jackson, 2010), which are themselves shaped by gendered and raced stereotypes about leaders and authorities. Since historically there has been a prevalence of members of particular social groups who have been sworn in as the president of the United States, then assumptions of what type of people (i.e., political party affiliation, class, gender, race, educational background) supposedly *belong* in that occupation stem from the prevalence of members of that group and the absence of members of different groups. These assumptions then inform meso-level practices (different political party nominations and deliberations) and individual behavior (voting practices), thus reifying the status quo ideology.

The issue of prevalence and absence lends itself to the third and most often cited component of token dynamics—numerical regularity versus rarity of members of certain social groups. More times than not, we find cases of researchers investigating workplaces or industries wherein a disproportionate, or "skewed," prevalence (and absence) of members of particular social groups work. For Kanter (1977), when groups are "skewed, ... there is a large preponderance of one type over another, up to a ratio of perhaps 85:15" (p. 208). She labeled members of the roughly 85% "dominants" and members of the roughly 15% "non-dominants" or tokens (pp. 208–209). Tokens are the "pink poodles" (Kelly, 2007, p. 237), or mascots, for their social group. As Kanter argued, if we see a great number of anything, and one or two of something different, that which is different will stand out. Moreover, the "something different" will be seen as aberrant and threatening to the greater number.

Scholars argue that when the issue of numerical disparities is taken into account with the first two elements (stereotypes of difference and occupational segregation), we get an increased possibility for token dynamics to become salient in employees', and specifically minority employees', day-to-day workplace experiences. In other words, when particular social stereotypes, occupational assumptions, and numerical rarity "meet," the conditions for tokenizing are ripe. This means that, according to the literature, individuals who face negative social stereotypes but who occupy a position in the workplace that stereotypically "fits" them will likely not feel that tokenism is an issue. Yet, someone who is subject to negative social stereotypes, holds a position at odds with the status quo, and is also one of a few at that level, will likely experience tokenism in the workplace.

Importantly, the lens created by understanding tokenism at the nexus of these three factors allows scholars and practitioners to scale down to investigate how these converging factors construct formal and informal structures and processes for individuals. Therefore, a macro-level approach to interrogating tokenism offers a useful starting point because it points scholars to research sites where the likelihood of finding marginalized groups is high. For instance, it is understandable that a scholar wanting to examine how female managers make sense of their disparate representation chooses a research site where women are disproportionately underrepresented. Likewise, identifying these three factors prompts practitioners to increase their awareness of token dynamics when such circumstances are present.

Yet, while a macro-level perspective on tokenism highlights the role of broad stereotypes in shaping micro-level experiences, this "top-down" approach runs the risk of offering deterministic, essential, and generalizable findings. When scholars present findings which suggest that all tokens at the nexus of the aforementioned factors in a given context report similar obstacles or enact similar strategies, such findings suggest that individuals in different contexts—although at the same nexus—will likely experience tokenism in the same ways. Why? Because, according to this line of thinking, broad stereotypes are determinants of how individuals experience token dynamics. This point thus undercuts individual agency, specifically resistance to tokenizing processes. Furthermore, although the data stem from the arguably varied experiences of individuals, the conclusions made about token dynamics tend only to point back to the dominance of broad stereotypes, overlooking individual agency and possibilities for changing the nature of token dynamics in a given context.

Additionally, we see a tendency in this approach to characterize stereotypes of difference and occupational status quo as located in binary, fixed social groups. Tokenism scholarship often traffics in functionalist ontological understandings, assuming that differences are fixed in the body and are the same across groups. In terms of race, scholars study African American tokens in job roles typically held by whites (Kelly, 2007; Turco, 2010; Wingfield, 2010). In terms of gender, scholars study women in jobs typically held by men (Simpson, 1997) or men in feminized jobs (Young & James, 2001). Macro-level perspectives have not allowed scholars to complicate our understandings about social groups and address intersecting social identities.

In this section, we have followed the lead of extant research by starting with an overview of a macro-level approach to investigating token dynamics. From this perspective, we have identified at least three factors that converge to create token dynamics in many workplaces: stereotypes of difference, occupational segregation, and numerical regularity versus rarity of members of particular social groups. As we noted earlier, this approach helps point researchers and practitioners to contexts where they are likely to find that token dynamics negatively shape the workplace experiences of tokens. However, this approach has the potential to overlook individual agency, resistance, and negotiated dynamics of tokenism. Furthermore, this top-down approach tends to treat individuals as members of one fixed social group, rather than as individuals navigating multiple intersecting social categories. Next, we introduce and discuss tokenism research that foregrounds individual responses to token dynamics and the problems and limitations this body of research faces.

Tokenism as a Micro-Level Experience

When scholars investigate token dynamics at the micro-level, the focus becomes how individuals report experiencing social consequences and challenges (Simpson, 1997) and/or enact strategies to mitigate, manage, or resist their token status (Kelly, 2007; Scott, 2005; Wingfield, 2010; Young & James, 2001). Over the previous three decades, scholars across disciplines have relied on the experiences of tokens to engage and extend Kanter's (1977) work. Much of this research supports the core tenet that token dynamics lead to negative social consequences for tokens (Kanter, 1977; Simpson, 1997; Spangler, Gordon, & Pipkin, 1978; Wingfield, 2009; Yoder, 1983). Scholars have extended this approach to explore token dynamics in numerous workplace contexts with various gendered and raced expectations. Some of the reported challenges faced by tokens continue to align with early conclusions and include a sense of isolation or exclusion, the internalizing of pressure to represent one's race and/or gender, and "boundary heightening" by members of the dominant group, where boundary heightening refers to acts by which dominants attempt to keep tokens in their place (see Kanter, 1977; Kelly, 2007; Simpson, 1997; Wingfield, 2009).

There are also a number of new findings regarding the consequences of tokenism, which extend the theory to include dynamics of emotion as well as positive outcomes of tokenism. For example, Young and James (2001) found that token dynamics lead to decreased job satisfaction and workplace detachment for token employees (p. 315). Wingfield (2010) honed in on the emotional labor practices of token employees and argued that token dynamics constrain the types of emotions tokens can display.

In his investigation of the experiences of black teachers, Kelly (2007) presented an argument which counters the assumption that token dynamics constitute negative social consequences for tokens. He found that some token teachers experienced both negative *and* positive consequences because of their token status. Although a great deal of research emphasizes negative consequences associated with token dynamics, Kelly's work illustrates a point often overlooked about Kanter's (1977) discussion of tokenism. As Kanter noted, tokenism may not *always* result in negative experiences, because their difference makes tokens "highly visible in a system where success is tied to becoming known" (p. 207).

Therefore, standing out in the workplace may help tokens get the recognition necessary for keeping their jobs or climbing the corporate ladder.

Micro-level research has also begun to address *how* tokens manage the negative social conditions created by token dynamics. More specifically, this literature focuses on the strategies that tokens develop and enact in order to mitigate, manage, or resist their token status. A number of strategies can be categorized under the umbrella of a common goal: to make non-tokens feel comfortable with the tokens' presence (Kanter, 1977; Kelly, 2007; Wingfield, 2010). According to the literature, this goal can be accomplished in a number of ways. Tokens can remain silent in interactions where race and/or gender become a salient issue (Wingfield, 2010). Tokens may also enact behaviors and emotions, such as smiling, to seem less threatening in front of dominants (Wingfield, 2010). In Wingfield's (2010) study, tokens chose to deflect attention away from their token status or chose not to make their difference an issue.

Additional strategies from the literature can be associated with added pressures that emerge from what Kanter (1977) referred to as the "two-edged sword of publicity" (p. 213). This double-edged sword suggests that while tokens may celebrate being noticed given their rarity, they also contend with the added pressure to perform as the highly visible, highly scrutinized Other. This situation often leads to tokens taking on additional non-job-related tasks. These additional tasks may include earning more advanced degrees or gaining additional credentials to stay ahead and continue to prove they belong (Simpson, 1997). Added pressures may also involve assumptions that tokens will function as "teachers" to dominants or mentors to other tokens (Kelly, 2007). From these examples, we are able to see that a micro-level approach to exploring tokenism, even across various contexts, tends to focus on how the token herself or himself manages personal status. This research therefore emphasizes and places the onus of resolving tokenism on the marginalized individual.

The micro-level perspective offers two ways of thinking about token dynamics in workplace contexts. First, scholars identify obstacles and negative consequences that tokens face, with hopes of drawing crucial attention to problematic work conditions. For instance, as noted previously, Wingfield (2010) investigated the emotion work of racial tokens and suggested that some tokens face the social obstacle of displaying emotions that counter negative cultural stereotypes while white colleagues function without fear that emotional displays like anger will be attributed to their inability to abide by social norms. Second, a micro-level approach offers a grounded approach to understanding tokenism from within the phenomenon, foregrounding lived experience rather than ideology. For these reasons, a micro, or interactional, perspective should be celebrated for highlighting individuals' agency in negotiating or resisting tokenizing stereotypes and practices.

Unfortunately, this perspective also runs the risk of positioning tokenism within individuals. Tokenism becomes seen as embodied in particular people, for example, women, ethnic minorities, and so forth, who "carry" token dynamics around with them, with the implication that difference is an issue only when historically marginalized people are present in the workplace. The effect is, first, to naturalize the workplace as the domain of men and white employees. Second, managing and navigating token dynamics becomes the responsibility of tokens—a practice that further tokenizes the token. Furthermore, this exaggerated expectation of agency overlooks the powerful role of organizational practices and societal stereotypes in sustaining such token dynamics. Third, inasmuch as tokenism is formulated as residing in the body, it is most often normalized as an issue that engages gender and race—differences that are ostensibly "visual"—but is not considered vis-à-vis other potential "differences" such as sexual orientation, religious identification, class background, abilities and disabilities, and so forth.

A Communicative Update to Tokenism Theory

A communicative perspective allows us to treat tokenism as a process constituted in and through communication. In other words, tokenism is not *in* people or organizations but emerges from our workplace interactions, themselves informed by societal stereotypes (of difference and occupational segregation) and organizational processes (hiring, firing, promoting). Thus, token dynamics turn on how difference is communicated and accomplished in everyday interactions. To explain this perspective, we turn to a discussion of organizations as communicatively constituted.

The communicative constitution of organizational processes begins with an understanding that reality is socially constructed. Through language and practices, people construct ideal and normalized assumptions about what it means to be an employee or have a particular job or career. Social constructionism suggests that continually reproduced patterns of behavior and speech lead to particular, taken-for-granted renderings of the world and that "all knowledge is historically and culturally specific. Labels, classifications, denotations, and connotations of social identity are always products of their time" (Allen, 2005, p. 37). Within organizational communication, scholars have turned to explaining the construction of organizations and organizational processes through the *communicative constitution of organizations*. Here, organizations and the processes and patterns taking place among them are themselves social constructs that are developed, shaped, and maintained by language and practice. Ashcraft, Kuhn, and Cooren (2009) explained as follows:

> As manager and employee interact, the conversation does not so much represent each party's internal states, but rather *jointly produces* reality by co-creating meanings that establish "what is" and coordinate and control activity accordingly. Simply put, outcomes are determined in communication....Communication acts on the world; it is a social practice alive with potential. Not "mere" talk or transmission, it (re)produces and alters current realities. (p. 5)

A communicative perspective on tokenism therefore insists that tokenism has a particular "communicational explanation" (Ashcraft et al., 2009, p. 4) and illuminates how difference, meaning, and identity are not only negotiated, but also constructed, in organizations.

From a communication perspective, the idea that one is different is not a "fact" but is born out of interaction. Difference is a social construct wherein the ways people are seen as different and the meanings ascribed to such difference are continually patterned and re-patterned so as to come to be seen as normal or the "truth" (Allen, 2011). Difference is formed in the way that words and ideas are ascribed to a person seen as different, thereby linguistically establishing that person as different. A simple example is found in the way that occupations typically held by men are qualified when women hold these positions. A "doctor" is assumed to be male, but a woman who is a doctor is referred to as a "female doctor." Similarly, saying someone is a pilot often assumes a male pilot, but women are qualified as "female pilots" or even "lady-fliers" (Ashcraft & Mumby, 2003). By qualifying occupations in this way, men are constructed as "natural" doctors and pilots whereas women are constructed as different or deviant (Acker, 1990).

Difference is not only constructed through language but is also accomplished through interactions. When we interact with others, we find ways to negotiate and account for what seems different to us, or perceived difference (West & Fenstermaker, 1995). This "accomplished" difference draws attention to how differences are manifested in interaction, usually around prominent markers such as gender, class, ethnicity, sexual orientation, and so on. Allen (1996) wrote compellingly about the assumptions by other academics that as a black woman in academia, she would naturally work with students of color. This suggestion, constructed in interaction with Allen, demonstrates how her blackness was understood by others as different and was therefore aligned with students also seen as different. Similarly, Adib and Guerrier (2003) demonstrated how individuals identify or dis-identify with one another when negotiating perceived differences and similarities. In their study, one hotel employee avoided sexual harassment, a situation based on gender difference, by appealing to the shared Spanish heritage between herself and her would-be harasser. As Adib and Guerrier pointed out with this example, it is possible for individuals to negotiate around similarities (the Spanish heritage) and not only around differences. Ultimately, this research points to the idea that difference (and sameness) is something we "do," where we are continually drawing from assumptions and bringing them to bear in our daily interactions.

Accordingly, identities in everyday performances are intersectional. Individuals are composed of multiple, fragmented, and competing identities consisting of religious identification, ethnic background, gender performance, native language, occupational identity, and so forth. In the case of the hotel workers (Adib & Guerrier, 2003), they were called to accomplish a number of intersecting differences and/or similarities at varying times. Staffers assumed that Pauline, as a black woman, would be the new housekeeper. But they also assumed that as an *educated* black woman, Pauline would be the housekeeping *manager* and not a maid. Adib and Guerrier observed, "In one context, that of receptionists, Pauline is considered different because of her race, while in another she is different because of her class" (p. 426). Important to note is that these identity positions are not experienced, embraced, or meshed the same way by all people, which further renders identity as situated and constructed in moments and interactions as people work with other people to figure out *who we are together*. This understanding gives credence to the idea that for tokens, the intersection of various and varying identity characteristics can change their experience. And yet, as noted previously, the tokenism literature tends to identify and study only one aspect of identity (e.g., black teachers in predominantly white schools or female managers in organizations where men hold the majority of upper management positions).

Organizational Communication and Tokenism

In the tokenism literature, scholars have tended to overlook how difference is constructed and tokenism is accomplished. Yet, it is apparent that these issues are addressed by today's communication scholarship. Research in gendered organizational communication, critical management studies, and related disciplines has looked to how majority and minority individuals negotiate gender and highly mythologized occupational identities such as aircraft pilots and entrepreneurs (Ashcraft, 2007; Ashcraft & Mumby, 2003; Bruni, Gherardi, & Poggio, 2004; Gill & Ganesh, 2007), how normative assumptions around professionalism versus "dirty work" are constructed and negotiated (Ashforth & Kreiner, 1999; Cheney & Ashcraft, 2007; Kreiner, Ashforth, & Sluss, 2006), and how gender, race and ethnicity, occupational identity, and/or religion are simultaneously navigated in everyday reactions and interactions (Allen, 1996; Essers & Benschop, 2007; Essers, Benschop, & Doorewaard, 2010). Simply by addressing difference in these and other studies, scholarship in our field has implicitly shed light on how tokenism is also constructed and negotiated.

We suggest, however, that there is more to learn about workplace interactions by reviving and reframing tokenism in communication and related literature. Tokenism represents a unique subject position for particular employees that cannot be captured solely by the study of difference or intersectionality. Instead, we propose that tokenism is a *particular* experience or accomplishment of difference and intersectionality that occurs under the circumstance of negative stereotyping, occupational segregation, and numerical rarity, leading to an "other's" being perceived as trespassing in an occupation. We are able to see how tokenism represents a unique instantiation of difference in the example of "female doctors" and "male nurses." While we might assume that a female doctor and a male nurse are in the same situation of being a numerical rarity, we can also point out that, broadly speaking, they are positioned differently within their respective occupations. The woman doctor's experience resides at the confluence of social stereotypes that suggest she is incompetent, occupational norms that suggest that doctoring is a prestigious job as well as a "man's job," and the likelihood that as a woman doctor, she is one of few (Hinze, 1999). While a male nurse similarly "trespasses" in a non-traditional occupation, he does not face the same professional scrutiny of his ability (though to be sure, his sexuality may be called into question; Lupton, 2000; Simpson, 2004).

The significant difference between the female doctor and the male nurse is that *the demands of the job do not change negatively for the male nurse*. The male nurse is not expected to represent his gender, and his mistakes will probably not be used as evidence that men should not be nurses. Rather, male nurses are assumed to be generally competent in most of the technological aspects of nursing and tend to move more often into higher positions in the hierarchy than female nurses (Bradley, 1993). That is, men are more likely to benefit from their token status than are women (Simpson, 2004). We suggest, then, the significance of a dimension of tokenism that we call "upward trespassing." Upward trespassing is at play when a member of a marginalized group enters a privileged occupation, typically occupied by the dominant group. When upward trespassing, members of the marginalized group face increased pressure and resistance. Yet, when members of a traditionally privileged group trespass *downward*, the result is quite different. In downward trespassing, dominant group members (e.g., white men) are positioned to ride a gendered and raced "glass escalator" that quickly moves them into upper level positions within that occupation (Wingfield, 2009). Thus, we want to underscore the importance of *associating tokenism exclusively with upward trespassing*, since it draws particular attention to privileged occupations and the degree to which they are protected and defended from outsiders. Tokenism is at play when someone "different" seeks to trespass upward. In this way, tokenism is a distinct kind of study of difference or minorities in the workplace because it not only attends to numerical rarity and social stereotypes, but it also attends to the relational power dynamics associated with individuals' positions and considers the status of the occupation.

This illustration admittedly draws on broadly sketched experiences of women and men in particular occupations (for instance, we did not consider implications of race, class, ability and disability, and other differences on the "female doctor" and "male nurse"). Nevertheless, we believe that this illustration demonstrates the need and potential for communication scholars to bring tokenism into the fold of communication studies and reframe it as an experiential process rather than as a numerical process. This perspective emphasizes that *there are no such things as tokens, only token dynamics*. In reframing tokenism within a communicative framework, tokenism is distanced (though, necessarily, not entirely severed) from its numerical roots, thus creating space to explore the interactive and accomplished processes involved in (re)producing token dynamics. Accordingly, gender and critical communication scholars can then take up tokenism as a lens for examining the unique positions of minority or "different" employees who are also engaged in high-status work. *In other words, tokenism would become not just the study of difference, but the study of "upward trespassers" within privileged contexts.*

In understanding tokenism as an accomplished, interactive dynamic in some workplace relationships, we are able to offer tentative theoretical and practical implications. It is our particular hope to begin to construct a diagnostic "worksheet" that employees and managers will be able to use in their efforts to identify and change the nature of token dynamics. We turn to implications and recommendations in this final section.

Token Dynamics: Theory and Practice

In offering observations and recommendations, we attempt to deviate from a more traditional "skills-based agenda" found in much management literature and practice (Ashcraft et al., 2009, p. 5). Our interest is directed more specifically toward developing a poststructuralist-inspired tool for assessing and responding to tokenizing dynamics in the workplace. A poststructural approach reminds us that language, meaning, interpretations, and identities are slippery, partial, and nuanced (Butler, 1997; Buzzanell & Liu, 2005; Weedon, 1997), and we suggest applying this approach to organizations as a way to emphasize the contingent, situated, and interactional aspects of token dynamics.

Theoretical Implications and Research Directions

First, by introducing tokenism to the field of communication, we advocate a closer investigation of the role of communication in sustaining token dynamics. For instance, scholars can interrogate organizational narratives for indications of the power dynamics (Martin, 1990; Mumby, 1987) between tokens and the organization, tokens and dominants, and tokens and other tokens. Such an investigation can reveal how particular organizational stories construct and constrain token employees' subject positions and deflect attention from organizational processes that sustain numerical token dynamics. Research foci might include specific attention to hyper-scrutiny in stories told about "upward trespassers" in highly protected occupations, the role of the organization in maintaining and/or mitigating these stories (see Martin, 1990), and the dominant and/or marginalized meanings that can be derived from these stories. Within these explorations, we must embrace a more sophisticated approach to understanding and studying subject positions, one that includes moving beyond unitary categories for interrogating experiences within token dynamics, and integrate an intersectional approach to understanding multiple social identities (see Turco, 2010).

Second, further research must be done to incorporate how members of *dominant* subject positions experience token dynamics. Richard and Wright (2010), for instance, explored the conditions that must be in place for dominant groups to support tokenizing policies. Their study is experimental, however, and does not assess *in situ* experiences. Thus, research that focuses on the involvement of "advantaged group" members as it plays out in the workplace can offer insight into how tokenism is maintained or challenged by others. Additionally, we wonder about the possibility of focusing a research lens on the tokenizing of dominant groups—that is, exploring how members of socially dominant groups (e.g., whites, men) are themselves tokenized based on competing identity markers such as sexuality, ability and disability, religion, and so forth. Research that explores "dominant tokenism" would reject the idea that tokenism resides in the bodies of people and offers revolutionary potential for our understanding of token dynamics as intersectional, processual, and context-based. In that tokens are typically assumed to be minorities, it is important first and foremost to explore how members of socially dominant groups may (or may not) be tokens in the workplace.

Along these lines, we challenge scholars and practitioners alike to shift our collective thinking of tokenism as an individual issue to a process issue. In other words, how do organizational practices themselves maintain token dynamics and problematic workplace relationships in a given context? This shift will involve, in part, identifying token problems present within the particular workplace. One can lean on current research in identifying such problems (e.g., numerical disparities, high turnover, emotional labor) but can also conduct inductive studies to identify hidden ways that tokenism is supported by the organization. The next steps then involve interrogating these organizational practices for how they implicitly design the conditions for tokenism.

Practical Implications: How Do We Begin to "See" Tokenism in the Workplace?

At this point, we turn to discuss how people negotiating tokenism in the workplace might begin to assess and address tokenizing processes. In turning toward practical suggestions, we synthesize our theoretical argument into a heuristic, or assessment tool, that illustrates the overlapping micro and macro conditions that constitute token dynamics and produce particular token experiences. Furthermore, we identify specific points of intervention within these token dynamics.

Our discussion of tokenism has suggested that token dynamics emerge at the intersection of six mutually reinforcing conditions: numerical rarity, negative stereotyping, and occupational segregation at the macro-level, and upward trespassing, heighted scrutiny, and demarcation of difference at the micro-level. The model we have developed (see Figure 1) illustrates the interplay of these dynamics as a set of conditions wherein *all conditions are necessary for creating tokenizing dynamics*. The model proposes that these dynamics operate as concentric circles, where the six conditions support and perpetuate the other

3 - Negative Stereotyping
Focus Areas:
- Silencing or lack of systems to challenge stereotyping
- "Tolerating" or "ignoring" those who perpetuate stereotypes
- Organizational narratives and informal information networks
- Confirmation bias

Interrupting Strategies:
+ Self-reflexivity/Perception checking
+ Developing strategies for open, honest, trusting conversations
+ Confronting problematic behaviors

5 - Heightened Scrutiny
Focus Areas:
- Communication of expectations
- Proof of worthiness
- Organizational narratives

Interrupting Strategies:
+ Maintaining consistent expectations via clear job descriptions
+ Challenging organizational narratives

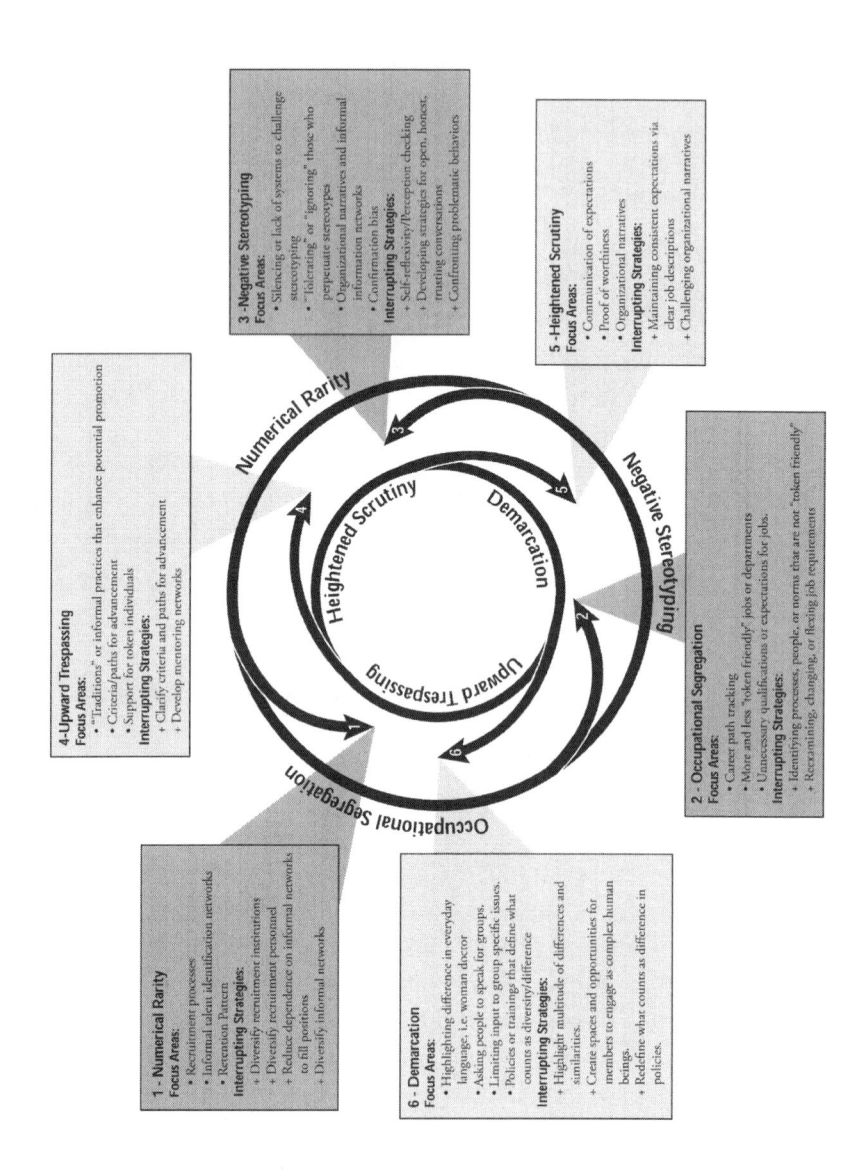

4 - Upward Trespassing
Focus Areas:
- "Traditions" or informal practices that enhance potential promotion
- Criteria/paths for advancement
- Support for token individuals

Interrupting Strategies:
+ Clarify criteria and paths for advancement
+ Develop mentoring networks

2 - Occupational Segregation
Focus Areas:
- Career path tracking
- More and less "token friendly" jobs or departments
- Unnecessary qualifications or expectations for jobs

Interrupting Strategies:
+ Identifying processes, people, or norms that are not "token friendly"
+ Reexamining, changing, or fixing job requirements

1 - Numerical Rarity
Focus Areas:
- Recruitment processes
- Informal talent identification networks
- Retention Pattern

Interrupting Strategies:
+ Diversify recruitment institutions
+ Diversify recruitment personnel
+ Reduce dependence on informal networks to fill positions
+ Diversify informal networks

6 - Demarcation
Focus Areas:
- Highlighting difference in everyday language, i.e. woman doctor
- Asking people to speak for groups.
- Limiting input to group specific issues.
- Policies or trainings that define what counts as diversity/difference

Interrupting Strategies:
+ Highlight multitude of differences and similarities.
+ Create spaces and opportunities for members to engage as complex human beings.
+ Redefine what counts as difference in policies.

Figure 1. Communicative Model of Tokenizing Dynamics

conditions. As such, the model allows us to visualize macro conditions and micro interactions as implicated in each other (such as with negative stereotyping and heightened scrutiny).

In addition to emphasizing the interplay of micro and macro conditions, the model also leaves space for a multiplicity of experiences that might emerge from these processes by offering an analytical framework that can adjust to situation-specific identities, occupations, and organizations. Most importantly, by framing tokenism as a dynamic process with interacting conditions, we point out that shifting the negative impact of token dynamics in the workplace requires that individuals and organizations *interrupt* these mutually reinforcing processes. In the remainder of this section, we address each of the six conditions that merge to produce token dynamics by offering specific diagnostic questions and points of intervention. Our discussion is not intended to be exhaustive or universally applicable but rather to demonstrate how our model helps to hone in on specific processes and points of intervention of token dynamics unique to a particular organization.

Interactional, micro-level. The interactional micro-level conditions, represented in the inner concentric circle, include upward trespassing, heightened scrutiny, and demarcation of difference. We emphasize that each of these are communicatively accomplished in interaction and that well-directed self-reflection can help to interrupt each of these conditions as they contribute to token dynamics. We begin with the notion of **upward trespassing.** Upward trespassing is different from simple advancement because it is characterized by the sentiment that the person who has advanced doesn't "really" belong. As mentioned earlier, upward trespassing is distinguished by the resistance one faces when crossing boundaries of occupational segregation (this resistance is, of course, manifested in mutually reinforcing processes of the demarcation of difference and heightened scrutiny). Although this resistance is in part due to the three macro conditions, it may also be accentuated by seemingly neutral organizational practices. For example, potentially troublesome practices include a lack of clear criteria for advancement in the organization that obscure why and how people have advanced in an organization, leading to the perception that elite ranks are just a "good ol' boys club" or that tokens are undeserving benefactors of affirmative action. This situation may be further exacerbated by a strong dependence on "traditions" or informal processes that increase likelihood for advancement, particularly when those informal processes are more difficult for one group to gain access to, such as playing golf or being invited to a weekend at the hunting lodge. These conditions can be interrupted by creating clear paths and criteria for advancement and by supporting people who want to pursue those paths. For example, if token dynamics are at work in the organization, are mentorship programs in place that partner people in token positions with colleagues who can help them identify paths and requirements to advance in the organization? Do clear criteria for advancement make it easier for token individuals and their allies to advocate and defend their belonging or, in the best case scenario, eliminate the need for them to defend their belonging at all?

Upward trespassing is both accentuated by and perpetuates issues of **demarcation.** In other words, if a difference is not marked, then one is not acknowledged as different and therefore not trespassing. Demarking difference not only sustains the notion that one does not belong but also reduces intersectional identities to a single aspect of identity. While we have already noted several of the language constructs that mark difference, such as female doctor, there are also specifically organizational exchanges that subtly mark difference. For example, individuals must be careful in meetings and less formal interactions to avoid tokenizing others by assuming they will act as social representatives of an entire social group. If a colleague is continually asked to speak on behalf of her or his social group, it is useful to ask, "Can we open up that question to the rest of the group?" or to ask the person being tokenized, "What are your thoughts about the other things we've been speaking about?" Too often, we see cases where tokens are silenced in formal and informal organizational interactions unless they are asked to speak on behalf of their social group. Such situations create patterns of behavior that not only mark difference but also restrict the value of a person to that difference.

Furthermore, we encourage both individuals and organizations to create strategies and opportunities for acknowledging the complexity in coworkers. No one is only male, only black, only wealthy, only a woman, only a shop floor manager, and so forth. We are all members of minority and majority groups in different contexts and at the intersection of multiple categories. Therefore, we are not suggesting that difference should be ignored; rather, we advocate that differences be multiplied. Rather than marking one kind of difference as significant, we advocate emphasizing a plethora of differences and similarities among all organization members, including those who are traditionally thought of as dominant group members. Organizations can also revisit policy to identify ways they support such complexity in interaction, by examining how the organization conceives of difference and diversity and what role the organization believes it should play in mitigating token dynamics. We might ask, then, how the organization defines minorities and how this definition might become more dynamic. For instance, does the organization incorporate and support additional instances of difference such as religious faith, sexual orientation, ability and disability, and so forth?

Finally, we suggest that token dynamics also emerge when individuals experience **heightened scrutiny** due to upward trespassing and demarcation as different. Heightened scrutiny may emerge in subtle organizational practices as raised expectations or insisting that members of token groups repeatedly or continually "prove" their competence. Individuals can mitigate intended or unintended scrutiny by reflecting on their own expectations of coworkers and employees and comparing those expectations to the job description. Is anyone asked to go beyond the description to an extent that is not expected of others? At the organizational culture level, one might pay close attention to the informal information networks and the narratives of the organizational culture. Are particular people's faults, successes, or potential being disproportionately emphasized in these informational circuits?

Macro-conditions of token dynamics. Although macro-conditions, represented in the external concentric circle, of numerical rarity, negative stereotyping, and occupational segregation, are also communicatively constituted, these conditions have a more structural character and stronger connection to broad social constructions of human difference. Nonetheless, individuals within organizations can make concerted efforts to challenge and change these structures. To begin, we suggest that practitioners can address **numerical rarity** of token groups by examining processes that sustain the regularity and rarity of members of certain social groups. Does the organization primarily recruit from schools and institutions wherein token dynamics and numerical unbalance are present? Does it recruit primarily from private institutions or white institutions? The demographic pool of potential employees will reflect demographics of the places from which the organization recruits. Does the organization send recruiters of a variety of identities to recruit at these schools? Aside from college recruiting, does the organization rely on personal and informal networks to fill open positions? If so, whose personal and informal networks?

If hiring does not seem to be an issue, one might examine retention issues. If the turnover rate is high for a particular social group, have exit interviews been conducted? Do these interviews include attention to how the organization can improve the experiences of future employees? Who conducts the exit interviews?

Occupational segregation is also a condition that has broad societal and structural roots that reach beyond the boundaries of the organization and into educational and training institutions. Yet there are still actions that individuals can take to reduce the ways these broad societal patterns emerge in an organization. One point of focus might be to examine career paths. Are token group members encouraged by each other or non-token supervisors to pursue career paths in jobs or departments that are considered to be more "friendly" to those who share their identity? If so, what makes a department or job more or less friendly to a particular group of people? Addressing the latter question might require organizations to revisit their assumptions about the competencies, skills, and expectations of particular jobs. Should a Hispanic person be expected to take a managerial job at a bank branch in a Hispanic neighborhood if his or her skills and interests are better used for a large commercial setting? Can a non-Hispanic Spanish-speaking employee fill the branch manager position? These forms of "tracking" career paths can cause identities to overshadow skill sets and interests, reinforcing occupational segregation and maintaining numerical rarity.

Finally, we address the issue of **negative stereotyping.** At the most basic level, we acknowledge that we are all influenced by broad social stereotypes, yet we challenge individuals to hold their assumptions about others lightly. This way of thinking involves a certain degree of self-reflexivity that involves asking oneself, "How did I come to these conclusions about others?" or "What behaviors has the other person exhibited that counter my assumptions?" Are we selectively perceiving things so that we can prove that our assumptions are correct (even if we don't know we are making the assumptions)? Do stories that circulate (formally or informally) throughout the organization import broad social stereotypes into the organization? These questions may lead to a greater degree of inquisitiveness or curiosity that will encourage conversation and a spirit of community that reduces reliance on stereotypes.

We also challenge individuals to be careful of becoming a bystander to the perpetuation of stereotypes and other tokenizing processes. It is important that organizations create spaces and processes through which individuals of all job titles, roles, and levels can challenge negative stereotypes (and other token dynamics) in their workplace without suffering negative consequences. Is the organizational culture one where employees can challenge problematic token dynamics without fear of being isolated, demoted, or fired? Suggesting that people should ignore or tolerate inappropriate behaviors from exceptionally offensive employees who sustain negative stereotypes and create hostile environments, rather than challenging those behaviors and risk "stirring things up," creates an environment where actions that sustain negative stereotypes are protected and challenges to negative stereotyping are cast as inappropriate. Of course, many people of dominant identities avoid confronting these stereotype-sustaining processes because they are uncomfortable and unsure about how to address them. Self-reflexivity, mutual trust, and open, honest conversations about issues of difference are necessary to create organizational spaces in which negative stereotypes can be challenged.

In our token dynamics model, we have marked each of these points of intervention and offered processes, questions, and possible interruptions one might consider when addressing tokenizing dynamics. Yet, rather than being a comprehensive model, this model, we anticipate, will provide focus for individual and collective self-reflection that leads to specific and actionable strategies for challenging token dynamics.

Conclusion

Our chapter has sought to (re)introduce token theory to the communication field and (re)invigorate token research in related fields. We contend that theorizing about token dynamics have remained relatively stagnant since Kanter's (1977) foundational work, save for a few exceptions, and that scholars in interdisciplinary social fields have not sufficiently pushed our understanding of tokenism. A communication perspective on tokenism as intersectional and accomplished problematizes this body of literature by shifting the discussion away from deterministic, numbers-based understandings of token dynamics toward more inclusive and situational understandings. Yet, at the same time, we believe that communication scholars can also take a page from our chapter to consider how we might ourselves study token dynamics. As we noted, communication scholars are studying relevant issues such as difference, intersectionality, and accomplishment. Yet, we contend that tokenism is a *particular subject position and workplace relationship* at the confluence of these dynamics. We concluded our chapter with a discussion of the theoretical and practical considerations related to token dynamics as we move forward in this area of research. We have also offered a model of tokenizing processes that we hope will aid practitioners in their own endeavors to identify and challenge these problematic workplace relationships.

Author's Note

> The authors contributed equally to the development of this chapter, and our names are listed in alphabetical order to reflect this equality of contribution. We would also like to express our appreciation to Heather Pitts of Bryan, Texas, for her excellent graphic design work on the tokenism model.

References

Acker, J. (1990). Hierarchies, jobs, and bodies: A theory of gendered organizations. *Gender and Society, 4*, 139–158.

Adib, A., & Guerrier, Y. (2003). The interlocking of gender with nationality, race, ethnicity and class: The narratives of women in hotel work. *Gender, Work & Organization, 10*, 413–432.

Allen, B. J. (1996). Feminist standpoint theory: A black woman's (re)view of organizational socialization. *Communication Studies, 47*, 257–271.

Allen, B. J. (2000). Learning the ropes: A black feminist standpoint analysis. In P. M. Buzzanell (Ed.), *Rethinking organizational and managerial communication from feminist perspectives* (pp. 177–208). Thousand Oaks, CA: Sage.

Allen, B. J. (2005). Social constructionism. In D. Mumby & S. May (Eds.), *Engaging organizational communication theory and research: Multiple perspectives* (pp. 35–53). Thousand Oaks, CA: Sage.

Allen, B. J. (2011). *Difference matters: Communicating social identity* (2nd ed). Long Grove, IL: Waveland Press.

Ashcraft, K. L. (2007). Appreciating the "work" of discourse: Occupational identity and difference as organizing mechanisms in the case of commercial airline pilots. *Discourse & Communication, 1*, 9–36.

Ashcraft, K. L., & Allen, B.J. (2003). The racial foundation of organizational communication. *Communication Theory, 13*, 5–38.

Ashcraft, K. L., Kuhn, T., & Cooren, F. (2009). Constitutional amendments: "Materializing" organizational communication. In J. P. Walsh & A. P. Brief (Eds.), *The Academy of Management Annals 3* (pp. 1–64).

Ashcraft, K. L., & Mumby, D. K. (2003). *Reworking gender: A feminist communicology of organization*. Thousand Oaks, CA: Sage.

Ashforth, B. E., & Kreiner, G. E. (1999). "How can you do it?": Dirty work and the challenge of constructing a positive identity. *The Academy of Management Review, 24*, 413–434.

Bank, B. J. (2009). Sex segregation and tokenism among teachers. In L. J. Sahn & A. G. Dworkin (Eds.), *International handbook of research on teachers and teaching* (pp. 291–302). New York, NY: Springer.

Bradley, H. (1993). Across the great divide. In C. Williams (Ed.), *Doing women's work: Men in non-traditional occupations* (pp. 10–28). London, England: Sage.

Bruni, A., Gherardi, S., & Poggio, B. (2004). Doing gender, doing entrepreneurship: An ethnographic account of intertwined practices. *Gender, Work & Organization, 11*, 406–429.

Butler, J. (1997). *Excitable speech: A politics of the performative*. New York, NY: Routledge.

Buzzanell, P. M., & Liu, M. (2005). Struggling with maternity leave policies and practices: A poststructuralist feminist analysis of gendered organizing. *Journal of Applied Communication Research, 33*, 1–25.

Cheney, G., & Ashcraft, K. L. (2007). Considering "The Professional" in communication studies: Implications for theory and research within and beyond the boundaries of organizational communication. *Communication Theory, 17*, 146–175.

Cloud, D. L. (1996). Hegemony or concordance? The rhetoric of tokenism in "Oprah" Winfrey's rags-to-riches biography. *Critical Studies of Mass Communication, 13*, 115–137.

Collinson, D. L. (1988). "Engineering humour": Masculinity, joking and conflict in shop-floor relations. *Organization Studies, 9*, 181–199.

Danaher, K., & Branscombe, N. R. (2010). Maintaining the system with tokenism: Bolstering individual mobility beliefs and identification with a discriminatory organization. *British Journal of Social Psychology, 49*, 343–362.

Essers, C., & Benschop, Y. (2007). Enterprising identities: Female entrepreneurs of Moroccan or Turkish origin in the Netherlands. *Organization Studies, 28*, 49–69.

Essers, C., Benschop Y., & Doorewaard, H. (2010). Female ethnicity: Understanding Muslim immigrant businesswomen in the Netherlands. *Gender, Work & Organization, 17*, 320–339.

Ferguson, K. E. (1984). *The feminist case against bureaucracy*. Philadelphia, PA: Temple University Press.

Gill, R., & Ganesh, S. (2007). Empowerment, constraint, & the entrepreneurial self: A study of white women entrepreneurs. *Journal of Applied Communication Research, 35*, 268–293.

Hinze, S. W. (1999). Gender and the body of medicine or at least some body parts: (Re)constructing the prestige hierarchy of medical specialties. *The Sociological Quarterly, 40*, 217–239.

Kanter, R. M. (1977). *Men and women of the corporation*. New York, NY: Basic Books.

Kelly, H. (2007). Racial tokenism in the school workplace: An exploratory study of black teachers in overwhelmingly white schools. *Educational Studies, 41*, 230–252.

King, E. B., Hebl, M. R., George, J. M., & Matusik, S. F. (2010). Understanding tokenism: Antecedents and consequences of a psychological climate of gender inequity. *Journal of Management, 36*, 482–510.

Kreiner, G. E., Ashforth, B. E., & Sluss, D. M. (2006). Identity dynamics in occupational dirty work: Integrating social identity and system justification perspectives. *Organization Science, 17*, 619–636.

Lupton, B. (2000). Maintaining masculinity: Men who do "women's work." *British Journal of Management, 11*, 33–48.

Martin, J. (1990). Deconstructing organizational taboos: The suppression of gender conflict in organizations. *Organization Science, 1*, 339–359.

Martin, J., Knopoff, K., & Beckman, C. (1998). An alternative to bureaucratic impersonality and emotional labor: Bounded emotionality at The Body Shop. *Administrative Science Quarterly, 43*, 429–469.

Mumby, D. K. (1987). The political function of narrative in organizations. *Communication Monographs, 54*, 113–127.

Mumby, D. K., & Putnam, L. L. (1992). The politics of emotion: A feminist reading of bounded rationality. *Academy of Management Review, 17*, 465–486.

Richard, N. T., & Wright, S. C. (2010). Advantaged group members' reactions to tokenism. *Group Processes & Intergroup Relations, 13*, 559–569.

Scott, E. K. (2005). Beyond tokenism: The making of racially diverse feminist organizations. *Social Problems, 52*, 232–254.

Simpson, R. (1997). Have times changed? Career barriers and the token woman manager. *British Journal of Management, 8*, S121–S130.

Simpson, R. (2004). Masculinity at work: The experiences of men in female dominated occupations. *Work, Employment and Society, 18*, 349–368.

Squires, C. R., & Jackson, S. J. (2010). Reducing race: News themes in the 2008 primaries. *The International Journal of Press/Policies, 15*, 375–400.

Spangler, E., Gordon, M. A., & Pipkin, R. M. (1978). Token women: An empirical test of Kanter's hypothesis. *American Journal of Sociology, 84*, 160–170.

Trethewey, A. (1997). Resistance, identity, and empowerment: A postmodern feminist analysis of clients in a human service organization. *Communication Monographs, 64*, 281–301.

Turco, C. J. (2010). Cultural foundations of tokenism: Evidence from the leveraged buyout industry. *American Sociological Review, 75*, 894–913.

Weedon, C. (1997). *Feminist practice and poststructuralist theory.* Oxford, England: Blackwell.

West, C., & Fenstermaker, S. (1995). Doing difference. *Gender & Society, 9*, 8–37.

Wingfield, A. H. (2009). Racializing the glass escalator: Reconsidering men's experiences with women's work. *Gender & Society, 23*, 5–26.

Wingfield, A. H. (2010). Are some emotions marked "whites only"? Racialized feeling rules in professional workplaces. *Social Problems, 57*, 251–268.

Yoder, J. D. (1983). Another look at women in the Army: A comment on Woelfel's article. *Sex Roles, 9*, 285–288.

Young, J. L., & James, E. H. (2001). Token majority: The work attitudes of male flight attendants. *Sex Roles, 45*, 299–319.

PART III

Maintaining and Restoring Effective Relationships

· 11 ·

"THE MOST VULNERABLE...[AND] MOST RESILIENT PEOPLE"

Communicatively Constituting Palestinian Refugees' Resilience

ABRAR HAMMOUD & PATRICE M. BUZZANELL

In October 2011, the Associated Press publicized Angelina Jolie's increased efforts on behalf of refugees and underserved people around the globe. The newsworthy item at that time was that Ms. Jolie was expanding her role beyond a goodwill ambassador and spokesperson with the United Nations refugee agency. Although the exact nature of her new work was unknown, she used the opportunity to draw attention to the lives and needs of refugees worldwide. As she explained, "Refugees [are] 'the most vulnerable people in the world, and they are also the most resilient people'" (Associated Press, 2011, p. D6). Although Angelina Jolie did not elaborate on why or how she perceives refugees to be resilient or to communicate in ways that enable them to construct resilience, our chapter discusses different ways in which refugees in a particular Palestinian refugee camp talk, interact, and create structures in ways that promote resiliency in their communities and for themselves as individuals. We take the position that resilience does not lie solely within a person or collectivity but is a complex and communicatively constituted phenomenon that is composed of several imbricated or interlocking processes adapted for and by different peoples and locales.

Moreover, we argue that resilience is not simply "bouncing back" or returns to normalcy after natural and/or human-made disasters or life traumas. Rather, it is a process whereby individuals, communities, nations, and global citizens exert agency and voice in the "new normal" that they organize through everyday discourses as well as macro or societal discourses and structures. As such, our aim is to discuss how refugee resilience is communicatively constituted as an imbricated system of interlocking processes embedded within particular cultures and spatio-temporal contexts. We draw upon the first author's research and personal experience in a Palestinian refugee camp to describe communicative resilience processes. We focus the ways in which refugee work has different meanings, meaningfulness, and material as well as discursive aspects that function productively and agentically in resilience processes.

Literature Review

In this section, we first discuss refugee communities and then provide an overview of the communicative construction of resilience and omissions in current literature in this area, particularly with regard to indigenous peoples.

Refugee Communities

In this section, we define "refugee" and then discuss how members of the Palestinian refugee camp we study both lack resources and experience marginalization similar to those of other "indigenous" populations.

The term refugee has been defined numerous ways. Malkki (1995) argued that the expression may have "analytical usefulness not as a label for a special, generalizable 'kind' or 'type' of person or situation, but only as a broad legal or descriptive rubric that includes within it a world of different socioeconomic statuses, personal histories, and psychological or spiritual situations" (p. 496). Jacobsen (2005) stated that "refugees are people displaced by persecution, war, or conflict, who have fled across an international border and are in need of international humanitarian assistance" (p. 4), while Grabska (2006) described refugees as individuals subject to forced migration. More specifically, Pont (2006) differentiated between various categories of refugees, with those living in exile over five years described as protracted refugees. As of 2006, there are 33 recognized protracted refugee situations, not including the largest protracted refugee situation, namely, Palestinian refugees.

"Jabal" (pseudonym) is a Palestinian refugee community with aspects similar in nature and definition to those of indigenous populations. Ellis (2000) noted that these populations are often overwhelmed and beleaguered by "modernity, capitalism, and expanding world religions, such as Christianity and

Islam"(p. 298). Native tribal systems of belief begin to weaken as the influence of incoming settlers increases and strengthens. With this in mind, Ellis reminded scholars that "monotheistic religions—Judaism but also Christianity and Islam—are born in a cycle of violence which emerges and stabilizes in a particular religion" (p. 299). Thus, the history of violence among these specific religions is at times in direct opposition to indigenous cultures and religions.

Conditions to which many indigenous populations are presently subjected may be comparable to those they previously imposed upon others: "Few histories of any duration are innocent and colonialism is hardly the property of any ethnic or religious group" (Ellis, 2000, p. 299). O'Faircheallaigh (1999) noted that indigenous people are oftentimes completely excluded from projects and missions, and they are directly affected and face challenges with social impact assessment. They find themselves frequently lacking resources that are not only financial in nature but also technical and professional. Across varying contexts and among differing cultures, examples of this type of marginalization with regard to voice and material resources are prevalent. Edelstein and Kleese (1995) shared an example pertaining to native Hawaiians. The specific community to which they referred places great significance on volcanoes and the surrounding land for spiritual and religious reasons. They were rebuffed and denied permission to voice their concerns when these regions were explored as sources of geothermal energy. Thus, decisions directly influencing their lives were made without their consent.

The relationship between indigenous Aborigines and Australian settlers provides yet another example of the marginalization imposed upon indigenous populations. Over the past 200 years, Australia's demographics rapidly changed as the Aboriginal population dramatically decreased while the settler population rapidly increased (Adger, 2000). Eventually, Aborigines' "rights were treated with disregard and contempt, and there was very little regret for their fate among those who set about building a new society in Australia" (Adger, 2000, p. 188).

Indigenous populations of refugees in Israel, Jordan, and Palestine compose yet another multi-faceted relationship between native inhabitants and settlers. The origins of issues facing these populations are quite complex and have been documented extensively. As Ellis (2000) noted, "The struggle in Israel/Palestine follows an ancient pattern of invasion and settlement, victory and defeat, but the pattern of integration and evolution of identity is also to be seen here" (p. 299). In our case, Jabal represents an indigenous population whose cultural identity is shaped by geographical region. In addition, much like the native Hawaiians and Aborigines previously mentioned, the refugees within this community are materially marginalized and fundamentally relegated to decision-making sidelines by settlers.

Resilience

Resilience processes are triggered by disruptions in people's lives—loss, disaster, trauma, upheaval in all one knows and values (for an overview, see Buzzanell, Shenoy, Remke, & Lucas, 2009; see also Lucas & Buzzanell, 2011). The processes whereby resiliences are constructed are not solely discursively and performatively based. Indeed, resilience has individual physiological and neurological bases, learning and development background and capacities, dependencies on social capital or networks, and so on. Early theories focused on the relationship between genetics and resilience. In the past, researchers described this relationship in ways that implied that individuals were simply born resilient. For example, studies centering on the growth and development of children within adversarial environments would note "something remarkable or special about these children, often described by words such as vulnerable, or invincible" (Masten, 2001, p. 227).

In contrast, existing literature supports notions of resilience as a process rooted within human adaptation and learning (Coutu, 2002). Additionally, recent research has emphasized the ordinary, rather than the extraordinary, nature of resilience (Bonnano, 2004; Masten, 2001). Bonnano (2004) noted how "resilience to the unsettling effects of interpersonal loss is not rare but relatively common, does not appear to indicate pathology but rather healthy adjustment" (p. 23). Even so, much resilience research continues to focus on what characteristics typify resilient structures, communities, and individuals; how children, survivors, and families adapt to hardship; and how resources and training might promote resilience for at-risk groups and those experiencing natural disasters or other life-changing events. In addressing resilience from a more ecological vantage point, Adger (2000) defined social resilience as "the ability of groups or communities to cope with external stresses and disturbances as a result of social, political and environmental change" (p. 347).

Buzzanell (2010) took a different angle on resilience by describing resilience as a process, not necessarily a quality of an entity or structure. This process may consist of multiple, as well as potentially unexpected, routes, phases, and triggers (Bonanno, 2004), but the primary characterization of resilience as processual lies in its nature as "dynamic, integrated, unfolding over time and through events, evolving into patterns, and dependent on contingencies" (Buzzanell, 2010, p. 2). Thus, resilience can be distinguished by "good outcomes in spite of serious threats to adaptation and development" (Masten, 2001, p. 228), although the meaning of "good" may change over the course of individuals' or communities' lifespan.

Resilience begins with and is sustained by five processes: (a) crafting normalcy, (b) affirming identity anchors, (c) maintaining and using communication networks, (d) putting alternative logics to work, and (e) legitimizing negative feelings while foregrounding productive action (Buzzanell, 2010). In crafting normalcy, individuals and collectivities "implicitly and sometimes explicitly produced a system of meanings that enabled them to maintain the mundane, the regularities in life that previously would have gone unnoticed" (Buzzanell, 2010, p. 3). Affirming identity anchors can be defined as "a relatively enduring cluster of identity discourses upon which individuals and their familial, collegial, and/or community members rely when explaining who they are for themselves and in relation to each other" (Buzzanell, 2010, p. 4). In maintaining and using communication networks, people build and use social capital or connections with others that may be helpful in disruptive times. As these people put their alternative logic to work, they "incorporate seemingly contradictory ways of doing organizational work through development of alternative logics or through reframing the entire situation" (Buzzanell, 2010, p. 6). Finally, when people legitimize negative feelings while foregrounding productive action, they note that there are more important roles or actions that they must undertake so they acknowledge that they should (and do) feel bereft, devastated, and lost, but they construct feelings of agency, hopefulness, and productive emotions so that they can carry on with life.

Although Buzzanell (2010) argued that these processes may be transferrable to many different human experiences, we argue that there are omissions in current resilience scholarship. These omissions can be addressed by taking an intersectional and culture-centered stance, such as the one we have taken here. Specifically, there is little research that looks at the varied identity, voice, and material struggles for viable "normalcies" in the lives of people whose very ways of knowing and being are misunderstood (e.g., intellectual, cultural, and material property rights; see Cannella & Manuelito, 2008; Pal & Buzzanell, 2008; Shome & Hegde, 2002). By definition, indigenous peoples are members of politically underprivileged groups who may be the original inhabitants of a particular space but who can operate as a collective with shared identity different from the nation or (later-arriving) groups in power. Toward the goal of understanding the lived experiences and constructions of resilience among members of a Palestinian refugee camp, we refer to culture-centered approaches (see Dutta, 2008, 2011).

These approaches operate at the intersections of culture, structure, and agency to offer insight into the deep contextual particularities and logics that can inform the adaptive and transformative potential of resilience processes.

Summary

We briefly described the vulnerabilities and experiences of refugees and indigenous peoples and then provided an overview of resilience as a theoretical framework for our case study. We question how we can make visible the imbricated layers of indigenous culture-centered resiliencies—both temporary, as some readers would expect from the label "refugee" camp, and the more routinized or longer-term "new normalcies" for members of the Palestinian refugee camp we studied in the Middle East.

Autoethnographic Case Study Method

We bring different experiences to our analysis of resilience in a Palestinian refugee camp. We developed our case study based on document analysis of websites and other materials, as well as on participant observations, conversations with camp and (unnamed) nongovernmental organization (NGO) members (we chose the acronym AMHA as a pseudonym for the nongovernmental organization to preserve anonymity; in Arabic, amal means "hope" and haya means "life"—"hope for life"—and the word amha means "a seed of wheat"), and our own ongoing conversations (via face-to-face, e-mail, and Skype communications) before, during, and after the first author's time in the Middle East (hereafter known as Abrar). We also brought our disciplinary and cultural expertise (e.g., Middle East and engineering). In these ways, we were not only able to question the nature and forms of resilience occurring in our Palestinian refugee camp, but we also interrogated culture through our drive to position ourselves as "others" through a collaborative questioning and reversing of "otherness" positionalities (Buzzanell, 2011). In doing so, we engaged with our subject matter through a critical empathic lens whereby we were mindful that we never could know the lives of the others whom we studied (Remke, 2006). We did our best to represent their lives through our scholarly expertise (see Foss & Foss, 1994).

Throughout, our metatheoretical and methodological lenses were social constructionist and autoethnographic. We employed social constructivism as a metatheoretical framework (see Craig, 1999) whereby we developed our understandings of our research in Jabal and our theoretical lens of resilience.

By doing so, we adhered to the main tenets of social constructionism (Allen, 2005; see also Bartesaghi & Castor, 2008).

The first of the four primary assumptions is that a social constructionist lens encourages us to be suspicious of our understandings about our research participants and context. We challenge and ask critical questions about previous findings and our own beliefs. Second, we acknowledge that contemporary constructions rely upon, but are not determined by, historical conceptualizations. Third, we focus on participants' language and interactions to locate subjective meanings and how participants create knowledge. Finally, we assume that knowledge and the social interaction that produces this knowledge are interconnected. We note not only that there are many stakeholders in refugee experiences and resilience processes but also that our primary participants, the refugees themselves, are affected by and affect public policy in their local region and in global politics.

In addition to being social constructionist, our case study also is autoethnographic. We relate personal narratives in which we "take on the dual identities of academic and personal selves to tell autobiographical stories about some aspect of their experience in daily life" (Ellis & Bochner, 2000, p. 740). In autoethnography, we operate in liminal and sometimes inverted and intermingled spaces—participant and observer, insider and outsider, privilege and marginalization. Ellis and Bochner (2000) advised that researchers start with personal life, pay attention to the embodiment of their feelings and thoughts, use "systematic sociological introspection and emotional recall" (p. 737), and write experiences as a story. We weave in our participants' stories, highlighting the material conditions in which they live and work and providing background on linguistic choices and our observations.

As a result of taking a social constructionist stance, we next present a brief overview of the specific context. We then provide information about ourselves. We were cognizant that we needed to recognize and articulate the influences of our own backgrounds—separately and together—on our interpretations (Creswell, 2007), as would befit social constructionism and autoethnography. We use these forms of knowledge to identify how and what factors contributed to the perspectives with which we viewed the community, context, and language choices of the individuals and of communities as a whole.

Context

According to the Palestinian Central Bureau of Statistics (PCBS, 2006), of the more than 3 million displaced Palestinians currently residing in the country in which our case study takes place, nearly 75,000 live in an area of East Amman called Jabal. The growth, development, and opportunities available to this community remain impeded by the prevalence of numerous social issues, particularly overpopulation.

The average Palestinian household in the location of our case study consists of 5.1 members (PCBS, 2009). However, nearly all the individuals we encountered and/or worked with belong to families containing at least 7 or 8 nuclear members. Dilapidated, graffiti-covered concrete and cement buildings have been partitioned and repartitioned over decades such that families are generally confined to living spaces of no more than four total rooms. During the winter season, when temperatures hover around the freezing point, kerosene lamps are used to heat homes. Those who cannot afford heaters often resort to building fires within their living spaces. Tragically, entire families often perish when these fires grow beyond control.

In addition to issues with residences, overpopulation issues permeating Jabal's schools confront the area. The lack of physical space to accommodate students has demanded fundamental changes to the educational system. The school day has been divided into one 4-hour morning session and one 4-hour afternoon session. Students are only permitted to attend school for the single 4-hour session to which they are assigned. Even after implementing these rules, three to four students are still required to squeeze next to one another and share desks that are nearly 25 years old. Additionally, the battered and worn texts and workbooks from which students read and write are significantly outdated. At the end of each school year, teachers erase the outgoing class's work and redistribute the material to the new incoming students when the next term commences.

Of the various other challenges facing this community, the increased and widespread prevalence of domestic as well as drug-related violence is among the most serious. Not only do children witness this violence, they have also been known to partake in it. For instance, during Abrar's initial stay in Jabal, she met a woman named Um Ahmed. We note that parents in the Middle East are often referred to as "the father of" or "the mother of" their oldest son. Thus, the name Um Ahmed translates to "the mother of Ahmed." Um Ahmed worked at the AMHA, the NGO that partnered with the institution of higher education in which Abrar was a student. As Um Ahmed worked at various tasks, long caftans concealed her round shape and a head scarf called a hijab covered her hair. Her round face was friendly, smiling more often than not, whether she was making photocopies or cups of coffee. Her reputation as an excellent cook was a great source of pride to Um Ahmed, and oftentimes, when Abrar would be wandering in and out of AMHA's offices, she would stop and ask Um Ahmed for tips on making one dish or another.

Um Ahmed was simply one of the many women and men whom Abrar met in the refugee community. Because Abrar speaks Arabic and knows local customs and rituals, she had both an insider's and outsider's view of community life. She engaged in many conversations with refugee community members as well as with AMHA staff of whom Jenna (pseudonym), the AMHA communication coordinator, was one.

One day, as Abrar shared something with Jenna from her latest conversation with Um Ahmed, she noticed a look of worry crossing the other woman's face. Abrar asked why Jenna seemed upset, and Jenna explained that Um Ahmed had, on numerous occasions, come to work with bruises. The marks on her body were not the result of abuse exclusively at the hands of her husband. The latest incident involved Um Ahmed's 17-year-old son. He had asked her to buy him hair gel, and when she explained she did not have enough money, he proceeded to strike her repeatedly.

This incident is not an isolated story of abuse. Each day that Abrar spent in Jabal, she heard similar stories. Many of the children with whom she interacted and played had bed-wetting problems, often a consequence of witnessing trauma, and physical appearances younger than their chronological age, often a consequence of malnutrition.

Because of these and other hardships, AMHA is dedicated to developing and implementing empowerment initiatives within the community. Founded in 2005 by a group of entrepreneurs, AMHA "operates through a network of partnerships with the private sector, civil society, government, and the target communities" (from the AMHA web site, 2011). Over the years, AMHA worked with the members of this particular refugee community to improve essential services in health, safety, education, employment, and legal aid.

Abrar's Story

My American mother and Lebanese father raised my older sister and me in Beirut, Lebanon, during the early portion of our childhood. My parents had each earned advanced graduate degrees in the United States and placed significant emphasis on the importance of education. Although my sister and I were fortunate to attend one of the premier schools in the Middle East, our home was located on the precarious Green Line that demarcated Muslim West Beirut from Christian East Beirut. When I was nearly 5 years old, my sister sustained a serious head injury when she was wounded by stray shrapnel from a nearby explosive. Shortly thereafter, my parents moved back to the United States, choosing to settle and continue raising us in a suburb near my mother's hometown of Toledo, Ohio.

As a young adult, I began visiting the Middle East on a yearly basis. The majority of my time in the region was spent in Lebanon, although I traveled for brief periods to Syria and Jordan. Nearly a year ago, I was introduced to AMHA while taking a course designed to address educational, entrepreneurship, and engineering solutions in sustainability for Jabal residents.

Patrice's Story (Second Author)

I am a middle-class white academician who grew up on the East Coast of the United States. I identify myself as European American because I grew up knowing and interacting with many of my first- and second-generation immigrant family members and their friends. As a child, my parents, siblings, and I attended Irish American parties, Russian Orthodox services, Italian American celebrations of Roman Catholic sacraments, and Austrian-Swiss family members' get-togethers. I have never been to the country in which this case study takes place, although I have visited Israel. I have seen dire poverty in India and Botswana as well as new wealth in Shanghai, Guangzhou, and Beijing. I lived for a few months in the Veneto region of Italy and have felt connections with passersby in Dublin, Copenhagen, Paris, Brussels, and other places.

My mom and dad, as well as my teachers, instilled an appreciation for difference and the responsibilities that come with privilege. I haven't always understood how privilege operates in different contexts. I am still learning. I also have muddled through various life experiences. Some of these experiences—the precarious neonatal and later course of my premature twins, Sheridan and Ashlee—are indelibly etched into my thinking about work, career, family, and other relationships. My thinking about how resilience is interactively constituted was born with Sheridan and Ashlee and emerged more fully when working with individuals who had lost their jobs (Buzzanell & Turner, 2003) and when reflecting on families whose members have disabilities (Buzzanell, 2006, 2008) and who have held onto meaningful activities, family rituals, and artifacts (Buzzanell & Turner, 2003; Lucas & Buzzanell, 2011, in press). In hearing Abrar's reflections on her time in the refugee camp as well as thinking about my own experiences, I've noted how people live through—sometimes even thrive during—incredible hardship.

Case Study of Jabal

Case Analysis

We use Abrar's voice to tell the story of Jabal.

I first met "Rima" in what would be considered the town square of Jabal. In the middle of the square is a large cemetery whose last burial was in 1938. Now members of the community use the cemetery to conduct drug deals, and teenagers spend their nights drinking within its perimeters. Across from the cemetery is a modest mosque from which men spill out into the street. It is a Friday, and Muslim men are required to pray the Friday afternoon prayer as a community and in a mosque if possible. I had heard about Rima from other women and asked "Lina," a trusted confidante of many women in Jabal as well as of her colleagues at NGO, if I could possibly meet her. As Lina and I walk through the square past the butcher shop, I laugh a bit to myself as I picture a U.S. Food and Drug Administration inspector and the fit he would likely have upon seeing carcasses sunning themselves in the window display.

Lina and I stop outside of a small convenience store located on the corner of the street. I curiously examine the inside of the store from one of two doors propped open, apparently to create a cross breeze. I reach into a poorly refrigerated case and grab juice for Lina and myself. Upon second thought, I pull out four more juices and toss some candy bars on the counter. As I pay, I look around the cramped store. The only light is provided by the sun streaming in from the dirty windows; however, it is clear that a number of customers pass through this space on a daily basis even though dust covers nearly every surface.

I walk out of the store and onto the sidewalk, involuntarily squinting my eyes at the contrast from dark store to bright street, and hand Lina the bag with the candy bars and additional juice boxes. She looks at me, surprised, and I explain that they are a token from "Aunt" Abrar to her children.

We continue our walk.

Rima had insisted that she meet Lina and me in the town square because she didn't want us to become lost on our way to her home. It is nestled somewhere deep within the concrete jungle of buildings. While we wait, Lina calls her son, "Hamza," to come pick up the snacks so they don't melt in the heat of the sun. No more than 10 minutes later, a boy turns the corner and approaches us. His slight frame and height indicate he is no more than 7 years old. When he tells me he is in fact 11, I hide my shock as best I can. The more I think about it, the more I realize a majority of the children look a great deal younger than their chronological ages, although they behaved with much more maturity. I can't help but think that malnutrition might have something to do with this discrepancy, and I start to pay more attention to what and when people eat.

Shortly thereafter, Rima appears. She is a little taller than my 5'5" height and wears a brown traditional *jilbab* (a long cloak that women wrap around themselves) that hides her somewhat generous build. Thin, sparse brows and lashes frame her dark eyes, and not a stitch of makeup conceals her tan and slightly sun-damaged complexion, the appearance of which indicates she is in her early to mid-40s. She walks with purpose and determination, but her eyes are hard to read. Prior to meeting her, my impression was that Rima was cautious and "cold" in interactions with her neighbors, so the fact she would entertain an "outsider" such as me was surprising.

Rima leads Lina and me through a maze of concrete corridors and stairwells, some covered in colorful, striking graffiti. Shards of glass remain jutting out from the once decorative windows of thick metal doors locked shut with chain-links. A mix of loud Arabic music and Quranic recitations spills out of various barred windows.

As we weave our way through the buildings and alleys, in nearly flawless English Rima describes how recycling transitioned from being a hobby to a profession for her. For the past 6 years, she has collected items that others throw away and "crafts them" into anything from dolls and purses to aprons and sponges. As she speaks, she recalls the numerous times she was ridiculed for her chosen career. Others within the community would scold her, telling her to get a "real job." However, Rima considers recycling her "real job" because she earns her living wage from this work.

After nearly 10 minutes of walking, we arrive at the top of a set of concrete stairs. Various containers and plastic baby bathtubs line the left or right side of every step. Each one is filled with potting soil from which herbs and flowers spring. The home is bustling with action as neighbors in adjacent buildings peer down from windows, asking Rima about her visitors and exchanging comments with one another. Clotheslines have been strung across the alleyway from one home to another. It is difficult to distinguish who lives in which apartment. However, it is clear that everyone knows everyone else and most are somehow related. I feel it would be too forward to ask Rima just how many people live in the four-room apartment she calls home, although from what I am able to determine, Rima lives with her parents, sister, and brother-in-law, and at least three children, presumably nieces and nephews.

As Lina and I sit at the top of the stairs, Rima goes inside her home to retrieve a few items she has made from recycled materials. She allows me to audio record our conversation as well as take pictures of her recycling projects. When she returns, she explains her position on the importance of community engagement and describes a competition she began in December 2010. In exchange for the opportunity to win a laptop, families in Jabal are encouraged to bring Rima their recyclable materials. After 1 year, in December 2011, the family that has donated the most is awarded the grand prize. Other participants are given a gift bag containing items such as an apron fashioned from donated pants and sponges created from discarded onion bags.

Although the afternoon sunlight is bright, Rima's home is quite dim. The kitchen is located on the left side of the entrance while the living room and another room extend from the right. Rima begins pointing out items in the entrance that she made from recycled materials. She points to a refurbished ironing board and a decorative wall hanging in the shape of a slipper that is used to store mail and keys. She also shows us an item resembling a cloth purse. She opens the purse, revealing the item to be a book cover with a Qur'an resting inside. A slip of matching cloth connected to the outside of the purse acts as a bookmark and a zipper compartment on the outside of the purse contains a pencil for note-taking while reading.

Looking beyond the items, I can see that the paint on the walls of the small, cluttered kitchen is peeling and a single small plastic table is covered with pots, pans, and food containers. A thick, black electrical cord drapes down from an outlet to the refrigerator that is situated next to a freestanding, ageing stove. Left of the stove rests a breakfront cabinet with missing glass panes and loose springs preventing the doors from closing. The visible parts of the cabinet contain mismatched plates, cups, and saucers. Rima directs us up three stairs into an annex off of the kitchen with a washer and dryer and points out two large, blue, plastic bins containing gray water that had been previously used for laundry or bathing. In another corner off of the kitchen, another receptacle containing food scraps operates as a compost bin. Rima explains that a nearby large, white, plastic bottle contains the homemade vinegar that she uses to wash dishes.

Next, we follow Rima outside and all the way up the concrete steps to the roof of the building. Numerous articles of clothing hang, drying listlessly from clotheslines, and we bow our heads to duck under them. In one corner of the roof, three brick walls and a roof have been constructed to resemble a small garage. Shelves lining the interior walls brim with scraps of wood and plastic containers. A large rug extends across the portion of the roof that is covered. Every space on the entire surface of the rug has pieces of drying bread. Rima explains that she collects the bread, dries it, and packages the crumbs in sacks weighing 30 kilos (approximately 66 lbs.). She is able to sell each sack for 2 to 3 dinars (approximately $2.80 to $4.25 USD).

The next day, Rima invites Lina and me to her workshop. The entrance is cluttered with tiles and concrete slabs. We walk under a ladder into a small, windowless room piled from floor to ceiling with overflowing cardboard boxes and plastic bags of various shapes and sizes. A quick peek inside them reveals that some contain empty cans and plastic food containers, old magazines, and olive oil tins. A broken fan is propped against the wall, and flies buzz in and out of the room. The workshop reminds me of the type of garage that would be featured on an episode of Hoarders, an A&E television show (see http://www.aetv.com/hoarders/). The inside of the workshop contains shelves stocked with more donated items as well as a used couch and a couple of tables and chairs. I sit across from Rima at the table as she describes more of her projects. As she speaks, I can't help but wish there were more time to learn about who she is, what she values, and how she perseveres.

Analysis

Resilient structures present in Jabal intertwine with the community's definitions of identity. The presence of both *resilience* and *social resilience* processes further influence our analysis such that we are concerned with both how the community *and* the individual shape and define resilience and its contributions to the meaningfulness of work. More specifically, our analysis focuses on how and in what ways both Jabal *and* Rima display resilience processes identified by, but also different from, those explicated by Buzzanell (2010). Indeed, our case study shows how the different processes intermingle and form new insights through ongoing continuities and discontinuities of establishing normalcy in ways that are adaptive and transformative individually and collectively, albeit not without resistance and identity considerations. Second, we show how resilience is predicated by continuities of disruptions and (re)constitutions of communication networks that offer alternative ways of living.

First, in establishing normalcy, Rima and the Jabal community construct resilience in varied ways. In Jabal, what constitutes "normalcy" in terms of work contrasts with Rima's individual actions, particularly the ways she goes about mundane actions and the ways she talks and interacts with others to frame their meaning to others (for frames, see Fairhurst, 2011). To begin, it's important to note that refugee camps are not always temporary holding spaces for people fleeing from hostility. Jabal has been a refugee community for many years. As such, Jabal members create their sense of home and belonging in a space and time between Palestine and their host nation, between their former homes and this community, between their former selves and everyday actions and their current situation. Jabal has continued for so many years that most of the people with whom Abrar interacted know no other home. What was normal before is held in collective memory, what is normal now is both anticipatory and grounded in current realities, and what may become the new normal in the future is held with resignation and hope. Within this liminal spatio-temporal milieu, people go about their everyday work—operating in past, present, and future with understandings of good work and real jobs operating differently among different Jabal stakeholders.

For Rima, work has become her personal "calling" as well as her way of actively transforming her environment and Jabal inhabitants' notions of who they are and what they can do. As recycling transitioned from her hobby into her primary source of income, Rima's sense of self and place in the world changed. She has endured ridicule from members of her community pressuring her to get a "real job." The conservative nature of Jabal suggests that elder community members dictate what constitutes work. This influence and the clout of community elders were evident during NGO Day, an event designed to raise awareness and support for Jabal. Business owners and potential investors were invited to tour the community and schools. In addition, they were asked to attend a debate and roundtable discussion. Panel members were well-established and influential individuals, including the founder and CEO of the corporation funding AMHA. Oftentimes, the panel moderator as well as participants would defer to the input and opinions of elderly audience members.

To the elders, acceptable work for women is limited to household maintenance and caregiving as well as to professions such as teaching. The limited financial, social, educational, and political resources available to those ascribed refugee status constrain opportunities to obtain other work. Rima engages in atypical work and identity constructions. She constantly (re)creates normalcy through the ways in which she deliberately (re)frames the recycling tasks in which she engages and the community education that she delivers in every interaction. Moreover, she embodies her work of offering alternative ways of interacting with camp environments. Rather than passively accepting her lived conditions, she actively changes and strongly advocates that others participate in such transformation. She is a realist insofar as she knows that camp members would most likely not engage in any part of her recycling activities without inducements. Therefore, she offers gift bags and chances for the laptop prize as extrinsic motivators.

Rima co-creates a new normalcy in which recycling, looking outward from one's own lived conditions to the betterment of the community, and offering different possibilities for work take place. In these ways, Rima socially constructs meaningfulness in work that both informs and is informed by her identity and that can have an impact on social challenges (i.e., responsible careers; see Tams & Marshall, 2011). Impact is derived from workers' strategic approaches to their tasks and goals, employment decisions, role behaviors, and other factors. Tams and Marshall (2011) delve into the discursive and material performance of career strategies and behaviors that include the different types of reflexivity needed by workers in responsible careers as well as the sensemaking, questioning, and negotiating of tensions. As Tams and Marshall noted, "Studying responsible careers requires attention to the ways in which work can be viewed by the individual as political, as a form of engaged citizenship and 'action' in the public sphere, outside the realm of formal political governance" (p. 111).

The push-pull tensions of change and resistance to change that operate in Rima's life and Jabal stakeholders' discourse offer insight into the very conceptualizations of resilience. For many, resilience captures the adaptation to new circumstances incurred through disaster, trauma, death, and other hardships. This adaptation and co-creation of a new normalcy that enables continuity in much that is precious to people is a profound accomplishment. Yet, Rima embodies the other sense of resilience as a transformational process whereby people can modify their lived conditions to benefit themselves and others. As such, they reinvent normalcy in their lives and in their own and others' identities. However, there are broader identity issues operating in Jabal.

Second, to show how resilience is predicated by continuities of disruptions and (re)constitutions of communication networks, we begin with regional history and then move into the ways these past and present socio-historical Discourses resonate in, change, and are shaped by resilience processes. We start by noting that Rima is among at least two generations of Palestinian refugees born and raised in the country. Following the 1948–1949 Palestinian War, the late king of this nation offered citizenship to Palestinians who had immigrated there. This country had also annexed a portion of central Palestine. In efforts to unite the areas, citizenship was extended to those who remained in the country (Brand, 1995). Nevertheless, despite their shared citizenship, tension and questions of identity persist among these groups.

In a 1995 exploration of intercommunal tensions between Middle Eastern countries, Brand (1995) reported "national as well as subnational identities are in a state of continuous adjustment, if not reconstruction" (p. 47). She noted that the issues that constitute nationality identification and values, such as "Jordanianness" or "Palestinianness," are "different today from what they would have been five, or certainly ten, years ago" (p. 47). Even so, the distinctions between national groups throughout the Middle Eastern region are increasingly more palpable; Palestinians generally share feelings of loss in regard to their homeland, they share the hope that they may one day return, and they share deeply rooted beliefs that the international community treated them unjustly (Brand, 1995).

These sentiments pervade Jabal, demonstrating the resilience process defined by subscribing and affirming aspects of identity. The impact this process of resilience has on the meaningfulness of work is substantial. The refugee community recognizes how notions pertaining to the meaningfulness of work are related to concessions that one's refugee status is more permanent than temporary. The consequences of such an admission rest in direct opposition to those constituting the generally shared Palestinians' identity. These consequences mean that resilience is (re)constituted communicatively through the continuities and disruptions of socio-historical and political economic conditions (and the meanings constructed by and affecting stakeholders) and (re)constitutions of communication networks.

In other words, communication is at the crux of resilience processes triggered by disruption and continued through networks. The refugee community *and* Rima are incredibly reliant upon communication networks. Moreover, these networks heavily inform attitudes about meaningful work and the ways in which it is executed. Rima's body of work is so entirely dependent upon continuously (re)formed, enlarged, and enriched communication networks that without them, her livelihood would be severely endangered. The raw materials that form the basis and substantial portions of her projects depend upon others. For the most part, inconsistent and undependable access to technology limits the methods she can employ when soliciting donations and recyclables and in doing her work. Thus, her communication networks consist mainly of word-of-mouth techniques with her as the central node in this network (and without the indigenous mass and new media campaigns and collaborations explored by others doing development work and indigenous research; e.g., see Dutta, 2008, 2011; Papa, Singhal, & Papa, 2006). There is both frustration and pride in her work and new identity. Rima and others realize that no matter how hard they work to improve their standards of living, a (literal) glance across the street into mainstream life in the nation that harbors these refugees indicates how much their lives are dependent upon an informal economy (i.e., economic activity determined by social convention and/or personal connections; see

Godfrey, 2011) and the beneficence of others (e.g., host country, AMHA, international interest). Rima's communication networks may be constrained to those internal to the camp, but her identity, meaningful work, and responsible career constructions, although not articulated by her as we have done, are expansive and resilient processes.

Discussion

In our case study of a long-term Palestinian refugee camp, we draw upon Abrar's participant observations and personal insights to describe how meaningful work and the creation of responsible careers can underlie and drive resilience. In particular, we note that the communicative construction of resilience is an imbricated structure whereby communication processes are more or less evident and instrumental in the adaptational and transformational forms and outcomes of resilience. Moreover, these interlocking processes are embedded within particular cultures and spatio-temporal contexts. In doing so, we not only demonstrate how refugee work can have different meanings, meaningfulness, and material as well as discursive aspects but also how people can operate productively and agentically in resilience processes.

Although we show how resilience functions within ongoing continuities and discontinuities, we note the need for further work in refugee resilience and lived conditions. We admit that the limited data on which our case is based offer more of a suggestive account rather than transferrable learnings. As a result, we encourage others from multidisciplinary and cross-cultural perspectives to construct a more complete accounting of resilience construction working with multiple voices. Furthermore, we see our theoretical and pragmatic implications lying within and between the two intersecting resilience processes described here. First, we showed how normalcy could be established adaptively and transformatively, individually and collectively, discursively and materially, and in collaborative and resistive forms. Second, we showed how resilience is predicated on and by continuities of disruptions and (re)constitutions of communication networks that offer possibilities for alternative ways of living and thinking about meaningful work.

In closing, we note that we have barely scratched the surface of refugee life and resilience. We offer this essay as one explanation for why Angelina Jolie described refugees as the "'most vulnerable people in the world, and they are also the most resilient people'" (Associated Press, 2011, p. D6).

References

Adger, W. N. (2000). Social and ecological resilience: Are they related? *Progress in Human Geography, 24*, 347–364.

Allen, B. J. (2005). Social constructionism. In S. May & D. K. Mumby (Eds.), *Engaging organizational communication theory ad research* (pp. 35–53). Thousand Oaks, CA: Sage.

Associated Press. (2011, October 5). Jolie considers bigger role with U.N. Lafayette, IN: *Journal & Courier*, p. D6.

Bartesaghi, M., & Castor, T. (2008). Social construction in communication. In C. Beck (Ed.), *Communication yearbook 32* (pp. 3–39). New York, NY: Routledge.

Bonanno, G. A. (2004). Loss, trauma, and human resilience: Have we underestimated the human capacity to thrive after extremely aversive events? *American Psychologist, 59*(1), 20–28.

Brand, L. A. (1995). Palestinians and Jordanians: A crisis of identity. *Journal of Palestine Studies, 24*, 46–61.

Buzzanell, P. M. (2006). Pondering diverse work-life issues and developments over the lifespan. *Electronic Journal of Communication, 16* (3, 4). Retrieved from http://www.cios.org/www/ejc/v16n34.htm

Buzzanell, P. M. (2008). Necessary fictions: Stories of identity, hope, and love. *Communication, Culture, & Critique, 1*, 31–39.

Buzzanell, P. M. (2010). Resilience: Talking, resisting, and imagining new normalcies into being. *Journal of Communication, 60*, 1–14.

Buzzanell, P. M. (2011). Interrogating culture. *Intercultural Communication Studies, 20*, 1–16.

Buzzanell, P. M., Shenoy, S., Remke, R. V., & Lucas, K. (2009). Intersubjectively creating resilience: Responding to and rebounding from potentially destructive organizational experiences. In P. Lutgen-Sandvik & B. Davenport Sypher (Eds.), *The destructive side of organizational communication* (pp. 530–576). New York, NY: Routledge.

Buzzanell, P. M., & Turner, L. H. (2003). Emotion work revealed by job loss discourse: Backgrounding-foregrounding of feelings, construction of normalcy, and (re)instituting of traditional masculinities. *Journal of Applied Communication Research, 31*, 27–57.

Cannella, G. S., & Manuelito, K. D. (2008). Feminisms from unthought locations: Indigenous worldviews, marginalized feminisms, and revisioning anticolonial social science. In N. Denzin, Y. S. Lincoln, & L. Smith (Eds.), *Handbook of critical and indigenous methodologies* (pp. 45–59). Thousand Oaks, CA: Sage.

Coutu, D. L. (2002). How resilience works. *Harvard Business Review, 80*(5), 46–51.

Craig, R. T. (1999). Communication theory as a field. *Communication Theory, 9*, 119–161.

Creswell, J. W. (2007). *Qualitative inquiry and research design: Choosing among five approaches.* Thousand Oaks, CA: Sage.

Dutta, M. J. (2008). *Communicating health: A culture-centered approach.* Malden, MA: Polity Press.

Dutta, M. J. (2011). *Communicating social change: Structure, culture, and agency.* New York, NY: Routledge.

Edelstein, M. R., & Kleese, D. A. (1995). Cultural relativity of impact assessment: Native Hawaiian opposition to geothermal energy development. *Society and Natural Resources, 8*, 19–31.

Ellis, C., & Bochner, A. P. (2000). Autoethnography, personal narrative, reflexivity: Researcher as subject. In N. K. Denzin & Y. S. Lincoln (Eds.), *Handbook of qualitative research* (pp. 733–768). Thousand Oaks, CA: Sage.

Ellis, M. H. (2000). Indigenous minority rights, citizenship, and the new Jerusalem: A reflection of the future of Palestinians and Jews in the expanded state of Israel. *Journal of Church and State, 42*, 297–310.

Fairhurst, G. (2011). *The power of framing: Creating the language of leadership*. San Francisco, CA: Jossey-Bass.

Foss, K. A., & Foss, S. K. (1994). Personal experience as evidence in feminist scholarship. *Western Journal of Communication, 58*, 39–43.

Godfrey, P. (2011). Toward a theory of the informal economy. *The Academy of Management Annals, 5*, 231–277.

Grabska, K. (2006). Marginalization in urban spaces of the global south: Urban refugees in Cairo. *Journal of Refugee Studies, 19*, 287–307.

Jacobsen, K. (2005). *The economic life of refugees*. Bloomfield, CT: Kumarian Press.

Lucas, K., & Buzzanell, P. M. (2011). It's the cheese: Collective memory of hard times during deindustrialization. In J. M. Cramer, C. P. Greene, & L. M. Walters (Eds.), *Food as communication: Communication as food* (pp. 95–113). New York, NY: Peter Lang.

Lucas, K., & Buzzanell, P. M. (in press). Memorable messages of hard times: Constructing short- and long-term resiliencies through family communication. *Journal of Family Communication*.

Malkki, L. H. (1995). Refugees and exile: From "refugee studies" to the national order of things. *Annual Review of Anthropology, 24*, 495–523.

Masten, A. S. (2001). Ordinary magic: Resilience processes in development. *American Psychologist, 56*, 227–238.

O'Faircheallaigh, C. (1999). Making social impact assessment count: A negotiation-based approach for indigenous peoples. *Society and Natural Resources, 12*, 63–80.

Pal, M., & Buzzanell, P. M. (2008). The Indian call center experience: A case study in changing discourses of identity, identification, and career in a global context. *Journal of Business Communication, 45*, 31–60.

Palestinian Central Bureau of Statistics. (2006). *Demographic and socioeconomic status of the Palestinian people at the end of 2006*. Ramallah, Palestine: Palestinian Central Bureau of Statistics.

Palestinian Central Bureau of Statistics. (2009). *Press release on household culture survey*. Ramallah, Palestine: Palestinian Central Bureau of Statistics.

Papa, M., Singhal, A., & Papa, W. (2006).*Organizing for social change: A dialectic journey of theory and praxis*. Thousand Oaks, CA: Sage.

Pont, A. (2006). A crisis in the dark: The forgotten refugees. *UN Chronicle, 43*(3), 38–39, 42–43. Retrieved from http://findarticles.com/p/articles/mi_m1309/is_3_43/ai_n17094055/

Remke, R. V. (2006). *(Ir)Rationalities at work: The logics, heart, and soul of Head Start* (Unpublished doctoral dissertation). Purdue University, West Lafayette, IN.

Shome, R., & Hegde, R. (2002).Culture, communication, and the challenge of globalization. *Critical Studies in Media Communication, 19*, 172–189.

Tams, S., & Marshall, J. (2011). Responsible careers: Systemic reflexivity in shifting landscapes. *Human Relations, 64*, 109–131.

· 1 2 ·

COMMUNICATION STRATEGIES TO RESTORE WORKING RELATIONS

Comparing Relationships That Improved with Ones That Remained Problematic

Jon A. Hess & Katelyn A. Sneed

When considering problematic workplace relationships, the question naturally arises of how people can deal most effectively with these challenges. What people most want with difficult relationships is a way to make the problems go away. That desire calls for research on strategies to transform problematic relationships into non-problematic relations. For this issue, there is both good news and bad news.

First, the bad news: There are few easy answers when dealing with problematic relations. Problematic relationships are difficult by definition. Relationships that involve challenges a person can easily resolve are not difficult relationships. The co-construction of these relationships often intertwines the weaknesses of both individuals. Given the infinite array of the resulting constructions, there are few actions that will improve every difficult relationship. Communication that makes one relationship less problematic might have no effect on another, or it could even inflame the problems. Thus, effective communicative responses to problematic relationships must be tailored to each individual case. Persons seeking a simple and universal fix are bound to be disappointed.

Now the good news: The variety of causes and difficult nature of these relationships do not preclude research generating insights into their resolution. An examination of problematic workplace relationships can offer essential background to help guide the improvement of almost any difficult relationship. Even though optimal responses vary across relationships, we can still craft useful strategies for identifying problematic issues and responding to them. And, despite the need to adapt communicative strategies to the specific people and situation involved, some behaviors may be documented to have fairly widespread utility. Research can identify those communicative approaches that seem applicable to a wide range of problematic relationships.

This chapter explores the experiences of working professionals who have wrestled with difficult relationships, sometimes seeing those relationships improve, sometimes finding no relief to the challenges of those relationships. Their stories offer useful insights into how people can communicate most effectively in the workplace when relationships become problematic.

Dealing with Difficult Workplace Relationships

There is no doubt about the prevalence of difficult workplace relationships. Across research conducted by the team of Hess, Fritz, and Omdahl (see Fritz & Omdahl, 2006), over a thousand people have reported on workplace relationships, and all but one participant readily identified a relationship viewed as problematic. While it is impossible to quantify precisely the proportion of relationships that can be considered problematic, some estimate that 10% or more of all employees can be deemed problematic, a figure that may cost American businesses several hundred billion dollars annually in reduced productivity, lost employee time, and other effects (Bruce, 1990). Levitt, Silver, and Franco (1996) simply referred to problematic relationships as "an integral part of the human experience" (p. 524). Problematic workplace relationships will always exist; the challenge is how best to handle them.

Despite agreement that problematic relationships are prevalent, researchers have not paid sufficient attention to the bigger question of how to deal with these relationships. The literature contains abundant scholarship on topics that could be useful for managing difficult relationships, but scholars have not always been intentional about seeking to integrate these studies into comprehensive answers to the question of how people can best respond to difficult relationships. However, scholars have at least begun to pay more attention in recent years to this question. This attention has resulted in a variety of books offering theory for scholars (e.g., Einarsen, Hoel, Zapf, & Cooper, 2011; Lutgen-Sandvik & Davenport Sypher, 2009) and advice for working professionals (e.g., Bruce, 1990; Hall, 2003). Taken together, these books offer useful information but do not provide a thorough survey of the landscape of problematic relationships at work. Many of these books focus only on certain contexts, based on industry, type of difficulty, or both. For instance, Higgerson and Joyce (2007) devoted an entire section of their book on leadership communication to managing difficult people, but because the book is directed toward academic department chairs and deans, it restricts attention to challenges of higher education. Einarsen et al.'s (2011) edited volume on workplace bullying and harassment is not restricted to one industry, but it is restricted to a single relational difficulty. Twale and De Luca's (2008) examination of incivility among faculty is bounded by both type of difficult relationship and industry.

Taken as a whole, the literature on difficult workplace relationships tends to exhibit a managerial bias, focusing on questions of how managers can best address problematic employees (e.g., Bruce, 1990; Hall, 2003; Higgerson & Joyce, 2007) and driven by organizational goals rather than by a desire to restore positive relationships. These sources are primarily concerned with using people to achieve organizational objectives, and while restoring working relationships is regarded as positive outcome, relationships themselves are often treated more as means than ends. Furthermore, while writers often offer advice for how to improve difficult relationships, researchers have rarely compared relationships that improved with those that did not. Doing so would offer a richer understanding of the forces shaping or preventing positive change in difficult relationships.

This project was undertaken to consider the bigger question of how communication can help restore relationships in the workplace—not just to improve the organization's bottom line but also because positive relationships have intrinsic merit. Furthermore, this study was designed to offer more general insights into how people can best address problematic relationships by comparing relationships that improved with those that did not. We addressed the following research questions:

RQ1: What communication helped improve problematic workplace relationships?

RQ2: What similarities and differences mark communication in problematic relationships that improved compared to those that did not?

This project used qualitative methods to glean a rich understanding of people's experiences in problematic relationships. We asked people to share their experiences in problematic workplace relationships that took a positive turn and in problematic relationships that did not. This comparison allowed us to understand the changes that took place and to see what communicative behaviors had a positive effect and what ones did not. By not restricting the scope to a specific industry or type of relational challenge, this study offers a broader viewpoint on challenging relationships.

Method

Participants

Participants for this study were 14 individuals who had experienced problematic workplace relationships. Although the requirement of having had a difficult workplace relationship could have been a screening variable, we did not encounter anyone who could not easily recall many such relationships. We used a convenience sample for this study, contacting people who were known to the researchers. This procedure risked producing a set of participants who had similarities due to their contact with the researchers. However, given the diverse experiences and range of strategies across an array of occupations, we believe the sample was not compromised due to the way we identified participants. Our sample was racially homogenous (all participants were Caucasian), but intentionally seeking variety in participants' age, sex, career paths, and type of relationship yielded a sample with notable diversity across those areas. As the results show, people's experiences in these relationships were identifiably different.

Respondents were seven men and seven women, ranging in age from 18 to 75, with a mean age of 38. Participants' occupations included sales, construction, banking, administrative support, farm labor, high school education, day care, bar and restaurant ownership, information technology, warehouse labor, and product delivery. To protect anonymity, all participants are identified in this chapter using pseudonyms.

Procedure

Prior to doing interviews, the researchers contacted potential participants to explain the study and seek their willingness to be interviewed. All people contacted agreed to participate. We met the participants at private, quiet locations agreeable to both parties, typically the home or workplace of the participant or researcher. Before the interview started, the participant read and signed a consent form and filled out a short demographic form that asked about age, sex, race, education, occupation, and duration of the difficult relationship. Two participants who were married co-owners of a business interviewed together, and while both shared their stories of their relationships (which improved) with the same pair of difficult employees, the husband also talked about a problematic relationship (which did not improve) with a former business partner.

We followed a semi-structured interview guide, which offered a set of general questions for each participant and allowed flexibility for follow-up probes specific to the topics raised in each interview. We began the interviews by asking participants to talk about themselves, their family of origin, and their jobs. These questions helped the participants settle into the interview and provided useful information to contextualize their descriptions of the problematic relationships. We then asked them to talk about two problematic relationships, one that took a positive turn and one that did not. Participants were asked to tell stories about the difficult interactions they had, what factors made the relationship challenging, and about the communication that took place. They were also asked to reflect on what communication behaviors worked well, which ones did not work well, and what might have caused these behaviors to produce the results that followed. All but one participant readily thought of relationships for both categories. One participant could not think of a problematic relationship that had taken a positive turn, so he discussed a pair of workplace relationships that had both remained problematic until he left the respective companies.

The interviews were digitally recorded, then transcribed with all identifying information removed. Interviews ranged from 8 to 61 minutes, with an average of 23 minutes. In the interviews, participants talked about a wide range of professional relationships that proved to be problematic. Most common were difficult bosses (15), followed by peers (8), and, least often talked about, subordinates (4). The category of peer relationships at work included any relationship that did not involve a direct hierarchical relationship between the two people. In some cases, the relationship involved people in the same department who reported to the same supervisor, but in other cases the two people were in different divisions of the company or even in different organizations who had contact but no authority over each other.

Results

The interviews were analyzed using thematic analysis (Lindlof & Taylor, 2002). Categories were identified when similar ideas recurred across multiple participants. Although our focus was on communication that could help restore working relationships, we also examined the cause of these relationship difficulties. A theoretical analysis of unwanted relationships suggested two main reasons why relationships can be unwanted: goal interference and negative affect (Hess, 2003). The former, rooted in logic and reason, suggests that relationships may be problematic when the other person does not share or support an individual's goals. The latter, rooted in emotion, suggests that problems arise when people dislike each other.

This distinction generally fit these problematic workplace relationships. People reported relationships to be problematic due either to lack of fit between their workplace goals or to behavior that showed disrespect, bred hostility, or was otherwise offensive. For example, people who experienced goal friction included Gina (50, a restaurant co-owner), who reported difficulties with a bar manager who was treating customers poorly (goal of retaining customers); Garrett (26, sales), whose boss was too busy to train him adequately but expected him to perform capably (goal of proper support so he could do his job well); and Jared (51, construction), whose business partner was hiding the fact that he was overcharging customers (goal of running business ethically).

In other cases, participants shared narratives in which the issues that made relationships problematic were not about the work that needed to be done but the way that people felt treated. Alex (32, medical supply delivery) had a boss who seemed to single him out unfairly to pick on him for his work. Abigail (52, administrative assistant) struggled with anger from a coworker who was upset when Abigail received a promotion the coworker had wanted. Lois (75, social worker) had difficulty with a younger male colleague who she believed was patronizing her due to her age. These problematic relationships resulted from feelings of disrespect and undue hostility from peers or supervisors.

Coping

Although the research focused on communication that influenced problematic relationships, the interviews also revealed two actions that seemed to be helpful in improving relationships. Even though these actions did not occur within the problematic relationship, respondents indicated that in many cases they influenced subsequent communication in the relationship. Therefore, they are worth attention in our investigation of communication that can improve problematic relationships. These two actions were doing the job well and talking with others.

Doing the job well. At least six of the respondents indicated that doing their job well was a major element in their approach to dealing with this difficult coworker. While excellence on the job is not necessarily a form of communication, in most cases it had a significant influence on the communication that took place in the relationship. Several reported that they were able to ease tensions by simply displaying competence in their organizational role; in some cases, doing the job well was a means of coping that reduced stress and made it easier for a person to deal with a difficult boss.

Examples of how doing the job well affected subsequent communication were varied. Garrett (sales) found that doing his job well earned the respect of his boss, who then began to treat him better:

> With this one [meeting with prospective customer], though, today, I was—I knew how this last one had gone, where he was just pissed off because he didn't think I was prepared, you know. So today, I kind of walked into his office, we kind of went over the whole thing. You know, I said, here is this whole big write up I've done on the whole company, you know, this is everything I know about them, this is where all their plant locations are in comparison to where we are located. You know, all this different stuff. And he goes, "Wow, this is actually really good. Nice job." And then, when he sees that, and then I hear that he already has a good impression of how this might go because of the work that I've done, and then I'm actually, tomorrow, for this meeting tomorrow, I'm actually finally, I'm actually pretty calmed down about it now, because I see that he doesn't already have it in his head that tomorrow is going to be a disaster.

Wade, 34, a banker whose boss was negative toward him, had an experience similar to Garrett's, noting, "I think really once she saw the value that I brought to the bank and my ability to do well and exceed in sales, that changed everything."

On the other hand, some people found that doing their job well reduced their reliance on a difficult coworker, and thereby took away some of the problems they faced with that person. Lois, a social worker, had a technical advisor who was difficult to work with. She worked hard to learn policies that she ordinarily had to discuss with this advisor so she would not have to go to him as often. This reduced her reliance on him and thereby eased some of the difficulty. Interestingly, when the advisor saw how well she learned this information, he began to show her more respect, and the relationship improved. So, even in cases where doing the job well was not undertaken to earn respect, it typically had that effect.

Talking to others. A second action appearing in the reports of at least three of the respondents was talking to others (third parties) about the problematic relationship. This helped them cope, often due simply to the social support of others. For example, Alex, whose boss seemed to pick on him unfairly, reported the following incident:

I would often ask Roger, who was my coworker doing the same job, but he had more years of experience than I did so he was sort of deemed in the office as my supervisor. And so oftentimes, I would say to Roger, "What's going on? Is there anything I'm doing wrong? What in the world—Why does he hate me so much?" And he'd say "I don't know. It doesn't make any sense. We're doing the same thing, and you're doing it as efficiently as I am, you know, I don't really see a difference. And yet—" So it was affirming to me, again, to find out I wasn't crazy, it wasn't me.

For Alex, and others, the support of peers altered their frames of mind, allowing them to better navigate the challenges of the difficult relationships.

Communication to Restore Relationships

Participants in this study reported a variety of communication behaviors that they believed led to improvements in problematic workplace relationships. These communication behaviors could be grouped into six categories, although some could fit into multiple categories: (1) showing civility or a positive demeanor, (2) confronting the other person directly about problems, (3) affirming the relationship, (4) avoiding conflict, (5) listening, and (6) adapting to the other person.

Civility and positive demeanor. One of the most common responses that people felt helped restore problematic relationships was to maintain civility, treat the other person well, and/or show a positive demeanor. Mindy, 23, a public relations intern, said of her approach to her difficult boss, "I just kind of sucked it up and I just tried to be friendly to her, and she, like, when I left, she gave me a gift card and was sad to see me go and said if ever I wanted to come back and work that I could [laughs], not that I ever did, but I thought that it was a nice gesture that it, it ended well." Lois, a social worker, relayed this experience about a difficult coworker who was a younger man: "It was an arrogance on his part and I had to become more humble, but by doing so, by remaining humble on my part and not becoming combative with him, I won him over."

While many people reported avoiding conflict, often due to anxiety or other avoidant tendencies, the people who talked about showing civility or positivity explained it as an active and intentional process. These people felt that they needed to model positive behavior and hoped that doing so would eventually yield more positive reactions from the other person. In many cases this approach worked, although, as we discuss later, some of this effect was mediated by the personalities of the people involved and the context of their difficult relationship. Some people also reported that being "nice" in some situations did not result in positive outcomes—although this situation was much less common than those who reported that civility and positive demeanor eventually had positive effects.

Directly confronting the problem. Another common response, noted by five participants, was to confront the problem directly. In this case, participants spoke openly with their problematic partner about the nature of the problem and sought ways to resolve the issues. Although this approach was not successful in all cases, more often than not, people reported that this strategy had a positive effect.

One example of how directly confronting the problem had a positive effect was when Mitch, 53, a computer salesman, had to deal with a new—and much younger—manager who seemed to think that older employees were not as capable as younger ones. After just a few months, this manager had to do a performance review on Mitch, and he did not submit a positive report. Mitch responded by addressing the issue with this supervisor. He reported the following events:

> I worked with him to educate him on my strengths and accomplishments. I spent time with him and tried to better understand his position so I could react to change his mindset. Basically, I spent several hours preparing a briefing for him on my performance for the previous 12 months. He appears to have somewhat of an attention deficit, so written communication seems to work best with him. Once he reviewed this and actually took the time to understand me, we ended up having a fairly positive relationship.

Abigail, an administrative assistant who received a promotion over a coworker who wanted the promotion, also talked about the situation directly with the coworker. She reported, "I think it was persistence in being straightforward and confronting her about it a few times that eventually made her realize that it wasn't my fault and that she was upset at me instead of being upset with HR or herself for not getting the position." These conversations resulted in an improved relationship between the two.

It is essential to note that in cases where direct confrontation was successful, the participants described conversations characterized by respect and civility. As is discussed later, many people reported angry and hostile confrontations that inflamed the problem and thus did not have positive effects.

Affirmation of the relationship. Four respondents reported that in their conversations with the partner, they expressed their commitment to that person and to improving the relationship. For example, Abigail expressed sympathy to her coworker who was passed over for the promotion, telling her she was sorry that she did not get the position. Rachel, 30, who co-owns a bar with her parents, recalled a difficult period with her mother where the two eventually took time away from each other while dealing with a significant conflict. Rachel noted, "I think for us it was trying to take a break from each other and take a few days apart and trying to sit down and say, you know, it's not that important, we'll work it out, work towards some sort of compromise where we're both happy because at the end of the day, our relationship is more important than anything else." Harrison, 42, a high school teacher, talked about a problem with another teacher in his department. Later they found out that the principal had been manipulating them, and he approached the other teacher to talk about his commitment to restoring their relationship: "When that happened, I thought, I need to talk to Jessie. So I did. And I said, 'Jessie, you know, this whole thing has been the worst thing between us, and I want to tell you things I know from my experience.' And so I did. And she told me things. And we realized that it was totally orchestrated." Their affirmation helped them restore a more positive relationship.

It is worth noting that all the respondents who reported affirming the relationship also talked directly to their coworker about the relational problems. This finding could suggest that affirmation is simply a part of the direct confrontation process. However, two of the respondents talked about directly confronting the issue without indicating any statement of their commitment to a good working relationship. Therefore, while confronting the problem was a prerequisite for affirmation, the latter can be seen as a distinct communicative response to a problematic relationship.

Avoiding conflict. Just as prevalent as directly confronting the problem was its opposite—avoiding conflict. Five respondents indicated that they avoided confrontation, and counter to conventional wisdom they believed this avoidance was useful in improving the problematic relations. For instance, Dawn, 27, a day care provider, talked about a boss who was not supportive of the workers:

> You know, it was frustrating, but I also look at it like that was my superior, and you know, I don't want to start an argument or have a bad relationship with her because she is my superior. You know, so I don't think I really did deal with it, I don't think I ever told her I was bothered by it, I never, she never knew I had any issues with it, I should put it that way. . . . I pretty much just did what she told me to do and I didn't argue [laughs], that usually works best, doesn't it?

Mindy relayed a similar experience, saying, "I wouldn't really battle her in anything, I would just sort of accept whatever she said, because I didn't feel, like even if I disagreed, I'd just be like ok, that sounds good! You know, just because I didn't want to deal with it. If I disagreed, she would not be happy with that, so more of just acquiescing to whatever she wanted."

While both of these respondents suggested that their behavior was motivated by a tendency to avoid conflict, Wade took a more philosophical approach. He noted that he sometimes avoided conflict not out of discomfort but out of a judgment about when conflict was beneficial in the workplace and when it was not. In his words, "You don't want to be in conflict at work all the time, so let it roll off your shoulders." He felt that by minimizing conflict and doing his job well he would contribute to an environment conducive to improved relations.

Listening. Although not as commonly mentioned as the previous strategies, four of the respondents spoke about listening to the other person as a means of restoring better working relations. Two cases of listening include Harrison's conversation with Jessie ("And she told me things.") and Mitch's conversation with his supervisor ("I spent time with him and tried to better understand his position. . ."). In another case, a restaurant co-owner, Gina, talked about listening to a chef and a bar manager who were causing problems. She noted, "And we were really ready to fire him and we went in and listened to his side, but realizing that they're ADD, both of them, we were really shocked." What was striking was the result of that conversation. After Gina and her co-owner listened to the employees and also shared their concerns, the employees made dramatic changes in behavior. Gina continued, "And they were both very apologetic. Apologized to the workers, coworkers, apologized to some of the customers that, that they were rude to. . . . And [the cook] is very good now, we've had him with us almost four years, and he very rarely blows up, and we just have to look at him, and you know 'Alright, alright, I know.'"

Listening seemed to offer respondents a variety of advantages in restoring the relationships. It helped them better understand and adapt to others, it established an environment that facilitated changes in behavior, and it allowed people to show commitment to their relationships.

Adapting to the other. The final behavior that was commonly mentioned as helpful was adapting to the other person. This strategy seemed to necessitate listening or at least careful attention to how the other person responded. Mitch found that using the best channel of communication led to better outcomes (written, instead of oral, for certain information). Garrett found that he needed to adapt to his boss's moods:

> I'm a person that tries to interject humor into most situations, you know, but he's not. If you can't tell right off the bat that he is in a good mood, being somebody that likes to interject humor into situations, it's just, it's never a good idea. So just trying to, you

know, if he seems like he is in more of a serious mood, trying to maintain a serious approach to the conversation on your end is probably the best thing to do. So, just kinda, really trying to work towards his mood, I guess.

In contrast, Patrick (18, worker at a farm) found that the right jokes were usually helpful with his boss. But in both cases, the person found success by understanding and adapting to the other person.

Ineffective Communication

In addition to talking about behaviors that were helpful, respondents also noted some behaviors that seemed to reduce the chances of improved relationships. Two were prominent: inflaming the problem and masking the problem. The former made matters worse, and the latter made the problem invisible.

Inflaming the problem. A number of the participants talked about behaviors they did that ended up inflaming the problem. These ranged from reciprocating antagonism or losing their temper to making accusations that could not easily be overlooked when the relationship took a turn for the better. For example, Rachel noted that when she and her mother (co-owners of the bar) would lose their tempers and yell at each other, they ended up making matters more difficult. Garrett noted that saying whatever was on his mind, regardless of what mood his boss was in, made the situation even worse. Harrison talked about restoring his relationship with Jessie, another teacher in his department. Although they were able to restore their relationship, he noted, some of the conversations they had during the difficult years had a lingering effect even when they reconciled:

> It nearly ruined the relationship I had with Jessie. And, I think it has definitely pockmarked it so that it can never be the same. But I think now we don't—I don't think she can ever look at me the same. Because I really did attack her motives in a way that revealed her in an unkind way. And I don't think she's ever really thought of herself in those terms. But she's not the most aware person, not the most self-aware person.

While Harrison was not trying to hurt Jessie during the time their relationship was difficult, his reflections on the events that took place and their impact at the present forms an important example of how actions in a problematic relationship shape options for the future relations between the relationship partners.

Shelly (25, secretary) had to work with a company owner who wanted more deference than she was willing to offer. However, while this owner's expectations created difficulties because they entailed an attitude she was not willing to offer, she was still careful to avoid inflaming the situation more than necessary in order to maintain her integrity. She noted the following:

> He thinks he is so important, that it is hard for me to have conversations with him without wanting to laugh [laughs]. I just don't think anyone is more important than anyone else, especially when they act that way. He gets irritated with me because I don't kiss his ass. I just won't do it....I never push the limit. I am respectful. I treat him as I would treat any boss. I respect him and all that he has accomplished, and he does know I feel that way. But really, I just don't kiss his ass and act all crazily impressed around him like everyone else does. So, I guess I respond by remaining true to myself and my values, and figure that I am good enough at my job that I am not going to get fired for being myself.

Thus, Shelly was able to keep a workable relationship despite the difficulties by being careful not to inflame the situation in ways she could avoid.

Masking the problem. The counterpoint to avoiding inflaming the problem is to mask difficulties completely. While hiding the fact that there are difficulties certainly avoids inflaming problems, it also takes away any opportunity the relational partner might have to contribute to better relations. Often, respondents noted that it was a change in situation or in actions done by the partner that made the relationship improve, not something that the respondent did. For instance, Abigail noted that her relationship got better when her coworker realized that Abigail was not the person at fault for the decision of who to promote. In Harrison's case, his relationship with Jessie improved when the principal who had caused the problems left the school. Lois noted that her problematic coworker became less antagonistic when he realized that he was wrong.

Completely hiding the problem would make it impossible to take initiative to solve the problem. Alex, whose relationship with his boss was difficult, wondered whether talking to his boss about the problem would have helped. While he agreed that it is possible that directly confronting the issue might not have improved the situation, he also noted that there is no way to know. But since Alex had never talked about it, his boss was unaware of the problem and could not have improved the relationship even if he had wanted to. Dawn, who felt that avoidance had helped her problematic relationship, also noted, "I think had I gone to her, maybe she would have been able to work on it, or say 'I don't think it's an issue.' But the fact that I never expressed my feelings to her, I think that was a challenge in itself, because she didn't even know." These examples show that when a person hides the problems skillfully enough that the partner is unaware of the issues, there is no possibility for the partner to improve her or his behaviors.

Taken together, these two observations suggest that people need to find an appropriate balance—they should neither make the problem so invisible the partner is oblivious to it, nor should they unnecessarily escalate problems. The experience of the participants in this study suggests that some constructive attempt to address problems could be useful but that it needs to be done with civility, exercising prudence with regard to how assertive to be.

Relationships That Did Not Improve

Clear distinctions from relationships that improved. When people contrasted relationships that did not improve with those that did, some differences were readily apparent. First, some relational qualities and situations made change more difficult. Relationships that started poorly were more difficult to change than relationships that started positively and took a bad turn due to circumstances. Second, more people talked about difficulties with their bosses than with subordinates. The organizational authority given to bosses can make it easier to effect change than for those who lack power over the problematic relational partner. Third, when people felt the relationship had a forthcoming end point, they were less motivated to improve it. Garrett talked about a problematic relationship at a job he had in college that did not improve: "And another thing with that job is that I didn't try because I knew that I was close to being done at school; I knew I never was going to work for this guy again. You know, there wasn't a future for me at this company, because I knew I went to college and I was going to go somewhere else and get a better job."

Finally, the less malleable a partner's offending qualities seem, the more difficulty people had in resolving the issues. Partners who exhibited a high degree of inflexibility, a mean-spirited nature, or evidence of psychological problems were harder for our respondents to deal with than those who were flexible, concerned with the respondent's well-being, or rational. Shelly, the secretary whose company owner wanted her to "kiss ass" more than she was willing to do, was able eventually to develop a better working relationship with him as they got to know each other better. She was unable ever to come to terms, however, with a coworker who seemed to have psychological issues. Shelly finally concluded that "arrogant" is easier to deal with than "crazy." Likewise, Harrison contrasted a coworker whom he was never able to win over, despite ongoing attempts to improve the relationship:

> The one that didn't make a positive turn was because the person involved—and it kind of became apparent—had issues, personal problems, and I think that it really had noth-

ing to do with me in the end. I think that I was just an outlet for the frustrations that this person was going through. So I think that it didn't make a positive change because this person *couldn't* change, wasn't able to deal with whatever it was she was dealing with. And she eventually left, which is, hopefully she went on to a happier life. The reason that Jessie and I reconciled was because we both realized that we were manipulated.

Dawn contrasted her non-supportive boss at a day care center with an unpleasant manager she had as a waitress. She eventually earned positive feelings from the former but not the latter. "Where she [day care boss] was never mean to me, I just felt like she wasn't listening, this one [restaurant manager] she was directly mean about it. And I think that was the biggest difference, her attitude about it."

Inconsistent effects. The greatest challenge to understanding how communication can improve or worsen a difficult relationship is the fact that some of the same behaviors that helped people restore troubled relationships were ineffective—or worse, counterproductive—in other situations. While many more people reported that civility and being nice to the partner was helpful, two people indicated that those behaviors did not help their problematic relationships, and one person indicated that being nice seemed to make matters worse. Jared recounted his attempts to talk to his business partner, who was falsely billing customers. Despite Jared's accounts of an approach that seemed rational and civil, the two could not come to an agreement, and Jared was unwilling to be party to this criminal behavior: "The way I extracted myself from that situation was I said, look, I'm not doing this anymore. We're disbanding the company, and that's what we did." Lois had a subordinate who would not follow proper procedures, and while she attempted to be nice to this person, she wondered whether being more businesslike and less friendly might have been more effective in that case.

Shelly, an attractive woman, found that it was being too nice that caused the problems she had with a coworker: "When I was in college, I worked at a little food shop in my small town. So, this kid started working there, and he was super weird, but I wanted to be nice to him because everyone else was rude to him. So I started being really nice, and he interpreted that as we were dating." Reflecting on their difficulties, she concluded, "Honestly, probably, I shouldn't have been so nice. This sounds mean, but this kid was kind of a dork…so he probably wasn't used to someone being so nice. I guess if I had just been cordial it could have ended up a little better. But, I was trying to make him feel welcome and gave off the wrong impression. . . ." For Shelly, civility blended with appropriate distance might have made the relationship less difficult than having shown too much friendliness.

In addition to showing civility or positive demeanor, participants also reported cases where directly confronting the problem, avoiding conflict, and attempting to adapt to the other person did not have restorative effects on the relationship. It is worth noting, however, that those behaviors had a positive impact in our sample much more than they had a negative impact or had no effect.

Discussion

The data presented in this study offer a unique insight into the way people managed problematic workplace relationships and to connections between communication and outcomes. The findings from this study offer both ideas worth further exploration and a useful lens for considering extant literature that can be related to difficult relationships. In the pages that follow, we discuss some potential implications of this study.

Although many of the relationships were presented as being nearly impossible to restore, it was clear from the stories of the participants that communication can do much to improve even the most difficult relationships encountered in professional life. While some communicative behaviors seem to offer high likelihood of positive outcomes, no matter the situation, it was also evident that there is not a set of behaviors guaranteed to offer positive effects in all situations. Therefore, the most important implication of these data is that researchers need to focus their attention in two areas to offer useful guidance to those in difficult relationships: (1) consistent strategies, which are behaviors identified by research as having a high likelihood of success regardless of situation or individuals involved; and (2) adaptive strategies, which include identification of factors that can help guide decision making among communicative choices.

Consistent Strategies

Not inflaming the problem. One consistent finding was that inflaming problems had a detrimental effect on problematic relationships and on the ability to repair them later. If people were able to avoid behaviors that were likely to make the problems worse, then the chances of eventually resolving the problems were increased.

The challenge for people in difficult relationships is that avoiding inflaming the problem is easier said than done. People's emotional responses often overwhelm their rational responses (Haidt, 2006). This makes it difficult to avoid actions that might inflame a problem even for the highly composed. Furthermore, people have a finite degree of self-control (Baumeister, Bratslavsky, Muraven, & Tice, 1998). Acting in ways that are difficult in order to avoid inflaming a relationship is hard work that eventually wears people out. It is difficult to make rational choices over emotional ones over a long period of difficult interactions. Furthermore, even when people make rational choices in the face of emotionally charged situations, they cannot foresee the consequences of their actions. Therefore, the ability to determine what actions will inflame a situation can often be judged only in retrospect. Finally, because problematic relationships are already somewhat inflamed, by definition, the issue is not a matter of avoiding any behaviors that could cause conflict or irritation but rather one of figuring out which behaviors are "unnecessary." Taken together, these issues raise a formidable challenge.

The suggestion raised by this study is that when people can identify behaviors likely to inflame a problem without apparent benefit, they should refrain from enacting them. Instead, they should choose behaviors that the best evidence suggests will be non-inflammatory, no matter how difficult those behaviors may be to carry out.

High likelihood practices. The data in this study pointed toward at least three communicative practices that seem to have had more positive than negative effects on problematic relationships: treating the other person with civility, affirming a commitment to the relationship, and listening to the other person. Although these behaviors are not guaranteed to have a positive effect in all cases, they offer high enough likelihood of success to be a good first approach in most situations.

Taken together, these three qualities reflect core principles of *dialogue*. Dialogue is a term whose horizon encompasses a range of activities, but it generally refers to a communicative process in which people of difference seek better understanding of each other's perspectives (e.g., DeTurk, 2006). It is characterized by sensitivity to the relationship between people as well as exploration of ideas, and it tends to establish a non-oppositional approach to exploring difference (Hyde & Bineham, 2000). Characteristics of dialogue include the behaviors mentioned here—civility, commitment to relationship, listening to understand—and related qualities, such as respect for the partner, open-mindedness, authenticity, attention to the partner, concern for each other's well-being, and an emergence of ideas "between" people (Arnett & Arneson, 1999; Arnett, Grayson, & McDowell, 2008).

Dialogue is a communicative construct that rose to prominence in the 1960s but fell from favor among theorists because of its theoretical foundations in therapeutic humanism that seemed unsuited to the times that followed (Anderson, 1982; Arnett, 1981). However, dialogue has seen a resurgence of scholarly attention since the mid-1990s, with scholars grounding dialogue in narrative and other philosophical foundations rather than in therapeutic perspectives (e.g., Arnett & Arneson, 1999; Baxter & Montgomery, 1996). The results of this study provide yet another form of support for the idea that dialogue is a powerful form of communication in the pursuit of positive relationships.

Adaptive Strategies

While certain communicative practices seem like a good bet in most situations, it was clear from our respondents' stories that people need to adapt their behaviors to each situation's specific qualities. We discuss two issues that were prominent in this data set: adapting to the situation and making the decision to confront the partner about relationship challenges.

Adapting to the person and situation. Participants in this study noted a variety of reasons for strained relations. These reasons included job-related topics, ranging from people's job performance to specific business decisions, and also personal topics, ranging from messages of disrespect to perceptions of differential treatment from coworkers. It was clear from respondents' experiences that restoration of good working relationships began with responses that were appropriate to the particular situation. For example, Abigail found that talking to her colleague who had been passed over for promotion about the issues led to a positive outcome, whereas Wade found that not bringing his concerns about preferential treatment of other employees to his boss eventually worked out for the better. Lois reported that her efforts to be friendly to a coworker who seemed to treat her disrespectfully helped set the stage for improved relations, whereas Shelly found that being too friendly with a coworker was what caused her relationship to become problematic. She had to distance herself in order to make the relationship more functional.

The clear implication of these outcomes is that people need to determine, as best they can, the cause of the relational difficulties and adjust their behavior accordingly. It is important to note that people cannot always be certain of the cause of difficulty, a point made clear by Harrison's experience with his colleague Jessie. Their problems appeared to have one cause at the time they emerged, and it was only after the departure of the school's manipulative principal that both Harrison and Jessie were able to piece together the actual source of the problems. Obviously, had more information been available to them, they could have dealt with the problem differently. Within the limits of available information, the better a person can assess the forces causing relational difficulty, the more effectively that person can tailor an effective response.

It is also worth noting that people needed to adapt to the perceptions of the difficult relational partner, regardless of the cause of difficulties. Mitch's problematic relationship with his new supervisor was caused by the boss's lack of understanding of Mitch's abilities. While his strategy of providing information to show the boss his contributions was a good adjustment to the cause of the problem, his observation that the boss absorbed written information more readily than oral reports allowed him to provide that information in a manner that would have the greatest impact. Put simply, a general awareness of the other person's perception is an important element of adaptation.

Confronting versus avoiding. One of the most fundamental decisions people have to make is whether to confront the person directly about the problem or to avoid bringing the issues to the fore. While more of our respondents found positive results from dialogue with the partner than found positive outcomes from avoidance of the issue, it was clear that in some cases, raising the issues could be counterproductive. Therefore, this decision will require thoughtful consideration.

Our data did not provide enough cases to begin to offer consistent reasons for a choice of whether to confront or to avoid. Future research will need to explore this topic. However, it is clear at this time that the choice of confronting or avoiding is one of the most fundamental decisions people need to make in dealing with problematic workplace relationships, a point that is consistent with the conflict management literature (e.g., Cahn, 1992; Kilmann & Thomas, 1975; Zietlow & Sillars, 1988) as well as other literature which suggests that the approach-avoid decision is fundamental to human social interaction (e.g., Mehrabian, 1981).

Skill

One issue that is not frequently explored in the relational maintenance literature is the skill with which people enact communicative behaviors. Yet there were indications throughout our interviews of the importance of the quality with which communication was enacted. Gina's conversation with the cook she was about to fire showed a genuine attempt to understand in her listening. Garrett's adaptation of his messages based on his boss's mood demonstrated sensitivity to another's emotions and appropriate adjustment. Mitch's efforts to understand his new boss's views and include that information in his messages showed an attempt to frame information in a manner most useful to the listener. All of these examples reveal the impact of not just what tactics were attempted but how *well* they were performed. In contrast, Shelly's coworker, who misinterpreted her friendliness, showed a lack of deftness in understanding social behavior, which led to problems between them.

Researchers often examine the presence or absence of behaviors without consideration for how well people accomplish those activities. The literature on communicative competence indicates that the skill with which certain communicative strategies are executed is likely to have more impact than any simple measure of how frequently a behavior is carried out (Spitzberg & Cupach, 2002). For example, relational maintenance is normally studied by assessing frequency of maintenance behaviors, but one study (Ramirez & Merolla, 2006) showed that the skill with which these strategies are enacted has a significant impact on their success. A concern for skillful communicative enactment is particularly salient when considering difficult situations. It is easy to imagine that a person who adroitly confronts the coworker will be more effective than a person who confronts that person in a clumsy or offensive manner. In some cases, a person's social skills may even mediate whether a strategy will work. Someone who does not handle conflict well might make a problem worse with an antagonizing attempt to address the issue, whereas someone who is remarkably skilled at dialogue might find success in direct confrontation where others would have failed. The results of this study show a need for more focus on how well certain strategies are executed, not just on what strategies were tried.

Taken together, the results of this study offer useful insights for communication scholars and practitioners on how to improve problematic workplace relationships. The results support re-emerging attention to dialogue in communication and allied disciplines. They also indicate that sensitivity and adaptation to others are critical to communicative success. Given the study's modest sample size, these results have limited generalizability. However, they offer a valuable springboard for future research on the actions and communication behaviors likely to contribute to the restoration or further deterioration of problematic relationships in the workplace.

References

Anderson, R. (1982). Phenomenological dialogue, humanistic psychology, and pseudo-walls: A response and extension. *Western Journal of Speech Communication, 46,* 344–357.

Arnett, R. C. (1981). Toward a phenomenological dialogue. *Western Journal of Speech Communication, 45,* 201–212.

Arnett, R. C., & Arneson, P. (1999). *Dialogic civility in a cynical age: Community, hope, and interpersonal relationships.* Albany, NY: State University of New York Press.

Arnett, R. C., Grayson, C., & McDowell, C. (2008). Dialogue as an "enlarged communicative mentality": Review, assessment, and ongoing difference. *Communication Research Trends, 27,* 3–25.

Baumeister, R. F., Bratslavsky, E., Muraven, M., & Tice, D. M. (1998). Ego depletion: Is the active self a limited resource? *Journal of Personality and Social Psychology, 74,* 1252–1265.

Baxter, L. A., & Montgomery, B. M. (1996). *Relating: Dialogue and dialectics.* New York, NY: Guilford Press.

Bruce, W. M. (1990). *Problem employee management: Proactive strategies for human resource managers.* New York, NY: Quorum Books.

Cahn, D. D. (1992). *Conflict in intimate relationships.* New York, NY: Guilford Press.

DeTurk, S. (2006). The power of dialogue: Consequences of intergroup dialogue and their implications for agency and alliance building. *Communication Quarterly, 54,* 33–51.

Einarsen, S., Hoel, H., Zapf, D., & Cooper, C. L. (2011). The concept of bullying and harassment at work: The European tradition. In S. Einarsen, H. Hoel, D. Zapf, & C. L. Cooper (Eds.), *Bullying and harassment in the workplace: Developments in theory, research, and practice* (2nd ed., pp. 3–39). Boca Raton, FL: CRC Press/Taylor & Francis.

Fritz, J. M. H., & Omdahl, B. L. (Eds.). (2006). *Problematic relationships in the workplace.* New York, NY: Peter Lang.

Haidt, J. (2006). *The happiness hypothesis: Finding modern truth in ancient wisdom.* New York, NY: Basic Books.

Hall, A. (2003). *Managing people.* Berkshire, England: Open University Press.

Hess, J. A. (2003). Maintaining undesired relationships. In D. J. Canary & M. Dainton (Eds.), *Maintaining relationships through communication: Relational, contextual, and cultural variations* (pp. 103–124). Mahwah, NJ: Lawrence Erlbaum.

Higgerson, M. L., & Joyce, T. A. (2007). *Effective leadership communication: A guide for department chairs and deans for managing difficult situations and people.* Bolton, MA: Anker Publishing.

Hyde, B., & Bineham, J. L. (2000). From debate to dialogue: Toward a pedagogy of nonpolarized public discourse. *Southern Communication Journal, 65,* 208–223.

Kilmann, R., & Thomas, K. W. (1975). Interpersonal conflict-handling behaviors as reflections of Jungian personality dimensions. *Psychological Reports, 37,* 971–980.

Levitt, M. J., Silver, M. E., & Franco, N. (1996). Troublesome relationships: A part of human experience. *Journal of Social and Personal Relationships, 13,* 523–536.

Lindlof, T. R., & Taylor, B. C. (2002). *Qualitative communication research methods.* Thousand Oaks, CA: Sage.

Lutgen-Sandvik, P., & Davenport Sypher, B. (2009). *Destructive organizational communication: Processes, consequences, and constructive ways of organizing.* New York, NY: Routledge.

Mehrabian, A. (1981). *Silent messages: Implicit communication of emotions and attitudes.* Belmont, CA: Wadsworth.

Ramirez, Jr., A., & Merolla, A. J. (2006, November). *The effect of skillful relationship maintenance* on *marital satisfaction, closeness, and commitment*. Paper presented at the annual convention of the National Communication Association, San Antonio, TX.

Spitzberg, B. H., & Cupach, W. R. (2002). Interpersonal skills. In M. L. Knapp & J. A. Daly (Eds.), *Handbook of interpersonal communication* (3rd ed., pp. 564–611). Thousand Oaks, CA: Sage.

Twale, D. J., & De Luca, B. M. (2008). *Faculty incivility: The rise of the academic bully culture and what to do about it*. San Francisco, CA: Jossey-Bass.

Zietlow, P. H., & Sillars, A. L. (1988). Life-stage differences in communication during marital conflicts. *Journal of Social and Personal Relationships, 5*, 223–245.

· 13 ·

PROTECTING AND PROMOTING WORKPLACE RELATIONSHIPS

Professional Civility

JANIE M. HARDEN FRITZ

Relationships are a significant and ubiquitous feature of life in the contemporary workplace. As Sias (2009) noted, nearly all organizational activities take place in the context of relationships, even for persons who engage the workplace remotely (e.g., through telework; see Fay, this volume). Research on workplace relationships and their communicative processes includes multiple areas of inquiry, ranging from relationship functions, such as social support, power, and influence, to relationship forms, including workplace friendships, mentorships, romances, and troublesome relationships of various types. Studies of workplace relationships emerge from multiple theoretical and methodological perspectives, including postpositivism, social construction, critical theory, and structuration theory (Sias, 2009).

Workplace relationships vary along a number of dimensions. Supervisor-subordinate relationships and peer relationships differ in relative hierarchical level. Kram and Isabella's (1985) information, collegial, and special peer relationship types vary in closeness and in what they provide for relational partners, as do mentoring relationships, friendships, and romantic relationships in the workplace. Relationships with liked and disliked others (Hess, 2006) highlight affective valence as a dimension relevant to workplace relationships. Customer and client relationships rest on the interface between the organization and the outside environment, suggesting an internal-external dimension for thinking about workplace relationships (Sias, 2009). These types of organizational relationships based on these dimensions take on particular discursive constructions within different workplace contexts, shaping and being shaped by the structure and culture of the organization (Myers, 2010).

Workplace relationships are subject to a number of identifiable forces contributing to their initiation, development, maintenance, and dissolution (Sias, 2009). Given their indispensable role in shared organizational life, scholars and practitioners benefit from understanding the role of these forces in workplace relationship processes, particularly threats to relational flourishing and how work relationships may be repaired when they take a turn for the worse (Hess, Omdahl, & Fritz, 2006; Hess & Sneed, this volume). Research on problematic and constructive relationships offers insight into the communicative processes that contribute to the formation, growth, decline, and rehabilitation of workplace relationships, equipping us with resources to promote healthy interpersonal environments in organizations (Omdahl, 2006). The underlying assumption of research on workplace relationships is that constructive interpersonal relationships are a "good" in, of, and for human life in organizations.

In this chapter, I offer a perspective on work relationships grounded in an understanding of professional civility as communicative virtue at work (Fritz, 2011a, 2012, in press). Professional civility becomes manifested through a phenomenological "turning" toward a number of "goods" emerging in and through communicative interactions in the workplace. Work, relationships with others in the workplace, the organization within which work is carried out, and the profession itself become these "goods" constituted through communication. Professional civility protects and promotes productivity, place (the organization), persons in the workplace, and the profession (Fritz, in press). Framed as an interpersonal communication ethic for the workplace, professional civility protects and promotes the "good" of workplace relationships by navigating the dialectic of distance and closeness between persons and embracing an understanding of roles as constitutive of "common places" in organizational life.

Professional Civility as Workplace Communication Ethic

Professional civility as an interpersonal communication ethic for the workplace incorporates the notion of responsibility for and with a relationship (Arnett, Fritz, & Bell, 2009) as embedded within the larger context of an organization to which the relationship and its participants are answerable. Professional civility as a modality of engaging work relationships is attentive to public and private sphere differentiation and assumes that organizations cannot fulfill every aspect of a life (Arnett, 2006); when one expects more than an organization can provide, cynicism from unmet high expectations is the likely outcome (Arnett & Arneson, 1999). Relational responsibility (Arnett et al., 2009) includes care for a relationship, accountability for a relationship's health, and attentiveness to the context within which the relationship is situated.

A professional civility perspective rooted in relational responsibility calls for thoughtful attention to work relationships as an integral part of the organization, which takes the role of a "third party" to whom the relationship and its partners are accountable (Arnett et al., 2009, p. 111; Fritz, in press). Relational responsibility in the workplace setting involves stewardship of the health of both the relationship and the organization. Organizations are sites of rich personal variation in domains ranging from interaction style differences to deep-seated diversity in core beliefs. In order to work together productively and constructively, organizational members need common interactive ground from which to engage everyday work life. An interpersonal communication ethic of professional civility is one response to the challenge of problematic relationships in the workplace.

Professional Civility: A Communication Ethics Perspective

A framework of professional civility both engages and moves beyond descriptive findings about work relationships into the realm of communication ethics, an arena offering multiple points of entry for engagement in a world of diversity and difference (Arnett et al., 2009). Just as different theoretical perspectives on workplace relationships rest on different ontological, epistemological, and axiological foundations (Sias, 2009), different theories of communication ethics rest on different sets of assumptions about the good for human beings (Arnett et al., 2009). Through the following discussion, my assumptions about the goods of work relationships will rest primarily within the context of a virtue ethics perspective based on the work of MacIntyre (2007). What I offer here suggests a way of thinking about communication in work life as a philosophy of communication (Arnett et al., 2009, p. 27; Arnett & Holba, in press).

Professional civility at work connects a conceptualization of civility as communicative virtue to an understanding of work grounded in the history of professions. Within this framework, professional behavior gains ethical traction from the assumption that everyday interactions can be reflections of the inherent dignity of all work (Hodson, 2001) and that work is an ontological element of the human condition (Arendt, 1958/1998). The work of the professions, originally identified as theology, education, medicine, and law (Kimball, 1995), can be understood as a tradition of practice marked by goods internal to that practice (MacIntyre, 2007). This tradition includes an implicit understanding of how professionals are to engage one another, their clients, and work itself (Fritz, in press) and sustains a professional ethic identifiable through the history of the professions (Kimball, 1995).

Relational Responsibility

Relationships define the warp and woof of the fabric of organizational life. As social beings, we engage shared work with others as part of the human condition. Although each historical moment is marked by particular ways of dividing labor to accomplish the human business of living in the world, a common thread running through the work of millennia is the common application of human physical and cognitive effort joined for purposes of sustaining human biological life, constructing the world we live in, and accomplishing action in the public sphere (Arendt, 1958/1998). Relationships remain a key motif in the narrative of human work life; they offer the potential to make everyday tasks light or heavy, pleasant or distasteful, and rewarding or distressing. The chapters in this volume and in the previous anthology (Fritz & Omdahl, 2006) devoted to problematic work relationships highlight the many ways relationships can go wrong and be put right. Resilience (Hammoud & Buzzanell, this volume), dialogic turning points (Hess & Sneed, this volume), and forgiveness (Waldron & Kloeber, this volume) all point to hope for relationships in the workplace as contributors to personal, corporate, and communal flourishing.

Arnett et al. (2009) offered a framework for understanding interpersonal communication ethics focused on protecting and promoting the good of relationships. Although relationships differ in type and in the contextual demands that provide their particular shape and texture, a major metaphor guiding the treatment of all relationships is "responsibility"—responsibility for the nurture of the relationship. When a goal other than the relationship is primary, such as accomplishing a work task, the type of communication emerging in such a relationship is closer to business and professional communication than to interpersonal communication (Arnett et al., 2009). Relational care, however, can become part of this communication, present in public as well as private settings.

Work relationships are characterized by elements relevant to both public and private spheres. In the typical workplace, we encounter a range of persons with whom we form functional relationships of varying intensity and duration. Some persons we end up knowing very well, in ways that overlap the private sphere, while others we engage at a public level. Marks (1994) noted that about half the population claims to have two or more close friends at work, which suggests that either the tendency or opportunity to seek close connections in the workplace is not uniform.

Work relationships that become friendships, or "blended" relationships, as Bridge and Baxter (1992) termed them, face a number of challenges, including balancing the demands of the friendship and the organizational role (Bridge & Baxter, 1992). These demands may be navigated in ways that permit the friendship to endure, but intervening circumstances may lead to relational deterioration (Sias, 2009). Other relationships, such as those with disliked others, are maintained for the sake of accomplishing tasks and are preserved through distancing strategies (Hess, 2006) that permit each party to work functionally with each other while bracketing personal disinclinations.

Hess's (2006) work on distancing provides important insights for a philosophy of work relationships underlying an interpersonal communication ethic of professional civility. Professional civility takes as one of its conceptual foundations the notion of civility as communicative virtue (Fritz, 2011a, in press), which is marked by some degree of distance and formality expressed verbally and nonverbally. Buber (1966) noted that friendship begins with distance; distance permits us to see another with greater clarity (Arnett et al., 2009). Forni (2011) pointed out that formality, which creates interpersonal distance, permits dignity and respect among persons who may have little in common and who do not know each other well. However, an ideology of intimacy (Sennett, 1974), pervasive in American culture, prescribes informality in most contexts. A focus on civility as communicative virtue provides an understanding of the role of distance and formality in protecting and promoting workplace relationships through the relational responsibility of professional civility.

Civility

Concerns about incivility in the public sphere and in the workplace have prompted increased attention to issues of civility (Arnett, 2006; Carter, 1998; Davenport Sypher, 2004; Davenport Sypher & Gill, this volume; Fritz, 2011a, 2012). Civility, traditionally understood as civic virtue (e.g., Shils, 1997), is a communicative virtue in its protection and promotion of human solidarity and interconnectedness through discursive interaction (Fritz, 2011a). Carter (1998) noted that civility consists of sacrifices we make for the sake of living with others and rests upon personal restraint for the good of something larger than the self—the community. Ironically, civility accomplishes its connective work through the creation and maintenance of interpersonal distance.

Civility permits persons sharing the same space to encounter one another without running over each other, to acknowledge one other's humanity without violating personal boundaries (Fritz, 2011a). Civility emerges as a product of the dialectic of closeness and distance; the interplay of the dialectic permits spaces between persons that both join and separate. Civility operates on behalf of a shared public space, protecting and promoting opportunity for public conversation, deliberation, and action; in this sense, civility is communicative care for institutions as well as for persons (Fritz, 2011a, 2011b). Civility permits joint action around a common center (Arnett, 1986), providing the shared ground of a worthwhile project to connect parties who may be very different from one another and who share no private or personal foundation for connection.

Professional Civility as Relational Responsibility: Protecting and Promoting Workplace Relationships

Professional civility as relational responsibility takes the communicative virtue of civility into the workplace, situating its action within a philosophy of work life sensitive to differences in personal boundaries for public and private communicative engagement and responsive to roles as public "common places" for shared organizational action. Professional civility differentiates types of relationships and discerns the operational salience of roles as guidelines for interactive routines in a given relationship and/or context. Professional civility protects and promotes workplace relationships through the practical wisdom of communicative *phronesis*.

Relational responsibility takes on various forms in different types of work relationships; relationships need different types of relational care (Arnett et al., 2009). The special peer is constructed from different patterns of interaction than the information or collegial peer (Kram & Isabella, 1985), and men's and women's collegial peer relationships are different in form and function (Fritz, 1997), which suggests that a different type of attentiveness is needed for each of these relationship types. The information peer is primarily a role-based relationship, without the closer connections found in the collegial or special peer relationship (Kram & Isabella, 1985), calling for a different type of relational responsibility and care. The problematic or troublesome relationship (Fritz, 2002, 2006) calls for yet a different type of engagement. Professional civility as relational responsibility exercises practical wisdom in discerning needs of different relational configurations.

Although relational responsibility varies from relationship to relationship, one principle underlying all relational responsibility is the recognition of the human face of the Other. Persons who strive to keep public and private spheres of life separate (Arnett, 2006) recognize the risks involved in investing more of life in the organizational context than a given institution can support. For this reason, some persons prefer to keep work and private life separate. Professional civility honors the wishes of those who prefer to maintain relationships at the public level (Omdahl, 2006). Professional civility, likewise, finds ways of carrying on work with others despite challenges to relationships arising from personal dislike, negative turning points, or other problematic behaviors. Professional civility as relational responsibility exercises practical wisdom in the face of relational difficulty.

In workplace relationships with those who wish to function at the public level or with whom we must function at the public level for the sake of the organization, we may not "look" directly into the face of the Other, but protect the Other's face, and perhaps our own, through respectful role distance that does not violate boundaries and permits a veil of privacy to screen shielded areas. In this manner, respecting the role's boundary management function works much like the engagement of Gadamerian "tact" (Kingwell, 1995, pp. 226–227) in its manner of "overlooking" in interaction by permitting role distance and circumspection to move or shield from the field of vision, and hence from remark, elements of the private or personal. In such relationships, the role is primary; the "depersonalization" does not dehumanize but protects. Professional civility as relational responsibility exercises practical wisdom through sensitivity to the "particular" of a given person and relationship.

In other work relationships, mutuality of interests and inclination lend potential for private friendship. In such cases, the relationship takes on many elements of the personal and private. When relationship partners in close relationships at work engage a professional civility perspective, they keep in mind the presence of the "third," the organization and its purposes, as a focus of attention in the context of the workplace. For example, to preserve the work of a team composed of multiple parties and to prevent ostracism emerging from clique formation (Sias, this volume), the formality of the role relationship is temporarily foregrounded to preserve equality of access and connection among all members, evidencing responsibility for multiple relationships and for the organization as a welcoming home for all. The role of a common center (Arnett, 1986) as a focus for joint labor upon common ground moves the source of connection from the personal and private to the realm of the public. Without threatening naturally occurring ties among persons who find commonality through private connections, a common center provides coordinates for connection among all. Professional civility as relational responsibility works through dialectical engagement, engendering care for both persons and the organization (Fritz, 2011b).

Conclusion

Work relationships serve multiple functions in the context of work life. They are pragmatically necessary for the accomplishment of tasks as well as an ontological element of the human condition, which includes the engagement of labor, work, and action (Arendt, 1958/1998) as existential demands (Arnett, in press). Communicative processes in work relationships give them their particular shape and texture, laying the groundwork for their contributions, both problematic and constructive, to the shared life of work. These communicative processes are, to a large degree, under our control, despite the exigencies of workplace complexities that may direct our perceptions toward others in particular directions and predispose our judgments of them as problematic or difficult (e.g., Duck, Foley, & Kirkpatrick, 2006).

As organizational leadership increasingly recognizes the destructive consequences of hostile relationships (Keashly, this volume), bullies in the workplace (Kinney, this volume), and incivility in general (Pearson & Porath, 2009), professional civility offers the possibility of functional and virtuous communicative interactions that protect and promote workplace relationships and their integral role in the organizing process (Sias, 2009). Professional civility offers an approach to engaging workplace relationships that honors difference and "the particular" in workplace relationships, ever mindful of the organizational background against which work relationships construct their relational patterns. Professional civility as relational responsibility protects and promotes workplace relationships as a "good" of and for the workplace as a site for human labor, work, and action in this historical moment. Through attentiveness to what is possible in a particular moment in time in a particular relationship and organization, professional civility works as an interpersonal communication ethic for the workplace.

References

Arendt, H. (1998). *The human condition* (2nd ed.). Chicago, IL: University of Chicago Press. (Original work published 1958)

Arnett, R. C. (1986). *Communication and community: Implications of Martin Buber's dialogue.* Carbondale, IL: Southern Illinois University Press.

Arnett, R. C. (2001). Dialogic civility as pragmatic ethical practice: An interpersonal metaphor for the public domain. *Communication Theory, 11*, 315–338.

Arnett, R. C. (2006). Professional civility: Reclaiming organizational limits. In J. M. H. Fritz & B. L. Omdahl (Eds.), *Problematic relationships in the workplace* (pp. 233–248). New York, NY: Peter Lang.

Arnett, R. C. (in press). *Communication ethics in dark times: Arendt's rhetoric of warning and hope.* Carbondale, IL: Southern Illinois University Press.

Arnett, R. C., & Arneson, P. (1999). *Dialogic civility: Community, hope, and interpersonal relationships.* Albany, NY: State University of New York Press.

Arnett, R. C., Fritz, J. M. H., & Bell, L. M. (2009). *Communication ethics literacy: Dialogue and difference.* Thousand Oaks, CA: Sage.

Arnett, R. C., & Holba, A. M. (in press). *An overture to philosophy of communication: The carrier of meaning.* New York, NY: Peter Lang.

Bridge, K., & Baxter, L. A. (1992). Blended relationships: Friends as work associates. *Western Journal of Communication, 56*, 200–225.

Buber, M. (1966). *The way of response: Martin Buber; selections from his writings* (N. N. Glatzer, Ed.). New York, NY: Schocken.

Carter, S. L. (1998). *Civility: Manners, morals, and the etiquette of democracy.* New York, NY: Basic Books.

Davenport Sypher, B. (2004). Reclaiming civil discourse in the workplace. *Southern Communication Journal, 69*, 257–269.

Duck, S., Foley, M. K., & Kirkpatrick, D. C. (2006). Uncovering the complex roles behind the "difficult" coworker. In J. M. H. Fritz & B. L. Omdahl (Eds.), *Problematic relationships in the workplace* (pp. 3–19). New York, NY: Peter Lang.

Forni, P. M. (2011, September). The case for formality. *Spectra, 47*(3), 8–10.

Fritz, J. M. H. (1997). Men's and women's organizational peer relationships: A comparison. *Journal of Business Communication, 34*, 27–46.

Fritz, J. M. H. (2002). How do I dislike thee? Let me count the ways: Constructing impressions of troublesome others at work. *Management Communication Quarterly, 15*, 410–438.

Fritz, J. M. H. (2006). Typology of troublesome others at work: A follow-up investigation. In J. M. H. Fritz & B. L. Omdahl (Eds.), *Problematic relationships in the workplace* (pp. 21–46). New York: Peter Lang.

Fritz, J. M. H. (2011a, September). Civility in the workplace. *Spectra, 47*(3), 11–14.

Fritz, J. M. H. (2011b). Women's communicative leadership in higher education. In E. Ruminski & A. Holba (Eds.), *Communicative understandings of women's leadership development: From ceilings of glass to labyrinth paths* (pp. 9–35). Lanham, MD: Lexington Books.

Fritz, J. M. H. (2012). Interpersonal crisis communication in the workplace: Professional civility as ethical response to problematic interactions. In S. A. Groom & J. M. H. Fritz (Eds.),

Communication ethics and crisis: Negotiating differences in public and private spheres (pp. 67–86). Madison, NJ: Fairleigh Dickinson University Press.

Fritz, J. M. H. (in press). *Professional civility: Communicative virtue at work*. New York, NY: Peter Lang.

Fritz, J. H., & Omdahl, B. H. (Eds.). (2006). *Problematic relationships in the workplace*. New York, NY: Peter Lang.

Hess, J. A. (2006). Distancing from problematic coworkers. In J. M. H. Fritz & B. L. Omdahl (Eds.), *Problematic relationships in the workplace* (pp. 205–232). New York, NY: Peter Lang.

Hess, J. A., Omdahl, B. L., & Fritz, J. M. H. (2006). Turning points in relationships with disliked coworkers. In J. M. H. Fritz & B. L. Omdahl (Eds.), *Problematic relationships in the workplace* (pp. 89–106). New York, NY: Peter Lang.

Hodson, R. (2001). *Dignity at work*. Cambridge, England: Cambridge University Press.

Kimball, B. A. (1995). *The "true professional ideal" in America: A history*. Lanham, MD: Rowman & Littlefield.

Kingwell, M. (1995). *A civil tongue: Justice, dialogue, and the politics of pluralism*. University Park, PA: The Pennsylvania State University Press.

Kram, K. E., & Isabella, L. A. (1985). Mentoring alternatives: The role of peer relationships in career development. *Academy of Management Journal, 28*, 123–140.

MacIntyre, A. (2007). *After virtue: A study in moral theory* (3rd ed.). Notre Dame, IN: Notre Dame University Press.

Marks, S. R. (1994). Intimacy in the public realm: The case of coworkers. *Social Forces, 72*, 843–858.

Myers, K. K. (2010). Workplace relationships and membership negotiation. In S. W. Smith & S. R. Wilson (Eds.), *New directions in interpersonal communication research* (pp. 135–156). Thousand Oaks, CA: Sage.

Omdahl, B. L. (2006). Towards effective work relationships. In J. M. H. Fritz & B. L. Omdahl (Eds.), *Problematic relationships in the workplace* (pp. 279–294). New York, NY: Peter Lang.

Pearson, C., & Porath, C. (2009). *The cost of bad behavior: How incivility is damaging your business and what to do about it*. New York, NY: Portfolio.

Sennett, R. (1974). *The fall of public man: On the social psychology of capitalism*. New York, NY: Vintage.

Shils, E. (1997).*The virtue of civility: Selected essays on liberalism, tradition, and civil society* (Steven Grosby, Ed.). Indianapolis, IN: Liberty Fund.

Sias, P. (2009). *Organizing relationships: Traditional and emerging perspectives on workplace relationships*. Thousand Oaks, CA: Sage.

· 1 4 ·

COMMUNICATING FORGIVENESS IN WORK RELATIONSHIPS

VINCENT R. WALDRON & DAYNA N. KLOEBER

Ed leads a department in a large research organization where office space is a precious resource. He was irate when a recent request for more space was held up by the "wicked witch" resource manager who requested a formal proposal complete with "color-coded graphs, bells, and whistles." When a member of another department confided that her unit had been quickly allocated extra space without even submitting a formal request, Ed was incensed. He shot off an e-mail demanding to see a copy of their formal request. "She writes me back with all of this BS on how they have all of these projects and how they don't have time for a proposal." He retaliated by sending a message through "the grapevine" that he intended to file a discrimination lawsuit based on the fact that the other department was largely female. "Now the almighty queen won't talk to me," Ed confides. He also reported that now all of a sudden he is receiving some of the space he requested. "She knows she picked favorites and I called her out on it." Ed thinks his confrontational approach was successful: "I feel pretty good that I did a big favor for my team by staying strong and calling her on her BS."

Why Forgiveness Is Important at Work

As suggested by the this example,[1] working life is sometimes punctuated by relational incidents that yield a sense of moral outrage, hostility or bitterness, grudges, and even acts of revenge (for one recent analysis, see Metts, Cupach, & Lippert, 2006). The incident described by Ed includes many of the elements of what could have become a forgiveness episode, although in this case forgiveness was eschewed in favor of retaliation. Ed views himself as the victim of a relational transgression attributed to arbitrary and unfair treatment by a more senior person who controls valued resources. The seriousness of the matter is marked by his apparent moral outrage. Ed feels wronged, and his response seems morally justified. As is typically the case at work, the trajectory of this episode is shaped by larger contextual considerations, including the organization's (apparently selective) preference for formalized communication and an "audience" of team members who may be evaluating Ed's response to a perceived sleight. Communication practices drive forgiveness episodes as well as retaliation episodes like this one: the exchange of demands and explanations, belittling and sexist language, Ed's use of the informal network to spread a threat, and the other party's cessation of interaction. If Ed had adopted a more forgiving approach and the resource supervisor had acknowledged the appearance of unfairness, the parties may have moved toward reconciliation. Instead, despite Ed's claim of victory, it is likely that the relational aftertaste of this episode will remain bitter, and a continuing cycle of retribution may ensue. This problematic relationship may have negative consequences not just for Ed but also for his team members.

In this chapter, we offer the process of forgiveness as a hopeful and potentially constructive response to the inevitable harmful and hurtful encounters that employees experience over the course of a career. Along with others who have advocated for a more positive framing of organizational behavior (Cameron, Dutton, & Quinn, 2003), we view forgiveness as an essential element of virtuous work relationships. In contrast to some misperceptions, forgiveness is neither a weak response to injustice nor a means of excusing wrongdoing (i.e., Enright, 2001; Waldron & Kelley, 2008; Worthington, 2005). When organizations foster the practice of forgiveness, members may feel encouraged to negotiate perceived violations of relational codes of conduct. The process may protect aggrieved employees from further harm, and it can provide a path by which transgressing employees may be restored to full membership in the workplace community. Further, the practice of forgiveness allows employees to work through negative feelings. It may restore their confidence in the organization and their coworkers. The result may be a working environment that is more humane, just, and, ultimately, productive.

Defining Forgiveness

Most definitions of forgiveness, including those offered by organizational researchers (Aquino, Grover, Goldman, & Folger, 2003), describe it as a psychological process whereby an individual recognizes that a transgression has occurred and makes a conscious decision to replace hostility and other negative emotional reactions with more positive feelings toward the offender (or, at least, less intensively negative ones). We agree that forgiveness is, among other things, an individual psychological decision. However, the communication practices that shape and enact forgiveness are of more interest to organizational communication scholars. A consciously communicative definition of forgiveness was offered by Waldron and Kelley (2008):

> Forgiveness is a relational process whereby harmful conduct is acknowledged by one or both partners, the harmed partner extends undeserved mercy to the perceived transgressor, one or both partners experience a transformation from negative to positive psychological states, and the meaning of the relationship is renegotiated, with the possibility of reconciliation. (p. 5)

When conceived in this way, forgiveness unfolds over time, often in a series of interactions. Indeed, in both personal and work relationships, the process can take not just days, but weeks, months, and even years as hurt subsides, grudges gradually erode, and the partners come to new understandings of the moral codes that will guide their interactions in the future. The process may be stalled, restarted, or replayed as the parties relive the past or commit new violations. The acknowledgment of harm and/or wrongdoing and the extending of mercy are crucial communicative components of this definition, and both of these communicative acts have been shown to vary considerably in both form and skill. Importantly, research suggests that, above and beyond the seriousness of the transgression, the communicative approach taken by the parties appears to have long-term relational effects (Waldron & Kelley, 2005). Forgiveness is a potentially transformative process, in that emotions and relational meanings typically change, for better or worse. As these authors found, some relational ties become deeper and stronger because coworkers give voice to strong emotions, rearticulate relational and organizational commitments, and incorporate the forgiveness episode into a larger narrative of relational resilience.

Several elements of this definition deserve further comment. First is the explicit acknowledgment of harm and/or wrongdoing. Often, the first communicative task of the parties is to acknowledge that something quite serious and wrong has apparently transpired—a relationally damaging event that must not be rationalized away or buried under the weight of bureaucratic obscurations that deny the victim his or her voice. The victim's response to these situations is quite understandably *emotional*, and the tendency to delegitimize it as "overly sensitive," "unprofessional," or "complaining" must be curbed if the process is to move forward (see Waldron, 2011). Second, although Waldron and Kelley (2008) focused on dyadic interactions, their model (see Figure 1) assumes that forgiveness episodes are shaped by the larger social context. At work, this context includes organizational norms that encourage workers to be more or less forgiving, the degree to which forgiving communication is hindered or hampered by formal procedures, and the "audience" of coworkers that has observed the wrongful behavior and is likely to pass judgment on its outcome. We see this last factor playing out in Ed's situation as he exploits the "grapevine" to cultivate support for his position.

A third factor is the notion of undeserved mercy. Although this term borders on redundancy, it makes clear the victimized party's right to eschew forgiveness in favor of other possible, and sometimes very appealing, alternatives: revenge, grudge holding, shunning, filing a grievance, whistle blowing, or, at the very least, lasting animosity. Typically, the offender has violated important, if sometimes informal, rules of relational conduct. He or she may have no "legitimate" claim to forgiveness. In that sense, forgiveness is a kind of gift, an act of altruism freely chosen by the victim. A fourth element of the definition is that forgiveness is made distinct from reconciliation. One or more parties may forgive but not commit to reconciliation because doing so would be unsafe or increase the possibilities for repeated violation. Partial reconciliation is a possibility, too, as when coworkers commit to restarting their collaborative activity while recognizing that feelings of friendship are unlikely to return. Fifth, Waldron and Kelley (2008) see forgiveness as a *moral* process, one in which the meanings of wrongful acts are negotiated by the parties with reference to the larger cultural, religious, familial, and organizational discourses that shape their understanding of moral relational conduct. Indeed, the words and emotions that make forgiveness episodes so meaningful and memorable are expressions of what workers consider to be good and evil, right and wrong, just and unjust, fair and unfair. As has been argued by others, perceptions of justice are inextricably woven into the fabric of workplace relationships and processes that restore justice, assuage negative feelings, and facilitate forgiveness (Hill, Exline, & Cohen, 2005).

A Model of Forgiveness in Organizational Relationships

The typical working career is punctuated by events that call for forgiveness, but they are sometimes crimped by restrictions on its practice. Figure 1 presents a model of the forgiveness process as practiced in work relationships. Adapted from Waldron and Kelly (2008), the model provides a structure of the current chapter.

Context

As suggested in Figure 1, forgiveness episodes at work are inevitably shaped by larger cultural and religious discourses about moral matters (see Arnett, Arneson, &Bell, 2006, on dialogic ethics). They are also influenced by the distinct qualities of the differing kinds of relationships found at work.

Cultural Understandings

Employees come to work with cultural understandings of, among other things, the nature of justice, the value of mercy, and the degree to which forgiveness or revenge is the proper response when one has been harmed. These values are often on display in popular television shows (e.g., *The Apprentice* or *The Office*), in which plots often turn on how merciful or vengeful workers will be when confronting the bad behavior of coworkers.

A more potent cultural influence throughout workplaces in the United States is religion. It is often spiritual concerns that motivate people to grant or seek forgiveness (Kelley, 1998). The extent to which these commitments are realized in work environments remains an open question as employees seek to rectify conflicts between religious ideals and business practices. Given questions about prioritizing values, it may be that faith-based organizations and those with highly religious leaders may more commonly invoke the language of forgiveness. It may even be that employees in faith-centric organizations will face greater expectations to be forgiving, and consequently, they may feel compelled to forgive transgressing coworkers or even the leaders themselves. This type of institutionally driven obligation is potentially problematic, as most theorists argue that true forgiveness is offered freely, under conditions determined by the victim (North, 1987). Forced forgiveness is a kind of "emotional tyranny" (Waldron, 2009) in which powerful people try to manipulate the emotional experiences of the aggrieved party. When people feel compelled to forgive, the

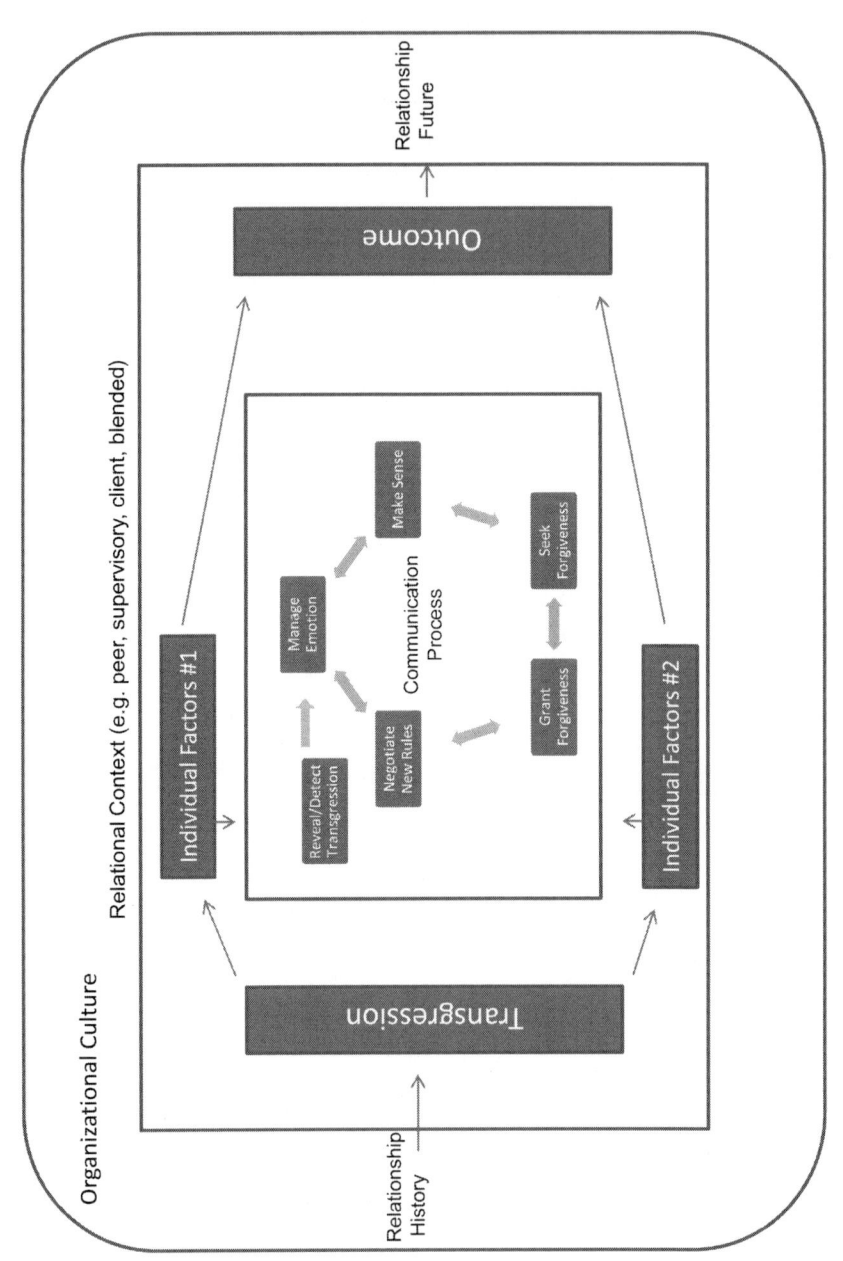

Figure 1. Organizational Forgiveness Model (Adapted from Waldron and Kelley, 2008)

process is unlikely to yield improved emotional and ethical conditions for the parties or the organization (Enright, Gassin, & Wu, 1992).

Popular culture is rich in clichés about forgiveness and revenge, and some of these sentiments will inevitably permeate organizational relations (e.g., "Forgive and forget"; "Don't get mad, get even"; "It is easier to ask for forgiveness than to ask for permission"; and "Take no prisoners"). Unless the organization itself addresses matters of forgiveness, adages may guide the behavior of members as they relate to one another, clients, and competitors.

At the same time, occupational culture can serve as an incentive or hindrance to forgiveness. In lines of work such as medicine, law, or property insurance, the admission of wrongdoing can have legal and financial consequences (Waldron, 2011). Certain professionals are understandably wary of informal processes of moral negotiation because they have been socialized to more formal and adversarial ways of addressing potential wrongdoing. Legal action and financial penalties may result if they admit wrongdoing and seek forgiveness. In contrast, some occupational cultures might encourage forgiveness seeking. Crisis management specialists may advise clients to "come clean" about mistakes in the hope that customers and clients will respond with mercy rather than grudge-holding. Numerous politicians have learned the same lesson (although many have not!), finding that their constituents can be forgiving when mistakes are admitted. Customer service representatives often seek forgiveness on behalf of their organizations by offering aggrieved customers apologies and compensation.

Organizational Context

The practice of forgiveness in the organizational context is unique. For example, task interdependence can make it necessary for members to work in close proximity, to communicate and cooperate. Relational blowups can endanger the productivity of the parties and those who work with them. This reality presumably provides an incentive for the practice of forgiveness. The alternatives, such as seeking revenge on a teammate, can be less constructive. Nonetheless, coworkers often do choose less productive responses, perhaps because forgiveness is rarely part of the repertoire of organizational interventions for coworker disputes (Stone, 2002). Another contextual feature is the networked nature of organizational communication. In the case of the denied resource request, Ed seems to view the resource manager's favoritism as harmful to his team, and news of this presumed wrongdoing reverberates across the organization's informal network. In this way, the magnitude of a transgression is intensified as additional parties take offense at an apparent breach of organizational justice. Another contextual factor is organizational memory, which assures that certain transgressions are documented or at least recorded in the collective memories of coworkers. Ed's senior colleague may seek to have the incident recorded in his personnel file and will certainly remember it when mulling over Ed's next resource request. For long-term employees, the accumulation of unforgiven offenses makes forgiving communication all the more difficult.

Relational Context

At work, forgiveness may be called for in varying types of relationships, including supervisory, peer, and client relationships. In the cases of supervisory relationships, differences in status can be problematic. Seeking forgiveness for one's transgressions almost always involves a willingness to cede power to the aggrieved party, who then decides when and if the process should proceed. This vulnerability may be uncomfortable for those who occupy powerful positions (but see Cameron & Caza, 2002). At the same time, employees who are willing to forgive may relinquish power that might be retained if they exercised other options, such as filing a formal grievance or issuing threats of eventual retaliation. In client or customer relationships, it may simply "be expected" that employees will seek forgiveness (by offering apologies or compensation) when damaging mistakes are made. However, the degree to which this ritualized form of forgiveness is perceived to be genuine may be a factor in a client's satisfaction with the organization and its representatives. Finally, many work relationships are blended, with the parties identifying as both friends and coworkers (Bridge & Baxter, 1992). A failure to negotiate forgiveness in this relational context can yield bad feelings that flow across the fluid boundary between personal and working life. The relational fallout may affect not just coworkers but also family members (e.g., spouses of the feuding parties) and extended friendship networks.

Relational History

The model notes the role of relational history in shaping the current episode. We have hinted at this earlier, noting that a history of repeated transgressions can complicate the process. Aggrieved parties feel more at risk when they perceive a continuing pattern of misbehavior (Waldron & Kassing, 2010), fearing that they will be victimized again. If they forgive at all under these circumstances, employees may choose to do so "conditionally," stipulating that certain changes in behavior must occur before the process can proceed. Based on a study of roughly 200 uses of conditional forgiveness, Kloeber (2011) reported that this approach is often used to balance the victim's desire to be merciful with the simultaneous need to make future interactions safe, predictable, and just.

More positively, a history of successful practice makes work relationships potentially more resilient and rewarding. Coworkers who have successfully worked through serious disagreements incorporate those episodes into their relational narratives. This tendency is reflected in language such as "we have our differences but we work them out" or "what doesn't kill us makes us stronger." This kind of relational history may breed optimism, mutual respect, confidence, and a tolerance for difference. These positive qualities may explain why some workgroups remain successful across time and changing circumstances while others experience disharmony and dysfunction (Cameron et al., 2003).

Transgressions

Forgiveness researchers consistently find that the perceived severity of the offense is among the most important predictors of how the parties will behave toward one another (Fincham & Beach, 2002). Eaton and Struthers (2006) suggested that transgressions at work were as consequential as those in friendships and romantic partnerships. Their findings indicate that coworkers are also less likely to repent than friends or romantic partners, which in turn makes forgiveness more difficult.

Indeed, forgiveness is considered applicable to and necessary for the most serious kinds of offenses. Misunderstandings, forgetfulness, mistakes, mildly annoying behavior—these offenses can be handled with forbearance, clarification, patience, or a willingness to "just let it go" (Waldron & Kelley, 2008). The transgressions that call for forgiveness are typically perceived to be deliberate acts that result in deeply felt hurt or undeniable harm. The victim (and often his or her peers) may view these actions as inexcusable acts of wrongdoing. Based on Harvey's (2004) analysis of transgressions, we conclude that they take one of three forms. First are those that communicate disrespect for the recipient. These acts threaten the identity of the victim and imply that he or she is devalued, inferior, or unworthy. Second are violations of spoken or unspoken organizational codes of conduct. Work relationships are often governed by a kind of covenant—a solemn sense of what behaviors are good, tolerated, and deeply wrong. The latter may include taking credit for another's work, criticizing a coworker or direct report in a public forum, "backstabbing," or undermining the performance of one's coworkers. Waldron (2009; Waldron & Krone, 1991) found that these acts are often described as a kind of "betrayal." Acts of injustice are a third type of serious transgression, often performed by people who have the power to manipulate or ignore the moral codes of the organization or the larger society. Abuses of power, sexism, and the manipulation of workers' emotions, such as guilt or shame, might be examples.

Eaton and Struthers (2006) found that coworkers reported forgiveness episodes that concerned poor work performance. Impeding the productivity of teammates, failing to perform a task as promised, or causing an egregious mistake—these are examples of performance that might require one to seek forgiveness from coworkers or supervisors. Poor task performance is typically unintentional. But forgiveness is sometimes expected and sought when significant harm results from negligent and even unintended acts. For example, a foreman reported transferring an employee (and family friend) to a more dangerous worksite, where he was killed in an industrial accident. The foreman was deeply distraught, not just by the loss, but by the fact that the company and the workers refused to forgive him for what they considered an act of negligence (Waldron, 2009).

Finally, some offenses are considered "unforgivable." In the realm of personal relationships, the most commonly identified unforgivable offense is infidelity, but organizations may deem as unforgivable a larger range of offenses. Some of these offenses are dictated by organizational procedure, as when a sexual harassment policy prescribes severe punishment for offenders. A case in point is that of Henry Stonecipher, a hard-charging executive at Boeing who was called out of retirement to lead the company back from a series of ethics scandals (Holmes, 2005). Boeing's board of directors fired Stonecipher after being tipped that he had initiated an affair with a female Boeing executive. She reported no harm, but the board apparently decided the offense was unforgivable, given the company's recent history of ethical blunders. In the realm of personal relationships, it appears that offenses are less likely to be considered unforgiveable as people age, gain experience, and have invested more in their network of relationships (Waldron & Kelley, 2008). A similar trend may occur at work, and perhaps organizations should gravitate toward more nuanced policies regarding employee relationships. Justice should be served and victims protected, but with the passing of time, and in certain instances, forgiveness, too, may be considered a more viable response.

Individual Qualities

Our model recognizes that individual qualities of employees can influence the course of the forgiveness process. On various survey measures, some people reveal a persistent tendency to be more or less forgiving (e.g., Brown & Phillips, 2005). As indicated in Figure 1, when faced with a particular kind of transgression, some employees may simply skip the "communication part" and move swiftly to enact a relationship outcome (e.g., requesting a transfer to a different supervisor or workgroup). Some existing research supports this proposed trajectory. In one study, employees with a high need for recognition were more likely to harbor negativity such as bitterness and dislike toward offenders, while those with a lower need for recognition were more disposed toward love and compassion (Butler & Mullis, 2001). We would add that the negotiation of forgiveness can require courage, empathy, and interpersonal communication—qualities that may vary considerably across individuals. For this reason, education and organizational encouragement would be needed if forgiveness practices are to be widely adopted (see Stone, 2002).

Communicative Practices

Figure 1 depicts the cycle of communicative tasks that constitutes the core of a forgiveness episode. These tasks need not occur in order (but they sometimes do), and the process can easily reverse itself, skip a step, or grind to a halt. The tasks are performed through the collective action of the parties; they are not actions performed individually. In some cases, they involve consultations with members of the larger community, such as team members, mentors, or human resource professionals.

Detecting/revealing the transgression. The discovery of the offense typically triggers the forgiveness episode. Discovery can involve such communicative acts as confessions, accusations, and blunders (the unintentional revelation of wrongdoing). Third parties sometimes report to the victim that a coworker has committed a harmful act. In some cases, the act is directly observed and then confirmed through an inquiry or "test" of some kind. Such was the case in this episode reported by a store manager (Waldron & Kelley, 2008):

> One morning I was in my store getting ready to open. I was so engulfed in work that I lost track of time. The store opened at 10:00 a.m. and at about 10:15 the phone rang and it was my district manager. She asked me why the store wasn't open. In a panic I

lied and said it was. But she knew it wasn't because she was at a pay phone across the hall from my store! I was mortified and she was extremely upset. (p. 102)

This situation was complicated by the two-tiered nature of the transgression. The failure to open on time was a performance problem, but the deception raised larger issues about trustworthiness and threatened the quality of the relationship with the supervisor. Coworkers are likely to be more forgiving when wrongdoing is acknowledged explicitly by the offender (Kelley & Waldron, 2005). Learning about transgressions from a third party can be highly face-threatening (Afifi, Falato, & Weiner, 2001), as when a coworker reveals that a peer has been covertly complaining to a supervisor about one's performance. In such cases, the negotiation of forgiveness may require the involvement of multiple parties, as the offender must help the victim restore his or her reputation.

Managing emotion. Although emotional expression is highly regulated in most workplaces, the parties to a forgiveness negotiation must find ways to communicate feelings. Approaches may involve communication behaviors such as listening for emotions, venting, labeling feelings, legitimizing emotions, proposing a "cooling off" period, and resisting the temptation to rush the process (with comments like "get over it"). Of course, emotions tend to dissipate over time, and the forgiveness process should not be an open-ended invitation to "dump" bad feelings on unsuspecting coworkers. Nonetheless, emotions such as indignation, guilt, and fear play an important signal function in organizations, as they are often a response to practices that are inhumane, deeply unfair, and ethically questionable. By voicing rather than suppressing them, forgiveness processes shed light on these unacceptable practices.

Sense making. Serious transgressions are highly disruptive in that the victimized employee questions long-held assumptions about work relationships and the organization's system of justice. Communication during this time may be designed to manage uncertainty and create meaning and may involve questioning the perpetrator (e.g., "Why did you do this?"), assessing the nature of the offense (e.g., "Is this as serious as it seems?"), and predicting the future (e.g., "In this organizational culture, am I likely to be victimized again?").Team members, mentors, family members, and other supporters may be consulted during this period, and the victimized employee will consider his or her own values and those endorsed by the organization (e.g., "What is the 'right' response to a transgression of this kind?" "Should I forgive the perpetrator or pursue some other response, such as avoidance or retribution?"). The counsel of human resource professionals and supervisors may be particularly helpful at this stage.

Seeking forgiveness. Although forgiveness-seeking communication is often associated with the perpetrator, it, too, is an interactive process. It may be demanded, encouraged, or discouraged by victims and their organizational allies, and a victim's response to initial forgiveness-seeking behaviors will influence the trajectory of the process. Was the initial effort judged to be authentic and sufficiently responsive? Does the victim need time to consider a response? A variety of forgiveness-seeking behaviors has been observed by researchers: apologies, offers of compensations/restitution, verbal and nonverbal assurances that the transgression won't be repeated, explanations and accounts for the bad behavior, and even the use of humor to lighten the emotional tone of the encounter or as an act of self-deprecation by the offender (Kelley & Waldron, 2005). It is no surprise that a sincere apology is the expected forgiveness-seeking response in such situations (see, e.g., Metts et al., 2006). However, the communicative qualities of sincere apologies have concerned forgiveness researchers (Waldron & Kelley, 2008). More positive responses have been observed when the perpetrator fully and explicitly acknowledges harm and wrongdoing, when the emotion of remorse is expressed, and when the perpetrator takes full responsibility for the harmful act.

Offers of compensation may be well received in some cases. The general approach is an offer to "make up" for the damage done to the work relationship. The risk is that the offer will be inadequate or even insulting to the wounded party. Compensation for serious personal offenses might include a pledge to help repair the damage done to a reputation or an offer to provide additional resources to help the victim. One study of workplace relationships compared the effectiveness of "mere talk" to offer of compensation ("penance") on the restoration of cooperative relationships (Bottom, Gibson, Daniels, & Murningham, 2002).Results showedthat a simple willingness to talk was less effective. Kelley and Waldron (2005) reported a similar finding with personal relationships. The willingness to discuss the offense with the victim is likely a necessary, but not sufficient, step in the forgiveness process. These authors reported that humor was typically an unsuccessful forgiveness-seeking strategy. In summary, it appears that the wounded partner must be convinced that the perpetrator "gets" the seriousness of the transgression and is willing to compensate for the damage. The expression of remorse and assurance may reduce uncertainty about the future by convincing the victim that the offense is unlikely to be repeated.

Forgiveness granting. Forgiveness is rarely enacted as an all-or-nothing act. Instead, it proceeds as a kind of negotiation, as the parties reassess the transgression, their moral commitments, and the nature of their relationship. In some cases, forgiveness is granted implicitly—it "just happens" as the process runs its course, negative emotion subsides, and normal patterns of interaction resume (Kelley, 1998). Nonverbal behavior cues (resumed eye contact, smiles) may be particularly important indicators that forgiveness has occurred, even if it has not been verbalized. However, forgiveness is also granted explicitly, often with statements such as "I forgive you," "Consider it in the past," or even "It's ok." Explicit forgiveness has been associated with positive relationship outcomes in at least one study of roughly 200 forgiveness episodes (Waldron & Kelley, 2005), perhaps because it reduces uncertainty about "where things stand" between coworkers. The wounded partner's willingness to discuss the offense with the perpetrator, to put hurt and harm into words, was also predictive of positive relational outcomes in that study. On the other hand, minimization strategies (e.g., "It's not that big of a deal") were significantly associated with relational deterioration. By using minimization, aggrieved workers may be denying their own emotional experience, substituting what previous writers have deemed "cheap" reconciliation for true forgiveness (see Volf, 2001). This approach may keep the peace in the short term, but hard feelings tend to persist and working relationships may be undermined.

A communicative approach called conditional forgiveness has been detailed in several descriptive studies (e.g., Kelley, 1998; Kloeber, 2011). It involves stipulations aimed at thwarting future transgressions. At work, the use of conditional forgiveness may supplement the rules and protections offered by the organization (i.e., retraining to improve awareness/knowledge). Among coworkers, conditions might include something like this: "I can move past this, but I need a promise from you—that you won't take credit for my work again." Some research suggests that conditional forgiveness is associated with relationship deterioration, but that might be an indication of the way the conditions were communicated. For example, there is a vast difference between an aggressive threat, such as "You better never do that again!" and a supportive message, such as "I'd like us to move forward with a shared understanding of our relational rules." Based on her analysis of over 200 episodes, Kloeber (2011) argued that this approach allows the parties to balance their commitments to mercy and justice, safety and risk, expression and suppression, and reconciliation with boundaries. A variety of other forgiveness-granting practices has been identified. The cultivation of empathy is one of those. Worthington (1998, 2001) showed that victims are more forgiving if they develop empathy for offenders. They might do so by inquiring about motives, feelings, and viewpoints. Also, by considering their own history of misdeeds, victims may come to appreciate those who have forgiven them—and, according to Worthington, be more likely to offer that "gift" to the undeserving offender.

In their study of very long-term relationships, Waldron and Kelley (2008) were struck by the length of time required by the forgiveness process. They concluded that successful forgivers "used time to advantage"; they allowed feelings to change with the passing of time, acted deliberately rather than hastily, and proposed that the parties live with uncertainty until feelings and desires could be sorted out. They also noted that those who "stuck with" the forgiveness process often cited values that transcended the interest of the parties. For some, it was a belief that forgiveness was a spiritually elevated response to worldly turmoil; others cited a belief in karma or a conviction that harmony should prevail in nature and in human relations. At work, these transcendent values might include a desire to enhance the goals of the organization or remain true to the spirit of cooperation that had otherwise prevailed in a successful career.

Finally, relational events serious enough to require forgiveness often overwhelm the participants. The counsel and emotional support of third parties are often required. At work, the third party might be a human resource professional, a mediator, or a skilled and trusted mentor (see Stone, 2002). The parties sometimes require counseling from a source outside the organization, such as a psychologist or mental health professional. In all cases, the victims must be protected from further harm if they choose to pursue a forgiveness process. The distinction between forgiveness and reconciliation must be preserved.

Relationship negotiation. Relationships are nearly always transformed by forgiveness episodes. Often, the incident prompts the parties to reassess communication rules and moral commitments presumed (perhaps inaccurately) to define their work relationship. It is entirely possible that this part of the process will simply result in a plan for the coworkers to coexist in the organization with as little direct interaction as possible. However, they might also make agreements to limit the chances of future harm. For example, team members might agree to discuss complaints before sharing them with a supervisor or peers. Coworker friends might agree that disclosures about their personal lives will not be shared with other coworkers. Clear restrictions on the use of sexual humor or touching might be agreed to. All of these actions constitute a bridge between forgiving and reconciling, although the relationship that emerges is likely to be different. Ideally, it will be a relationship that both parties, but particularly the victim, will experience as safe, just, and conducive to high levels of work performance.

Relational Outcomes

Work relationships can deteriorate when individuals simply can't bring themselves to forgive or when the communication process fails due to poor communication practices, limited motivation, or organizational obstacles. This last factor might include an unforgiving organizational culture that lacks a support system for employees who feel hurt or wronged. Under even the best of circumstances, forgiveness is a daunting process. In some cases, the best outcome may simply be that one of the parties is relocated or the perpetrator is terminated. Leaders may choose to downplay the incident, hoping that the outcome will be an eventual return to normal relations. Indeed, sometimes the passing of time facilitates the forgiveness process.

However, it is more likely that, left to fester, serious relational incidents will have harmful consequences for people and their organizations. In some cases, the incidents as well as the consequences may remain largely invisible to the larger organization. The harmed employee subtly withdraws from the workgroup, becomes more cynical about prospects for organizational justice, or quietly begins a search for a new and more humane working environment. However, those who feel victimized by coworkers or supervisors may react in ways that are more obviously damaging. Long-simmering resentments may boil to the surface in the form of hostile reactions to minor impositions. A sustained effort to undermine the offending coworker may ensue. In rare but tragic cases, the victim may seek to even the score through an act of violence. At this writing, another report of workplace violence is reverberating through the national media—a disgruntled employee of a North Carolina lumberyard who resolved his long-held grievances with a gun rather than his words. Violence is often the result of mental illness. Nonetheless, organizations that encourage forgiveness practices at least provide aggrieved employees with a constructive way to voice their concerns and, perhaps, experience a peaceful resolution.

The practice of forgiveness has been associated with improved mental health and reduced stress, and some evidence suggests physical health may be improved as well (e.g., Lawler, Younger, Piferi, Jobe, Edmondson, & Jones, 2005; Witvliet, 2001). When contrasted with the mental and physical toll taken by unaddressed grievances, these mental health benefits should be associated with improved employee morale, wellness, cooperation, and productivity. Based on findings in other contexts, it seems quite likely that forgiveness-based interventions should help estranged coworkers with the task of relationship repair (Rusbult, Hannon, Stocker, & Finkel, 2005). Therefore, we would expect improvement in team functioning, especially when dyadic conflicts are hampering team processes. Perhaps the most significant outcome, however, relates to an organization's moral vitality. Forgiveness processes can surface acts of wrongdoing and harm, clarify standards of moral conduct and civil behavior, and provide a path to redemption for offenders. The result may be a workforce committed to moral vigilance, justice, and compassion.

Research Directions

Although research on forgiveness has accelerated in recent decades, as recorded in such volumes as the *Handbook of Forgiveness* (Worthington, 2005), investigation of workplace forgiveness remains in its infancy. In terms of theoretical development, Waldron and Kelley (2008) proposed a framework that highlights the role of communication practices as parties in a forgiveness episode negotiate the individual, relational, and cultural values that are called into question when serious transgressions occur. Their Negotiated Morality Theory (NMT) suggests that communication serves a variety of moral functions in forgiveness episodes (Table 1) and other morally tinged encounters. At work, these include such functions as *defining moral standards*—the surfacing of the values that define right and wrong coworker relations and prioritizing individual and organizational values. For example, in our opening example, the senior employee might have been unfair in the allocation of resources. By speaking up (albeit inappropriately), Ed was essentially calling attention to what he considered a violation of an organizational value—the impartial treatment of working groups.

NMT helps us conceptualize how coworkers *engage moral tensions*. For example, in forgiveness episodes, the parties often express concerns for mercy and justice (Kloeber, 2011; Waldron & Kelley, 2008). Melissa, as a young bank teller, experienced this tension when a fellow employee stole from her "cash drawer," causing her months of both personal and professional anguish. Initially, Melissa was angry and focused on justice, but over time she came to feel compassion toward the other woman. "When I was finally told she had been caught stealing at another branch and had been fired, I'll admit I was relieved. But it was also then that I felt very sad for her too."

Redirecting hostility is another function proposed by NMT. Tragically, there is abundant evidence of hostility toward persons and organizations escalating to catastrophic ends. As we seek to make sense of these tragedies, the abnormal psychiatric pathology of the villain is often the most "digestable" explanation. Take, for instance, Amy Bishop, the Harvard-educated professor described

Table 1. The Moral Functions of Forgiving Communication in Organizations (Adapted from Waldron & Kelley, 2008)

Moral Function	Characteristics/Example(s)
Defining moral standards	Requesting equitable treatment; identifying abuses of power
Establishing accountability	Accepting responsibility for poor performance; truth telling
Engaging moral tensions	Mercy versus justice; safety versus risk
Restoring relational justice	Offering a public apology to team members; seeking restitution
Reimagining a moral future	Offering a path to redemption; promising more civil behavior
Honoring the self	Claiming respect from coworkers; recognizing the dignity of individual employees
Redirecting hostility	Safely venting anger; forgoing aggression
Increasing safety and concern	Creating formal processes of forgiveness; protecting victims from retribution
Finding closure	Halting negative rumination; reestablishing a task-oriented focus
Possible reconciliation	Instituting new relational boundaries; conforming to revised communication rules

as both "brilliant" and an "oddball," who went on a spree at the University of Alabama, Huntsville, shooting and killing three colleagues and wounding three others (Canning, McPhee, Netter, & Donaldson-James, 2010). We don't know if Ms. Bishop devalued merciful responses to perceived transgressions or if she was aware of options for negotiating her grievances peacefully. However, as organizations seek ways to avert such tragic acts of violence, it is worth considering that in numerous settings, from the Rwandan genocide to the schools of Northern Ireland, forgiveness processes have provided "a mechanism for persons to express negative emotion rather than retaining it or ruminating over its causes"(Waldron & Kelley, 2008, p. 87).

If Amy Bishop had been an active participant in such a process, might she have eschewed violence and vengeance? Much empirical research remains to be done on questions such as this one. Among those empirical questions are some that relate to organizational contexts: Which organizations tend to be more or less forgiving? How is forgiveness cultivated in these organizations? To what degree is forgiveness embedded in policy, ethics guidelines, and conflict resolution systems? How are religious and cultural values related to forgiveness, and how are they expressed, repressed, or oppressed by an organization's culture? Other questions relate to history (e.g., What role does the organization's or relationship's history of transgressions play in shaping the tendency to be forgiving in the present time?). Researchers should build on existing work (e.g., Metts et al., 2006) on the nature of transgressions in coworker relationships: What kinds of transgressions do employees believe could be best addressed through forgiveness processes? Which are considered unforgivable by employees or their organizations?

Research on the communication processes that enact forgiveness remains scant, especially in comparison to the large body of research on its psychological dimensions. Nonetheless, communication scholars have become more active in investigating this area (e.g., Bachman & Guerrero, 2006; Guerrero & Bachman, 2010; Kloeber, 2008, 2011; Merolla, 2008; Merolla & Zhang, 2011). The nature and effectiveness of various forgiveness-seeking and forgiveness-granting practices need to be evaluated further in the various types of work relationships. The discourse of forgiveness has yet to be studied in naturalistic organizational settings. The role of communication-related individual differences (e.g., perspective taking or communication apprehension) in shaping forgiveness episodes requires further study, as does their responsiveness to education and training. Studies of this kind could be building blocks for employee training programs and interventions. Of course, these approaches remain to be evaluated as alternatives or supplements to traditional forms of mediation and dispute resolution. Finally, the degree to which the practice of forgiveness yields improvements in employee well-being and organizational functioning deserves study.

Imagining a More Forgiving Workplace

Returning to the anecdote introduced at the beginning of this chapter allows us to imagine a more forgiving workplace. What if Ed's organization encouraged employees in disputes to approach disagreements and disputes with open-mindedness to the possibilities of forgiveness? Could Ed have approached the resource manager personally to share his perception that he and his unit were being treated in an unjust manner? Could his feelings of resentment have been expressed and his concerns explored through an informal conversation rather than an outraged e-mail? Would Ed's peers have gently suggested that he negotiate his differences directly rather than cultivate their support for his vengeful response? Might the resource manager have entertained the options of admitting a mistake and offering an apology? The process might have been facilitated if the organization encouraged employees to seek third-party assistance when work conflicts threatened personal and organizational productivity. Although the process may have been difficult at first, the parties may have come to an improved understanding of the rules that regulated their relationship. When would formal resource requests be needed, and when could the process be expedited? How could decisions be appealed, what kinds of reasons should be offered, and who should be consulted for help if the parties could not come to an agreement about resource priorities?

A more forgiving organization might leave employees such as Ed feeling more confident that organizational values would be upheld and that individual members would be approached with dignity and fairness. Rather than stressed or cynical, they might feel more hopeful and optimistic that real differences in values could be negotiated in a spirit of mutual respect. The options of seeking revenge or wallowing in feelings of alienation may seem less appealing in an organization that fosters forgiveness and justice as complementary and fundamentally important moral commitments.

Note

1. This and other anecdotes presented in this chapter are fictionalized to disguise identifying information. However, they are similar in tone and structure to accounts posted to the public Internet site http://jobmob.co.il/ or shared with us by students and research participants.

References

Afifi, W. A., Falato, W. L., & Weiner, J. L. (2001). Identity concerns following a severe relational transgression: The role of discovery method for the relational outcomes of infidelity. *Journal of Social & Personal Relationships, 18*, 291–308.

Aquino, K., Grover, S., Goldman, B., & Folger, R. (2003). When push doesn't come to shove: Interpersonal forgiveness in workplace relationships. *Journal of Management Inquiry, 12*, 209–216.

Arnett, R. C., Arneson, P., & Bell, L. M. (2006). Communication ethics: The dialogic turn. *Review of Communication, 6*, 63–93.

Bachman, G. F., & Guerrero, L. K. (2006). Forgiveness, apology, and communicative responses to hurtful events. *Communication Reports, 19*, 45–56.

Bottom, W. P., Gibson, K., Daniels, S. E., & Murningham, J. K. (2002). When talk is not cheap: Substantive penance and expressions of intent in rebuilding cooperation. *Organization Science, 13*, 497–513.

Bridge, K., & Baxter, L. A. (1992). Blended relationships: Friends as work associates. *Western Journal of Communication, 56*, 200–225.

Brown, R. P., & Phillips, A. (2005). Letting bygones be bygones: Further evidence for the validity of the tendency to forgive scale. *Personality & Individual Differences, 38*, 627–638.

Butler, D. S., & Mullis, F. (2001). Forgiveness: A conflict resolution strategy in the workplace. *Journal of Individual Psychology, 57*, 259–272.

Cameron, K. S., & Caza, A. (2002). Organizational and leadership virtues and the role of forgiveness. *Journal of Leadership and Organizational Studies, 9*, 33–48.

Cameron, K. S., Dutton, J. E., & Quinn, R. E. (Eds.). (2003). *Positive organizational scholarship*. San Francisco, CA: Berrett-Koehler.

Canning, A., McPhee, M., Netter, S., & Donaldson-James, S. (2010, February 15). Alabama shooting suspect's husband: "I'm no psychologist." Retrieved from ABC Good Morning America website: http://abcnews.go.com/GMA/alabama-university-shooting-suspect-amy-bishops-husband-idea/story?id=9839348

Eaton, J., & Struthers, C. W. (2006). The reduction of psychological aggression across varied interpersonal contexts through repentance and forgiveness. *Aggressive Behavior, 32*, 195–206.

Enright, R. D. (2001). *Forgiveness is a choice*. Washington, DC: American Psychological Association, APA Life Tools.

Enright, R. D., Gassin, E. A., & Wu, C. R. (1992). Forgiveness: A developmental view. *Journal of Moral Education, 21*, 99–114.

Fincham, F. D., & Beach, S. R. H. (2002). Forgiveness in marriage: Implications for psychological aggression and constructive communication. *Personal Relationships, 9*, 239–251.

Guerrero, L. K., & Bachman, G. F. (2010). Forgiveness and forgiving communication in dating relationships: An expectancy-investment explanation. *Journal of Social & Personal Relationships, 27*, 801–823.

Harvey, J. (2004). *Trauma and recovery strategies across the lifespan of long-term married couples*. Phoenix, AZ: Arizona State University West Press.

Hill, P. C., Exline, J. J., & Cohen, A. B. (2005). Social psychology of justice and forgiveness in civil and organizational settings. In E. L. Worthington, Jr. (Ed.), *Handbook of forgiveness* (pp. 477–490). New York, NY: Routledge.

Holmes, S. (2005, March 8).What Boeing needs to fly right. Retrieved from the Bloomberg Business Week Los Angeles website: http://www.businessweek.com/bwdaily/dnflash/mar2005/nf2005038_1218_db042.htm

Kelley, D. (1998). The communication of forgiveness. *Communication Studies, 49*, 255–271.

Kelley, D. L., & Waldron, V. R. (2005). An investigation of forgiveness-seeking communication and relational outcomes. *Communication Quarterly, 53*, 339–358.

Kloeber, D. N. (2008). *The language of conditional forgiveness*. Paper presented at the annual conference of the Western States Communication Association, Denver, CO.

Kloeber, D. N. (2011). *Voicing the knot of conditional forgiveness*. Paper presented at the annual conference of the National Communication Association, New Orleans, LA.

Lawler, K. A., Younger, J. W., Piferi, R. L., Jobe, R. L., Edmondson, K. A., & Jones, W. H. (2005). The unique effects of forgiveness on health: An exploration of pathways. *Journal of Behavioral*

Medicine, 28, 157–167.

Merolla, A. J. (2008). Communicating forgiveness in friendships and dating relationships. Communication Studies, 59, 114–131.

Merolla, A. J., & Zhang, S. (2011). In the wake of transgressions: Examining forgiveness communication in personal relationships. Personal Relationships, 18, 79–95.

Metts, S., Cupach, W. R., & Lippert, L. (2006). Forgiveness in the workplace. In J. M. H. Fritz & B. L. Omdahl (Eds.), Problematic relationships in the workplace (pp. 249–278). New York, NY: Peter Lang.

North, J. (1987). Wrongdoing and forgiveness. Philosophy, 62, 499–508.

Rusbult, C. E., Hannon, P. A., Stocker, S. L., & Finkel, E. J. (2005). Forgiveness and relational repair. In E. L. Worthington, Jr. (Ed.), Handbook of forgiveness (pp. 185–205). New York, NY: Routledge.

Stone, M. (2002). Forgiveness in the workplace. Industrial and Commercial Training, 34, 278–286.

Volf, M. (2001). Forgiveness, reconciliation, and justice: A Christian contribution to a more peaceful social environment. In R. Helmick & R. L. Petersen (Eds.), Forgiveness and reconciliation: Religion, public policy, and conflict transformation (pp. 27–49). Philadelphia, PA: Templeton Foundation Press.

Waldron, V. R. (2009). Emotional tyranny at work: Suppressing the moral emotions. In P. Lutgen-Sandvik & B. Davenport Sypher (Eds.), The destructive side of organizational communication: Processes, consequences and constructive ways of organizing (pp. 9–26). New York, NY: Routledge.

Waldron, V. R. (2011). Communicating emotions at work. San Francisco, CA: Polity.

Waldron, V. R., & Kassing, J. (2010). Managing risk in communication encounters: Strategies for the workplace. Thousand Oaks, CA: Sage.

Waldron, V. R., & Kelley, D. L. (2005). Forgiving communication as a response to relational transgressions. Journal of Social & Personal Relationships, 22, 723–742.

Waldron, V. R., & Kelley, D. L. (2008). Communicating forgiveness. Thousand Oaks, CA: Sage.

Waldron, V. R., & Krone, K. (1991). The experience and expression of emotion in the workplace: A study of a corrections organization. Management Communication Quarterly, 4, 287–309.

Witvliet, C. V. (2001). Forgiveness and health: Review and reflections on a matter of faith, feelings, and physiology. Journal of Psychology and Theology, 29, 212–224.

Worthington Jr., E. L. (1998). An empathy-humility-commitment model of forgiveness applied within family dyads. Journal of Family Therapy, 20, 59–76.

Worthington, E. L. (2001). Unforgiveness, forgiveness, and reconciliation and their implications for societal interventions. In R. G. Helmick & R. L. Petersen (Eds.), Forgiveness and reconciliation (pp. 171–192). Philadelphia, PA: Templeton Foundation Press.

Worthington, E. L. J. (Ed.). (2005). Handbook of forgiveness. New York, NY: Routledge.

· 15 ·

RESILIENCE, CIVILITY, POSITIVE COMMUNICATION, AND FORGIVENESS IN THE ACADEMY

BECKY L. OMDAHL

"Connie seems to challenge everything her nursing professor says. During small-group work, Connie text messages her friends and rarely pays attention. The professor is impatient and uses harsh language with Connie in front of other students" (Clark & Springer, 2007, p. 93). Over the last two decades, an increasing number of researchers are pointing out uncivil behaviors like the interaction between Connie and her instructor (e.g., Alexander-Snow, 2004; Amanda, 1999; Carbonne, 1999; Hirschy & Braxton, 2004). Some books and articles offer causal explanations for the rise. For example, Twale and DeLuca (2008) offered a detailed explanation of the factors in institutions of higher education contributing to the rise of the "Academic Bully Culture." Other scholars are focusing attention on empirical studies that document the nature, prevalence, and costs of behaviors ranging from incivility to hostile work relationships (e.g., Bjorklund & Rehling, 2010; Clark & Springer, 2007; Fox, 2008).

The reported rise in incivility among students, faculty, and employees in institutions of higher education arguably impacts relationships and the overall quality of work life (e.g., Boice, 1996; Dechter, 2007). As a backdrop for inviting the academy to build strong collegial relationships and resolve problematic ones, it seems only fitting to begin this concluding chapter with a section on the scope, severity, and costs of the problem faced by the academy.

The Scope and Severity of Incivility in Higher Education

The research on incivility in the academy presents a clear picture of the scope and severity of the behavior running across students, faculty, and staff.

Student Incivility

Incivility among students is broad ranging and frequent. Bjorklund and Rehling (2010) surveyed 3,616 students, asking them to rate the incivility (1= not uncivil to 5 = extremely uncivil) and frequency (1 = never to 5 = frequently) of 23 behaviors. These students identified the following behaviors as the most uncivil: "continuing to talk after being asked to stop" (mean = 4.50), "coming to class under the influence of alcohol or drugs" (4.45), and "allowing a cell phone to ring" (4.14). Midrange were actions like "text messaging" (3.30) and "packing up books before class is over" (3.29); "using a palm-pilot, iPod, or computer for non-class activities" (3.25); and "getting up during class, leaving and returning" (2.99). Least uncivil were actions like "nose blowing" (1.86) and two manipulation checks, "nodding or smiling in response to others' comments" (1.72) and "displaying attentive posture or facial expressions" (1.60; Bjorklund & Rehling, 2010, p. 16). In terms of frequency of occurrence, the top three nominees were "texting" (4.00), "packing up books before class is over" (3.76), and "yawning" (3.47). Bjorklund and Rehling (2010, p. 17) concluded from their comprehensive survey at a mainstream, public, Midwestern university that "students recognize and perceive that they experience incivility in the classroom." The authors noted that while the more egregious behaviors were rare (e.g., "coming to class under the influence of alcohol or drugs" [1.65]), midrange incivilities, such as "text messaging" or "packing up to leave class early," occurred relatively often (Bjorklund & Rehling, 2010, p. 16).

Similar in-class behaviors were identified in a study of 168 nursing students and 15 nursing faculty members (Clark, 2008; Clark & Springer, 2007). Faculty identified the following student uncivil behaviors (in order from highest to lowest frequency): disrupting others by talking in class, making negative remarks/disrespectful comments toward faculty, leaving early or arriving late, using cell phones, sleeping/not paying attention, bringing children to class, wearing immodest attire, and coming to class unprepared. In addition, faculty identified several out-of-class student behaviors they regarded to be uncivil (from most to least frequent): verbally discrediting faculty, turning in late assignments without proper notification, sending inappropriate emails to faculty, not keeping scheduled appointments, complaining about constructive feedback from faculty, stealing/driving too fast on campus, and making veiled threats toward faculty (Clark & Springer, 2007).

Some studies go beyond the identification of behaviors and their frequencies and offer explanations for why students are more likely to direct uncivil/bullying/harassing behavior at some faculty to a greater extent than other faculty. "Contrapower harassment," or harassment by a "person with lesser power within an institution [of]...an individual with greater power," is arguably more commonly directed at members with less social-cultural or socio-economic power (Lampman, Phelps, Bancroft, & Beneke, 2009, p. 331). Several studies have looked at sexual harassment of female faculty, and some offer alarming statistics. Grauerholz (1989) found that nearly half of the female faculty at Purdue University could identify one or more experiences that could be considered sexual harassment from a student. Similarly, more than half of the faculty in a study conducted by DeSouza and Fransler (2003) could identify sexually harassing student behavior directed at them by a student. Other studies found that male faculty received more sexual attention from students than did female faculty (Carroll & Ellis, 1989; McKinney, 1990, as cited by Lampman et al., 2009), although women are more likely to see the attention as harassing (McKinney, 1990).

In the most recent study looking at student behaviors ranging from incivility to harassing behaviors directed at faculty, Lampman et al. (2009, p. 337) surveyed 399 faculty at a large public university. They found that 96% of women and 99% of men indicated having experienced one or more acts of student incivility/bullying. The highest percentages of faculty indicated less egregious behaviors (e.g., 78.3% "reported that a student had slept during class," and 71.3% reported that a student had "engaged in non-class activity during class"). However, 67.5% of faculty reported "continual interruption" by a student and 65.7% reported a student "showing disdain" (Lampman et al., 2009, p. 338). Nearly half of all faculty (47%) reported receiving hostile or inappropriate comments on course evaluations, and nearly a quarter of faculty (29.1%) responded that they had a student scream or yell at them and (25.7%) violate their personal space. In comparison to their male counterparts, female faculty indicated being more upset by all types of incivility (Lampman et al., 2009).While the findings indicate that student incivility is prevalent and experienced by most faculty, the research did not support the hypothesis that women receive more student incivility than men. It did, however, identify faculty working toward tenure, female faculty teaching women's studies, and male faculty in the arts and sciences (presumably because of the high proportion of general education courses) as more likely targets of uncivil and harassing actions than counterparts. The findings that faculty working toward tenure and women teaching women's studies were the more common targets of uncivil to bullying behavior were regarded as evidence of contrapower harassment in the academy. Counter to the predictions of this study, but consistent with the earlier research (i.e., Carroll & Ellis, 1989; McKinney, 1990), more men than women reported sexual behaviors from students (men = 37%, women = 26%).

The student entitlement research is another look at the power dynamics underlying incivility. This approach argues that students, due to factors like customer-service orientations, grade inflation, and bolstered self-esteem and narcissism, engage in uncivil acts of communication sending the message, "I deserve better/more"(Lippman, Bulanda, & Wagenaar, 2009).The authors noted that "student entitlement is often reflected in students' priority of grades over learning and the appearance of achievement over achievement itself" (Pollio & Beck, 2000, cited by Lippman et al., 2009, p. 203). Communication from a position of entitlement can be very attacking:

> Do you really think it is absolutely necessary to require the completion of SOC151 to remain in this class? You're not teaching Finance 400 buddy. You teach Women's Studies. Do you seriously have nothing better to do than personally check the transcripts of everyone registered for your class? I dont [sic] mean to sound venomous, but ive [sic] just grown weary of the whole class registration process....(Lippman et al., 2009, p. 197)

Probably not at all shocking to readers is that my own mailbox contains very similar messages (e.g., one sent to the director of placement assessment):

> I am an accountant, and you are telling me that I need to take a math placement? Do you not know the meaning of the word "accountant"? You say you have a math Ph.D., but I can't imagine what kind it is if you don't understand that accountants do math.

Faculty and staff receiving messages reflecting an attitude of entitlement are often shocked, offended, and not eager to engage with the aggressive student.

Overall, research on student behavior to date reveals that students recognize a wide array of behaviors as uncivil, and they identify many of these behaviors as occurring with moderate to high regularity in their classrooms. Evidence of both contrapower and student entitlement exists as a driver of uncivil student behaviors.

Faculty and Staff Experiences with Incivility

The research on incivility among faculty and staff in the academy has focused less on the breadth of behaviors and more on severe forms of behavior like aggression, mobbing, and bullying. As clarified by Keashly (this volume) and Kinney (this volume), aggression and bullying are behaviors targeted with the intention of controlling or hurting the other, and with bullying, hurtful behaviors are repeated over time. Common examples of aggressive and bullying behavior include persistent criticism, insults, or ridicule, being treated as nonexistent or ignored, or being set up to fail with impossible or demeaning tasks (see Lewis, 2004, for a review).

In an extensive review of the prevalence and nature of aggression and bullying in academic settings, Keashly and Neuman (2010) reviewed ten empirical studies (i.e., Bjorkqvist, 1994; Court, 2008; Fox, 2008; Keashly & Neuman, 2009; Kinman & Jones, 2004; Lewis, 1999; McKay, Arnold, Fratzl, & Thomas, 2008; Raskauskas, 2006; Simpson & Cohen, 2004; Times Higher Education Supplement, 2005). Overall, they reported that the rates of bullying seem high in the academic samples compared to bullying levels for the general population: Scandinavia general population, 2%–5%, Scandinavian academics, 20.5%; UK general population, 10%–20%, UK academics, 25%–42%; U.S. general population, 10%–14%, U.S. academics, 32%–52% (Keashly & Jagatic, 2011, cited in Keashly & Neumann, 2010; Rayner & Cooper, 2006).

These high percentages speak to the many drivers of aggression and bullying in the academy. In a major treatise on faculty incivility, Twale and DeLuca (2008, p. 30) identified "motivating structures and processes" at universities (e.g., governance structures, campus politics), which combined with "precipitating circumstances" (e.g., scarce resources, consumer orientation) to drive "enabling structures and processes" (e.g., isolation, peer review, faculty/administration tension, ambiguity). Left unchecked, these enabling structures and processes increase the likelihood of workplace incivility, harassment, camouflaged aggression, and bullying. The model (originally proposed by Salin, 2003), in conjunction with current trends in higher education, offers an explanation of why the academy is particularly prone to becoming a "bully culture."

Many tensions play out at institutions of higher learning in the context of "motivating structures and processes" (Twale and DeLuca, 2008, p. 30). For example, Twale and DeLuca (2008) described the academy as one in which elitism is pitted against democratization (with merit thrown in to spice up the debate). In addition, tensions between the liberal arts and vocationalism have grown over the years. Both the liberal arts and professional program faculty present eloquent arguments for their curriculums, and as Twale and DeLuca (2008) reminded us, we now live in a time when the student as consumer chooses between them. Gouldner (1957, 1958, as cited by Twale and DeLuca, 2008) pointed out another major tension: competition for loyalty between one's discipline and one's institution. Given that faculty own their own means of production, and team effort is not required, the loyalty bias is often swung toward the discipline. As Twale and DeLuca (2008) described it, this poses extreme challenges to collegiality. Yet another struggle is between academic freedom and paternalism. While the American Association of University Professors (AAUP) has defended "autonomy, academic freedom, promotion and tenure, basic treatment by administrators and inclusion in campus decision making," the reality is that there are many pressures for individuals as well as collectives of faculty to acquiesce to normative standards. The pressures may be more keenly felt by members of non-dominant ideologies and groups (Twale & DeLuca, 2008, p. 44).

The list of "precipitating circumstances" (stressors) proposed in the conceptual framework reads like a list of the top challenges facing academe today: (1) scarce resources (nearly all public institutions have watched the proportion of state funding steadily decrease from the early to mid-1970s until today; private and public institutions have watched economic downturns impact gifts, grants, and foundation funding), (2) consumer orientation (increasingly, competition and consultants are encouraging customer service orientations), (3) market orientation (decisions throughout universities are increasingly driven by student demand for classes, certificates, and programs), (4) corporate cultural influence (advisory boards and industry connections increasingly guide programmatic and curricular decisions), (5) quest for excellence (formerly a qualifier and now a desired end state), (6) mission creep (motivated by quests to claim market shares of students, meet the demands of employers, and attain excellence), (7) changes to the face of the profession (e.g., diversity in the academy has been steadily increasing; however, tokenism and marginalization are challenging the environment for many), and (8) shift to online education (advocated to increase flexibility for students, attract new audiences, and reduce the need for bricks and mortar). The bottom line is that the precipitating circumstances increasing stress are at all-time historical highs, and the model argues that these "precipitating circumstances," along with the "motivating structures and processes," contribute to "enabling structures" that allow for bad behavior in the academy (Twale & DeLuca, 2008, p. 30).

The enabling structures are perhaps most within the control of institutions. They include isolation, peer review, ambiguity, lack of policy on incivility, strong academic culture, tension between administration and faculty, high stress, and competition (Twale & DeLuca, 2008). However, they are difficult to change given the structures and circumstances already identified. Isolation makes people more vulnerable to attack, but in the academy, faculty members are often more aligned with their discipline than with their colleagues, and the means of production can be achieved alone. Peer review sets up a system where influence and votes matter, but it is a celebrated structure within the academy. Ambiguity is ubiquitous given the autonomy associated with faculty positions (e.g., Should I serve on this committee? How much scholarship is required for promotion?). Strong academic culture, what is described in the book as built on a male-preferred form of aggressive competition, is also entrenched. Finally, faculty-administrative tensions are often increased as more requirements and protections are instituted to address competition and avoid legal risk. Market pressures reducing the number of tenure-track positions and the resulting pressures on the tenure-track faculty to mentor and coordinate increasing number of adjuncts is only one of the increasing stressors. Competition for recognition and limited grant dollars is likely to increase as university rewards stagnate and faculty look outside for factors that make their jobs valuable. According to the predictions of Salin (2003, as presented by Twale & DeLuca, 2008), if the conditions reviewed in the preceding paragraph are in fact at high levels, academic institutions are enabling incivility, aggression, bullying, and mobbing to flourish.

As numerous studies reveal, the costs of aggression and bullying are not borne equally. "Faculty recognize that tenure offers relatively secure employment. Some may presume they can do anything they please. Left unchecked, however, any aggressive behavior not reprimanded may escalate into increasingly more serious behaviors" (Twale & DeLuca, 2008, p. 149). Consistent with this inference that those with tenure have greater license for doing "anything they please," there is evidence that those with power are the more likely aggressors. Based on research to date, Keashly and Neuman (2010) proposed that aggression is controlled, in part, by the effect/danger ratio. Specifically, more powerful people are likely to aggress against less powerful people, and as the power becomes more equal or the aggression is directed at a more powerful person, the forms used will be increasingly indirect (Keashly & Neuman, 2010, p. 57).

The Costs of Incivility in the Academy

The growing evidence from empirical research indicates that thousands of students, staff, faculty, and administrators are feeling disrespected and even threatened in the academy. The costs of this behavior go far deeper than the momentary inconvenience, frustration, or hurt feelings of an isolated episode. These behaviors erode the quality of workplace relationships, eating into trust, goodwill, collegiality, and organizational commitment (Keashly & Neuman, 2010; Lester, 2010). Personal stories offer glimpses of how trust and relationships are impaired by problematic behaviors:

> I worked very hard in school. I was afraid for my grade and felt totally out of control. I realized that no matter how hard we worked in our clinical group, that it was the instructor's way or no way. . . . If we embarrassed her, she would squash us, she would fail us. . . . We felt helpless. I was angry with her. I thought, "How dare she use her power to stifle and control us like that?" (Clark, 2008, p. 287)

> This guy who headed up the department was sending these wild letters to a VP he did not like. Just vile letters and there was no response. There was no response from the administrative level. One [a letter] just came to us saying that "Your buddy is gone, you better watch your back." (Lester, 2010, p. 457).

In their first volume, *Problematic Relationships in the Workplace*, Fritz and Omdahl (2006) presented the high costs associated with problematic work relationships: stress, burnout, impaired mental health (Omdahl & Fritz, 2006), reduced job satisfaction, diminished organizational commitment, workplace cynicism (Fritz & Omdahl, 2006), emotional demands (Kramer & Tan, 2006), and distress and jeopardized well-being (Kinney, 2006). This volume identifies yet a new set of behaviors incurring significant costs to workplace relationships. Hostile work relationships and bullying damage well-being, mental health, and organizational commitment (Keashly, this volume; Kinney, this volume). Incivility diminishes both interpersonal trust and organizational trust (Davenport Sypher & Gill, this volume). Bureaucratic behavior instead of true leadership compounds cynicism and decreases organizational commitment and engagement (Arnett, this volume). Isolation and distance create emotional and well-being costs as well as less effective employees (Fay, this volume; Sias, this volume).

With an eye toward restoring valued workplaces and ending the deleterious effects arising from problematic work relationships, the last section of this chapter focuses on contributions individuals and organizations can make to create constructive communities. For the individual contributions, we focus on resilience, civility, positive communication, and forgiveness. The organizational contributions emphasize making the mission matter, cultivating mutual respect and civility, valuing diversity, engaging everyone, and developing skilled leaders.

Individual Contributions to Constructive Work Relationships

As readers of this chapter, what can we personally do to foster healthy work relationships?

Practice resilience. Across our working lives, stressful situations will inevitably arise. To the extent that we build the processes of resilience in the good times, we will be prepared for adversity in the worst times. Hammoud and Buzzanell (this volume) offer an excellent case study bringing to life five processes sustaining resilience. First, resilience requires crafting normalcy, which is defined as producing a system of meaning that sustains maintenance of the mundane. We must strive to give meaning to the actions we regularly carry out in everyday situations. Second, resilience is built up through identity anchors. We should affirm the identities constructed in social relationship that reflect who we are as unique beings and who we are in collectives. Third, resilience calls for using and maintaining communication networks. We are encouraged to build the social capital that we will need during stressful times by nurturing effective communication that serves a variety of functions (social support, task effectiveness). Fourth, resilience invites alternative logics. As we reframe situations and explore contradictory ways of thinking and getting tasks accomplished, we develop what is talked about in the coping literature as valuing change and flexibility. Finally, resilience demands "legitimizing negative feelings while foregrounding productive action" (Hammoud & Buzzanell, this volume). Seligman, a founding researcher of "learned helplessness" (Abramson, Seligman, & Teasdale, 1978), now studies "learned optimism" (Seligman, Steen, Park, & Peterson, 2005). Dweck (2007), a researcher of the impact of ability versus strategy attributions on children, now advocates fostering a mastery orientation in everyone. The core concept of both approaches is that mental health is sustained by focusing on specific strategies rather than global abilities or emotions. They join with Hammoud and Buzzanell (this volume) in admonishing us to validate feelings but stay focused on cycles of planning, doing, reviewing, and adopting improved strategies as needed.

Treat everyone with respect and civility. In the book titled *Civility*, Stephen Carter (1998) tells the story of the interdependence of passengers sharing a train car on a cross-country trip. To the extent they choose courtesy and kindness as opposed to rudeness and selfishness, the trip is made more enjoyable for all. The realization is this: We are all passengers on a much bigger train for a very long ride.

If I were to offer the greatest simple truths I have learned aboard the train, they would be these: Everyone wants to feel valued, and everyone is more sensitive than anyone knows. These realizations lead to a predicament: We want to be valued and respected by everyone else, but, as humans, we are sufficiently sensitive that when we experience hurt or unfairness, we often feel the right to respond badly. In committing to respect and civility, we choose a different path than responding badly; we choose to care consistently for both the self and the other, adopting the I-Thou relationship characterized by deep positive regard and commitment to authentic dialogue (Arnett, 2006; Buber, 1937/2004). In our weak moments, it is easier to be civil if we have honed perspective taking, empathy, social skill, and genuine positive regard for those we encounter on a daily basis. Arnett (2006) encouraged us to commit to the unseen neighbor—in Levinas's words, remembering "I am my brother's keeper," (p. 98)—to guide our actions toward respect and tolerance.

While we must become tolerant of the individual differences, foibles, and glitches that are part of being human, we must not be tolerant of disrespect in all its forms. The question is not whether to address the repeated acts of incivility enacted by individuals and groups, but how. Civility calls us to a greater investment. We may need to have honest conversations, contact others more appropriately situated to address particular instances, be willing to work with mediators, and/or acknowledge our failures and wrongdoing.

Communicate in ways that build secure, supportive relationships. Hess and Sneed (this volume) provide a wealth of valuable information on how to engage in communication that builds secure, supportive relationships. First, they encourage us to take a close look at why a workplace relationship has become problematic. Are we experiencing goal incompatibilities or do we simply dislike the other person? The answers may offer insight into the true nature of the problem and how it may be resolved. The research findings of Hess and Sneed would encourage us, first, to keep doing our jobs well, regardless of the situation or cause of the challenges. Second, they found that talking with trusted people capable of facilitating better navigation of the difficulties was a constructive action. Third, the research findings indicate that maintaining civility and a positive demeanor "as an active and intentional process" is crucial. Fourth, the research findings suggest that in moving forward with a conversation, it is important to affirm the relationship with the other, listen carefully, adapt to the other, and find "an appropriate balance [between masking and confronting problems]—neither make the problem so invisible the partner is oblivious to it, nor . . . unnecessarily escalate problems" (Hess & Sneed, this volume). Looking across the successful and unsuccessful relationship-repair attempts, competence in interpersonal communication clearly resulted in greater success. Therefore, we should all hone the social and emotional skills necessary to carry out sensitive conversations with high regard for the other while effectively articulating concerns important to self (Hess & Sneed, this volume).

Forgive feet of clay. "This image's head was of fine gold, his breast and his arms of silver, his belly and his thighs of brass, his legs of iron, his feet part of iron and part of clay" (Daniel 2:32–33). This account of King Nebuchadnezzar's dream highlights the plight of even the most magnificent of imagined humans: feet of clay. Humans are destined to blunder, bumble, fail, act in self-centered ways, attempt revenge, and behave with aggression.

Most days, we find paths through the array of human oversights and mistakes. Ultimately, we forget about them, accepting them as a part of the intricate fiber of human interactions. However, "working life is sometimes punctuated by relational incidents that yield a sense of moral outrage, hostility or bitterness, grudges, and even acts of revenge" (Waldron & Kloeber, this volume). What do we do with the situations smacking of deep disrespect?

Forgiveness may be the most rewarding path, but it is also a process calling for moral and social deliberations, personal growth, and time and energy. The process of "extending undeserved mercy to the perceived transgressor" invites deep thought over right and wrong, mercy and justice, responsibility and irresponsibility in the context of one's own mind, family, social network, and broader culture (Waldron & Kloeber, this volume).

Waldron and Kloeber (this volume) approach forgiveness as a process. It typically involves acknowledging the harm and experiencing all the emotion that acknowledgment elicits, being encouraged to move forward or discouraged from moving forward in the process by organizational and cultural messages, understanding that the mercy to be extended will never be "earned," sorting out forgiveness ("letting go," the transformation) and reconciliation (actions toward restoring the relationship), and working through the moral issues (Waldron & Kloeber, this volume).

In situations in which we want to move toward forgiveness, we can invite the process. We can acknowledge the harm, working through it alone or with trusted others. We can respectfully share it with the person who created the pain or sense of unfairness. While conversing with our transgressor, we can listen carefully, accepting that the other is also working through a complex chain of emotions and sense-making. We can clearly state what we need from the other (e.g., a direct acknowledgment of what the person did, an apology), recognizing that whether he or she provides it or not, it is that person's decision, not ours. Perhaps most importantly, we can ponder human fallibility—our own and that of others—gaining deeper insights that, given we all fall short, we all need undeserved mercy over and over as we walk the earth with our feet of clay.

As was noted in the story about the South African tribunals granting amnesty after years of apartheid (Tippett, 2012, cited in Omdahl, Chapter 2, this volume), if we seek to be forgiven, there are steps that we can take. Openly acknowledging the harm we caused and apologizing for it, while maintaining focus on the pain/sense of injustice experienced by the other, is an important first step. It is essential to listen to any description of the other person's experience that is offered. Finally, it is important to respect that granting or not granting forgiveness is totally the offended party's decision. It is a gift that cannot be demanded or expected. If we make such demands or hold such expectations, we have not yet fully realized the pain or feelings of injustice our behavior has caused.

Organizational Contributions to Constructive Work Relationships

While we can individually elect to engage in many thoughts and practices that increase our resilience, civility, positive communication, and ability to forgive and be forgiven, the discussions in all of these chapters have emphasized the importance of the organization in fostering their enactment. If we really want civil, respectful, supportive workplaces, we must engage entire organizations. What can organizations do to contribute?

Make the mission matter. Institutions exist to accomplish missions (Arnett, 2006), and it serves both the organization and individual well-being to have a clear mission orienting all workers to important shared tasks and responsibilities. Calling attention to the highest purposes of the organization clarifies the need for professional civility: The ability to work effectively with one another is the most direct path to achieving the mission.

Cultivate a culture of mutual respect and civility. Just as individuals must commit to behaving in respectful and civil ways, we must call organizations to make respectful and civil behavior an essential feature of the organizational culture. The founders of Mayo Clinic established five ideals: teamwork, collegiality, professionalism, mutual respect, and a commitment to progress for the organization and for individuals (Mayo Clinic, 2012).These ideals, which are still held high, reflect a commitment to a culture of mutual respect and civility.

The importance of organizational support for respect and civility cannot be overestimated. Hutchinson (1997) analyzed the degree to which employees' perceptions of organizational support served as a link between problematic actions of the organization (e.g., creating roles with ambiguity and conflict, centralizing decision making, allowing employees to be supervised by people who are not considerate, and failing to foster participation in decision making) and organizational commitment. Hutchinson found that perceptions of organizational support mediated between organizational action and organizational commitment. Specifically, when the overall organizational culture is supportive and when that support is understood, the problems that will inevitably emerge in human endeavors will not destroy organizational commitment.

In contrast to the benefits of organizational support are the costs of not ensuring respect and civility. Oore, LeBlanc, Day, Leiter, Spence Lashinger, Price, and Latimer(2010) examined two forms of stress, high work overload and low levels of control, in seventeen units of hospital workers ($n = 478$). These stressors were associated with lower mental health and more negative physical symptoms. However, incivility significantly exacerbated the deleterious effects while respect moderated the harmful effects of incivility.

In this volume, Davenport Sypher and Gill present research testing important predictions about the relationship between civility and different forms of trust. While 84.4% of respondents indicated trusting relationships with their immediate supervisors, workplace incivility from supervisors negatively correlated with interpersonal trust. This incivility impacted both affect-based and cognitive-based trust, but affect-based trust was impacted to a greater degree by increasing incivility. Over 40% (42.5%) of employees reported incivility in the organization, and workplace incivility was strongly negatively associated with organizational trust (Davenport Sypher & Gill, this volume). The conclusion is clear: We need supervisors and organizational leaders who model and cultivate respect and civility and take an active and systematic role in curbing incivility.

Value diversity. This volume has presented a wealth of evidence on the importance of honoring and valuing diversity. In her exploration of factors influencing exclusion, Sias (this volume) identifies dissimilarities (i.e., ethnic and racial minorities, geographic location, sexual orientation, disability) as leading causes for employees to be excluded from others in the work environment. The personal costs of exclusion include loss of self-esteem, loneliness, alienation, stress, and anxiety (Sias, this volume). The organizational costs are also significant: tardiness, absenteeism, impaired performance, and increased aggression and sabotage in the work unit.

Millhous (this volume) points to the strength heterogeneity brings to larger social groups, but she also points out that the failure to embrace and work with differences occurs in many forms and at great costs. She notes common misattributions around cultural differences, making individuals "the problem" and increasing the likelihood that stereotypes and prejudicial attitudes will undermine work relationships. As Sillars (1980, 1981) has pointed out, people are less likely to work at resolving conflicts when they attribute problems to the other rather than the situation. The process of acculturation may also pose challenges, leaving employees feeling apprehensive and leaving organizations uncertain about how to respond. Yet another challenge due to cultural differences is incompatible role expectations, in which two people are asked to play culturally defined roles while disagreeing on the definitions. However, just as these challenges are rooted in the discursive practice of communication, they can be addressed through discursive communication practices. Millhous (this volume) invites organizations to consider creating third cultures (which bridge the backgrounds of people involved) and seeing cultural differences *not* as problems but as "normal" and "functional" opportunities for creativity and learning.

As a third call for a genuine commitment to honoring diversity, Collins, Gill, and Mease (this volume) explicate the prevalence and costs of "tokenism" in workplaces. They point to studies documenting the continued marginalization of women in leadership positions and the use of individual or small numbers of women to present an image of accepting the under-represented group. The costs of tokenism are great for those who become "tokens." Specifically, their values and behaviors remain non-normative, and they are likely to experience heightened scrutiny, greater judgment, more negative stereotyping, and greater occupational segregation than their peers (Collin, Gill, & Mease, this volume).

Engage everyone. Reading the three chapters addressed in the preceding paragraphs leads to a realization of the loss of human potential incurred by organizations that fail to embrace diversity. When organizations bring everyone to the table and strive for the true engagement of all, both individuals and organizations benefit from the bounty of talent and energy.

Both Sias (this volume) and Fay (this volume) include an overview of research on the impact of working remotely from colleagues. Being out of sight and out of mind creates significant costs for employees in the form of loneliness, lack of formal and informal networks, greater difficulty in learning and staying current with organizational culture, lack of consistent supervision cues, and potentially impaired career advancement opportunities. The number of workers telecommuting, working at physical locations separated from peers, and/or spanning work sites is growing, and for the sake of those already operating at a distance as well as those soon to be, we must find ways to fully integrate and engage these employees.

Valuing diversity and engaging everyone requires a special commitment on the part of organizational leaders to genuine dialogue and authentic listening. As documented by Sias (this volume), Millhous (this volume), and Collins, Gill, and Mease (this volume), experiences of marginalization, exclusion, isolation, and tokenism are not equally distributed across all workers in most organizations. The fact that those afforded less cultural power and socio-economic status are more likely to be pushed out of the circles of engagement means that leaders must find ways to ensure access and participation for all.

Research on how to engage workers abounds. Many studies draw on Oldham's five-factor theory of work engagement calling for feedback, skill variety, task significance, task identity, and autonomy (Hackman & Oldham, 1980). Newer research (Chen & Chiu, 2009) on engagement offers a more complicated picture: Task significance, task identity, and autonomy continue to predict engagement. However, feedback emerged as only minimally important, and variety was negatively associated with engagement. In subsequent research, Chen, Zhang, and Vogel (2011) determined that while task conflict contributes to experienced safety and availability and engagement, relationship conflict negatively impacts experienced safety, availability, and meaning, as well as engagement.

There is broad agreement that engagement is fostered when everyone in organizations sees the meaning in their work, recognizes the ways in which tasks they perform contribute to the overall mission, and feels trusted to perform high quality work while working autonomously. We must succeed at inviting these conditions for engagement within our workplaces.

Develop skilled leaders. Arnett (this volume) makes it very clear that skilled leaders are not advancement-seeking bureaucrats. Arendt's warning calls us to ponder the rise of the bureaucrat as the "problematic other" of the modern age (1963/2006, as cited in Arnett, this volume). Bureaucrats prize career advancement over genuine concern for tasks; they reflect modernity's belief that individuals can rise above and separate themselves from community, and through these values, they fail to nurture and sustain the soil of the community that allows others to grow and thrive (Arnett, this volume).

Other researchers have also pointed out leadership styles that are problematic. Skogstad, Einarsen, Toscheim, Aasland, and Hetland (2007) emphasized the failure of laissez faire leaders to address incivility, and Kelloway, Sivanathan, Francis, and Barling (2005) asserted that many leaders invite stress by failing to check disrespectful behavior. Overall, we need engaged leaders who are committed to building the workplace community.

Finally, organizations must support the restoration of healthy work relationships. Much has been said in this volume about how to do that, and it requires the kind of leaders advocated by Arnett (this volume), persons who genuinely care about community and communicate on all levels (mission, vision, values, speeches, newsletters, training, resources such as skilled consultants, facilitators, and mediators; Fisher & Keashly, 1991; Grieg, 2005; Kolb, 1986; Sheppard, 1984) that we are an institution committed to healthy working relationships.

As evidenced by research throughout this volume, without this backdrop, broken relationships break further, individuals struggle with myriad costs that steal their productive energy, and absenteeism and turnover increase. However, with the assurance that the organization is committed to a healthy and vibrant community, transgressions can be shared and understood, apologies can be extended and received, and those too broken to heal themselves but still hopeful can reach to trustworthy, powerful others for assistance or protection.

Summary

This chapter began with a review of the research and reasons for incivility at all levels of the academy. The conclusion was that the academy faces levels of incivility and bullying unmatched in broader global societies. Research consistently reveals a relation between forms of incivility and problematic workplace relationships and between problematic workplace relationships and deleterious outcomes. In this final section, we have explored steps that both individuals and organizations can take to create vibrant, engaged communities characterized by meaningful work and strong relationships.

Note

1. For those who want to learn more about the topics covered in this book, there is a growing list of books based on careful scholarship addressing problematic behaviors and relationships in the workplace (e.g., Fritz & Omdahl, 2006; Kinney &Pörhölä, 2009; Namie & Namie, 2000; Pörhölä & Kinney, 2010; Lutgen-Sandvik & Davenport Sypher, 2009; Sias, 2009; Waldron, 2011, 2012). In addition, there are many other books not based on scholarly research (Branch, 2011; Cava, 2004; Gill, 1999; Lilley, 2002; Lubit, 2003; Shepard, 2005; Solomon, 2002; Sutton, 2007; Warner & Klemp, 2011).

References

Abramson, L. Y., Seligman, M. E. P., & Teasdale, J. D. (1978). Learned helplessness in humans: Critique and reformulation. *Journal of Abnormal Psychology, 87,* 49–74.

Alexander-Snow, M. (2004). Dynamics of gender, ethnicity, and race in understanding classroom incivility. *New Directions for Teaching and Learning, 99,* 21–31.

Amanda, G. (1999). *Coping with misconduct in the college classroom: A practical model.* Asheville, NC: College Administration.

Arendt, H. (2006). *Eichmann in Jerusalem: A report on the banality of evil.* New York, NY: Penguin Books. (Original work published 1963)

Arnett, R. C. (2006). Professional civility: Reclaiming organizational limits. In J. M. H. Fritz & B. L. Omdahl (Eds.), *Problematic relationships in the workplace* (pp. 233–248). New York, NY: Peter Lang.

Bjorklund, W. L., & Rehling, D. L. (2010). Student perceptions of classroom incivility. *College Teaching, 58,* 15–18.

Bjorkvist, K. (1994). Sex differences in physical, verbal, and indirect aggression. A review of recent research. *Sex Roles, 30,* 177–188.

Boice, B. (1996). Classroom incivilities. *Research in Higher Education, 37,* 453–485.

Branch, T. (2011). *The drama-free work week: How to manage difficult people for workplace and career success.* Bloomington, IN: Trafford Publishing.

Buber, M. (1937/2004). *I and thou.* New York, NY: Scribner.

Carbonne, E. (1999). Students behaving badly in large classes. *New Directions for Teaching and Learning, 77,* 35–43.

Carroll, L., & Ellis, K. (1989). Faculty attitudes toward sexual harassment: Survey results, survey process. *Initiatives, 52,* 35–41.

Carter, S. L. (1998). *Civility: Manners, morals, and the etiquette of democracy.* New York, NY: HarperCollins.

Cava, R. (2004). *Dealing with difficult people: How to deal with nasty customers, demanding bosses, and annoying coworkers.* Richmond Hill, Ontario, Canada: Firefly Books.

Chen, C. C., & Chiu, S. (2009). The mediating role of job involvement in the relationship between job characteristics and organizational citizenship behavior. *Journal of Social Psychology, 149,* 474–494.

Chen, C. C., Zhang, Z., & Vogel, D. (2011). Exploring the underlying processes between conflict and knowledge sharing: A work engagement perspective. *Journal of Applied Social Psychology, 41,* 1005–1033.

Clark, C. M. (2008). Student voices on faculty incivility in nursing education: A conceptual model. *Nursing Education Perspectives, 29,* 284–289.

Clark, C. M., & Springer, P. J. (2007). Thoughts on incivility: Student and faculty perceptions of uncivil behavior in Nursing Education. *Nursing Education Perspectives, 28,* 93–97.

Court, S. (2008, November). *The extent of bullying and harassment in post-16 education.* Paper presented at the Tackling Bullying Conference, University and College Union (UCU), London, England.

Dechter, G. (2007, January 8). Not so long ago most college instructors were treated with dignity and respect. *The Baltimore Sun,* p. 1F.

DeSouza, E., & Fransler, G. A. (2003). Contrapower sexual harassment: A survey of students and faculty members. *Sex Roles, 48*, 529–542.

Dweck, C. (2007). *Mindset: The new psychology of success.* New York, NY: Ballatine.

Fisher, R. J., & Keashly, L. (1991). The potential complementarity of mediation and consultation within a contingency model of third party intervention. *Journal of Peace Research, 28*, 29–42.

Fox, S. (2008). Academic bullies. *Chronicle of Higher Education, 55*, B10.

Fritz, J. M. H., & Omdahl, B. L. (2006). Reduced job satisfaction, diminished commitment, and workplace cynicism as outcomes of negative work relationships. In J. M. H. Fritz &B. L. Omdahl (Eds.), *Problematic relationships in the workplace* (pp. 131–152). New York, NY: Peter Lang.

Gill, L. (1999). *How to work with just about anyone: A 3 step solution for getting difficult people to change.* New York, NY: Simon & Schuster.

Gouldner, A. (1957). Cosmopolitans and locals: Toward an analysis of latent social roles—I. *Administrative Science Quarterly, 2*, 281–305.

Gouldner, A. (1958). Cosmopolitans and locals: Toward an analysis of latent social roles—II. *Administrative Science Quarterly, 2*, 444–480.

Grauerholz, E. (1989). Sexual harassment of women professors by students: Exploring the dynamics of power, authority, and gender in a university setting. *Sex Roles, 21*, 789–801.

Greig, J. M. (2005). Stepping into the fray: When do mediators mediate? *American Journal of Political Science, 49*, 249–266.

Hackman, J. R., & Oldham, G. R. (1980).*Work redesign.* Reading, MA: Addison-Wesley.

Hirschy, A. S., & Braxton, J. M. (2004). Effects of student classroom incivilities on students. *New Directions for Teaching and Learning, 99*, 67–76.

Hutchinson, S. (1997). A path model of perceived organizational support. *Journal of Social Behavior and Personality, 12*, 159–174.

Keashly, L., & Jagatic, K. (2011). North American perspectives on hostile behaviors and bullying at work. In S. Einarsen, J. Hoel, D. Zapf, & C. L. Cooper (Eds.), *Workplace bullying: Developments in theory, research, and practice* (2nd ed., pp. 41–74). Boca Raton, FL: CRC Press/Taylor & Francis.

Keashly, L., & Neuman, J. H. (2009). Building a constructive communication climate: The Workplace Stress and Aggression Project.In P. Lutgen-Sandvik & B. Davenport Sypher (Eds.), *Destructive organizational communication: Processes, consequences, and constructive ways of organizing* (pp. 339–362). NewYork: Routledge.

Keashly, L., & Neuman, J. H. (2010). Faculty experiences with bullying in higher education: Causes, consequences, and management. *Administrative Theory & Praxis, 32*, 48–70.

Kelloway, E. K., Sivanathan, N., Francis, L., & Barling, J. (2005). Poor leadership. In J. Barling, E.K. Kelloway, & M. R. Frone (Eds.), *Handbook of work stress* (pp. 89–112). Thousand Oaks, CA: Sage.

Kinman, G., & Jones, F. (2004, November).*Working to the limit: Stress and work-life balance in academic and academic related employees in the UK.* Publication of the AUT Higher Education Union. Retrieved from www.ucu.org.uk/media/pdf/4/7/workingtothelimit.pdf

Kinney, T. A. (2006). Should I stay or should I go now? The role of negative communication and relational maintenance in distress and well-being. In J. M. H. Fritz & B. L. Omdahl (Eds.), *Problematic relationships in the workplace* (pp. 179–204).New York, NY: Peter Lang.

Kinney, T. A., & Pörhölä, M. (2009). *Anti and pro-social communication: Theories, methods, and applications*. New York, NY: Peter Lang.

Kolb, D. M. (1986). Who are organizational third parties and what do they do? In R. J. Lewicki, B. H. Sheppard, & M. H. Bazerman (Eds.), *Research on negotiations in organizations, volume 1* (pp. 207–278). Greenwich, CT: JAI.

Kramer, M. W., & Tan, C. L. (2006). Emotion management in dealing with difficult people. In J. M. H. Fritz & B. L. Omdahl (Eds.), *Problematic relationships in the workplace* (pp. 153–178). New York, NY: Peter Lang.

Lampman, C., Phelps, A., Bancroft, S., & Beneke, M. (2009). Countrapower harassment in academia: A survey of faculty experience with student incivility, bullying, and sexual attention. *Sex Roles, 60*, 331–346.

Lester, J. (2010). Not your child's playground: Workplace bullying among community college faculty. *Community College Journal of Research and Practice, 33*, 446–464.

Levinas, E. (1998). *Ethics and infinity: Conversations with Philippe Nemo* (R. Cohen, Trans.). Pittsburgh, PA: Duquesne University Press.

Lewis, D. (1999). Workplace bullying: Interim findings of a study in further and higher education in Wales. *International Journal of Manpower, 20*, 106–118.

Lewis, X. (2004). Will the real bully please stand up. *Occupational Health, 56*, 22–26.

Lilley, R. (2002). *Dealing with difficult people*. Philadelphia, PA: Kogan Page.

Lippman, S., Bulanda, R. E., & Wagenaar, T. C. (2009). Student entitlement: Issues and strategies for confronting entitlement in the classroom and beyond. *College Teaching, 57*, 197–204.

Lubit, G. (2003). *Coping with toxic managers, subordinates, and other difficult people: Using emotional intelligence to survive and prosper*. Englewood Cliffs, NJ: Prentice Hall.

Lutgen-Sandvik, P., & Davenport Sypher, B. (Eds.). (2009). *Destructive organizational communication: Processes, consequences, and constructive ways of organizing*. New York, NY: Routledge.

Mayo Clinic. (2012). The Mayo culture. Retrieved from http://www.mayoclinic.org/physician-jobs/culture.html

McKay, R., Arnold, D. H., Fratzl, J., & Thomas, R. (2008). Workplace bullying in academia: A Canadian study. *Employee Responsibilities and Rights Journal, 20*, 77–100.

McKinney, D. (1990). Sexual harassment of university faculty by colleagues and students. *Sex Roles, 23*, 421–438.

Namie, G., & Namie, R. (2000). *The bully at work: What you can do to stop the hurt and reclaim your dignity on the job*. Naperville, IL: Sourcebooks.

Omdahl, B. L., & Fritz, J. M. H. (2006). Stress, burnout, and impaired mental health: Consequences of problematic work relationships. In J. M. H. Fritz & B. L. Omdahl (Eds.), *Problematic relationships in the workplace* (pp. 109–130). New York, NY: Peter Lang.

Oore, D. G., LeBlanc, D., Day, A., Leiter, M., Spence Lashinger, H. K., Price, S. L., & Latimer, M. (2010). When respect deteriorates: Incivility as a moderator of the stressor-strain relationship among hospital workers. *Journal of Nursing Management, 18*, 878–888.

Pollio, H. R., & Beck, H. P. (2000). When the tail wags the dog: Perceptions of learning and grade orientation in, and by, contemporary college students and faculty. *Journal of Higher Education, 71*, 84–102.

Pörhölä, M., & Kinney, T. A. (2010). *Bullying: Contexts, consequences, and control*. Barcelona, Spain: Editorial Aresta.

Raskauskas, J. (2006, April). *Bullying in academia: An examination of workplace bullying in New Zealand universities*. Paper presented at the annual meeting of the American Education Research Association, San Francisco, CA.

Rayner, C., & Cooper, C. (2006). Workplace bullying. In E. K. Kelloway, J. Barling, & J. Hurrell (Eds.), *Handbook of workplace violence* (pp. 121–146). Thousand Oaks, CA: Sage.

Salin, D. (2003). Ways of explaining workplace bullying: A review of enabling, motivating, and precipitating structure and processes in the work environment. *Human Resources, 56*, 1213–1232.

Seligman, M. E. P., Steen, T. A., Park, N., & Peterson, C. (2005). Positive psychology progress. *American Psychologist, 60*, 410–421.

Shepard, G. (2005). *How to manage problem employees: A step-by-step guide for turning difficult employees into high performers*. New York, NY: Wiley.

Sias, P. M. (2009). *Organizing relationships: Traditional and emerging perspectives on workplace relationship*. Thousand Oaks, CA: Sage.

Sillars, A. (1980). Attributions and communication in roommate conflicts. *Communication Monographs, 47*, 180–200.

Sillars, A. (1981). Attributions and interpersonal conflict resolution. In J. H. Harvey, W. Ickes, & R. Kidd (Eds.), *New directions in attribution research* (Vol. 3, pp. 281–306). Hillsdale, NJ: Lawrence Erlbaum.

Simpson, R., & Cohen, C. (2004). Dangerous work: The gendered nature of bullying in the context of higher education. *Gender, Work & Organization, 11*, 163–186.

Skogstad, A., Einarsen, S., Toscheim, T, Aasland, M. S., & Hetland, H. (2007). The destructiveness of laissez faire leadership behavior. *Journal of Occupational Health Psychology, 12*, 80–92.

Solomon, M. (2002). *Working with difficult people*. Englewood Cliffs, NJ: Prentice Hall.

Sutton, R. I. (2007). *The no asshole rule: Building a civilized workplace and surviving one that isn't*. New York, NY: Hachette Books.

Times Higher Education Supplement. (2005, June 3). Times higher survey: Experiences of bullying in academia survey. Retrieved from http://www.timeshighereducation.co/uk/story.asp?storyCode=196514.

Tippett, K. (2012, February 12) On being: An interview with Desmond Tutu [Radio broadcast]. Retrieved from American Public Media (podcast).

Twale, D., & DeLuca, B. M. (2008). *Faculty incivility: The rise of the academic bully culture*. San Francisco, CA: Jossey-Bass.

Waldron, V. R. (2011). *Managing risk in communication encounters: Strategies for the workplace*. Thousand Oaks, CA: Sage.

Waldron, V. R. (2012). *Communicating emotions at work*. Malden, MA: Polity Press.

Warner, J., & Klemp, K. (2011). *The drama free office: A guide to healthy collaboration with your team, coworkers, and boss*. Austin, TX: Greenleaf.

CONTRIBUTORS

Ronald C. Arnett (PhD, Ohio University) is chair and professor of the Department of Communication & Rhetorical Studies and the Henry Koren, C.S.Sp, Endowed Chair for Scholarly Excellence at Duquesne University. He is the author/coauthor of six books and three edited books, including *Communication Ethics Literacy: Dialogue and Difference* (with Janie M. Harden Fritz & Leeanne M. Bell, Sage, 2009), and *Dialogic Confession: Bonhoeffer's Rhetoric of Responsibility* (Southern Illinois University Press, 2005; Everett Lee Hunt Award winner, 2006). His most recent book, *Communication Ethics in Dark Times: Hannah Arendt's Rhetoric of Warning and Hope*, is in press with Southern Illinois University Press.

Patrice M. Buzzanell (PhD, Purdue University) is a professor in the Brian Lamb School of Communication at Purdue University. She has published three books and over 100 articles and chapters in areas such as gender and feminism, leadership, career, work and family, and resilience communication theory and practice, as well as on children's career aspirations. International Communication Association Fellow and National Communication Association Carroll C. Arnold Distinguished Lecturer, she has delivered keynote addresses around the globe. She currently coadvises an engineering team on women's empowerment in Ghana through the Engineering Projects in Community Service (EPICS) at Purdue University.

Brittany L. Collins (MA, University of Cincinnati) is a doctoral candidate in communication at Texas A&M University. Her research focuses on issues of difference and leadership, diversity narratives, organizational token dynamics, and organizational identity. More specifically, Brittany's dissertation work addresses the framing processes of leaders of nondominant social groups. She is interested in how leaders draw on particular discourses to frame their difference when it becomes a salient issue in organizational interactions.

Beverly Davenport Sypher (PhD, University of Michigan) is the vice provost for Faculty Affairs, Susan Bulkeley Butler Professor of Leadership, and a professor in the Brian Lamb School of Communication at Purdue University. Her recent book with Lutgen-Sandvik (2009), *Destructive Organizational Communication*, won an Outstanding Book Award from the National Communication Association. In addition to numerous articles and chapters, she also has published three books on long-standing interests in quality of work life issues, directed the evaluation of a health-related entertainment education initiative in the Peruvian Amazon, and published reports on e-health projects including telemedicine and telehospice.

Martha J. Fay (PhD, Ohio State University) is Associate Professor in the Communication and Journalism Department at the University of Wisconsin–Eau Claire, specializing in organizational communication. Dr. Fay's research interests include leadership, informal communication in the workplace, conflict, and identity/identification processes, as well as family communication in specialized contexts. Her work has been published in the *Journal of Applied Communication Research*, *Southern Communication Journal*, and *Qualitative Research in Organizations and Management*.

Janie M. Harden Fritz (PhD, University of Wisconsin–Madison) is associate professor of Communication & Rhetorical Studies at Duquesne University. She coedited (with Becky L. Omdahl) *Problematic Relationships in the Workplace* (Peter Lang, 2006), coauthored (with Ronald C. Arnett & Leeanne M. Bell) *Communication Ethics Literacy: Dialogue and Difference* (Sage, 2009), and coedited (with S. Alyssa Groom) *Communication Ethics and Crisis: Negotiating Differences in Public and Private Spheres* (Fairleigh Dickinson University Press, 2012). Her work appears in *Management Communication Quarterly, Communication Research Reports, Journal of Public Management and Social Policy, Communication Monographs, Journal of Business Communication, Journal of Business Ethics*, and several edited volumes. Her current book, *Professional Civility: Communicative Virtue at Work*, is forthcoming with Peter Lang.

CONTRIBUTORS

Abrar Hammoud (MA, Purdue University) is a Knox Fellow and current graduate student in the Brian Lamb School of Communication at Purdue University. The focus of her research is meaningful work and social change in the Middle East. As part of Purdue's Global Engineering Program (GEP) Global Design Teams (GDT), her work abroad focused on identifying and implementing sustainable entrepreneurship, engineering, and educational opportunities in underserved communities. Additionally, she has examined the influence of political instability upon children's conceptualizations of work. Abrar's thesis explored the various implications of the work refugees engage in and how material and discursive aspects of this work function within resilience processes.

Jon A. Hess (PhD, University of Minnesota) is professor and chair of the Department of Communication at the University of Dayton. His research has examined how people constructively handle relational challenges—including unwanted and problematic relationships—and how people manage closeness and distance in relationships. He has over 25 articles and book chapters, in such publications as *Human Communication Research*, *Personal Relationships*, *Communication Education*, *Journal of Social and Personal Relationships*, and *Management Communication Quarterly*.

Matthew J. Gill (PhD, Purdue University) is an assistant professor in the Department of Communication Studies at Eastern Illinois University. His research interests include organizational trust, workplace incivility, worklife quality, and how organizations interact with society. His recent research has examined the role organizational history plays as a socializing agent within collectives and the causes and consequences of trust in organizations, particularly how organizational communication can damage trust. His work has been published in the *International Journal of Sports Marketing and Sponsorship* and in edited volumes such as *Sports Fans, Identity, and Socialization: Exploring the Fandemonium* and *Destructive Organizational Communication: Processes, Consequences and Constructive Ways of Organizing*.

Rebecca Gill (PhD, University of Utah) is assistant professor at Texas A&M University, where she examines the intersections among organizing and organizational identity, gender and difference, and enterprise and entrepreneurship. Additional interests include globalization, consumption, social justice, and organizational methods. Her work has been published in the *Journal of Applied Communication Research*, *Qualitative Research on Organizations and Management*, *Organization*, the *Electronic Journal of Communication*, as well as in the edited books, *The Debate over Corporate Social Responsibility* and *Public Address and Moral Judgment: Critical Studies in Ethical Tensions*.

Loraleigh Keashly (PhD, University of Saskatchewan) is associate professor and interim chair of the Department of Communication at Wayne State University, Detroit. Her current research focus is the nature, effects, and amelioration of uncivil and bullying behaviors in the workplace. Her numerous articles are published in such journals as *Work & Stress*, *Journal of Emotional Abuse*, *Violence and Victims*, *Employee Rights and Employment Policy Journal*, and the *Journal of Management and Organizations*. Her book chapters have appeared in such books as *Bullying and Harassment in the Workplace* (Taylor & Francis), *Counterproductive Work Behavior* (American Psychological Association), the *Handbook of Workplace Violence* (Sage), and *The Destructive Side of Organizational Communication* (Routledge/LEA).

Terry A. Kinney (PhD, University of Wisconsin–Madison) is an independent consultant who examines the association among exposure to verbal aggression, emotional reactions, and aspects of well-being. Most recently Kinney's work has focused on aspects of bullying and verbal harassment, including workplace and cyber-bullying. In addition to research articles and book chapters on various aspects of verbal aggression, Kinney, with coauthor Maili Pörhölä, has published two books that examine how prosocial and antisocial communication manifest and affect individuals: *Anti- and Pro-Social Communication: Theories, Methods and Applications* and *Bullying: Contexts, Consequences, and Control*.

Dayna N. Kloeber (MA, Arizona State University) enjoys her work as a communication studies faculty associate and holds a fellowship with Arizona State University's Family Communication Consortium. Her research primarily examines how relational partners communicate conditions and boundaries during the forgiveness process and how these reflect the theoretical intersections between forgiveness and reconciliation. In addition to nearly a dozen conference papers, Dayna has been a chapter contributor in *Marriage at Mid-Life: Counseling Strategies and Analytical Tools*. Her other coauthored work has appeared in *Environmental Communication: A Journal of Nature and Culture*.

Jennifer J. Mease (PhD, University of North Carolina at Chapel Hill) is a consultant with the Center for Intentional Leadership, a management consulting firm in Charlotte, North Carolina. Her research and practice address how social bias is built into organizational structures and how individuals and groups develop strategies for coping with, challenging, and changing those structures. Jennifer's work has been published in several journals and books including *Text* *and Performance Quarterly, Communication Monographs, Reframing Difference in Organizational Communication Studies: Research, Pedagogy, Practice,* and *Intercultural Communication: A Reader.* Her consulting work spans across corporate, not-for-profit, and government organizations and includes leadership development, change initiatives, diversity work, and career coaching.

Lisa M. Millhous (PhD, University of Minnesota) is associate professor at West Chester University who studies the complex facets of micro- and macro-cultures that individuals experience when they work in groups. Her articles and chapters appear in such publications as *Small Group Research, Communication Research Reports,* and *Perspectives and Methods of Political Discourse and Text Research (Vol. 2).* She also works with a variety of international and multicultural organizations around the world.

Becky L. Omdahl (PhD, University of Wisconsin–Madison) is dean of the College of Arts and Sciences and professor at Metropolitan State University. Her research explores the communication of emotion and its impact on empathy, stress, and burnout, and problematic relationships in the workplace. She has articles and chapters in such publications as *Communication Monographs, Western Journal of Communication, Journal of Advanced Nursing,* and *Advanced Interpersonal Communication,* a book, *Cognitive Appraisal, Emotion, and Empathy* (Lawrence Erlbaum), and a coedited anthology (Janie Harden Fritz), *Problematic Relationships in the Workplace* (Peter Lang).

Patricia M. Sias (PhD, University of Texas–Austin), having served as professor of the Edward R. Murrow School of Communication at Washington State University for many years, recently joined the University of Arizona as Senior Lecturer of Leadership and Organizational Communication in the McGuire Center for Entrepreneurship at the Eller College of Management and director of the McGuire Entrepreneurship academic program. Her research centers on workplace relationships and uncertainty, and she is currently conducting a broad, multiyear research project examining communication and innovation in entrepreneurial teams. She has over 50 articles and chapters in such publications as *The Handbook of Organizational Communication (3rd ed.), Communication Monographs, Communication Research, Human Communication Research,* and the *Journal of Applied Communication Research.*

Katelyn A. Sneed (MA, University of Dayton) is a graduate student studying interpersonal and health communication. She has presented a paper at the National Communication Association 2011 conference entitled, "Listening to Voices often Overlooked: Stories of Maintaining Difficult Relationships."

Vincent R. Waldron (PhD, Ohio State University) is professor of Communication and associate director of Social and Behavioral Sciences at Arizona State University. His research and teaching focus on communication practices that make relationships satisfying, lasting, and good—in the moral sense of that word. Professor Waldron is the author or coauthor of 50 articles and chapters and four recent books, including *Communicating Forgiveness* (Sage, 2008), *Managing Risk in Communication Encounters* (Sage, 2010), and *Communicating Emotion at Work* (Polity, 2012). He has served as chairperson of both the Interpersonal Communication Division and Applied Communication Division of the National Communication Association.

AUTHOR INDEX

Aasland, M. S., 9, 10, 11, 14, 303, 308
Abalkina, M., 172, 188
Abramson, Y. L., 297, 305
Acker, J., 192, 198, 210
Adger, W. N., 217, 218, 233
Adib, A., 199, 210
Adorno, T, W., 171, 184
Afifi, W. A., 278, 286
Agathangelou, A. M., 181, 182, 184
Ageyev, V. S., 172, 188
Aichholzer, G., 127, 140
Albert, R., 167, 184
Alberts, J. K., 7, 16, 56, 67
Albrecht, T. L., 128, 140
Alexander-Snow, M., 289, 305
Alger, C. F., 180, 184
Allen, B. J., 181, 184, 190, 197, 198, 200, 210, 221, 233
Allen, D. G., 61
Allen, J. A., 24, 35
Alred, G., 163, 184
Altemeyer, B., 171, 172, 184
Amanda, G., 289, 305

Anastasiou, L., 133, 143
Anderson, C. M., 12, 15
Anderson, J. W., 70, 81
Anderson, R., 252, 254
Andersson, L. M., 7, 16, 23, 35, 44, 48, 49, 60, 61, 88, 90, 102, 104
Aquino, K., 4, 6, 13, 34, 35, 44, 46, 49, 50, 51, 52, 53, 56, 60, 61, 64, 115, 121, 269, 286
Arendt, H., 145, 146, 147, 148, 149, 150, 151, 152, 153, 154, 155, 156, 157, 158, 159, 160, 161, 260, 264, 265, 303, 305
Argyris, C., 116, 118
Arneson, P., 251, 252, 255, 259, 265, 271, 286
Arnett, R. C., x, xi, 29, 145, 147, 151, 161, 251, 252, 255, 258, 259, 260, 261, 262, 263, 264, 265, 271, 286, 296, 298, 300, 303, 304, 305, 309, 310
Arnold, D. H., 293, 307
Arnold, M. B., 27, 35
Arnseth, H. C., 140

AUTHOR INDEX

Arora, R., 135, 142
Ashburn-Nardo, L., 58, 61
Ashcraft, K. L., 181, 184, 190, 198, 200, 202, 210
Ashford, S. J., 137, 144
Ashforth, B., 46, 61
Ashforth, B. E., 200, 210, 211
Ashforth, N., 9, 10, 11, 13
Avtgis, T. A., 59, 61

Bachman, G. F., 285, 286, 287
Baeyens, C., 25, 39
Baillien, E., 49, 51, 54, 61
Baldwin, D. C., 66
Ballard, D. J., 125, 140
Baltes, B. B., 132, 140
Bancroft, S., 291, 307
Bank, B. J., 190, 192, 210
Barber, B., 165, 184
Barling, J., 21, 23, 35, 45, 48, 49, 61, 63, 304, 306
Barnes-Farrell, J. L., 136, 141
Baron, R. A., 4, 5, 6, 7, 8, 13, 16, 45, 51, 54, 61, 75, 78, 80, 81, 88, 89, 102, 104
Bartesaghi, M., 221, 233
Bartlett, J. A., 74, 82
Baruch, Y., 132, 140
Bassman, E., 48, 61
Bauer, C. C., 132, 140
Baumeister, R. F., 28, 29, 35, 38, 39, 44, 61, 113, 115, 118, 121, 251, 255
Baxter, L. A., 70, 81, 252, 255, 261, 265, 274, 287
Beach, S. R. H., 275, 287
Beck, H. P., 292, 307
Beckman, C., 190, 211
Beehr, T. A., 46, 49, 62
Bell, L. M., 258, 265, 271, 286, 309, 310
Bell, R., 109, 120
Bell, R. A., 111, 118
Bellah, R. N., 151, 158, 161
Belschak, F. D., 33, 36
Belton, L. W., 60, 65, 78, 83
Beneke, M., 291, 307
Benhabib, S., 151, 158, 161

Bennett, J. M., 175, 187
Bennett, M. J., 171, 175, 184, 186, 187
Bennett, R. J., 5, 6, 7, 8, 13, 16, 17
Benschop, Y., 200, 211
Berscheid, E., 27, 35
Biddle, S. J. H., 184, 185
Bies, R. J., 5, 13, 34, 35, 56, 61, 85, 86, 100, 102
Bimber, B., 132, 140
Bineham, J. L., 251, 255
Bishop, A., 283, 284
Bjorklund, W. L., 289, 290, 305
Björkqvist, K., 46, 62, 89, 102, 293, 305
Blau, P., 128, 140
Blustein, D. L., 43, 62
Bochner, A. P., 221, 234
Bochner, S., 165, 189
Boice, B., 289, 305
Bonanno, G. A., 218, 233
Boon, S. D., 87, 103
Bormann, E. G., 180, 185
Bottom, W. P., 279, 287
Boulton, M. J., 70, 74, 75, 82
Bowes-Sperry, L., 57, 62
Bowling, N. A., 46, 49, 62
Bradac, J. J., 132, 140
Bradfield, M., 61
Bradley, H., 200, 210
Bradley, L., 125, 142
Brake, T., 111, 118
Branch, T., 304, 305
Brand, L. A., 230, 231, 233
Branscombe, N. R., 190, 211
Brass, D. J., 115, 118
Bratskavsky, E., 28, 29, 35, 44, 61, 251, 255
Braxton, J. M., 289, 306
Brewer, M. B., 87, 103
Brickner, R. K., 179, 185
Bridge, K., 261, 265, 274, 287
Brislin, R. W., 166, 172, 185
Brocklehurst, M., 132, 140
Brodsky, C. M., 3, 10, 13, 46, 62
Brotheridge, C. M., 55, 64
Brown, K., 125, 142
Brown, P., 1, 101, 103

Brown, R. P., 277, 287
Bruce, W. M., 236, 237, 255
Bruch, M.A., 75, 81
Bruni, A., 200, 210
Buber, M., 261, 265, 298, 305
Buell, F., 165, 185
Bulanda, R. E., 292, 307
Burke, K., 148, 161
Burkhardt, M. S., 115, 118
Burleson, B. R., 128, 140
Burnazi, L., 47, 62
Burnstein, E., 187
Burt, R. S., 86, 87, 103, 104
Buss, A. H., 13, 45, 62
Butchart, A., 69, 80, 81
Butler, D. S., 277, 287
Butler, J., 202, 210
Butler, J. K. J., 87, 103
Buzzanell, P. M., x, xi, xii, 29, 31, 126, 142, 190, 202, 210, 215, 218, 219, 220, 228, 233, 234, 260, 297, 309
Byram, M., 163, 184

Cahill, D. J., 105, 106, 107, 108, 110, 114, 118, 120, 128, 143
Cahn, D. D., 253, 255
Camerer, C., 86, 104
Camerer, C. F., 166, 189
Cameron, K. S., 4, 13, 268, 274, 275, 287
Canary, D. J., 70, 81
Cannella, G. S., 219, 233
Canning, A., 284, 287
Cannon, W. B., 25, 35
Carbonne, E., 289, 305
Carr, J. C., 54, 67
Carroll, L., 291, 292, 305
Carter, S. L., 261, 262, 265, 297, 305
Cashman, J. F., 105, 119
Casmir, F. L., 180, 185
Castor, T., 221, 233
Catanese, K. R., 115, 121
Cava, R., 304, 305
Caza, A., 274, 287
Cerda, M., 69, 81
Cesaria, R., 85, 87, 88, 92, 100, 104

Chen, C. C., 303, 305
Cheney, G., 200, 210
Chiu, S., 303, 305
Chory, R. M., 59, 61
Chou, B. R., 149, 161
Chua, E., 177, 186
Ciarocco, N. J., 113, 121
Clark, C. M., 289, 290, 291, 296, 305
Clore, G. L., 27, 38
Cloud, D. L., 190, 210
Coffee, P., 184, 185
Cohen, A. B., 270, 287
Cohen, C., 293, 308
Cohen, S., 74, 75, 76, 81, 82
Coie, J. D., 115, 118
Cole, J. D., 109, 118
Collier, M., 168, 185
Collier, M. J., 176, 179, 183, 185, 187
Collins, A., 27, 38
Collins, B. L., xi, 29, 190, 302, 303, 310
Collins, J., 5, 15, 29
Collinson, D. L., 190, 211
Cook, K. S., 85, 100, 103
Cooper, C. L., 6, 7, 8, 13, 14, 15, 59, 62, 65, 71, 82, 236, 255, 293, 308
Cooren, F., 198, 210
Corman, S. R., 133, 137, 143
Cortina, L. M., 47, 48, 54, 62, 63, 65, 89, 90, 91, 93, 103, 104
Court, S., 293, 305
Coutu, D. L., 218, 233
Cox, T., 31, 35
Cragan, J. F., 180, 185
Craig, R. T., 220, 233
Craig, W., 172, 185
Crandall, W., 111, 119
Creed, W. E. D., 92, 103
Creswell, J. W., 221, 233
Crossley, C. D., 6, 17, 34, 35, 56, 62
Cupach, W. R., x, xii, 3, 13, 17, 34, 38, 56, 65, 70, 81, 84, 168, 185, 254, 256, 268, 288

Dahlberg, L. L., 69, 83
Dahlin, E., 125, 140

Dalal, R. S., 51, 67
Danaher, K., 190, 211
Daniels, S. E., 279, 287
Darley, J., 72, 83
Darwin, C., 19, 25, 36
Davenport Sypher, B., xi, 4, 5, 9, 12, 13, 14, 15, 29, 59, 65, 85, 86, 89, 103, 104, 236, 255, 261, 265, 296, 301, 304, 307, 310
Davey, L., 59, 62
Davies, J., 172, 188
Day, A., 301, 307
Day, N. E., 109, 119
Dechter, G., 289, 305
De Cuyper, N. A., 49, 61
DeLuca, N. M., 237, 256, 289, 293, 294, 295, 308
Den Hartog, D. N., 33, 36
de Pedro, M. M., 70, 74, 75, 81
de Rivera, J., 27, 36
Derkacs, D., 72, 83
Derlega, V. J., 125, 144
DeSanctis, G., 126, 128, 133, 134, 140
Desmarais, S., 10, 17
DeSouza, E., 291, 306
De Turk, S., 251, 255
Deutsch, M., 87, 103
DeWitte, H., 49, 54, 61
Dhar, S., 164, 188
Dickson, M. W., 132, 140
Diestel, S., 29, 36
Dillard, J. P., 70, 71, 81
Dimmick, J., 133, 143
Dindia, K., 70, 81
Dirks, K. T., 99, 104
Dofradottir, A., 78, 82
Dolan-Pascoe, B., 115, 121
Donaldson-James, S., 284, 287
Doorewaard, H., 200, 211
Dostaler, S., 185
Dotan, O., 110, 119
Douglas, S., 4, 13
Douilliez, C., 25, 39
Dovidio, J. F., 170, 185
Drum, M. L., 66

Dubinsky, A. J., 111, 119
Duck, S., x, xi, 168, 186, 264, 265
Duffy, M. K., 4, 10, 14, 16, 46, 51, 62, 67
Dunham, P., 132, 141
Dupre, K. E., 49, 61
Duriuz, B., 172, 186
Dutta, M. J., 219, 231, 233
Dutton, J., 43, 62
Dutton, J. E., 4, 13, 268, 287
Dweck, C., 297, 306
Dyrenforth, S. R., 60, 65, 78, 83

Eaton, J., 275, 276, 287
Edelstein, M. R., 217, 233
Edmondson, K. A., 282, 287
Eibl-Eibesfeldt, I., 25, 36
Einarson, S., 6, 9, 10, 11, 14, 23, 32, 36, 38, 46, 48, 49, 50, 52, 53, 54, 62, 63, 67, 72, 73, 74, 75, 81, 89, 103, 236, 237, 255, 303, 308
Eisenberg, E. M., 137, 141
Ekman, P., 20, 24, 25, 26, 36
Ellis, C., 221, 234
Ellis, D., G., 171, 186
Ellis, K., 85, 87, 88, 92, 100, 103, 104, 291, 292, 305
Ellis, M. H., 216, 217, 234
Ellis, P., 27, 36
Ellison, N. B., 127, 141
Ellsworth, P., 20, 27, 36, 39
Elon, A., 153, 161
Embrick, D. G., 109, 119
Enright, R. D., 268, 273, 287
Erickson, K., 113, 119
Escartin, J., 45, 62
Essers, C., 200, 211
Exline, J. J., 270, 287

Fairhurst, G., 228, 234
Falato, W. L., 278, 286
Faragher, B., 71, 82
Fay, M. J., xi, 12, 29, 111, 125, 128, 129, 130, 131, 135, 141, 257, 296, 302, 310
Feldman, J., 109, 119

AUTHOR INDEX

Feldman, M. S., 126, 137, 141
Felson, R. B., 50, 66
Fendrich, M., 66
Fenstermaker, S., 198, 212
Ferguson, K. E., 192, 211
Ferris, S. P., 127, 142
Fincham, F. D., 275, 287
Fineman, S., 24, 36, 100, 103
Finkel, E. J., 282, 288
Finkelstein, S., 166, 186
Finkenauer, C., 28, 35, 44, 61
Fisher, R. J., 304, 306
Fitzgerald, L. F., 70, 73, 84
Fix, B., 175, 189
Flaherty, J. A., 47, 52, 66
Fleming, M., 163, 184
Fletcher, C., 4, 16, 18, 38
Floyd, K., 133, 143
Foer, F., 151, 161
Fogel-Grinvald, H., 185
Foley, M. K., x, xi, 168, 186, 264, 265
Foley, S., 108, 119
Folger, R., 5, 17, 44, 55, 62, 66, 269, 286
Folkman, S., 31, 32, 38
Fonner, K. L., 129, 138, 141
Fontaine, J. R., 20, 36
Forni, P. M., 261, 265
Foss, K. A., 60, 65, 220, 234
Foss, S. K., 220, 234
Foster, D. A., 176, 186
Fox, S., 5, 6, 7, 8, 9, 14, 62, 289, 293, 306
Francart, B., 25, 39
Francis, L., 304, 306
Franco, N., 236, 255
Fransler, G. A., 291, 306
Fratzl, J., 293, 307
Frederickson, B., 44, 62
Fredrickson, J. W., 69, 82
Freels, S., 52, 66
Frenkel-Brunswik, E., 171, 184
Friedman, H. S., 74, 75, 76, 81
Friesen, W. V., 20, 24, 25, 26, 36
Frijda, N. H., 20, 27, 36
Fritz, J. M. H., ix, x, xi, xii, 3, 4, 5, 7, 8, 9, 10, 11, 12, 13, 14, 18, 19, 20, 29, 37, 46, 49, 52, 63, 70, 81, 108, 119, 126, 141, 142, 145, 151, 161, 163, 166, 186, 187, 236, 255, 257, 258, 259, 260, 261, 262, 263, 264, 265, 266, 296, 304, 306, 307, 309, 310, 313
Frone, M. R., 45, 66
Fruzetti, A. E., 28, 37
Furnham, A., 10, 14, 165, 189

Gagnon, M. A., 105, 119
Gainey, T. W., 127, 141
Gajendran, R. S., 127, 141
Gambetta, D., 86, 100, 103
Ganesh, S., 200, 211
Ganster, D., 10, 14, 46, 62
Gao, L., 111, 119
Garud, R., 126, 144
Gassin, E. A., 273, 287
Genkova, P., 187
George, J. M., 190, 211
Gherardi, S., 200, 210
Giacolone, R. A., 4, 6, 7, 8, 14
Gibson, K., 279, 287
Giesberg, J., 116, 119
Gilboa, E., 165, 183, 186
Gill, L., 304, 306
Gill, M. J., xi, 9, 12, 29, 85, 86, 103, 261, 296, 301, 311
Gill, R., 190, 200, 211, 302, 303, 311
Ginossar, T., 72, 83
Giroux, H., 137, 143
Glew, D. J., 4, 7, 16, 45, 65
Glick, P. S., 170, 185
Glomb, T. M., 21, 23, 24, 37, 45, 47, 48, 50, 52, 63
Godfrey, P., 232, 234
Goffman, E., 131, 141
Golden, T. D., 129, 136, 141
Goldhaber, G. M., 91, 103
Goldman, B., 269, 286
Goldsmith, D., 128, 140
Gonnerman, M. E. Jr., 75, 82
Goodwin, S., 58, 61
Gordon, M. A., 195, 212
Gossett, L. M., 125, 134, 140, 141

Gottman, J., 37, 44, 61, 63
Gouldner, A., 294, 306
Gover, S., 61
Grabska, K., 216, 234
Graen, G., 105, 108, 119
Grandey, A. A., 24, 35
Granovetter, M., 163, 186
Grauerholz, E., 306
Gray, A., 177, 186
Gray J., 109, 119
Grayson, C., 251, 255
Greenberg, J., 4, 5, 6, 7, 8, 14, 16
Greenhaus, J. H., 108, 119
Greig, J. M., 304, 306
Griffin, R. W., 3, 4, 5, 6, 7, 9, 14, 15, 16, 17, 45, 65
Groom, S. A., 310
Gross, C., 47, 52, 54, 55, 59, 67, 69, 77, 84
Grotevant, H. D., 176, 186
Groth, M., 24, 35
Grover, S., 61, 269, 286
Grunewald, T. L., 114, 121
Gudykunst, W. B., 174, 177, 186
Guerrero, L. K., 285, 286, 287
Guerrier, Y., 199, 210
Gurung, R. A. R., 114, 121

Hackman, J. R., 303, 306
Hadeed, L., 183, 185
Haidt, J., 250, 255
Hall, A., 237, 255
Hall, S., 165, 186
Hammer, M. R., 184, 186
Hammoud, A., xi, 29, 31, 215, 223, 225, 260, 297, 311
Hammoud, S., 172, 188
Hancock, J., 132, 141
Hannon, P. A., 282, 288
Hanraham, S. J., 184, 185
Harden, J. M., 71, 81 (see also Fritz, J. M. H.)
Harel-Fisch, Y., 185
Harris, P. R., 175, 187
Harrison, D. A., 127, 141
Hart, W. B., 165, 188

Hartman, R. C., 135, 142
Harvey, J., 275, 287
Harvey, S., 47, 48, 63, 64
Hauge, L. J., 52, 63
Hawker, D. S. J., 70, 74, 75, 82
Hawkins, A., 135, 142
Hazler, R. J., 47, 63
Heath, R. G., 175, 189
Hebl, M. R., 190, 211
Hecht, M., 164, 168, 176, 183, 187
Hegde, R., 219, 234
Hegde, R. S., 179, 185
Heimer, C. A., 85, 103
Henle, C. A., 51, 67
Herbert, T. B., 74, 75, 76, 82
Herington, A. D., 12, 15
Hershcovis. M. S., 45, 63
Hershcovis, S., 44, 67
Hess, J. A., x, xi, 18, 23, 29, 37, 52, 53, 55, 60, 63, 72, 77, 82, 83, 126, 142, 166, 175, 187, 235, 236, 240, 255, 257, 258, 260, 261, 266, 298, 299, 311
Hetland, J., 185, 303, 308
Higgerson, M. L., 237, 255
Higgins, E. T., 25, 34, 37, 75, 76, 82
Hill, E. J., 135, 142
Hill, J. A., 127, 141
Hill, P. C., 270, 287
Hills, M. D., 165, 187
Hinze, S. W., 200, 211
Hirschy, A. S., 289, 306
Hirshberg, M., 187
Hitlan, R. T., 109, 119
Hjelt-Back, M., 46, 62, 89, 102
Hochschild, A. R., 23, 24, 29, 37
Hodson, R., 51, 63, 109, 110, 119, 120, 260, 266
Hoel, H., 6, 14, 53, 59, 62, 63, 65, 71, 72, 82, 236, 255
Hoel, W., 105, 119
Hofstede, G., 164, 165, 170, 173, 175, 187
Hogh, A., 78, 82
Holba, A. M., 148, 151, 161, 259, 265
Hollinger, R. C., 3, 15
Holmes, J., 128, 142

AUTHOR INDEX

Holmes, J. G., 87, 103
Holmes, S., 276, 287
Holmes, T. H., 174, 187
Hommen, L., 109, 119
Hornstein, H. A., 98, 103
Hosmanek, A. J., 169, 187
Huff, J., 75, 82
Huijser, M., 175, 176, 187
Hunter, S., 48, 64
Hutchinson, S. R., 87, 104, 301, 306
Hyde, B., 251, 255
Hylmo, A., 126, 132, 142

Ibarra, H., 108, 120
Ilgen, D. R., 69, 74, 82
Imahori, T. T., 168, 185
Infante, D. A., 12, 15
Isabella, L. A., 105, 108, 120, 257, 262, 263, 266
Izard, C. E., 25, 26,37
Izquierdo, M. G., 70, 81

Jablin, F. M., 70, 74, 77, 83, 84, 92, 103, 106, 112, 120
Jackson, M. H., 126, 142
Jackson, S. E., 31, 38
Jackson, S. J., 192, 211
Jacobs, G., 139, 142
Jacobsen, K., 216, 234
Jacobson, N. S., 28, 37
Jagatic, K., 5, 6, 7, 15, 46, 47, 52, 53, 58, 64, 293, 306
James, E. H., 192, 194, 195, 212
James, W., 25, 37
Jamieson, K. H., 177, 178, 187
Janson, G. R., 47, 63
Jarvenpaa, S. L., 133, 142
Jex, S. M., 46, 66
Jobe, R. L., 282, 287
Johnson, T. P., 66
Jolson, M. A., 111, 119
Jones, F., 293, 306
Jones, W. H., 282, 287
Joyce, T. A., 237, 255

Ka'imikaua, C. I., 169, 187
Kanagawa, C., 187
Kanner, A. D., 31, 38
Kant, I., 152, 159, 161
Kanter, R. M., 191, 192, 193, 195, 196, 209, 211
Karol, S. H., 111, 118
Kassing, J., 274, 288
Keashly, L., xi, 5, 6, 7 , 8, 10, 12, 15, 20, 21, 22, 23, 29, 30, 32, 34, 37, 43, 45, 46, 47, 48, 49, 52, 53, 55, 57, 58, 59, 60, 62, 63, 64, 65, 264, 293, 295, 296, 304, 306, 312
Keller, S. E., 74, 75, 76, 82
Kelley, D., 287
Kelley, D. E., 127, 141
Kelley, D. L., 34, 40, 268, 269, 270, 271, 272, 275, 276, 277, 278, 279, 280, 281, 283, 284, 287, 288
Kelley, H. H., 166, 187
Kelloway, E. K., 10, 17, 45, 49, 57, 59, 61, 66, 304, 306
Kelly, E., 125, 140
Kelly, H., 190, 192, 193, 194, 195, 196, 211
Kelly, K. M., 109, 119
Kemmelmeier, M., 172, 187
Kenagawa, C., 187
Kets de Vries, M. F. R., 9, 15
Kidwell, R. E., Jr., 7, 15
Kiesler, S., 133, 143
Kilmann, R., 253, 255
Kim, J., 12, 15
Kimball, B. A., 260, 266
King, E. B., 190, 211
Kingwell, M., 263, 266
Kinman, G., 293, 306
Kinney, T. A., x, xi, 8, 9, 12, 15, 16, 20, 21, 22, 29, 30, 68, 71, 74, 75, 78, 80, 82, 83, 264, 293, 296, 304, 306, 307, 312
Kirkpatrick, D. C., x, xi, 168, 186, 264, 265
Kirschbaum, K., 164, 188
Kleese, D. A., 217, 233
Klein, L. C., 114, 121
Klein, R., 75, 82
Klemp, K., 304, 308

Klimoski, R. J., 7, 15
Kline, S. L., 128, 129, 130, 131, 133, 141, 143
Kloeber, D. N., xi, 29, 30, 34, 260, 267, 275, 280, 283, 285, 287, 299, 312
Kluckhohn, F. R., 165, 187
Knape, J., 33, 38
Knez, M., 87, 103
Knobloch, L. K., 70, 81
Knoke, D., 128, 142
Knopoff, K., 190, 211
Kolb, D. M., 304, 307
Koslowsky, M., 5, 17
Kossowska, M., 172, 186
Kowalski, R. M., 70, 83
Kram, K. E., 105, 108, 120, 257, 262, 263, 266
Kramer, M. W., x, xii, 72, 83, 296, 307
Kramer, R. M., 85, 87, 100, 103, 104
Kreiner, G. E., 200, 210, 211
Kristoff, N. D., 159, 161
Krone, K., 276, 288
Krone, K. J., 106, 120
Krug, E. G., 69, 83
Krumov, K., 187
Kuhn, T., 198, 210
Kumar, V., 73, 84
Kurihara, T., 109, 119

LaGanke, J. S., 132, 140
Lambert, L. S., 51, 67
Lamertz, K., 44, 46, 49, 50, 51, 52, 60, 61, 64
Lampman, C., 291, 307
Landis, D., 175, 187
Langan-Fox, J., 7, 15
Langhout, R. D., 89, 103
Latane, B., 72, 83
Latimer, M., 301, 307
Latour, B., 182, 187
Laurenti, H. J., 75, 81
Lauring, J., 167, 179, 187
Lavine, H., 75, 82
Lawler, K. A., 282, 287
Lazarus, R. S., 31, 32, 37, 38

Leary, M. R., 115, 118
LeBlanc, D., 301, 307
Lee, J., 70, 83
Lee, R. T., 55, 64
Lee, W., 179, 185
Leeds-Hurwitz, W., 165, 188
Leibowitz, A., 66
Leidner, D. E., 133, 142
Leiter, M., 301, 307
Leiter, M. P., 31, 38
Leonardi, P. M., 126, 142
Lesniak, R., 91, 103
Lester, J., 296, 307
Levenson, R. W., 26, 36
Levinas, E., 158, 161, 307
Levinson, D. J., 171, 184
Levinson, S., 101, 103
Levitt, M. J., 236, 255
Lewis, A. P., 109, 120
Lewis, B. P., 114, 121
Lewis, D., 57, 64, 86, 87, 97, 104, 293, 307
Lewis, R. D., 175, 188
Lewis, X., 293, 307
Leymann, H., 46, 64, 72, 74, 75, 83, 89, 104
Liao, H., 52, 63
Liden, R., 105, 119
Lieberman, M. A., 31, 38
Lilley, R., 304, 307
Lim, S., 48, 65, 88, 90, 104
Lind, T., 48, 65
Lindoff, T. R., 239, 255
Ling, L. M. H., 181, 182, 184
Linnehan, F., 108, 119
Lipman-Blumen, J., 10, 15
Lippert, L., x, xii, 34, 38, 56, 65, 268, 288
Lippman, S., 292, 307
Liu, M., x, xi, xii, 190, 202, 210
Lockhart, D. E., 54, 67
Lombardo, M. M., 10, 15
London, H., 20, 39
Lopez, S. H., 51, 63, 109, 120
Lopez, Y. P., 3, 4, 6, 7, 14
Lozano, R., 69, 83
Lubit, G., 304, 307
Lucas, K., 218, 224, 233, 234

AUTHOR INDEX

Ludvigsen, S., 140
Lupton, B., 200, 211
Lutgen-Sandvik, P., 4, 5, 7, 8, 13, 15, 16, 18, 19, 32, 38, 47, 51, 55, 57, 59, 60, 65, 72, 74, 75, 83, 104, 236, 255, 304, 307, 310
Luthans, F., 4, 16
Lyche, L. F., 115, 121

MacIntryre, A. C., 151, 158, 161, 259, 260, 266
MacLean, L. M., 10, 15, 46, 64
Madlock, P. E., 165, 177, 188
Madsen, R., 151, 161
Magley, V. J., 54, 62, 88, 89, 90, 103, 104
Malkki, L. H., 216, 234
Mallia, K. L., 127, 142
Mandler, G., 26, 38
Mann, S., 24, 38
Manuelito, K. D., 219, 233
Maoz, I., 171, 186
March, A., 137, 140
March, J. G., 87, 104, 137, 141
Marks, S. R., 261, 266
Marshall, G W., 111, 120, 125, 142
Marshall, J., 230, 234
Martin, C. L., 7, 15
Martin, J., 165, 181, 188, 190, 202, 211
Martin, J. L., 171, 172, 188
Martin, M. M., 12, 15
Martin-Pena, J., 45, 62
Marx, K., 148, 161
Mascharka, P. B., 136, 141
Maslach, C., 31, 38
Masten, A. S., 218, 219, 234
Matthiesen, S. B., 89, 104
Matusik, S. F., 190, 211
May, S. K., 135, 143
McAllister, D. J., 86, 87, 92, 104
McCall, M. W., 10, 15
McCroskey, J. C., 109, 118
McDaniel, P. A., 109, 120
McDonald, P., 125, 142
McDowell, C., 251, 255
McFarland, S. G., 172, 188

McHale, B., 151, 162
McKay, R., 293, 307
McKinney, D., 291, 292, 307
McManus, S. E., 125, 142
McPhee, M., 284, 287
Meares, M. M., 72, 74, 83
Mease, J. J., xi, 29, 190, 302, 303, 312
Meeussen, V., 33, 38
Meglich-Sespico, P. A., 45, 65
Mehrabian, A., 253, 255
Menaghan, E. G., 31, 38
Mercy, J. A., 69, 83
Merolla. A. J., 254, 255, 285, 288
Messick, D. M., 85, 104
Metts, S., x, xii, 34, 38, 56, 65, 268, 279, 285, 288
Michael, J. H., 105, 119
Michaels, C. E., 111, 120, 125, 142
Michela, J. L., 166, 187
Miike, Y., 165, 188
Mikkelson, E. G., 32, 36, 38
Miles, R. E., 92, 103
Miller, B., 135, 142
Millhous, L. M., 163, 177, 180, 188, 302, 303, 313
Miner, A. G., 21, 23, 37, 48, 63
Mishra, A. K., 88, 104
Mitchell, T. R., 69, 82
Moen, P., 125, 140
Monge, P., 126, 128, 133, 134, 140
Montgomery, B. J., 252, 255
Montgomery, M. J., 125, 144
Montoya, L. A., 109, 121
Moore, S. C., 78, 83
Moran, R. T., 175, 187
Morgan, S. J., 126, 133, 134, 135, 142
Morris, K. A., 58, 61
Moss, S. E., 54, 67
Mulki, J. P., 111, 120, 125, 142
Mullan, J. T., 31, 38
Mullis, F., 277, 287
Mumby, D. K., 190, 198, 200, 202, 210, 211
Muraven, M., 29, 35, 38, 251, 255
Murningham, J. K., 279, 287
Musson, G., 125, 143

Myers, K. K., 258, 266

Nakayama, T. K., 179, 185
Namie, G., 8, 10, 15, 16, 47, 51, 57, 65, 304, 307
Namie, R., 8, 10, 15, 16, 304, 307
Nathaniel, K., 183, 185
Navarro, M. C. S., 70, 81
Nawyn, S. J., 66
Nelson, T. D., 170, 188
Netter, S., 284, 287
Neuliep, J. W., 174, 188
Neuman, J. H., 4, 5, 6, 7, 8, 13, 16, 45, 46, 47, 51, 52, 54, 55, 57, 58, 60, 61, 62, 64, 65, 88, 89, 102, 104, 293, 295, 296, 306
Neyens, I., 49, 61
Nie, M., 133, 142
Niedl, K., 69, 70, 74, 75, 76, 83
Nishii, L. H., 48, 65
Niven, K., 44, 67
Noels, K. A., 187
North, J., 271, 287
Nowell, N. L., 21, 23, 37, 48, 49, 52, 58, 59, 60, 64

Oakes, P. J., 108, 121
Oatley, K., 26, 38
Odden, C. M., 108, 112, 120
Oesterreich, D., 171, 173, 188
Oestreich, D. K., 46, 66
Oetzel, J., 163, 164, 176, 183, 188
Oetzel, J. G., 72, 83
O'Faircheallaigh, C., 217, 234
Oldham, G. R., 303, 306
O'Leary, A., 74, 75, 76, 83
O'Leary-Kelly, A., 3, 4, 5, 6, 7, 9, 15, 16, 45, 57, 62, 65
Olsen, J. P., 87, 104
Olson, M. H., 126, 142
Olweus, D., 69, 70, 78, 80, 83
Omdahl, B. L., ix, x, xi, xii, 4, 5, 8, 13, 14, 18, 29, 37, 46, 49, 52, 63, 70, 81, 126, 141, 142, 166, 187, 236, 255, 258, 260, 263, 266, 289, 296, 300,

304, 306, 307, 310, 313
O'Meara, A., 172, 188
Oore, D. G., 301, 307
Ortony, A., 26, 27, 38
Osatuke, K., 60, 65, 78, 80, 83
Oster, H., 25, 36
Österman, K., 46, 62, 89, 102
Ozcelik, H., 99, 104

Pagon, M., 10, 14, 46, 62
Paige, R. M., 184, 188
Pal, M., 219, 234
Panteli, N., 139, 143
Papa, M., 231, 234
Papa, W., 231, 234
Park, N., 297, 308
Parker, C. P., 75, 82
Parks, M. R., 133, 143
Parsons, R. J., 183, 185
Payne, J., 24, 38
Pearson, C. M., 7, 9, 11,16, 23, 35, 44, 48, 49, 60, 61, 73, 80, 83, 88, 89, 90, 102, 104, 264, 266
Pearson D., 9, 11, 16
Pelled, L. H., 108, 120
Pena, D. C., 178, 179, 188
Perlin, L. I., 31, 38
Perry, T., 128, 143, 175, 189
Peterson, C., 297, 308
Pfeffer, J., 98, 100, 101, 104
Pfeifer, R., 26, 38
Phelps, A., 291, 307
Philippot, L., 25, 27, 39
Phillips, A., 277, 287
Piferi, R. L., 282, 287
Pilkington, C., 125, 144
Pipkin, R. M., 195, 212
Pitts, H., 209
Pitts, M. J., 4, 17
Poggio, B., 200, 210
Pollio, H. R., 292, 307
Pont, A., 216, 234
Poortvilet, M., 115, 121
Porath, C. L., 7, 9, 11, 16, 73, 80, 83, 264, 266

AUTHOR INDEX

Pörhöla, M., 12, 15, 71, 78, 80, 82, 83, 304, 307, 312
Porrua, C., 45, 62
Porter, D. T., 91, 103
Postmes, T., 132, 143
Price, S. L., 307
Price Spratlen, L., 46, 65
Pryor, J. B., 70, 73, 84
Pugh, S. D., 24, 35
Putnam, L. L., 190, 211

Quinn, R. E., 4, 13, 268, 287
Qvortrup, L., 127, 143

Rafaeli, A., 126, 137, 141
Raghuram, S., 126, 144
Rabe, R. H., 174, 187
Rainivaara, S., 12, 16, 23, 39, 49, 55, 65, 76, 77, 84
Raknes, B. I., 72, 74, 81, 89, 103, 104
Ramirez, A., Jr., 254, 255
Rancer, A. S., 12, 15
Raskauskas, J., 293, 308
Raver, J. L., 48, 65
Ray, E. B., 114, 120
Raymond, N., 114, 120
Rayner, C., 57, 59, 65, 70, 73, 84, 293, 308
Reed, A., 6, 13 (OK TO DELETE "II"?)
Rehling, D. L., 289, 290, 305
Reich, T., 44, 67
Reinking, K., 109, 111, 120
Reinsch, N. L., Jr., 126, 134, 143
Remke, R. V., 218, 220, 233, 234
Retzinger, S., 21, 22, 23, 39
Ribeau, S., 176, 187
Richard, N. T., 202, 211
Richman, J. A., 46, 47, 48, 52, 56, 66
Richman, J. M., 135, 143
Riforgiate, S., 4, 16, 18, 38
Riley, P., 137, 141
Rivera, K. D., 56, 67
Rivet, K. M., 75, 81
Robichaud, D., 137, 143
Robinson, S. L., 4, 5, 6, 7, 8, 13, 16, 99, 104
Rodriquex-Carballeira, A., 45, 62

Roesch, E. B., 20, 36
Rogers, E. M., 165, 188
Rokkum, O., 89, 104
Rolloff, M. E., 78, 84, 111, 118, 129, 133, 138, 141, 143
Roscigno, V. J., 51, 63, 109, 120
Roseman, I. J., 27, 39
Rosenfeld, L. B., 135, 143
Rospenda, K. M., 47, 48, 52, 54, 66
Rousseau, D. M., 8, 13, 86, 104
Rowe, M., 57, 66
Rubin, Y., 110, 119
Rubinstein, G., 172, 188
Rudman, L. A., 170, 185
Rusbult, C. E., 282, 288
Russell, J. E. A., 125, 142
Ryan, D. J., 174, 188
Ryan, K. D., 46, 66

Sable, M., 178, 189
Sagie, A., 5, 17
Sakai, A., 32, 40
Salin, D., 53, 54, 59, 63, 66, 70, 71, 72, 73, 74, 82, 84, 295, 308
Sanchez, M. I. S., 70, 81
Sanford, R. N., 171, 184
Sartre, J. P., 148, 162
Schacter, S., 26, 39
Schat, A. C. H., 10, 17, 45, 57, 59, 66
Scheff, T. J., 22, 39
Schein, E. H., 165, 170, 189
Schepman, S., 110, 119
Scherer, K. R., 20, 25, 27, 36, 39
Schleifer, S. J., 74, 82
Schmidt, K. H., 29, 36
Schneider, K. T., 110, 119
Schoenrade, P., 109, 119
Scott, E. K., 190, 195, 211
Scully, M., 57, 66
Sczesny, S., 6, 17
Segrin, C., 71, 81
Seidenberg, R., 112, 120
Seligman, M. E. P., 297, 305, 308
Sellars, C. N., 184, 185
Selye, H., 30, 31, 39

Sennett, R., 261, 266
Sha, B., 171, 189
Shackleton, V., 10, 17
Shannon, C. A., 47, 66
Sheehan, D. V., 66
Sheehan, K. H., 46, 66
Shenoy, S., 218, 233
Shephard, G., 304, 308
Sherif, M., 108, 120
Sherman, M. P., 132, 140
Shields, D. C., 180, 185
Shifflett, S. C., 74, 82
Shils, E., 261, 266
Shockley-Zalabak, P., 85, 87, 88, 92, 100, 103, 104
Shome, R., 219, 234
Shook, V. E., 169, 189
Sias, P. M., x, xi, xii, 12, 17, 21, 29, 74, 77, 84, 105, 106, 107, 108, 110, 111, 112, 113, 114, 115, 118, 120, 125, 128, 143, 175, 189, 257, 258, 259, 261, 263, 264, 266, 296, 301, 302, 303, 304, 308, 313
Sillars, A., 77, 84, 302, 308
Sillars, A. L., 253, 256
Silva, D., 175, 189
Silver, M. E., 236, 255
Simons-Morton, B., 185
Simpson, R., 190, 192, 194, 195, 196, 200, 211, 293, 308
Singer, J. E., 26, 39
Singhal, A., 231, 234
Sitkin, S. B., 86, 104
Sivanathan, N., 304, 306
Skarlicki, D. P., 5, 17, 55, 66
Skogstad, A., 9, 10, 11, 14, 63, 72, 74, 75, 81, 303, 308
Sluss, D. M., 200, 211
Sminkey, L., 69, 81
Smith, A. P., 75, 81
Smith, C. A., 27, 39
Smith, G., 160, 162
Sneed, K. A., xi, 23, 29, 235, 258, 260, 298, 299, 313
Socha, R. J., 4, 17

Solomon, M., 304, 308
Sommer, K. L., 107, 110, 113, 119, 121
Soule, K. P., 78, 84
Spangler, E., 195, 212
Spangler, W. D., 111, 119
Spector, P. E., 5, 6, 7, 8, 9, 14, 46, 66
Spence Lashinger, H. K., 301, 307
Spitzberg, B. H., 3, 13, 17, 70, 81, 84, 254, 256
Spratlen, L. P., 77, 84
Springer, P. J., 289, 290, 291, 305
Sproull, L., 133, 143
Squires, C. R., 192, 211
Stafford, L., 70, 81, 133, 143
Stallworth, L., 58, 62
Stashevsky, S., 5, 17
Steen, T. A., 297, 308
Steinburg, A., 109, 121
Stevenson, R., 151, 162
Stocker, S. L., 282, 288
Stone, M., 273, 277, 281, 288
Stoner, C. R., 135, 142
Strauman, R., 75, 82
Stride, C., 44, 67
Strodtbeck, F. L., 165, 187
Struthers, C. W., 275, 276, 287
Sullivan, V. J., 109, 121
Sullivan, W. M., 151, 161
Sutton, R., 11, 17
Sutton, R. I., 304, 308
Swidler, A., 151, 161
Symon, G., 126, 133, 134, 135, 142

Tajfel, H., 174, 189
Tams, S., 230, 234
Tan, C. L., x, 296, 307
Tanis, M., 132, 143
Taylor, B. C., 239, 255
Taylor, C., 145, 162
Taylor, J., 10, 14
Taylor, J. R., 137, 143, 167, 189
Tylor, S. E., 114, 121
Teasdale, J. D., 297, 305
Tedeschi, J. T., 50, 66
Tepper, B. J., 9, 10, 11, 17, 46, 51, 54, 55,

AUTHOR INDEX 327

56, 66, 67
Tews, M. J., 24, 37
Thatcher, S. M., 129, 132, 137, 143
Thau, S., 6, 13, 17, 49, 53, 61, 115, 116, 121
Thomas, K. W., 253, 255
Thomas, M., 168, 185
Thomas, R., 293, 307
Tice, D. M., 28, 29, 35, 38, 39, 251, 255
Tietze, S., 125, 143
Ting-Toomey, S., 168, 189
Tippett, K., 33, 39, 300, 308
Tipton, A. M., 151, 161
Tocqueville, A. de, 149, 159, 162
Toffolo, C. E., 183, 189
Tomkins, S. S., 25, 39, 40
Tompkins, P. K., 134, 141
Torres, A., 72, 83
Toscheim, T., 303, 308
Totterdell, P., 44, 67
Tracy, S. J., 7, 16, 56, 67
Treem, J. W., 126, 142
Tretheway, A., 133, 137, 143, 190, 212
Triandis, H. C., 169, 189
Tripp, T. M., 5, 13, 34, 35, 56, 61, 85, 86, 100, 102
Trompenaars, F., 165, 189
Trott, V., 10, 15, 46, 64
Turco, C. J., 190, 192, 194, 202, 212
Turner, J. C., 108, 121, 174, 189
Turner, L. H., 224, 233
Tutu, D., 33, 34
Twale, D. J., 237, 256, 289, 293, 294, 295, 308
Twenge, J. M., 115, 121
Tyrrell, D. A. J., 75, 81

Uchida, K., 32, 40
Uchitelle, L., 158, 162
Uhl-Bien, M., 108, 119
Updegraff, J. A., 114, 121
Uzzi, B., 87, 104

Van Camp, K., 111, 188
Van Dam, K., 33, 38
Van Fleet, D. D., 6, 17

Van Hiel, A., 172, 186
Van Zundert, A., 33, 38
Vardi, Y., 3, 4, 5, 6, 7, 8, 17
Vartia, M., 72, 84
Venkataramani, V., 51, 67
Villaveces, A., 69, 81
Voegelin, E., 148, 162
Vogel, D., 303, 305
Vohs, K. D., 28, 35, 44, 61
Volf, M., 280, 288

Wagenaar, T. C., 292, 307
Waldron, V. R., xi, 29, 30, 34, 40, 46, 67, 133, 143, 260, 267, 268, 269, 270, 271, 272, 273, 274, 275, 276, 277, 278, 279, 280, 281, 283, 284, 287, 288, 299, 304, 308, 314
Walther, C. S., 109, 119
Walther, J. B., 132, 133, 144
Ward, C., 60, 65, 78, 83, 165, 174, 175, 189
Warmington, P., 182, 189
Warner, J., 304, 308
Warren, D. E., 5, 17
Wasson, B., 140
Weber, M., 158, 162
Weber, R. A., 166, 189
Webster, C., 166, 189
Weedon, C., 202, 212
Weer, C. H., 108, 119
Wegner, J. W., 89, 104
Weick, K. E., 137, 144
Weigert, A., 86, 87, 97, 104
Weiner, B., 27, 40
Weiner, J. L., 278, 286
Weitz, E., 3, 4, 5, 6, 7, 8, 17
West, C., 198, 212
Westhues, K., 54, 57, 67
Wheatley, M., 106, 121
Whimster, S., 162
White, A., 166, 189
White, K., 66
Wickens, C. M., 109, 119
Wiener, Y., 3, 5, 17
Wiesenfeld, B. M., 126, 130, 134, 144
Williams, J. H., 89, 103

Williams, K. D., 107, 113, 121
Wilson, C. B., 69, 76, 84
Wingfield, A. H., 190, 192, 194, 195, 196, 201, 212
Winstead, B. A., 125, 144
Wiseman, R., 184, 186
Wislar, J. S., 47, 66
Witvliet, C. V., 282, 288
Wolf, J., 20, 39
Woodman, P., 73, 84
Worthington, E. L., Jr., 268, 280, 283, 288
Wright, S. C., 202, 211
Wright, S. L., 113, 121
Wu, C. R., 273, 287

Xin, K. R., 108, 120

Yamada, D., 46, 67
Yamasaki, K., 32, 40

Yammarino, F. J., 111, 119
Yates, M. P., 91, 103
Yep, G. A., 179, 185
Yoder, J. D., 195, 212
Young, J. L., 192, 194, 195, 212
Younger, J. W., 282, 287

Zapf, D., 6, 14, 45, 47, 52, 54, 55, 59, 62, 67, 69, 77, 84, 109, 121, 236, 255
Zarate, M. A., 110, 119
Zhang, L., 28, 39, 115, 121
Zhang, S., 285, 288
Zhang, Z., 303, 305
Zhu, X., 129, 132, 137, 143
Zietlow, P. H., 253, 256
Zucker, L. G., 87, 104
Zwi, A. B., 69, 83

SUBJECT INDEX

Abrasive harasser, as type of problematic/troublesome other in the workplace, x, 20
Academic incivility. *See* Incivility
Affect. *See* Negative affect; Positive affect
Affect-based trust, 87
    relationship to incivility, 94, 95, 97, 98, 99, 301
    study results, related to incivility, 94–95
    subscale, 92
Aggression, 3, 9, 11, 21, 44, 45
    affective, 50
    emotion, 19, 22–23, 35. *See also* Emotion
    as core of relationship, 50
    as cost of exclusion, 302
    as form of bullying, 72
    as form of compliance gaining and influence, 20, 70, 71, 72
    as having communicative dimensions, 13
    as human response, 299
    as precursor to violence, 48
    as response to alienation/normlessness, 116
    as response to exclusion/isolation, 115, 116, 117
    as response to negative behaviors, 55
    Buss's framework, 11
    in academia/among faculty and staff, 293, 295
    in hostile relationships, 51
    institutionalized, 50
    instrumental aggression, 50
    marginalized minority groups as targets of, 172
    negative outcomes from, 46
    organization motivated, 3, 7
    progressive, 49
    psychological, 45
    relational nature of, 46
    relationship to other concepts/constructs, 9
    response to perceived norm violation, 54
    workplace. *See Workplace aggression*
Aggressive behavior. *See* Aggression
Ambition as source of problematic behavior. *See* Career

SUBJECT INDEX

Antisocial (work/place) behavior, 3, 4, 6, 7, 8
  as organizing concept/construct, 7
  relationship to other concepts/constructs, 7
Antisocial communication, 12
Anxiety
  about "coming out" at work, 109
  about communicating with others, 109
  as cause of avoiding conflict, 242
  as cause of exclusion, 118
  as intercultural communication apprehension, 174
  as result of harassment, 89
  as result of hostile workplace relationships, 51
  as result of incivility, 89
  as result of organizational changes, 54
  as result of problematic work(place) relationships, x, 126
  as result of relational exclusion, 113, 114, 302
  as result of workplace bullying, 32, 75, 76, 89
  effects on employee health, 114
  effects on organizational and personal outcomes, 89
  effects on work performance, 115
  relief from, provided by social support from high quality interpersonal relationships, 114
  social, 118
Apology
  sincere, features of, 279
  See also Forgiveness
Artificial light, 148
  of modernity, 149

Banality of evil, 150, 152, 157, 159, 160
Bias(es), x, 170
  anti-social, 72
  attribution, 51, 174
  interpersonal communication, 182
  loyalty, 294
  managerial, 168, 237

  perceptual, 72
  performance, 132, 136
Boss(es), 43, 99, 248
  as troublesome other, 9, 10, 11
  bullying, 11, 74
  civil, 98
  difficult, 239
  intolerable, 10
  micromanaging, ix
  preying, 98
  uncivil, 98
Bully, 57, 77
  as type of problematic/troublesome other in the workplace, x
  predatory, 50
Bullying, xi, 3, 6, 7, 9, 12, 19, 20, 21, 23, 29, 30, 32, 49, 68, 70, 76, 79, 80, 172, 237, 293
  and emotion, 20, 22, 23, 29, 30, 32
  and emotional labor, 29
  and organizational policy, 12, 79, 80
  and suicide, 78
  as anti-social influence strategy, 71
  as conflict/disagreement, 77, 78, 80
  as distinct from conflict, 52
  as contrapower harassment, 292
  as dominating perpetrator/predatory role, 50
  as driven by shame, 22
  as exclusion, 32, 107
  as functional response, 53
  as hostility, 46
  as interpersonal process, 76
  as popular/academic term, 8
  as social problem, 73
  as (interpersonal) violence, 12, 68, 69, 75, 78, 79, 80
  by bosses/supervisors, 9, 11
  cases, high-profile in media, 78
  classified as workplace aggression, 8, 9
  coping strategies for, 32, 49, 56, 77
  definition, 32, 69, 79
  definition, implications/importance of, 79
  direct, 73

SUBJECT INDEX

dispute-related, 73
effects on personal outcomes, 32, 33, 74, 75, 76, 89, 296
European research, 48
examples of, 19, 20, 32, 69, 71, 73, 74, 75, 293
formal prevention/intervention programs, 79, 80
in academic settings, 291, 292, 295, 304
indirect, 73, 74
informal prevention/intervention programs, 80
interpersonal pathway to, 52
intervention strategies, 79
intragroup/organizational pathway to, 53
intrapersonal pathway to, 51
legislation regarding, 68, 78, 79
linked to/as social influence, 70, 71, 72
minority groups as targets, 172
organizational factors contributing to, 71, 72, 293
"plausible deniability," 73
predatory, 50, 73
prevention strategies, 79
prevention/intervention programs, 78, 79, 80
relationship, 77
relationship to other concepts/constructs, 8, 9
school as context for, 78
student-to-faculty, 291, 292
types of, 73
victims of, as contributing to likelihood of, 72, 73
women-bullying-women, 60
See also Negative affect
Bureaucrat, 29, 145, 146, 150, 152, 153, 154, 155, 156, 157, 158, 159, 160, 303
as character type, 145, 151, 158
as communicative agent of modernity, 152
as problematic other, 145, 146, 147, 149, 157, 159, 303
career obsession, 158

clichés, 159
communicative practices, 146, 147, 150, 153, 155, 156, 157, 160n
connected to individualism, 149, 150
connected to modernity, 146, 153, 303
differentiated from leadership, 147
Burnout, 31
as result of isolation, 125
as result of problematic workplace relationships, x, 125, 126, 296
definition, 31

Career(s), 197, 224, 226, 230
and tokens, 208
damaged by workplace aggression, 89
responsible, 230, 232, 268, 271, 281
Career advancement
as characteristic of bureaucrat, 146, 147, 151, 152, 157, 159, 303
as source of problematic behavior, 146, 147, 151
harmed by being out of sight/out of mind/exclusion, 113, 303
helped by good relationship with supervisor, 105
helped by inclusion in workplace relationships, 106
Career ambition, as source of problematic behavior, ix, 154
Career enhancement
and impression management, 131, 132
Career obsession. See Bureaucrat
Career progression. See Career advancement
Career opportunities
damaged by aggression, 89
damaged by one's own incivility, 98
Civility, x, xi, 101, 102, 261
as characteristic of approach to addressing problems in relationships, 248
as civic virtue, 261
as communicative care for institutions, 262
as communicative virtue, 259, 261, 262
as connection through distance, 262
as failing to lead to improvements in

SUBJECT INDEX

problematic work relationships, 249
as helpful for communities and persons, 100, 101
as influence strategy, 71
as individual contribution to constructive community, 297, 298, 300
as leading to improvements in problematic work relationships, 242, 243, 249, 250, 251
as organizational contribution to constructive community, 300, 301
as protective of public space, 262
as sacrifice and personal restraint, 262
as workplace norm, 101
in relation to different forms of trust, 301
professional. *See* Professional civility
Cognition-based/cognitive-based trust, 87
relationship to incivility, 97, 98, 99, 301
study results, related to incivility, 94–95
subscale, 92
Commitment, 139, 269, 301
affective, 33
organizational, as outcome, x, 33, 85, 89, 102, 125, 126, 128, 129, 130, 131, 138, 165, 296, 301
to authentic dialogue, 298
to community, x
to culture of mutual respect and civility, as ideal of Mayo Clinic
to education, 159
to equality (on the part of the organization), 191
to genuine dialogue and authentic listening on the part of organizational leaders, 303
to honoring diversity, 302, 303
to individual/organizational progress, as ideal of Mayo Clinic, 301
to institutions, 151
to person in relationship, 243
to (restoring/working) relationship, 244, 245, 251, 269
to self-promotion, 154
Commitments

moral, 280, 281, 286
operative in conditional forgiveness, 280
to religious/spiritual ideals in relation to forgiveness, 271
Communication ethic(s)
and assumptions about the good, 259
as protecting and promoting goods, 260
professional civility, for the workplace, 258, 259, 261, 264
Communication Ethics in Dark Times: Hannah Arendt's Rhetoric of Warning and Hope, 147
Communication and Community: Implications of Martin Buber's Dialogue, 151
Communication process(es)
and emotion, x
and exclusion, 109
and resilience, 232
failure of, 282
in relation to problematic behaviors/relationships in the workplace, 12, 13
informal, 129
interdependence with individual and organizational outcomes, 139
maintaining relationship with a bully, as complex and demanding, 77
that enact forgiveness, 285
Communicative Model of Tokenizing Dynamics, 204
Compliance gaining. *See* Strategies
Contrapower harassment. *See* Harassment
Coping responses/strategies, 19, 30, 31, 297
and emotion, 33
and emotional labor, 29
and resilience, 31, 32, 35, 297
as mediators between stressful events and outcomes, 31, 32
behavioral, 31
cognitive, 31
conflict management, 77, 78
emotion-focused, 31
exit, 55
gender differences, 32
in response to bullying, 32, 69, 77

in response to negativity, 76
in response to problematic work relationships, 240–242
physiological, 31
problem-focused, 31, 54
role of, 31
stress-coping framework, 174
unsuccessful, in response to hostile behavior from others, 51, 53
Counterproductive (work) behavior, 3–4, 6, 8, 9
and emotion, 33
as organizing term, 7
relationship to other concepts/constructs, 7, 9
Coworker(s)
abrasive, incompetent harasser, type, 20
and blended relationships, 274
and forgiveness, 269, 270, 273, 274, 276, 277, 280, 282, 283
and perception of differential treatment, 112
and perception of special privilege/slacking, in context of telework, 132
and social support, 125, 130
and telework, 130, 131, 134, 135, 137, 138, 139, 140
as challenging/difficult, ix, 140, 240, 241, 242, 243, 244, 245, 249, 252, 254
as friends, 105, 114, 125, 281
as observer(s) of wrongful behavior, 270
as target of displaced frustration, 51
bullying by, 32, 74
causes of strained relations with, 252, 254
communication/conversation with, 106, 111
complexity, 206
difficulty in communicating with, leading to isolation from, 109, 110
disliked, 52, 77
disputes, 273
estranged, 282
exclusion of, 116, 117
liked, 131
less likely to repent of transgressions than friends or romantic partners, 275
offending, 282
problematic/problems with, 125, 247, 252
providing informal help to parties to hostile relationship, 57
proximity to, leading to relationship development, 110
negative relationships with, 126
receiving verbal abuse or undermining from, 55
relationship(s), 106, 112, 113, 115, 125, 126, 134, 135, 137, 138, 139, 247, 285
satisfaction with, 131
sensitive, 19
shunning by, 74
support/social support from, 114, 130
taking informal action to assist hostile relationships, 57, 58
transgressing, 54, 271
unprofessional, ix
upset, 240
with psychological issues, 248
Coworker liking , 128, 130, 131
Culture(s)
and attributions, 166–167
and bullies, 172
and conflict, 167
and cross-national teams, 180
and problem relationships, 173, 183
and resilience, 216
and role expectations, 174–175
as cognitive construct, 167
confounded with individual attributes, 170, 171, 172, 173
definitions of, 164–165
difference(s), 165, 167, 169
dimensions of difference, 167
feature of every workplace relationship, 182
high power distance, 173

indigenous, 217
influence on relationships, 170
interrogating, 220
intersection with larger social dynamics, 179
macro, 164
meaning, 166
micro, 165, 181
national, 165, 166, 181
occupational. *See* Occupational culture
organizational. *See* Organizational culture(s)
problematic nature of, 182
shock, 174, 175, 176
systemic, 181, 182
third, 180, 183, 184, 302
See also Stereotype(s)
Culture-difference hypothesis, 165
Cultural diversity. *See* Diversity
Cultural distance, 174
Cynicism/cynical, 282, 286, 296
from unmet high expectations, 259
See also Workplace cynicism

Dark side of interpersonal communication behavior, 3
Dark side of organizational behavior, 3, 7, 9
Dark times, 148
Depression, 32
as eventual outcome of bullying, 75
as effect on personal/organizational outcomes, 89
as outcome of harassment, 89
as outcome of incivility, 90
as outcome of problematic work relationships, x, 126
Destructive leadership behavior, 9, 11
definition, 10
types, 10
Destructive organizational communication, 5
Deviance, 7
organizational. *See* Organizational deviance
relationship to other concepts/constructs, 9
workplace. *See* Workplace deviance.
Deviant behavior(s), 3, 9
as element of incivility, 88, 89
Dialogue, 251, 253, 254
authentic, 298
characteristics of dialogue, 251
cross-cultural, 167
genuine, 303
reflected by three qualities of high-likelihood practices with positive effects on problematic relationships, 251
resurgence of scholarly attention to, 252
Disliked coworkers. *See* Coworkers
Disliked others/people, x, 31, 257, 261, 279
Distance, 110, 125
and civility, 262
and closeness, dialectic of, 258, 262
and formality, 261
and personal relationships, 127, 249, 261
as creating costs, 296
as element of professional civility, 261
cultural. *See* Cultural distance
friendship beginning with, 261
in context of telecommuting/telework, 125, 133, 134, 138, 139, 303
power. *See* Power distance
role. *See* Role distance
Distance worker, 127
Distancing
and the bureaucrat, 159
as maintenance strategy in hostile, problematic, or undesired relationships, x, 29, 54, 55, 126, 140, 252, 261
examples of, 29
from bullies, 77
Diversity, xi
and emotion, 29
and tokens/token dynamics, 206
as source of creativity for groups, 163
cultural, 180
honoring, 302
in the academy, 294

increasing, related to episodes of hostility and aggression, 54
managing, 181
organizations as sites of, 259
problems with, workplace, 183
training, 80
valuing, 297, 301, 302, 303
Dysfunctional behavior(s), 3
relationship to other concepts/constructs, 7
Dysfunctional leadership, 9

E-mail, 130, 133, 220
as bullying, 73
as distancing behavior, 77
as problematic behavior, ix, 129, 135, 136, 267, 286, 291
Eichmann in Jerusalem: A Report on the Banality of Evil, 146, 151, 152, 153, 157–158
Emotion(s), 19, 20, 24, 31, 33, 60, 190, 192, 195, 253, 276, 297
and attributions, 26
and bullying, 30, 75, 76, 79
and forgiveness, x, 30, 34, 35, 46, 269, 270, 279
and resilience, 219
and unwanted relationships, 240
as drivers of patterns of problematic interaction, 19, 21, 22 35
as experience to be managed, 19, 23
as mediator, 30, 32, 33, 35, 46
as signal function, 278
as transformative/transformation, 33, 34
and problematic relationships in the workplace, xi, 18, 29, 30, 251, 296
as problematic behaviors, 18, 19, 20, 35
cognitive appraisal theories of/process, 27, 28, 34
cognitive approaches to, 25, 26
coping strategies, 31, 32, 33
dimensions of, 20
Emotions in Man and Animals, 19
flooding, 28

multi-level approach to, 27
negative, x, 28, 34, 75, 76, 77, 269, 280, 284
physiological nature of/approach to, 25, 26
positive, 18, 29, 33, 34
regulation, 28, 29
roles played by, 18, 19
schema discrepancy theory of, 27
tipping point, 28
Emotion management, 23, 24, 25, 28, 30, 35, 278
Emotional abuse, 46
Emotional attachments/bond(s)/connection(s)/disconnection/investment, 88, 95, 97, 98, 99, 100, 101
Emotional demands, 296
Emotional deterioration, 58
Emotional distance/distancing, 126
Emotional distress, 78, 79
Emotional exhaustion, 31
Emotional investments, 87
Emotional labor, 23, 24, 29, 35
and token employees, 195, 196, 203
Emotional recall, 228
Emotional responses/choices, 27, 30, 33, 250, 251
Emotional states, 20, 25, 27, 75, 76, 79. *See also* Emotion(s)
Emotional support, 57, 114, 281
Emotional transformation, 34, 46. *See also* Emotion(s)
Emotional tyranny, 46, 271, 273
Employee isolation. *See* Isolation.
Employee misconduct, 3
Employee theft, 6
Employee vice, 7
Employee well-being/needs
as threatened by problematic behavior, ix
damaged by incivility, 102
trust as fundamental to, 86
Employee characteristics/status leading to exclusion/ostracism
being boss's pet, 112

communication apprehension, 109
dissimilarity, 108
gender, 108
homosexuality, 109
language differences, 109, 110
minority status 108, 109
physical disability, 109
shyness, 109
tasks and position, 111
unfavorable differential treatment, 111
Enabling structures and processes, in academia, 293–295
Excluded employee(s). *See* Exclusion
Exclusion, 12, 21, 68, 117, 301, 303
aggression and sabotage as response to, 115, 116
alienation as outcome of, 113, 116
and intent, 116–117
and social networks, 107
and telework, 130, 136, 138, 139
and tokenism/tokens, 192, 193, 195
as complex, 106
as element/form of bullying, 32, 69, 73, 74, 107
as incivility, 89
as inherent to workplace relationships, 105
as requiring attention from organizational leaders, 303
communication as defining feature of, 12
consequences of, 112–115
contextual elements as cause of,110
costs of, 301
demographic dissimilarity as cause of, 108
forms of, 107
impaired performance as consequence of, 115
interdependent nature of consequences of, 117
lack of communication ability as cause of, 109
language differences as cause of, 109–110
linked to problematic outcomes, 106

loneliness as outcome of, 113
options to mitigate, 117–118
personality traits/personal characteristics/factors as cause of, 109, 110
physical disability as cause of, 109
physical proximity as cause of, 110
process of/features of, described, 107
sexual orientation as cause of, 109
stress and anxiety as outcome of, 113, 114
supervision/leadership as affecting, 111–112
tardiness and absenteeism as outcome of, 114
task and position as cause of, 111
work environment as contributing factor to, 112
See also Ostracism
Existential homelessness, 147

Forgiveness, xi, 30, 34, 268, 271, 273, 281, 282
and emotion, x, 30, 33, 34, 35, 56, 269, 273, 278, 284
and empathy, 280
and incivility, 99
and individual differences, 285
and individual qualities, 277
and justice, 270
and moral tensions, 283
and occupational culture, 273
and offense type, 275–276
and organizational culture, 282, 285
and organizational outcomes, 283, 285
and personal/individual outcomes, 282, 283, 285, 286
and relational flourishing, 260
and relational transformation, 281
and religious/spiritual concerns, 271, 281
and victim protection, 281
as communicative process, 269, 285
as cultural understanding, 271
as element of virtuous work relationships, 268

SUBJECT INDEX

as gift, 270, 300
as individual contribution to constructive community, 297, 299
as moral process, 270
as (potentially) transformative process, x, 269, 281, 299
as protecting productivity, 273
as response to harmful/hurtful encounters, 268, 276
clichés, 273
conditional, 275, 280
definition (communicative), 34, 269, 270
differentiated from reconciliation, 34, 270, 281
discourse of, 285
discussing offense with victim as part of process of, 279
episodes, communication as driver of, 268, 269
explicit, 280
forced, as emotionally tyranny, 271
granting, 279, 280
Handbook of. See Handbook of Forgiveness
implicit, 280
in different types of organizational relationships, 274
in relation to offense severity, 275
in work relationships, compared to nonwork relationships, 275
model of process, 272
negotiation of, 277, 278, 279
research, 283
ritualized, 274
-seeking. *See* Forgiveness seeking
shaped by social context, 270
temporal features of, 281, 282
true, 271, 280
workplace, research on, 283
Forgiveness episode. *See* Forgiveness
Forgiveness-seeking
apology as expected behavior, 279. *See also* Apology, features of
communication/behaviors of, 279

humor, as unsuccessful strategy for, 279
Friendship(s), 44 , 275
beginning with distance, 261
feelings of, in forgiveness, 270
in the workplace, 106, 108, 110, 112, 114, 128, 129, 132, 139, 257, 261
networks, as affected by failure to negotiate forgiveness, 274
private, 263
See also Coworker(s); Workplace relationships

Gender
and token(s)/ism, 191, 194, 195, 196, 197, 198, 199, 200, 201
as source of stereotypes, 192
Gender differences in coping strategies, 32
Genuine light, 148

Handbook of Forgiveness, 283
Harassment, 46, 237
and policy, 68, 70
as accepted organizational behavior, 53
as result of enabling structures and processes, 293
as social influence, 70, 72
as type of bullying, 71, 75
as type of exclusion, 107
contrapower, 291, 292
criminal, 78, 79
forms of, 48
organizational policies and reporting, 58
policies, 79
sexual. *See* Sexual harassment
status blind, 46
victims of, 89
workplace, 46, 89
Harm, vs. hurt, 74
Harms
from problematic relationships in the workplace. *See* Problematic relationships in the workplace
Hostile supervisory behavior, 9
Hostile work relationships, xi, 12, 57, 58,

338 SUBJECT INDEX

60, 289
and aggression, 21
and emotion, 30
and emotional labor, 29
and emotional displays, 20
and turning points, 53
as negative relationships characterized by hostility and aggression, 44
as embedded in organizational context, 53
distinguished from relationships with occasional hostile episodes, 46
pathways to, 51–53
role relations perspective/theory, 49–51
shame as emotional drive of, 21
Hostility, 11, 21, 46, 49, 51, 55, 58, 59. 268, 299
and forgiveness, 269
and incivility, 23
as characteristic of problematic relationship, 240
as response to perceived norm violation, 51
as triggered by precipitating factors, 54
enduring forms of, 46
episodic, 50
faculty, 57
institutionalized, 50
persistent, 54
preceded by covert/subtle forms of aggressive behaviors, 21, 22–23
redirecting, as component of Negotiated Morality Theory, 283
Hurt, vs. harm, 74

Incivility (in the workplace), 7, 8, 54, 88, 98, 102, 264, 298
among faculty, 237, 293
and emotional labor, 29
and faculty gender, 292
and power, in the academy, 292
and problematic relationships, 304
and trust, 12, 86, 87, 90, 93, 94, 95, 96, 97–98, 99, 100, 101, 296, 301 *See*
also Interpersonal trust; Organizational trust; Trust
as characteristic of work environment, 90
as communication phenomenon, 90
as "dark side" behavior in organizations, 3
as a form of harassment, 48
as popular/academic term, 8
as problematic (workplace) behavior, xi, 11
as psychological mistreatment, 89
as trust violation, 86. *See also* Trust
costs of, in the academy, 296
damage/harm from, 89, 90, 101, 102, 301
definition, 88
distinguished from workplace aggression, 88
employee observation of, 92
in higher education/the academy, 289, 290, 293, 296, 304
in the classroom, 290
in the public sphere, 261
in relationships, explained away, 99
leaders must address, 301, 304
low levels of, associated with trust in supervisor, 92
more prevalent in academia than in other locations, 304
relationship to other concepts/constructs, 9
spiral, 49, 90
student, 290, 291
supervisory, associated with lower levels of trust, 93, 96, 98, 301
tolerated, as part of organizational culture, 72
Insidious workplace behavior, 5, 6, 8, 9
Interpersonal trust, 86, 87
and incivility, in connection to, harms/negative outcomes, 90, 96, 99, 101, 102, 296, 301
and organizational/interpersonal outcomes, 85
contrasted with organizational trust, 87

SUBJECT INDEX

engendered by civility, 102
factors affecting, 88
measured, in study, 92
nature of, 86–87
study results, related to incivility, 93–95
Isolated employee(s). *See* Isolation
Isolation, xi
   and emotional labor, 29
   and stress and anxiety, 113
   and telework, 126, 137
   and tokens/tokenism, 195
   as costly, 296
   as an element of bullying, 69, 74
   as enabling circumstance driving aggression and bullying in the academy, 293, 295
   as requiring attention from organizational leaders, 303
   as a result of bullying, 76
   as a result of incivility, 89
   as a result of workplace context, 111
   associated with deleterious outcomes, 125
   from social networks, 107
   racial and minority group, 109
   shame, as caused by, 22

Job satisfaction, 33, 128, 129, 130, 131, 139
   and cultural values, 165
   as result of liking for coworkers, 131
   as result of relationships, 92, 105
   predicted by trust, 85
   reduced, as eventual outcome of managing intense negative emotional states, 76
   reduced, as result of isolation, 125
   reduced, as result of problematic workplace relationships, x, 125, 126, 296
   reduced, as result of stress, depression, and anxiety, 85
   reduced, as result of token dynamics, 195
Jolie, Angelina, 215, 232

Leader-member exchange (LMX) relationship. 108
   in-group relationship, 108
   See also Supevisor(s)
Listening. *See* Strategies
Loneliness
   as cost of exclusion, 301
   as result of exclusion, 113, 114
   distinguished from alienation, 113
   managerial 111
   workplace, 113

Macro-cultures, 154
Marginalization
   and the academy, 294
   and indigenous peoples, 217, 218
   and refugee communities, 216
   See also Ostracism; Isolation
Marginalized groups, 192
   and gender, 192, 302
   and tokens/tokenism, 191, 196, 197, 201
   as requiring attention from organizational leaders, 303
   cultural minority, 172
   immigrant status, 110
Misbehavior in the workplace. *See* Organizational misbehavior
Mission
   creep, 294
   organizational, x, 297, 300, 303, 304
Mobbing, 6, 9, 46, 54
   in the academy, 294, 295
Modernity, 145, 147, 152, 156, 158, 159, 160
   and artificial light, 148
   and the bureaucrat, 146
   deconstruction of, as Arendt's project, 147
   and dark times, 148
   and progress, 147
   Arendt's critique of/warning about, 146, 147, 148, 152, 153, 158
   as secular trinity, 147
   characterized by banality/commonness, 148, 152

compared to eclipse, 147
dangers of, 151–152
given shape by communication practices of the bureaucrat, 151

Negative affect
  as cause of unwanted relationships, 240
  as core of victim and perpetrator characteristics in hostile relationships, 51
  as result of bullying, 32
  as result of (inter)cultural contact/interaction, 167, 174, 175
  as result of negative messages, x
  See also Emotion(s)
Negative affectivity, as characteristic of provocative victim role in hostile relationships, 50
Negotiated Morality Theory, 283

Occupational culture
  and forgiveness, 273
Organizational commitment. See Commitment
Organizational culture(s)
  and forgiveness, 278
  and teleworkers, 136, 137, 138, 303
  and tokens/token dynamics, 207, 208
  destructive/unhealthy, 11
  dysfunctional. See Dysfunctional organizational culture
  research, and importance of difference in/to, 166
  (supportive) of mutual respect and civility, 300, 301
  supportive of problematic behaviors/relationships, 53
  unforgiving, 282
Organizational deviance, 5, 6, 7, 8
  See also Deviance; Workplace deviance
Organizational Forgiveness Model, 272
Organizational interests/well being, as threatened by problematic behavior, ix, 102
Organizational misbehavior, 3, 5, 7

as organizing concept/construct, 8
Organizational retaliatory behavior, 5
Organizational trust
  and organizational identification, 88
  and organizational/interpersonal outcomes, 85
  and (workplace) incivility (connection to, harms, etc.), 86, 90, 98, 99, 102, 296, 301
  contrasted with interpersonal trust, 87
  engendered by civility, 102
  factors affecting, 88
  Index (OTI), 92
  measured, in study, 92
  Mishra's four-factor model, 88
  study results, related to incivility, 95–96
Ostracism, xi, 12, 263
  and emotional labor, 29
  as type of relational exclusion, 107
  definition, 107
  ethnic/minority group members as likely targets of, 109
  homosexual employees as likely targets of, 109
  intentional, 118
  physical, 107
  physical disability as cause of, 109
  social, 107
  supervision/leadership as affecting, 111–112
  See also Exclusion

Peer(s), 43, 115, 278, 281, 286, 302
  and aggressive behavior, 46
  and emotional labor, 24
  and social support, 114
  as challenging/difficult. . See Coworker
  as target of attack by authoritarian personality, 172
  collegial, 262
  friendships with, 105, 108
  harassing, ix
  hostility/disrespect from, 240
  in context of telecommuting/telework,

128, 129, 130, 131, 132, 138, 139, 303
 information, 262
 of victim of transgression, 275
 relationship types, 105
 relationships, 107, 257, 274
 review. *See* Peer review
 special, 105, 108, 257, 262
 support from, 242
 troublesome, 163
 uncivil, 98
Peer review, 293, 295
Petty tyranny, 9, 10, 11, 46
Phobe Prince case, 78
Pink poodles. *See* Token(s)
Positive affect, 32
 and cognitive reappraisal, 31
 and (inter)cultural contact, 175
 and problem solving, 31
 See also Emotion(s)
Positive emotional experiences. *See* Emotion(s)
Positive organizational behavior, 4
Positive organizational scholarship, 4
Positive side of interpersonal communication, 4
Power distance, 165, 173, 177
Pregnancy as source of bias, x
Precipitating circumstances, 293, 294
Problematic others in the workplace, types, x
Problematic relationships in the workplace, xi, 5, 12, 13, 18, 19, 30, 33, 126, 254, 259
 as cause of stress, x
 harms from, x
Problematic Relationships in the Workplace, ix, 296
Productivity, 11
 as affected by negative/corrosive relationships, 44
 as purpose of abusive supervision, 11
 as response to bullying, 56
 damaged by bullying, 60

damaged by incivility (potentially), 101
decreased, due to cultural differences, 166
decreased, due to problematic/difficult work relationships, 236
endangered by relational blow-ups, 273
group, related to technology, 127
hurt, due to stress, depression, and anxiety, 89
impeding, as example of performance requiring seeking forgiveness, 276
improved, as eventual result of forgiveness, 282
increased, due to telework, 127, 140
lost, as result of decreased trust, 85, 100, 101
lowered, as result of managing intense negative emotional states, 76
perceptions of teleworkers,' on part of others, 136
personal and organizational, threatened by work conflicts, 286
protected and promoted by professional civility, 258
reduced, as a way of coping with frustration, 51
Professional civility, xi
 and civility as communicative virtue, 259
 and communicative *phronesis*, 262
 and/as relational responsibility, 259, 261, 262, 263, 264
 as communicative virtue at work, 258
 as interpersonal communication ethic for the workplace, 258, 259, 264
 protecting and promoting goods, 258
Public communicative engagement/ conversation, 262
Public relationships, 263, 264
Public sphere, x, 153, 230, 259, 260, 261
 as context for bullying, 68
 of a life, 263
Public space, 262

Quality of work life

damaged by incivility, 98, 289

Refugee(s), 215, 217, 220, 231
  community, 216
  definitions, 216
  indigenous, 217
  Palestinian, 216, 230
  protracted, 216
  resilience and/or, 232
  resilience processes of, 221
  work, 232
Refugee camp(s), 220, 224, 228
  Palestinian, 215, 216, 219, 220, 232
Relational responsibility, 259, 263
  and professional civility, 261, 262, 263, 264
Resilience, xi, 260
  and emotions, 29
  as communicatively constituted/constructed, 216, 231, 232
  as opposite of burnout, 31
  as ordinary, 218
  as a process, 218
  conceptualizations of, 230–231
  constructing, 213, 228, 232
  genetics and, 218
  human adaptation and learning and, 218
  in Palestinian refugee camp, 219, 220
  interactive constitution of, 224
  multiple bases for constructing, 218
  practicing, 297, 300
  processes, 218, 221, 231
  processes of sustaining, 31, 219
  refugee, 216
  relational, 269
  social, 218, 228
Role distance, 263

Sexual harassment, 3, 10, 11, 48
  bullying as on par with, 69, 80, 199
  of female faculty members, 291
  policy, 276
Shame, x, 22, 35
  as driver of aggressive/hostile behaviors, 19–22, 23, 35

  and bullying, 22, 76
  as result of act of injustice, 276
  cues, 23
Shame-rage spiral, 22
Special peer relationship. See Peer(s)
Stereotypes, x
  about leaders and authorities, 192
  and behavior, 171
  and cultural identity, 176
  and cultural misattribution, 170, 302
  and double-bind dilemma, 178
  and real cultural differences, 171
  and prejudiced behavior/individuals, 170
  and problematic relationships at work, 171
  and tokens/tokenism/token /tokenizing dynamics, 192, 194, 196, 197, 200, 201, 203, 204, 205, 208, 209, 302
  cultural, 170
  education to address, as approach to workplace diversity problems, 183
  identity-based, 192
  of "ideal worker," 192
  of occupational segregation, 193
  role in shaping micro-level experiences, 194
  social, about women, 192
Strategies
  active, in response to persistent hostility, 55
  adapting to the other, 245
  adaptive, for restoring working relations, 252–253
  aggressive behavior as, in response to hostile relationships, 52
  avoidance communication, 177
  avoidant, in response to persistent hostility, 55
  communication, xi, 29
  communicative, 236
  compliance gaining, 20, 71
  conflict management, 77
  consistent, for restoring working relations, 250–252
  coping. See Coping responses/strategies

SUBJECT INDEX

directly confronting the problem, 243
distancing, in response to aggression, 54
emotion-focused, 31
in response to bullying. *See* Coping responses/strategies; Bullying
listening, 245
low-involvement, in response to bully, 57
maintenance, 54, 55, 56
mediation/alternative dispute resolution, 58
mobbing, as means of establishing social dominance, 54
skill at enacting, 253–254
to transform problematic relationships into nonproblematic, 235, 236
types, in response to aggressive action, 56
used by tokens, 196

Stress, 30, 31, 53, 74, 76
as result of bullying, 76, 77
as result of emotional labor, 24
as result of organizational change, 54
as result of problematic workplace relationships, x
as result of relational exclusion, 113, 114
effects on organizational and personal outcomes, 89
management, as skill preventing entrenched relational hostility, 59

Subordinate(s)
as challenging/difficult, ix
as perpetrators of problematic behaviors, 32, 46
difficulty with, compared to bosses, 248
expectations of, for management/leadership, 176–177
perceptions of challenging bosses, 11
troublesome, 163

Suicides from school bullying, 78

Supervisor(s), 242, 243, 245, 268, 276, 277, 278, 281, 282
abusive, 10, 11
aggression, 10, 46
and communication anxiety, 109
and teleworkers, 134, 135, 136, 137, 138
and tokens, 208

and trust, 87
as bully/bullies, 9, 74
as challenging/difficult, ix
as models of informal bully-prevention strategies, 80
as models of respect and civility, need for, 301
emotional connection with, 97, 98
experience of incivility with, 93, 95, 96
in multinational organizations, 179
leader-member exchange (LMX), 108
"out of the loop," 111
perceptions of, 97
performance bias, 136
problematic/problematic relationship with, 10, 179
relationship(s) (with), 91, 92, 97, 105, 107, 108, 112, 113, 114, 115, 253, 257, 274, 278, 301
trust in immediate, 92, 93, 97, 301
uncivil, 97, 98
undermining, 10
See also Leader-member exchange; Supervisory behavior

Supervisory behavior
abusive, 9
aggressive, 46
and destructive leadership, 10
challenging feedback, 33
destructive, 9
differential treatment, 112
dysfunctional, 9
hostile, 9
hostility, 240
incivility, 98
negative, 4, 9, 11, 32
problematic, 10
See also Supervisor(s)

Token(s), 191, 193, 194, 195, 196, 199
African-American, 194
and emotion, 29, 196
and emotional labor, 195
and gender, 200
as pink poodles, 193

challenged/obstacles faced by, 195, 196
consequences for, 195
non-tokens and, 196
numerical rarity, 193, 200, 201, 203, 207, 208
racial, 196
status, 195
strategies used by, to manage token dynamics, 196
Token dynamics, 191, 192, 193, 194, 195, 197, 201, 202, 203, 205, 206, 207, 208, 209
Tokenism, xi, 191, 192, 194, 197, 203, 209
and upward trespassing, 201
as dynamic process, 205
communicative perspective, 197, 198, 200, 201, 202, 209
conditions of, 203
demarcation, 206
heightened scrutiny, 207
macro-level issue/conditions, 192, 193, 194, 203, 204, 207
meso-level practices/processes, 192–193
micro-level approach, 191, 192, 194, 195, 196, 197, 203, 205
positive outcomes of, 195
theory, 190, 191, 193
Tokenizing dynamics, 202, 205, 206, 208, 209
communicative model of, 204, 208
Tokenizing processes, 191, 192, 193, 194, 197, 200, 202, 206, 208
of dominant groups as "dominant tokenizing," 203
stereotypes. *See* Stereotype(s)
Toxic supervisory behavior, 9
Transgressions, x, 274, 280, 283, 284, 285, 304
at work, compared to those of as compared to those of friends and romantic partners, 275
history of, shaping tendency to forgive in present moment, 285
history of repeated, complicating forgiveness episode, 274

learning about, from a third party, 278
nature of those that call for forgiveness, 275
relational, as linked to aggression and development of hostile relationships, 53
serious, effect on sense making, 278
three forms of, 275–276
Trust, 87, 100
affect-based. *See* Affect-based trust
affected by emotional displays, 19
affected by incivility, 12, 101, 296
and coworker relationships, 138
and incivility, 86, 98, 99, 101, 301
and relational closeness, 132
and self-disclosure, 131
as characteristic of coworker friendship, 125
as fundamental to employee and organizational well-being, 86, 101
as fundamental to/necessary for organizational relationships, 85, 101, 129
as fundamental to social action/interaction, 86, 100
as necessary to form interpersonal relationships, 133
as predictor of organizational/personal outcomes, 85, 100
as protective mechanism, 86
as requirement of social interactions, 86
characteristic of high-quality connections, 43
conditions of, 87
damaged by workplace incivility, 86, 87, 97, 100, 101, 102
decreased, as result of market-like, transactional relationships, Pfeffer, 100
engendered by civility, 102
impaired by problematic behaviors, 296
in artificial light, 148
interpersonal. *See* Interpersonal trust
McAllister's 11-item scale, 92
mutual, as necessary for challenging stereotypes, 209
organizational. *See* Organizational trust

overall, in organization, shaped by managers, 91
peer, 139
relationship to various organizational/interpersonal variables, 86
"swift," 85
too much supervisory contact interpreted as lack of, 135
violations, 86
Tyler Clementi case, 78

Unforgivable offenses, 276
Upward trespassing, 200–201, 202, 203, 205, 206

Workplace aggression, 4, 5, 8, 57, 89
abusive supervision as distinct from, 11
and instrumental aggression, 50
as having relational face, 45
as organizing/integrating construct, 6–7
bullying as type of, 8
characteristics of research on, 7
defined, 45
distinguished from workplace incivility, 88–89
See also Aggression
Workplace cynicism
as result of problematic workplace relationships, x, 126, 296
Workplace deviance, 5, 6
relationship to other concepts/constructs, 7
See also Deviance; Organizational deviance
Workplace friendship(s), x, 106, 108. 110, 112, 114, 128, 129, 132, 139, 257, 261
close, 108
See also Coworker(s); Friendship(s)
Workplace harassment. See Harassment
Workplace incivility. See Incivility (in the workplace)
Workplace Incivility Scale, 91
Workplace relationships, 106
and emotion, 18
and justice, 270
and relational responsibility, 261
as good of/for workplace, 264
central to workplace functioning, 106, 131
defined by social context, 110
development of, 108
embedded in multiple social structures, 182
good of, 258
involuntary, 167
problematic. See Problematic relationships
social support functions of, 114
theoretical perspectives on, 259
varying along multiple dimensions, 257
See also Coworker(s); Friendship(s); Peer(s); Workplace friendship(s)